ART AS DEMONSTRATION

ART AS DEMONSTRATION

A REVOLUTIONARY RECASTING OF KNOWLEDGE

SVEN SPIEKER

THE MIT PRESS
CAMBRIDGE, MASSACHUSETTS
LONDON, ENGLAND

The MIT Press would like to thank the anonymous peer reviewers who provided comments on drafts of this book. The generous work of academic experts is essential for establishing the authority and quality of our publications. We acknowledge with gratitude the contributions of these otherwise uncredited readers.

This book was set in Bembo Book MT Pro and PF DinText Pro by New Best-set Typesetters Ltd. Printed and bound in the United States of America.

Library of Congress Cataloging-in-Publication Data

Names: Spieker, Sven, author.
Title: Art as demonstration : a revolutionary recasting of knowledge / Sven Spieker.
Description: Cambridge, Massachusetts : The MIT Press, [2024] | Includes bibliographical references and index.
Identifiers: LCCN 2023015505 (print) | LCCN 2023015506 (ebook) | ISBN 9780262048712 (hardcover) | ISBN 9780262377553 (epub) | ISBN 9780262377546 (pdf)
Subjects: LCSH: Arts—Political aspects. | Artists—Political activity. | Political art. | Art and social action.
Classification: LCC NX180.P64 S65 2024 (print) | LCC NX180.P64 (ebook) | DDC 701/.03—dc23/eng/20230801
LC record available at https://lccn.loc.gov/2023015505
LC ebook record available at https://lccn.loc.gov/2023015506

10 9 8 7 6 5 4 3 2 1

CONTENTS

1

INTRODUCTION: ART-AS-DEMONSTRATION IN THE 1960S AND BEYOND

The Enlightenment was a magnificent revolution in itself.

—*Antonio Gramsci*

The literary and artistic heritage of humanity should be used for partisan propaganda purposes.

—*Guy Debord, "A User's Guide to* Détournement*"*

During the infamous student-organized Festival der neuen Kunst that took place at Technical University in Aachen, Germany, on July 20, 1964—timed by its organizer, Latvian artist Valdis Abolins, to coincide with the twentieth anniversary of the unsuccessful attempt to kill Adolf Hitler—the artist Bazon Brock stepped up to a lectern and started to deliver a lecture entitled "Do You Want Total Life?," standing on his head.

The festival itself was conceived as a demonstration and art-infused protest against consumer capitalism and totalitarianism; apart from Brock, it included Joseph Beuys, Stanley E. Brouwn, Henning Christiansen, Robert Filliou, Ludwig Gosewitz, Arthur Koepcke, Tomas Schmit, Ben Vautier, Wolf Vostell, and Emmett Williams, among others. Brock's headstand, his

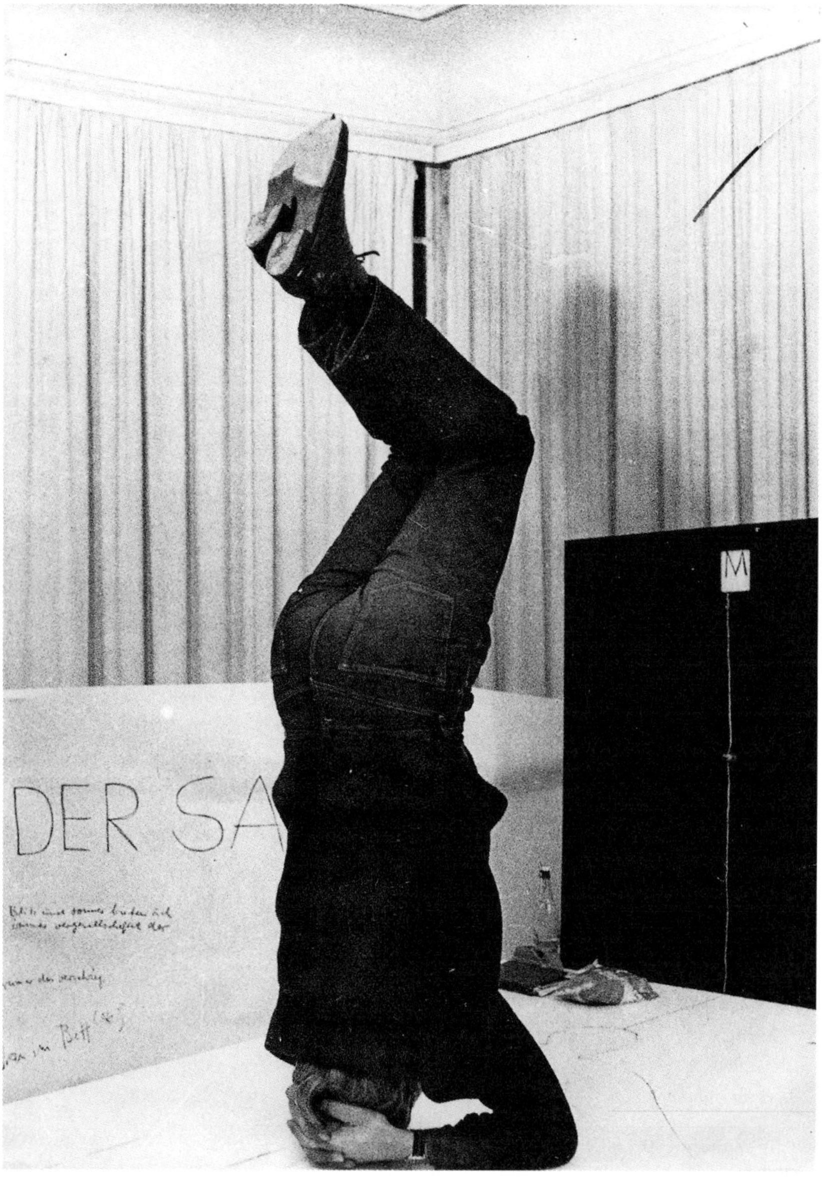

Figure 1.1 Bazon Brock, *Der Satz*, Wuppertal, June 5, 1965. Photo: Ute Klophaus.

signature stunt since 1959, grotesquely combined references to Goebbels's infamous 1943 speech at the Berlin Palace of Sports ("Wollt ihr den totalen Krieg?") with the Marxian desire to stand the Hegelian dialectic from its head onto its feet. As the artist explained, "the headstand demonstrated the falseness of a so-called critique of idealism that was widespread at the time, and which alleged that Hegel had to be 'turned from his head onto his feet.' . . . In fact, the head continues to remain on top for the person who is standing on his head . . . even as the observers of such a person may be inclined to think that only what is on top has the capacity to think, even if it's the feet."[1] Brock's wisecracking provocation does not disagree with the Marxian critique of Hegelian idealism, nor with Marx's reversal of the relationship between thinking and material reality. On the contrary, the artist remains faithful to Marx, who saw himself as a student of Hegel even as he critiqued parts of the philosopher's system. However, Brock points out, whether we stand on our head or on our feet, it is always the head that retains the capacity to think, even as it may reset the parameters for how we interpret the world.

Brock's demonstration reminds us that much of what we associate with revolutionary or alternative culture during the expanded 1960s[2]—a period stretching from the mid-1950s to the mid-1970s—had its origin in different permutations of instruction and the didactic, of which demonstration is one crucial element. Brock's affirmation of thinking (the head) is, as such, as emblematic for my book as is his use of affect and surprise, providing an apt illustration of how during the 1960s a young generation of artists pivoted to demonstration as a way of combining their "heads with their feet," stressing the importance of instruction in order to change the status quo.[3]

This book, then, deals with the ways in which demonstration has helped (re-)shape art and politics from the height of the cold war to the late twentieth century.[4] I analyze what I am calling art-as-demonstration in two regions: Western Europe (especially Germany) and the US—the "West"—and the countries of Eastern Europe and the former Soviet Union—the so-called "East"—paying close attention to how demonstration manifests in

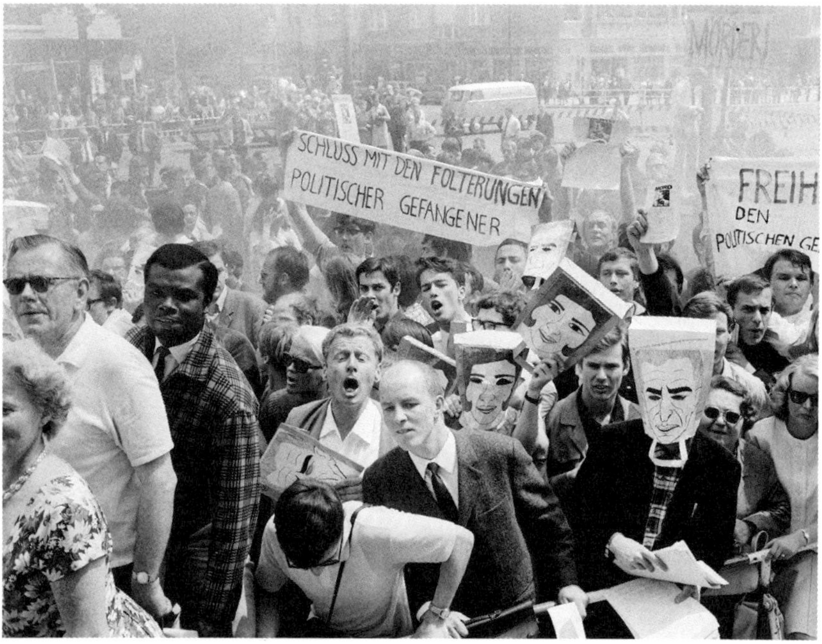

Figure 1.2 Max Scheler, protesters and spectators during the official visit of the shah of Iran in Berlin-Schöneberg, 1967. © Max Scheler.

or as art on either side of the Berlin Wall. Indeed, while the emancipatory agenda of the 1960s used to be identified squarely with the West—the 1967 anti-shah protests in the Western half Berlin, the Berkeley Free Speech Movement and the Civil Rights Movement, May '68 in Paris, Germany's *außerparlamentarische Opposition* (APO), and so forth—a more comprehensively oriented take on the era has now emerged that not only includes the nations of the former Eastern Bloc but is also mindful of the many ways the two sides remained connected, defying the cold war's binary logic.

The chapters that follow aim to give added traction to contemporary discussions of art as protest, activism, and resistance, assuming that a closer, more historical look at art's connection with demonstration may help us reconnect with earlier efforts to marshal art for instructional purposes, notably by the early twentieth-century avant-garde.[5] While it is commonly associated with street protest, demonstration ultimately aims to teach. And while "protest art" is frequently associated with the educational work undertaken by activist groups and social movements, as *art* it is often considered irrelevant or secondary. By contrast, in this study, I argue that any post-art position that draws on instruction—as post-art positions tend to do—also has to account for demonstration's specificity as art, both thematically and formally.

What is demonstration? Briefly put, "to demonstrate" is to show or point out.[6] And while to our modern ears the term is mostly associated with mass political protest, it has a long pedigree in a variety of other disciplines, ranging from philosophy to rhetoric and the sciences. For instance, in science and the legal sphere, demonstration refers to a process of proving the existence of something, while in rhetoric, *demonstratio*—Greek *enargía*—points to a particularly vivid description, so vivid indeed that what is being described may appear before the listener's eyes in the form of an image (*ad oculos*). Demonstration also has an intimate connection with knowledge. After all, in its classic Aristotelian definition, the term refers to the production of knowledge not merely by emphasizing what is factual, but by gesturing at the reasons why something is considered factual or true. In other words, while in one sense a demonstration may serve as a vehicle for pointing out that something is the case, in another sense it highlights the process of truth production itself, for example, by helping us identify an object or concept for which there is not as yet a stable name or definition, or by withholding that definition for greater effect. As one science educator writes, "an effective demonstration should promote good observation skills, stimulate thought, arouse curiosity, present aspects of complex concepts on a concrete level, and, most important, be the basis for class discussion. Explanations should contain enough information to satisfy the audience's curiosity as to what took place and why, and should serve as a starting point for further inquiry for those individuals who need more details."[7] The reference made in this statement to the affective aspects of demonstration, the various strategies instructors may use to arouse the curiosity of their viewers, is crucial. After all, a demonstration is always more than a technical procedure for showing something to be the case. It's not by coincidence, in this context, that for the playwright Bertolt Brecht, who used "demonstration" to refer to his nonmimetic theory of acting, the assumption that what was being shown (*demonstriert*) on stage was already known to both actors and audience alike freed up both to concentrate on other aspects of the performance, such as their shared social environment.

The legendary infatuation of the 1960s with (street) demonstrations, too, has some relation with the decade's overall obsession with learning and education, impulses that pervade its countercultures like few others. The anthropologist Marshall Sahlins even went so far as to subsume all countercultural phenomena of the era, including "the sexual revolution, verbal obscenity in public places, marijuana, LSD, beatniks, long hair, folk rock, acid rock, Bob Dylan, Joan Baez, Jerry Rubin, 'let's rap' college classes, back-to-nature, Black Panthers, hippies, etc., etc." under what he calls a "common anthropological pedagogy."[8] In his article about the periodization of the decade, Fredric Jameson even notes the demonstrative nature of terrorism, which, in his estimate, "aimed not at any classical seizure of state power, but rather at essentially pedagogical or informational *demonstrations*, e.g., forcing the state to reveal its fundamentally fascist nature."[9]

In many ways, the 1960s attitude toward education and knowledge was radically iconoclastic. In one recent book, this is referred to as the decade's "fantasy that we can 'be new.' That we can . . . wipe the slate clean."[10] However, while the 1960s certainly do gesture at such a zero point—a point where everything can be made new, where existing knowledge is erased and nullified—at the same time, they pursue deeducation as a prerequisite for new kinds of instruction and knowledge, untarnished by class and gender injustice, racism, and inequality, and subject to new forms of distribution that would make such knowledge available to all. In other words, the decade that fights like no other against ossified forms of instruction at the same time embarks on an alternative education project all its own, albeit one that seeks to subject all existing curricula to a radical rewriting. Much like Marx who vigorously rejected Bakunin's educational nihilism, so activists, student protesters, and artists during the expanded 1960s are focused not merely on the destruction of knowledge, but also on its *revolutionary recasting*, with demonstration serving as one of its principal conduits.[11]

In this spirit, artists joined student and worker demonstrations against colonial rule and the war in Vietnam, but also against dysfunctional universities and art institutions (the Art Workers Coalition or the "Art Strike" in the US), inequality, and worker exploitation. Research has shown the profound impact of artistic formats such as performance, happenings, action readings, street theater, vaudeville, and Situationist *dérives* on these protests. In West Berlin, for instance, the radical actionist student group Subversive Aktion, with student leader Rudi Dutschke as a member, frequently borrowed from a vocabulary that included elements of Dada and Situationism, while also drawing on the thinking of Nietzsche, Freud, and Marx. As the West German artist Wolf Vostell noted in 1969, "today, demonstrations have the character of art."[12] Yet the reverse was also true: art increasingly assumed the character of a demonstration, forming part of what Claire Bishop has identified as a pervasive "scholastic attitude" in contemporary art.[13]

Of course, in some sense all art demonstrates, in that by designating an object or an action to be looked at—by pointing to it—artists perform a more or less explicit act of instruction. We owe the artistic analysis of this process to Duchamp's readymades and their desublimation of art's demonstrational aspects. For example, for his *Unhappy Readymade* (1919–1920), Duchamp instructed his sister Suzanne to hang a textbook of geometry with strings outside her balcony so that it would gradually be worn down by the elements.[14] Geometry being an area of mathematics where demonstration is of particular importance, with *Unhappy Readymade*, while the object of the textbook's demonstration—its instructional content—is gradually worn down by the accident of the weather, what remains is the act of showing itself, preempting Jacques Lacan's insight that the real—the part of reality that defies symbolization, such as chance or accidents—cannot be methodically known or represented, only demonstrated. As Lacan noted, "the real differs from reality. This is not to say that it's unknowable, but that there's no question of knowing about it, only of *demonstrating* it."[15]

The art practices I discuss in this book pursue the real in demonstration, but they also charge that art-as demonstration can help refashion reality, from Dada-inspired anti-art—think of Oswald Wiener and Peter Weibel's 1968 *Art and Revolution* at Vienna University, a series of raucous interventions that included an action lecture about the Austrian finance minister and a speech entitled "What Is to Be Done" by Peter Weibel—to formally more sedate forms of (auto-)instruction such as Adrian Piper's reading performance *Food for Thought* (1967), during which the artist sought to establish a sense of self through her sustained study of Immanuel Kant's second *Critique*. Between these extremes, we find practices that challenge educational institutions such as school or the university and their systemic entanglement with power; action readings; lecture performances; demonstrations of scientific knowledge as a form of semiotic communication untainted by the distortions of the media; and unique demonstrational formats such

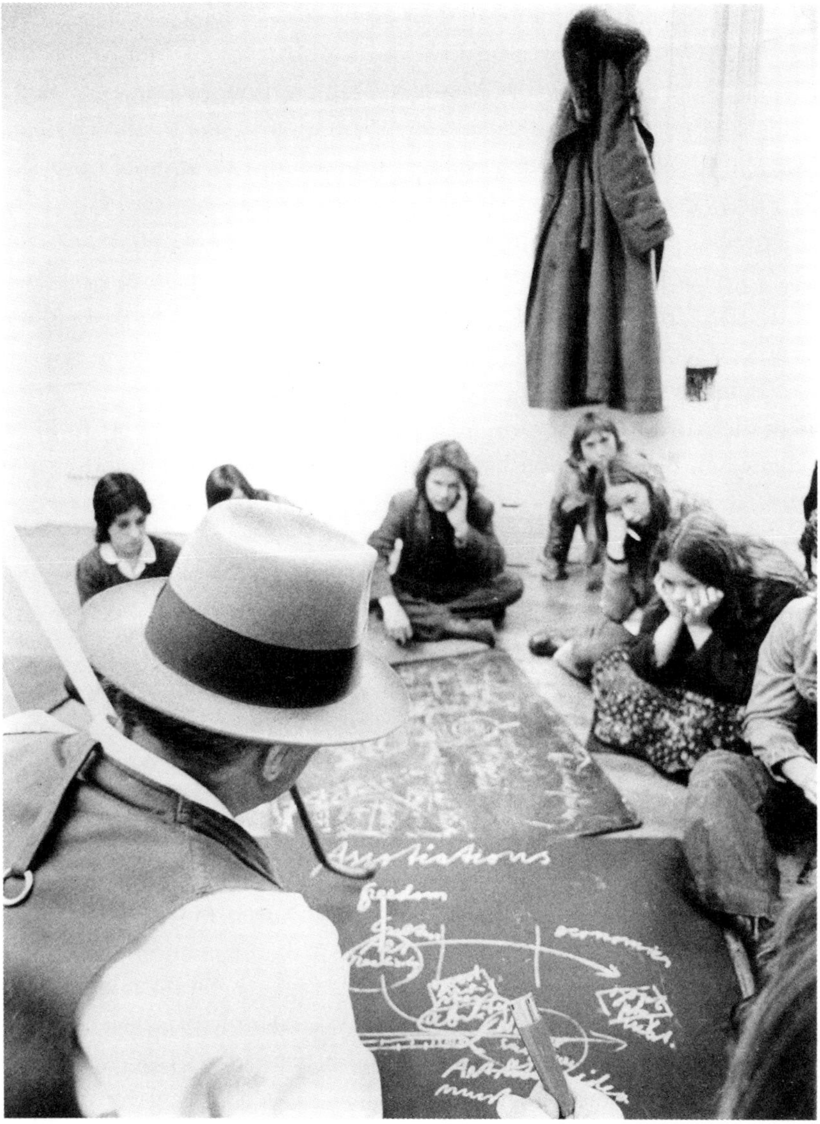

Figure 1.3 Joseph Beuys with students, Institute of Contemporary Art, London, November 1974. Stiftung Museum Schloss Moyland. Photo: Chris Schwarz. © 2024 Artists Rights Society (ARS), New York / VG Bild-Kunst, Bonn.

as Harun Farocki's agitational flyer films (*Flugblattfilme*), which mobilize the medium of film as an instrument of direct agitation, or Ulrike Meinhof's documentary film *Bambule* (1972), a striking example of a militantly expanded cinema that uses demonstration to agitate the residents of a reform school for young women. I supplement these more historical examples of art-as-demonstration with more recent iterations, especially where these explicitly or implicitly revisit the expanded 1960s, as is the case with Clemens von Wedemeyer's reexamination of Meinhof's *Bambule*, or Ciprian Homorodean's didactic approach to stealing as a way to address structural social injustice.

While the above examples of art-as-demonstration generally use demonstrational techniques without explicitly referring to them as such, in other cases, demonstration became part of an artwork's title and formal remit, as with *Georg Metzger's First Public Demonstration of Auto-Destructive Art* (1961); Milan Knížák's demonstrations on the streets of Prague, such as the 1963 *Demonstration of Objects*; Gerhard Richter and Konrad Lueg's 1963 *Living with Pop—A Demonstration for Capitalist Realism*; or Joseph Beuys's *Auschwitz Demonstration* (1956–1964).[16]

Far from describing a precisely defined genre or technique, demonstration during the expanded 1960s was the designation of choice for non-object-focused, progressive art practices with an appellative character for which no other description seemed appropriate. Witness a review published in 1964 of an action by West German artist Günther Uecker during which he drove nails into a piano at a family residence: "When he [Uecker] started to drive the first nail into the old piano, he was no longer in the home of the Kohl family. . . . He was somewhere. But completely himself. He was transfixed, and he transfixed others. Maybe he is not aiming at such transfixing . . . he is not a magician. Rather a *demonstrator*, albeit a highly sensitive one."[17] The term "demonstrator" here addresses the artist's relationship with his work, shifting the weight of the action away from expression and intention toward an attitude characterized by ostension, implying the detached display of an action that seems to unfold by its own laws.

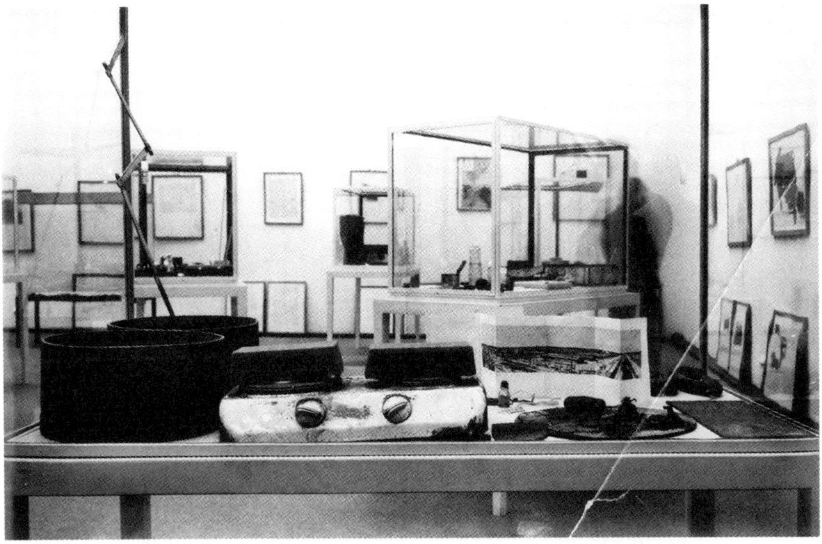

Figure 1.4 Joseph Beuys, *Auschwitz Demonstration in the Collection Karl Ströher*, 1958. Photo: Ute Klophaus. bpk/Stiftung Museum Schloss Moyland/Ute Klophaus. © 2024 Artists Rights Society (ARS), New York / VG Bild-Kunst, Bonn.

Demonstration certainly forms part of a broader trend toward teaching in post-World War II art. As Howard Singerman has impressively shown, artists in the postwar era not only more and more frequently took on the role of instructors at universities and arts schools, they also viewed their own work in the context of teaching and instruction.[18] On the one hand, as Peter Weibel has observed, this may be linked to the breakdown of the humanist Kantian educational program in the wake of the traumatic twentieth century, as artists

> realized that they needed to study . . . the way in which verbal and visual fictions and representations created reality in order to get to the bottom of the barbarity. They realized that . . . the only way they could hope to possibly heal the wounds of a sick society was through . . . demonstrations, didactic exercises and seminars, action teachings, . . . propaganda, protest, . . . education, and explanation. In short, they . . . invented the performance, action, interaction, happening, and the viewers' participation in art's production.[19]

As a result, as Allan Kaprow wrote in 1964, "essentially, the task is an educational one. . . . [The artist's] job is to place at the disposal of a receptive audience those new thoughts, new words, the new stances even, which will enable his work to be better understood."[20] According to Kaprow, it is the professional artist's role to educate their audience regarding the innovative nature of a work whose progressive nature is no longer a function of its formal innovation: "If he [the artist] does not [explain his work to the audience], the public's alternative is its old thoughts and attitudes, loaded as they are with hostilities and stereotyped misunderstandings."[21] What changes during the later 1960s, especially in the context of the student revolts, is that Kaprow's perspective is put to a rigorous institutional test: henceforth, demonstrational art, explicitly or implicitly, has an ineluctably political and emancipatory rather than a merely aesthetic remit.

The question of what kind of public the artist might be addressing was central during this era, when the problem of what constitutes the public sphere in the age of mass media was becoming more and more urgent. On the one hand, artists were grappling with the fact that there was neither a knowledgeable audience nor a developed art criticism. As Lucy R. Lippard noted, communication between artists and a "broader audience was vague and undeveloped."[22] On the other hand, left-leaning artists and intellectuals such as Oskar Negt and Alexander Kluge in West Germany questioned the very nature of this audience, especially the hegemony of the bourgeois public sphere, with its instrumentalization not only of the mass media—from newspapers to film and television—but also of the different modes of reception that correspond to them, and argued for the need to think through the possibility of a separate public sphere for the proletariat alone.[23] Demonstrations would play a crucial role in the production of such a sphere. As an element of deliberate *Störung* (disruption), they intervene in the machinations of what Negt and Kluge refer to as the "consciousness industry" (*Bewusstseinsindustrie*), and they do so with deliberate recourse to the one means of production that, according to Negt and Kluge, is resistant to the capitalist interest in drawing everything into the production process: the imagination (*Phantasie*). Negt and Kluge associate *Phantasie* with a specific form of labor that capitalism seems to have overlooked, namely "the changing of the relations among individuals, and between humans and nature."[24] This, however, is precisely the terrain on which art-as-demonstration operates.

Yet at the same time, and without denying or diminishing the crucial agency of *Phantasie*, revolutionary change also relies on the need to grasp reality intellectually, roughly in the spirit of Gramsci, who wrote in an early article, "the fact is that only by degrees, one stage at a time, has humanity acquired consciousness of its own value . . . and this consciousness was formed not under the brutal goad of necessity, but as a result of intelligent reflection, at first by just a few people and later by a whole class, on why certain conditions exist and how best to convert the facts of vassalage into a sign [*segnacolo*] of rebellion and social reconstruction."[25] Demonstrations during the 1960s are an attempt to turn oppression into "signs of rebellion and social reconstruction," an operation that relies both on *Phantasie* and on the demonstrators' access to what Herbert Marcuse referred to as "authentic information" so they can "deliberate and choose on the basis of knowledge" rather than preformatted truths that suit the powers that be.[26]

In the way it combines imagination with thinking, then, demonstration points to the need for careful *preparation* when it comes to revolution and change, militating (with Gramsci) against the idea that higher consciousness can be the result of a spontaneous evolution independent of will and intellectual reflection. This was particularly important for the way that artists such as Harun Farocki, Joseph Beuys, or Bazon Brock, for all their differences, tied demands for revolutionary change in the colonized world—in the countries of Africa, Palestine, or Vietnam—to the analysis of social and political oppression in their home country.

The instructional, awareness-raising mission of demonstration also has a self-reflexive aspect: designed to educate the public, demonstrations, so the theory went, instructed the demonstrators as well. This autodidactic element was directly addressed by Dutschke when he wrote in 1968 that "all the fights with the police and the frustrations and increased aggressions that resulted from them . . . should be understood as a permanent learning process, as a continuous effort to change the structure of one's own character structure."[27] Dutschke elsewhere calls this autodidactic process *Selbstaufklärung*, or self-enlightenment, a designation that, while it certainly had its detractors, corresponded to an understanding of demonstration widespread during the 1960s.[28]

Self-reflexive demonstration desublimates and redefines experientially the confluence of art and social action by reflecting on the value of pointing itself.[29] Here, demonstration becomes deliberately *ostentatious*, a term I understand literally as an emphasis on the act of showing that was as such of particular interest to artists. Demonstration's self-referential side rarely erupted as bluntly as in a photograph that shows student protesters on the streets of West Berlin in 1967, during a protest against the right-wing Springer newspaper group. As Robert Stockhammer has argued, the fact that one participant carried a sign with the inscription "DEMONSTRANT" was motivated both instrumentally—caricaturing as it did a city ordinance that had mandated a certain number of security personnel to accompany the demonstration—and performatively, with the latter aspect neatly addressed by a protester who urged his colleagues to "demonstrate in order to demonstrate!"[30]

Throughout this book, I juxtapose examples of art-as-demonstration from Western Europe and the United States with Eastern European examples. It is routinely assumed that the attitude of nonofficial Eastern European artists toward politics was antipolitical or even "dissident," suggesting that these artists subscribed to practices that helped them shore up art's autonomy in the face of a public sphere where art was being instrumentalized for propaganda purposes. However, it must not be forgotten that the term "antipolitical," in the way it negates politics, still retains a crucial connection with what it opposes, and "antipolitics" must not be confused with "no politics." In fact, nonofficial demonstrations in Eastern Europe generally reflected widespread dissatisfaction with real existing Socialism and Western liberal democracy alike. In Hungary, for example, a clandestine circle of Maoist students registered their dissatisfaction with their country's Socialism *and* denounced the war in Vietnam by creating a mural portrait of leftist civil rights icon Angela Davis.[31] Elsewhere, reform-minded rather than flatly anti-Communist or "dissident" youth and student cultures targeted the oppressive policies of economic and bureaucratic elites and the educational establishment, but not necessarily the abolition of the Socialist system per se.[32] Jacek Kuroń and Karol Modzelewski's famous 1964 "Open Letter for the Party" lamented ossification and bureaucratization, as well as the existence of state capitalism, worker exploitation, and class privilege, in Poland and in the other countries of the Eastern Bloc, yet this did not imply that the authors preferred the Western model of democracy over Socialism.

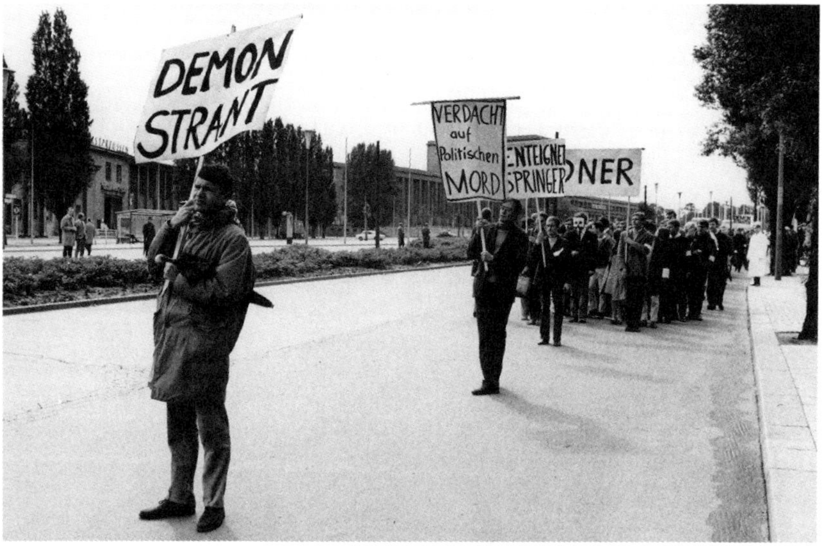

Figure 1.5 *Demonstrant*, student demonstration against the police on the occasion of the shah's visit to West Berlin, June 13, 1967. Photo: Ludwig Ehlers. Landesarchiv Berlin, F Rep. 290 (04) Nr. 0121667.

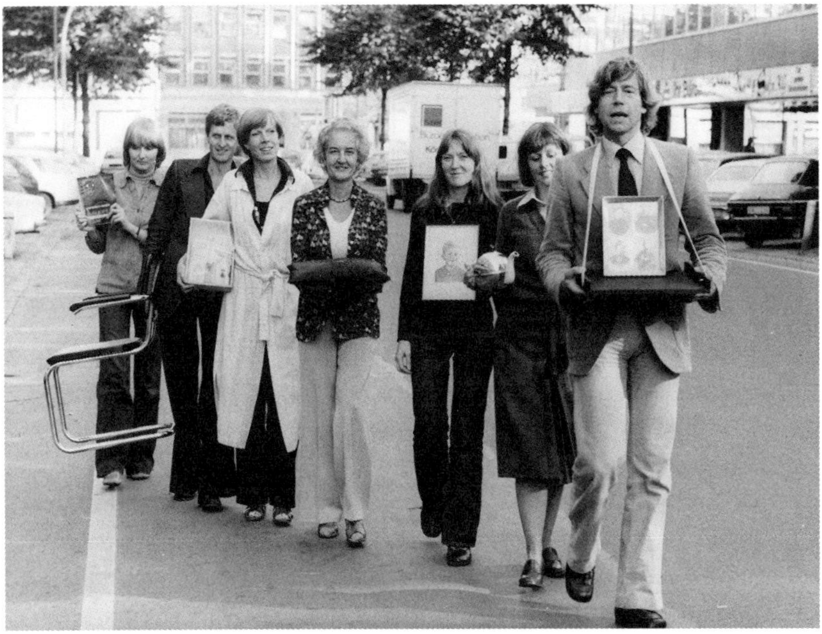

Figure 1.6 Bazon Brock, *Zeig Dein liebstes Gut* (*Show Your Dearest Possessions*), 1977. © and image courtesy of Bazon Brock. Photo: Ludwig Binder.

Rather, their letter was written in the name of a refreshed Communist project that would be based on workers' self-management and proletarian solidarity across the world:

> Our ally against the intervention of Soviet tanks is the Russian, Ukrainian, Hungarian, and Czech working class. Our ally against the pressures and threats of imperialism is the working class of the industrial West and the developing colonial revolution. . . . Against an eventual accord between the international bureaucracy and the international imperialist bourgeoisie, which maintains systems of anti-people's dictatorship in its sphere of influence, we utter the traditional worker's slogan: "proletarians of all countries, unite!"[33]

This passage is less an instance of dissidence than of the painful experience of the gulf that separated the reality of life behind the Iron Curtain from the promises of Communism. The Slovak art critic Tomáš Štrauss surely spoke for many artists and intellectuals in his assessment of the intellectual merits of state Socialism when he wrote that "I could not understand at all how it was possible that they transformed one of the intellectually most ambitious sophisticated philosophical systems of the 19th century [Marxism], into such primitive and illustrative art without any spirit or form."[34]

A few years later, Kuroń's and Modzelewski's call for international solidarity, which by the mid-1960s had been translated into major West European languages and had actively influenced Western protest leaders as well, found a receptive audience among members of an underground group of rebellious Marxist students that included the future Solidarność leader Adam Michnik. The group formed in 1967 under the name Komandosi and began to organize campaigns against state-sponsored anti-Semitism and censorship. On March 8, 1968, following the expulsion from the university of two prominent student leaders—among them, Michnik—and the cancellation of a play by the Polish national poet Adam Mickiewicz, violent clashes broke out at universities all over Poland between security forces and university students who demanded freedom of speech, the press, and demonstration.[35] The art historian Luiza Nader has argued that despite obvious similarities, it's important that we remain mindful of what separates these protests from their counterparts in the West: "The character of the 1968 political events in Poland was thoroughly different from the student demonstrations in France or on university campuses in the United States" because, according to Nader, they mark the end of an era rather than a new beginning: the end of the hopes for a reform-minded system that had been raised in the wake of the post-Stalinist thaw.[36]

In early June 1968, student demonstrations also broke out in the Yugoslav capital, Belgrade. Again, far from demanding an altogether different system, demonstrators paraded through the streets of the Yugoslav capital with posters showing the country's leader Josip Broz Tito from the days of his Partisan fight against the German invaders. Their intent was to remind onlookers of the disparity between past promises and the current state of affairs, whereby the foundations on which the Yugoslav federation had been built seemed to be subject to progressive erosion.[37] The tensions between the students and the government resulted, among other things, in the creation of the Student Cultural Center in Belgrade in 1968, the first in a network of semiautonomous cultural institutions run by students that became crucial staging grounds for the development of the so-called New Practices.[38]

While some of the examples of Eastern European art-as-demonstration I discuss in the following chapters are more or less strictly private—consider GDR artist Ruth Wolf-Rehfeldt's *Didactic Typewritings* from the early 1970s, which served the artist as a way to demonstrate the broad range of forms available on the typewriter for the production of visual poetry[39]—others appeal to their audience directly. I am thinking, for instance, of Milan Knížak's aforementioned demonstrations on the streets of Prague's old town in the first half of the 1960s, Włodzimierz Borowski's *Syncretic Demonstration* (1966), or Jiří Kovanda's actions in the center of Prague. In

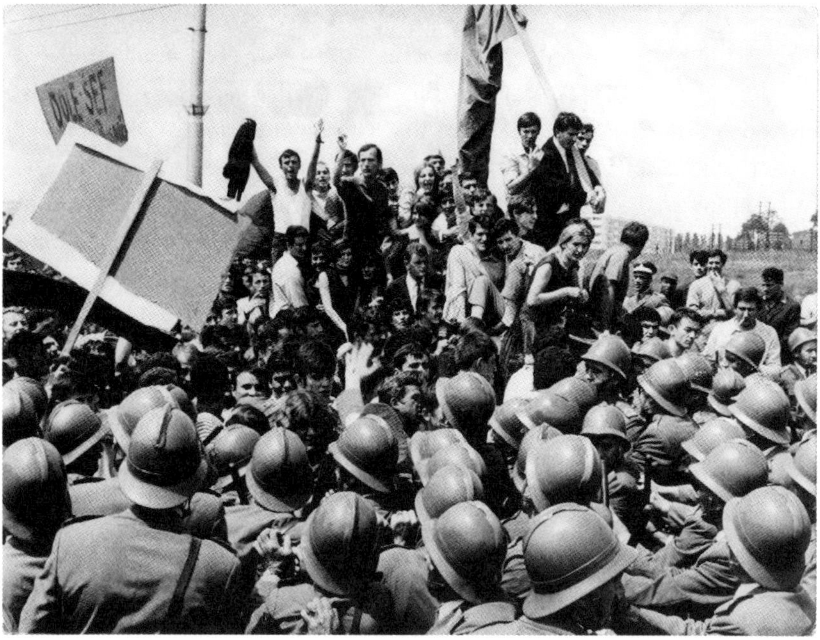

Figure 1.7 Student demonstrations in Belgrade, 1968. Image courtesy of Museum of Yugoslavia. Photo: Stevan Kragujević.

another crucial demonstration-based artwork from the period, Bálint Szombathy, in a public action called *Lenin in Budapest* (1972), carried a hand-held sign he had appropriated from an official Party rally with a blown-up image of Lenin through the streets of Budapest. Meanwhile, Hungarian Gyula Pauer's legendary *Forest of Protest Signs* was an installation realized in 1978 in the artist settlement in the Hungarian countryside at Nagyatád that had been established in the second half of the 1960s to advance cultural life in the countryside. The installation consisted of a dense "forest" of tall wooden poles with square boards on top that bore a variety of inscriptions in Hungarian. These inscriptions were quickly deemed subversive by government officials, and the installation was taken down only a few days after its creation.[40]

Eastern European instances of art-as-demonstration such as Pauer's offer the intriguing case of an "antipolitical" art practice with a clear political charge. In their appeal to the public, such demonstrations exceed the confines of what is unambiguously antipolitical, even if that does not make them squarely political.[41] This is the case even where, as was frequently the case in Eastern Europe, art-as-demonstration limits itself to intervening in the instrumental means-ends logic of daily life without promoting any far-reaching political goals for the rebuilding of society as a whole.

In their study *The New Spirit of Capitalism* (1999), Luc Boltanski and Ève Chiapello distinguished, for the 1960s, between artistic and social critique, viewing both as responses to four fundamental sources of indignation: capitalism as a source of disenchantment and inauthenticity, as a source of oppression, as a source of poverty and inequalities, and as a source of opportunism and egoism. And while, according to the authors, the first two sources are at the heart of artistic critique, the last two are more characteristic of social critique.[42] The difference between social and artistic critique is formative for my argument, even as I will be particularly interested in art that undermines their strict separation. For example, *Metzger's First Public Demonstration of Auto-Destructive Art* (1960) was as closely related to the history of painting—and to the need to react to that history—as to the

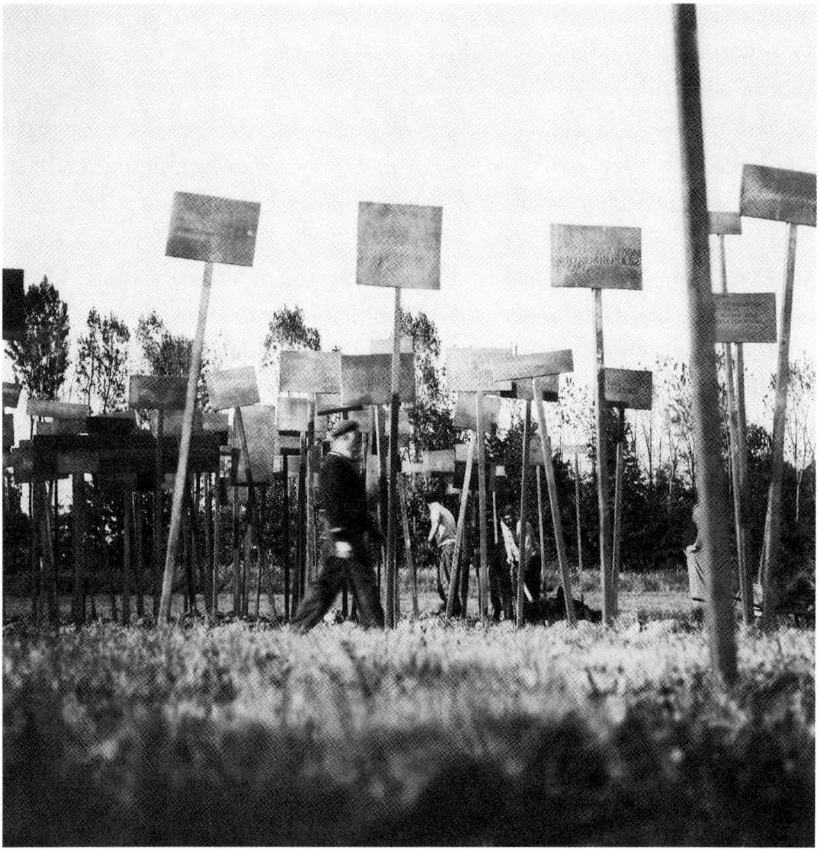

Figure 1.8 Gyula Pauer, *Forest of Protest Signs*, 1978. Image courtesy of Emánuel Pauer.

artist's critical attitude toward nuclear proliferation. Another prominent demonstration from the early years of the decade, Beuys's *Demonstration: Hand* (1961) further deepens this ambiguity, presenting two images of a hand in such a way that we are unsure whether what we are seeing is a single hand (for making things) or two demonstrating hands in the plural, perhaps as part of a street demonstration.

Beuys seems to deliberately conflate the two readings in a bid to present the two sides of demonstration as being either self-reflexive (demonstration *of* a hand) or as a form of protest (demonstration *by* a hand).[43] Other demonstrations adopted a more metaphysical perspective, including Düsseldorf-based Klaus Rinke's *Primary Demonstrations* from the mid-1960s where the artist used bodily gestures and motions to create "drawings in space" in order to explore binary concepts like "the masculine" and "the feminine."

Meanwhile, in Eastern Europe, while the sources of disenchantment Chiapello and Boltanski identify as being root causes for artistic and social critique applied to real existing Socialism in equal measure, there was more separation, behind the Iron Curtain, between the social and the artistic side of critique than was the case in the West, and with good reason. Whereas in the West, artists and protesters worked together to develop demonstrative formats that battled the capitalist public sphere and its production of false consciousness in the name of Mao and Che Guevara, in Eastern Europe, artists and intellectuals—even the few who sympathized with the New Left in the West—suffered from the fact that many of the New Left's slogans and icons had long since been used by their own regimes, regimes that betrayed the ideals of Communism even as they claimed to represent them.[44] As a result—and not only because of the artists' preference for artistic autonomy—many nonofficial Eastern European artists and intellectuals did not use these slogans and were weary of enlisting art in a project of political renewal.[45] Noemi Smolik, drawing on Gayatri Spivak's theorization of the subaltern, has described this dilemma in reference to the pre-1968 Czechoslovak Socialist Republic as a "discursive impasse."[46] As Slovak art historian Andrea Bátorová has noted of the reaction by one

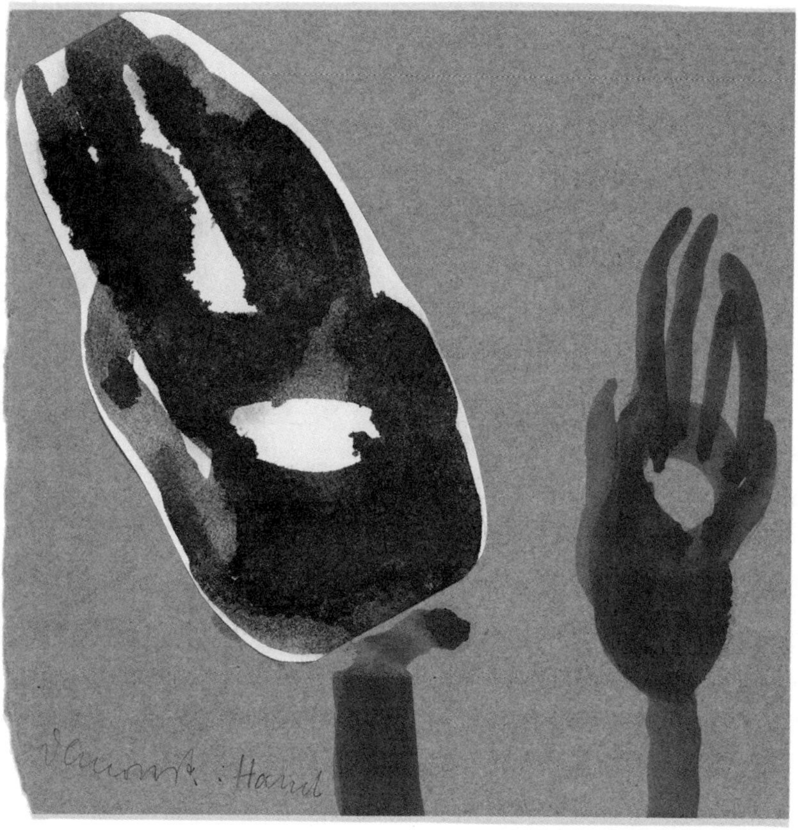

Figure 1.9 Joseph Beuys, *Hand*, 1961. © 2024 Artists Rights Society (ARS), New York / VG Bild-Kunst, Bonn. Photo Tate.

of Slovakia's most important performance artists, Alex Mlynárčik, to the 1968 invasion of Czechoslovakia: "Basically for him as a citizen of a Socialist state who knew all the consequences of a totalitarian system from experience, it was very difficult to get worked up about the . . . revolutionary ideas in the West."[47]

DEMONSTRATION AND THE DIDACTIC

As an instance of instruction, demonstration is closely linked with the didactic, a concept derived from the Greek verb διδάσκειν that translates into English as "to teach." While traditionally didactics has tended to be associated with particular *methods* of teaching, in the 1960s, scholars of education more broadly began to associate the term with the contents and subjects of instruction, thus expanding its remit to include *what* was being taught.[48]

Didacticism in or as art has traditionally been met with widespread disdain whose basis is the fear that art with a stake in instruction is, or may be perceived as, heteronomous, thus lowering its status as art. Yet the denial of art's didactic dimension overlooks the fact that in the premodern and early modern eras, the notion that art was didactic was commonplace. In antiquity, didactic poems were a genre in themselves, and works such as Hesiod's *Works and Days* often used meter as a mnemonic device so that the hearer could assimilate the technical (in Hesiod's case, agricultural) knowledge conveyed by the verse. Indeed, according to the Princeton *Encyclopedia of Poetry and Poetics*, "the seed of all poetry is the proverb, the gnomic line, the memorizable rhyme,"[49] with the purest forms of didactic poetry reserved for verse that both conveys information and provides for a pleasurable experience in the listener, as in Horace's formulation: "The man who mingles the useful with the sweet carries the day by charming his reader and at the same time instructing him,"[50] a formula that was, in the words of Norbert Kössinger and Claudia Wittig, a "universal phenomenon" in ancient literature and the arts.[51] The history of art too is replete with examples of didacticism. This frequently involved an iconography that instructed viewers in certain articles of religious or other dogmas: think of the religious iconography of the Middle Ages, including such curiosities as the demonstrative display of Christ's genitals in Renaissance paintings (*ostentatio genitalium*), whereby baby Jesus' penis is not only present but demonstrated in a variety of ways, arguably in order to highlight the Christian dogma of his humanness.[52] Other well-known examples of a historical art practice focused on instruction and demonstration include Baroque (Jesuit) theater and, more generally, all art focused on a virtuous lifestyle.

For instance, the so-called *Tabula cebetis*, a large 1568 painting created in a Bruges painting workshop, combines episodic series of images with descriptive text focused on human life as a journey composed of lessons whose goal is to enable the traveler to distinguish between what is right and what is wrong, so that true education can be attained. In this scheme, even the seven *artes liberales* are nothing but temporary waystations on the way to a virtuous life.

In modern times, tolerance for the didactic increasingly competed with demands that art and literature exist for their own sake, encapsulated in Edgar Allan Poe's resounding denunciation of heteronomy as a form of heresy:

> a heresy too palpably false to be long tolerated, but one which, in the brief period it has already endured, may be said to have accomplished more in the corruption of our Poetical Literature than all its other enemies combined. I allude to the heresies of *The Didactic*. . . . We have taken it into our heads that to write a poem simply for the poem's sake . . . would be to confess ourselves radically wanting in the true Poetic dignity and force:—but the simple fact is that would we but permit ourselves to look into our own souls we should immediately there discover that under the sun there neither exists nor *can* exist any work more thoroughly dignified, more supremely noble, than this

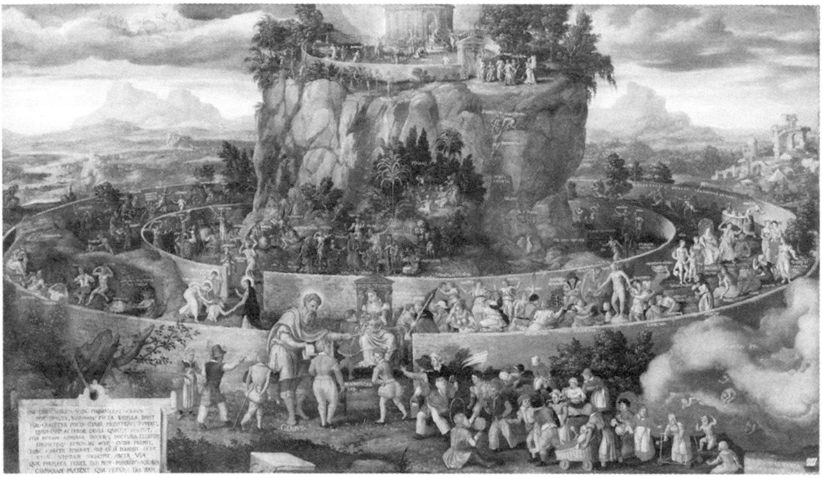

Figure 1.10 Peter Claeissens, *Cebestafel*, 1568. Museumslandschaft Hessen Kassel, Gemäldegalerie Alte Meister. Photo: Ute Brunzel.

> very poem—this poem *per se*—this poem which is a poem and nothing more—this poem written solely for the poem's sake.[53]

In so many ways, Poe's invective set the tone for didactic art's modern detractors who have tended to associate the didactic with an unseemly overload of heteronomous elements that distract from art's presumed essence. As Luis Camnitzer has argued, "didactics is generally considered a dirty word . . . it is the primacy of formalism and the promotion of art for art's sake that led to a very simplistic definition of didactics and to its blacklisting. In formalism's dismissive definition of 'didacticism,' explicit messages are viewed as *dumbed down*."[54]

Didactic art reentered the vocabulary of twentieth-century art criticism in 1967, with the publication, in *Artforum*, of an article by the young critic Barbara Rose entitled "The Value of Didactic Art." Rose uses "didactic" as a way of identifying some of the positions that would come to be associated with concept or idea art. In an effort to theorize the work of US neo-avant-garde artists, including Jasper Johns, Robert Rauschenberg, Andy Warhol, Robert Morris, Carl Andre, and Ad Reinhardt, Rose argues that while all art teaches a lesson in a broad sense ("all valid art, of course, teaches something"), didactic art has a more specific function: "I am defining didactic art as art whose primary intention is to instruct. Within the terms of this definition, Jasper Johns's 1955 flag, based on a diagrammatic drawing of the US flag, is a 'didactic' work, whereas a painting by Barnett Newman, which also teaches a lesson, is not."[55] While the precise parameters of this distinction remain somewhat blurry, it's clear that Rose hinges didactic art to the development of heteronymous "propositions" (her term) about the nature of art: "Works of didactic art are, in other words, illustrations of theoretical esthetic positions condensed into a single object, which stands for the entire argument. They represent abstract ideas made concrete in works of art. Their value is relative to the cogency, clarity and originality of the argument they illustrate."[56] The verb "illustrate" is key here, for much like a teacher's demonstration of a mathematical formula on a blackboard, didactic art does not *embody* its argument; it serves as a way of initiating a conversation (according to Rose, didactic art's "principal value is as dialogue, not as object").[57] Rose sees the purest examples of didactic art in Duchamp's unassisted readymade: "Pure didactic art includes that whole class of found objects which Duchamp termed 'unassisted ready-mades'; it includes virtually nothing else."[58]

Around the time Rose published her piece, *Artforum* was running a series of articles entitled "Problems of Criticism" in which contributors reflected on the challenges that post-Abstract Expressionist art created for critics. Rose's article belongs within the orbit of these reflections, even if it did not explicitly appear under the same rubric. Clearly, her use of the term "didactic" in a positive sense was in itself a novelty on the pages of the magazine, where the word was generally treated as a synonym of "pedantic" or "academic."

In 1968, one year after the publication of Rose's article, didactic art was taken up again in *Artforum*, this time by the young Jack Burnham, in a well-known article entitled "System Esthetics."[59] Burnham begins by identifying the dilemma that had also driven Rose's investigation: the fact that there was as yet no name for what he calls "post-formalist" tendencies in art that he, like Rose, wants to theorize. However, Burnham's approach is broader than Rose's: where Rose's goal, based in large part on the phenomenology of postformalist art, was to argue for a plurality of "beautiful arguments," Burnham is convinced that the erosion of the boundaries between art and other disciplines—science, research, the natural environment, social life—necessitates a new critical approach based on "research and production" and a new type of art as a form of organization and information-handling. Burnham seeks a new critical framework in order to account for "unobjects, these being either environments or artifacts which resist prevailing critical analysis," a category under which he subsumes expanded sculpture as well as "some gallery kinetic and luminous art, some outdoor works, happenings, and mixed media presentations."[60] As artistic activities increasingly cannot be distinguished from other types of social production, the artist now acts as an organizer of society's productive forces, using information to model the relations between people and environments.

Burnham theorizes this state of affairs with the help of systems aesthetics, a cutting-edge line of scientific inquiry he had recently culled from biological theorist Ludwig Bertalanffy's book *General System Theory* (1968), where the author argues that every part of a given system can be understood only with respect to the other parts in the same system, and the system as a whole only as a function of the other systems within which it is embedded. Systems theory, designed among other things to facilitate teaching in the sciences, opened the way toward understanding art, too, as a system that can be understood only in its relationship with other systems and disciplines. As Burnham writes, systems analysis implies "the creation of stable, on-going relationships between organic and non-organic systems, be these neighborhoods, industrial complexes, farms, transportation systems, information centers, or any of the other matrixes of human activity."[61] He is convinced that "intuitively many artists have already grasped these relatively recent distinctions" and that the environmental, context-oriented approach of recent postformalist art—in line with Bertalanffy's idea of "open systems" whose exchange with their surrounding environment he qualifies as "organized complexity"—further reflects this fact.[62]

Burnham, who mentions some of the same artists as Rose, takes her understanding of didactic art a step further by broadening what Rose had identified as (didactic) art's predisposition toward dialogue and exchange into a more systematically understood notion of the environment. If, as Burnham reminds us, capitalist society exists in a state of alienation ("society thus estranged") then the idea, central to modernism, that art production can be exempt from such a state of affairs and exist in a state of unadulterated reconciliation and authenticity is no longer tenable.[63]

A case in point is Burnham's discussion of the work of his friend Hans Haacke, whose 1967 solo show at MIT's Hayden Gallery had included *Rain Tree*, a tree dripping water in patterns (1967); *Sky Line, Central Park*, a 1,400-foot suspended string of helium-filled balloons (1967); and other works indebted to systems theory, to which Burnham had introduced the artist.[64] If in these works Haacke had attempted to create art based on systems theory, in another, slightly later work entitled *Photo-Electric Programmed Viewer Coordinated System* (1968), the artist went beyond a purely technical approach by including a didactic element. The installation featured a white cube with infrared beams that set off rows of light bulbs based on the visitor's movements ("environmental feedback," in Haacke's description); this "learning curve" was interrupted when another visitor entered the space:

> Then another person enters the white cube and begins on the same short learning curve. Lights switch on and off. You pause. An expression of annoyance flickers across your face. The requirement to share space, recognize another with the same basic skills and claim to a luminescent reward. . . . You settle back on your heels patiently. Resolution. You suspect new possibilities. Waiting for an appropriate moment you catch the other person's eyes—a playful invitation. The stranger catches your hint immediately. Together you begin an impromptu performance.[65]

The learning curve is mediated at first by the technical feedback mechanism inside the cube, but then extended to the relationship between the two visitors as a result of their interaction with the system. The two rivals are turned into collaborators, illustrating Burnham's view that "the specific function of modern didactic art has been to show that art does not reside in material entities, but in relations between people and between people and the components of their environment."[66]

Burnham praises Haacke's work as an instance of technical self-sufficiency and lack of empathy ("He [Haacke] insists that the need for empathy does not make his work function as with older art. Systems exist as ongoing independent entities away from the viewer"),[67] corroborating the impression that for Burnham, the didactic is a way for contemporary art to assimilate the technological possibilities of the modern age beyond the teleological format of modernism and its implicit Hegelianism, a position not ultimately so distant from Brecht's assertion that art comprises the desire to "make the world controllable" through science.[68] The artist, for Burnham, is not a maker of objects but a mediator between different forms—in his article Burnham uses the term "homo arbiter formae"—whose decision making based on criteria derived from art will, in the critic's optimistic assumption, help redirect the ecologically fatal course taken by advanced industrial society.[69]

During the 1970s, systems theory came under attack from, among others, artists with a feminist agenda for whom mediation was not a politically neutral form of arbitration, and who did not view the social system as being calibrated in a just and equitable way. While demonstration and didacticism remained key to these feminists, they now served to highlight the unequal distribution of power, and demonstration was used, often ironically, as a way not only to pinpoint women's functionally subservient social position but also to highlight ways in which the problem might be addressed.[70] In a now-iconic, highly demonstrative performance from the mid-1970s, *Semiotics of the Kitchen* (1975), for instance, artist Martha Rosler confronted her audience in the role of a TV cooking show host who demonstrates various kitchen utensils by picking them up by their names, from A to Z (there is no object-equivalent for the last letters). Adopting a role similar in form to Julia Child's then-popular cooking demonstrations, Rosler defamiliarizes the format not only by picking up her tools in alphabetical order—a reference to a seemingly neutral, systematic form of signification—but also by using these tools to visibly vent her anger and exasperation, in motions more akin to fighting than to cooking. If this signals emancipation from the tight pressure of patriarchal gender roles—the apron Rosler puts on at the beginning of her film resembles a straitjacket more than anything—the success of her lesson ultimately hinges on the artist's successful establishment of distance between herself and the "female" tasks she is expected to carry out, even as she stays within the bounds of the system that oppresses her (the kitchen).

In another example of feminist art-as-demonstration, Sanja Iveković's 1979 *Triangle* (*Trokut*), the artist's protest against patriarchy and exclusion is staged as a reading performance. Composed of four photographs accompanied by a text penned by the author, *Triangle* documents a performance in which Iveković lounges and reads a book on the balcony of her Zagreb apartment on May 10, 1979, the day of Yugoslav president Tito's official visit to the city.

People who lived along the motorcade's route had been ordered to stay away from their windows and balconies, and to close the shutters of their windows.[71] Iveković's refusal to comply with these orders by lounging on her balcony (in a pose the artist related to masturbation) amounts to open defiance, especially if we assume that the artist is aware of the fact that she is being watched.[72] The four photographs that an (invisible) photographer takes of the scene add visual context by revealing—or so we presume—what is behind the balcony, and below it: Tito's motorcade as seen from the (same?) balcony; the crowds in the street with a large Yugoslav flag in the foreground; and, finally, a large modernist building with a small figure on top who, equipped with a camera, is observing what we presume is the artist on the balcony.

By declaring her work a triangle—encompassing the observer on the roof, the artist herself, and Tito—Iveković engages geometry, a discipline that uses didactic diagrams to solve mathematical problems related to, among other things, the relative position of figures and the properties of space. On the one hand, the artist's choice of this title may be seen as a vaguely Duchampian move: letting geometry brush up against the chance-filled events that happen in the street.[73] On the other, it allows her to connect her triangle's three extension points (Tito and his motorcade, the artist on her balcony, and the observer with the camera on the roof) into one and the same geometrical figure (the triangle), so that in effect they all become

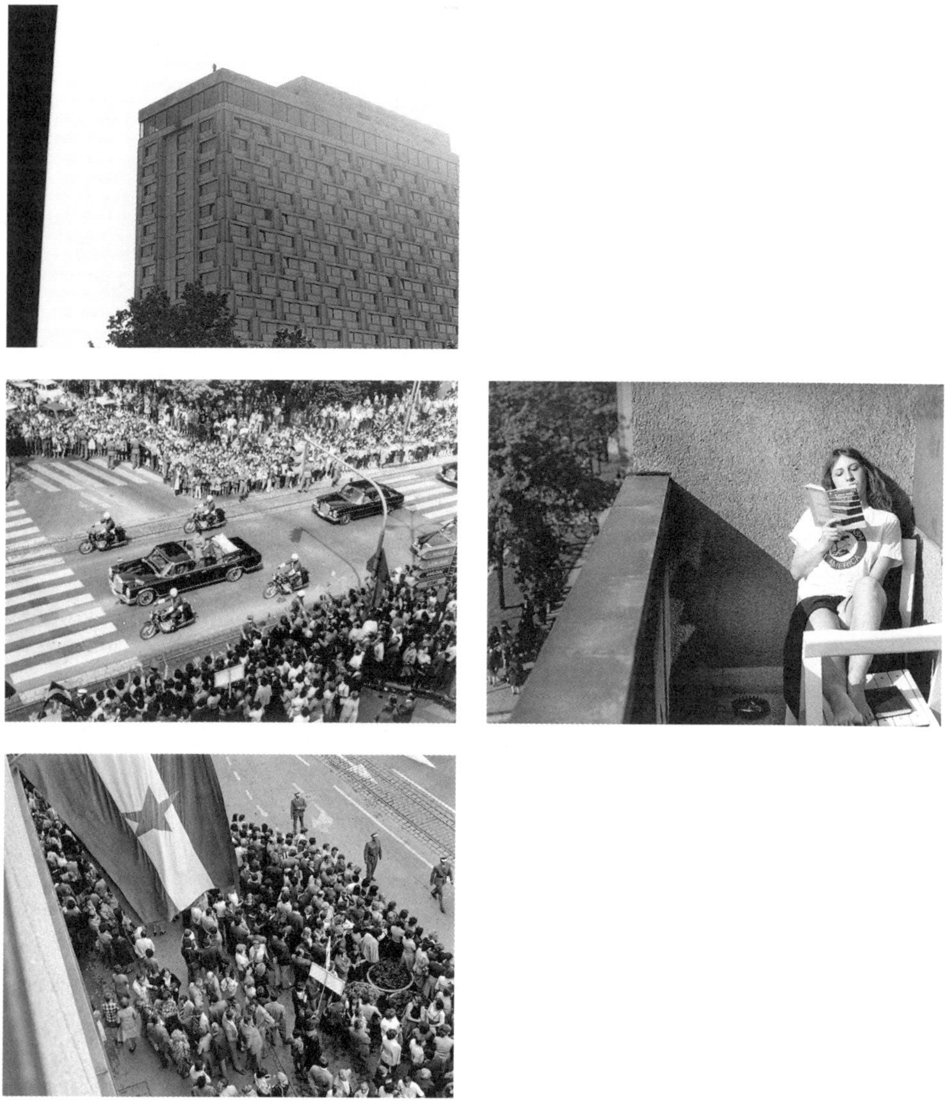

Figure 1.11 Sanja Iveković, *Triangle* (*Trokut*), 1979. Museo Nacional Centro de Arte Reina Sofía, Madrid. Image courtesy of Sanja Iveković.

part of her performance, now encompassing knowledge (Iveković reading a book), politics and its representation (Tito's motorcade, the street demonstrations), and, third, what in the broadest sense we may refer to as the imaginary (the observer with the camera on the roof). What to make of this transformation?

In commentaries on *Triangle*, neither the fact that the artist is reading nor *what* she is reading—T. B. Bottomore's classic *Elites and Society* (1964)—has received much attention.[74] As a book, Bottomore's study marks a counterpoint to *Triangle*'s more cinematic aspects, represented by the observer on the roof. This cinematic mode implies a way of looking at the scene on the balcony that turns that scene—roughly in the vein of the Lacanian Imaginary—into a chronologically coherent (film) sequence. The person on the roof observes the artist and communicates his or her findings to other members of the police, who in turn proceed to knock on Iveković's door and ask her to remove "all the objects" from her balcony.[75] In open contrast to this cinematic reading of the performance, the book in the artist's hand produces knowledge very differently: with recourse to language primarily, more systematically and discursively, and without the kind of cathexis we might associate with a gripping story involving the police, recalcitrant artists, fetishized politicians, and long motorcades.

Iveković makes herself part of both these scenes or modes rather than positioning herself outside of their triangular structure, as if her goal was to demonstrate them rather than choose between them. In this way, the artist demonstrates that diagrams are what Brian Rotman, in his semiotic analysis of mathematics, calls "the work of the body," and that they are "created and maintained as entities and attain significance only in relation to human visual-kinetic presence, only in relation to our experience of the culturally inflected world. As such, they not only introduce the historical contingency inherent to all cultural activity, but . . . they call attention to the materiality of all signs and of the corporeality of those who manipulate them in a way that ideograms . . . do not."[76] In his analysis of diagrams in Dada, the art historian David Joselit has extrapolated from these remarks—and from Deleuze and Guattari's theory of the diagrammatic machine—what he terms the diagram's "embodied utopianism," that is to say, the way in which diagrams combine "phenomenological corporeality" with "pure semiosis."[77] Perhaps it would not be too far-fetched to claim for Iveković's use of the diagram in *Triangle* a similarly embodied feminist perspective, one that combines the phenomenological emphasis on concrete space and temporality with an open utopian horizon.

I argue that demonstration is more than a technical device in the armor of global modernism, functioning as it does as a powerful means for artists to intervene in the reality that surrounds them. In saying this, I am mindful of the ways in which discourses of learning and education have been and are being instrumentalized, not least by a variety of neoliberal and neonationalist regimes in present-day Eastern Europe, where populist governments are using instruction to push a retrograde nationalist cultural agenda.[78] By comparison, the 1960s may seem like a time of unbridled optimism when it comes to trust in the ability of education to raise consciousness and give individuals—indeed, entire societies—a sense of what it would mean to exercise their rational judgment. Yet the 1960s were also the time when the intractable co-dependence of critical art and market-driven economics that is so familiar to us today began to take hold. Not coincidentally, even an alternative project like the famous 1968 *Whole Earth Catalog*—a decidedly instructional project that aimed to create knowledge networks focused on solving practical problems in late capitalist society—reflects a hybrid legacy, basing its existence on two diametrically opposed principles: first, military-industrial research and its emphasis on flat hierarchies and collaborative work between individual scientists; and second, the pedagogical counterculture that had been forming since the 1950s.[79] Art-as-demonstration then presents us with a conundrum: while on the one hand, it is inextricably connected to an optimistic belief in dialogue, progress, and instruction as an emancipatory force, on the other hand, its optimism is forever threatened by an equally intractable blind spot with regard to its proclivity for being manipulated.

2

OSTENTATIOUS NEUTRALITY (BERNAR VENET, DANIEL BUREN, ADRIAN PIPER)

One significant exception to the disdain in which the didactic has generally been held is Bertolt Brecht's concept of epic theater (*episches Theater*). The playwright's major theoretical texts became available to an English-speaking audience in the 1960s through John Willett's pathbreaking volume of translations, *Brecht on Theatre: The Development of an Aesthetic* (1966). Brecht understood epic theater explicitly as following in the tradition of the didactic arts of the past, including their "expository character and . . . emphasis on virtuosity."[1] As he argues, "didactic tendencies are to be found in the medieval mystery plays and the classical Spanish theatre, and also in the theatre of the Jesuits," but he also counts avant-garde theater and (montage) film, with their daring display of "right and wrong courses of action," among the forerunners of his own brand of *Lehrtheater*. Brecht notes that while "there is nothing all that new about the epic theatre," the reemergence of didactic theatrical forms, after being violently shut down by fascism, needed "a powerful movement in society . . . interested to see vital questions freely aired with a view to their solution."[2] In this spirit, for Brecht, the didactic theater is a form for which the distinction between art, on the one hand, and scientific knowledge, on the other, has no meaning ("I have to admit that I cannot get along as an artist without the use of one or two sciences") and, as such, he wants theater to fight the capitalist instrumentalization and commodification of knowledge for the benefit of the disadvantaged: "There are . . . strata 'waiting their turn' who are discontented with conditions, have a vast interest in the practical side of learning, want at all costs to find out where they stand, and know that they are lost without learning; these are the best and keenest learners. . . . Thus, the pleasure of learning depends on all sorts of things; but none the less there is such a thing as . . . cheerful and militant learning."[3] For Brecht, the playwright has a claim to power and control—"a desire to make the world controllable" (to use Burnham's words)—whose medium is the use and demonstration of ideas from a broad variety of disciplines, at the service of an anticipated better, more just world. As Fredric Jameson has argued, the delight Brecht takes in science is motivated less by science's representation or mimesis than by his (Brecht's) interest in the demonstration of ideas, in teaching: "The delight in learning lies ultimately in the *gestus* of showing as such. . . . Teaching is thus showing. . . . The dramatic representation of teaching is the showing of showing, the showing of how you show and demonstrate."[4] Being militant and partisan—with a clear sense of who might benefit from its lessons—Brechtian didactic theater, which as Jameson notes is not really interested in teaching "something," stands in the tradition of Friedrich Schiller's view of the theater stage as a "moral institute" (*moralische Anstalt*) where the distinction between pleasure or amusement, on the one hand, and useful moral instruction, on the other, has no purchase.[5]

In this and other respects, Brecht's understanding of instruction is close to what his friend Walter Benjamin outlined in his 1934 lecture "The Author as Producer," where he describes the nonexpert artist as collating and connecting knowledge from a broad variety of fields and disciplines in an effort to redirect its meaning. Benjamin refers to this, with Brecht, as *Umfunktionierung* (retooling), by which he means that an artist changes the conditions for the production of text and images—for example, by becoming a photographer—rather than using them to illustrate a progressive political standpoint (a *Tendenz*, in Benjamin's wording). Benjamin's authors-as-producers are teachers in a double sense: first in that, by acquiring new skills in which they have no expertise, they expand literature's technical capabilities; and second in that, through writing, they animate others to follow their example. In his view, instruction leads by example, not by dispensing specialist knowledge or by illustrating a political *Tendenz*, however progressive it may be: "This further requires a directing, instructing stance on the part of the writer. And today this must be demanded more than ever before. *An author who teaches writers nothing teaches no one.* What matters, therefore, is the exemplary character of production, which is able, first, to induce other producers to produce, and, second, to put an improved material apparatus at their disposal."[6] Such exemplary art production appeals to readers or viewers to become producers themselves, thus further eroding the difference between writers and readers.

The return, to art of the expanded 1960s, of various inflections of Brechtian/Benjaminian didactic *Umfunktionierung* manifests itself, among other things, in a thorough reexamination of the artist's competence and expertise. Benjamin's artists-as-producers overcome the limitations of traditional artistic skill and competence in line with technical progress and political necessity. As a reward, they are able to communicate "with certain other producers who earlier seemed scarcely to concern [them],"[7] resulting in forms of instruction that persistently blur the line separating teachers from students. As an example of how this played out in art of the 1960s, I want to turn to the young Bernar Venet, who arrived in New York City for a first visit in 1966, and whom Burnham discusses in his book *The Structure of Art* (1971). A self-taught artist from the south of France, Venet felt alienated from the object-focused approach of the *Nouveaux réalistes* and decided to leave France for the US. During his first trip to New York, he saw the works of the minimalist US avant-garde in the Lipman collection at the Whitney, including Donald Judd's. According to Thierry de Duve, this experience showed Venet that a work of art could be "conceived by an artist and executed by an engineer whose role it was to clear the work of any romantic, expressive, or artisanal connection with its author."[8] Already before coming to the States, Venet had experimented with various forms of non-art and nonrelational sculpture, including black works on canvas made from tar. The artist denied that these black tar works had anything to do with artistic expression, a fact that he claimed distinguished them sharply from contemporary (anti-)painting in the manner of, say, Ad Reinhardt's black paintings.[9]

Especially notable instances of Venet's earliest interest in didactic art are the beveled sections of pipes the artist produced in the mid-1960s: made of either industrial polyvinyl or painted cardboard, some of these objects were accompanied by wall-mounted information that related to their material and structure. As Venet comments,

> the pipe was designed as a minimal form without multiple signification, a piece that existed objectively only through its volume. It appeared to me . . . that I might present a piece of information about this pipe, an analysis of the pipe that would be its diagram (precisely indicating its dimensions, its color, its material) instead of the pipe itself. Within the logic of my thinking, the presentation of this diagram was tantamount to the object itself, from the point of view of its signification within the context in which I inserted it.[10]

The diagrams accompanying the pipes were meant to act as a representational limitation designed to prevent these objects from functioning symbolically or otherwise expressively (this is what Venet calls a "rational image").

During his second trip to the United States in 1967 Venet visited the mathematics and physics departments at Columbia University. What he saw and heard there inspired him to think that, even though he was not an expert in either discipline, mathematics and physics offered an "objective, rational way of analyzing the world"[11] that could help him in his quest for an art beyond representation and expression. Venet's idea of a

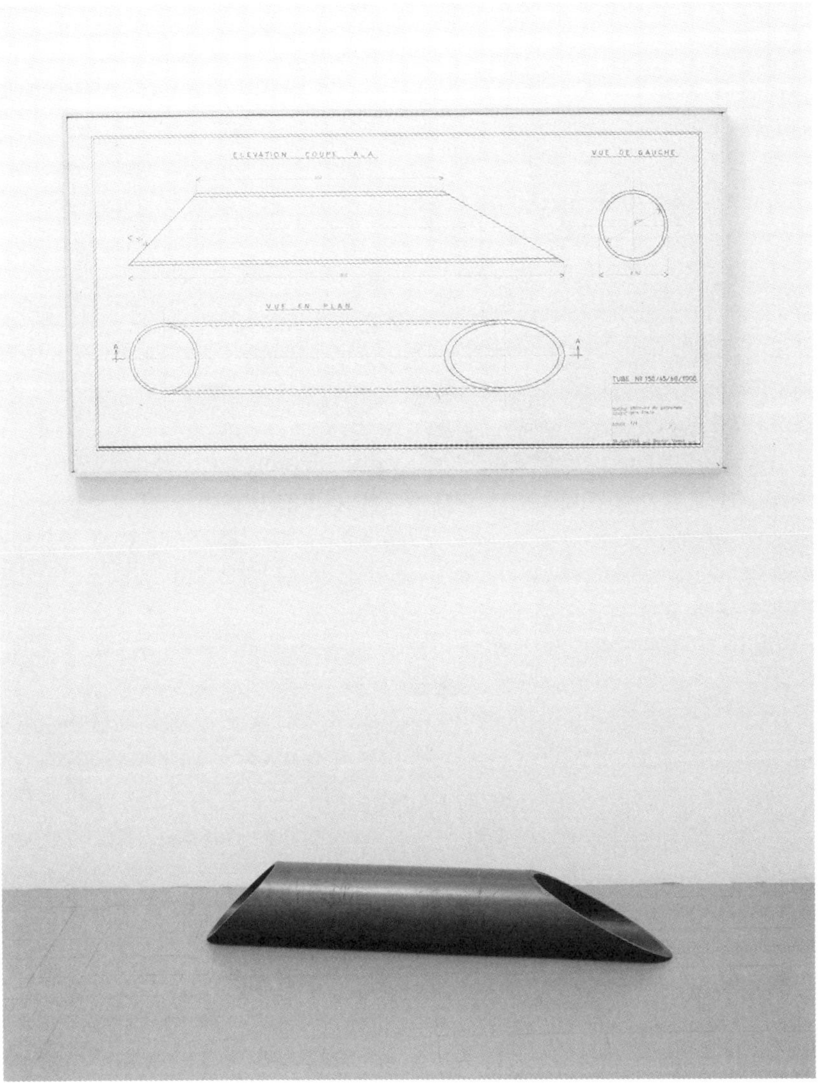

Figure 2.1 Bernar Venet, *Tube n° 150 / 45 / 60 / 1000*, June 18, 1966. Drawing on tracing paper and Bakelite tube, 83 × 153 cm (drawing); 15 cm diameter × 100 cm (tube). © Bernar Venet.

neutral communication borrowed from mathematical notation must be read alongside other efforts in the 1960s to use mathematics to purge art of expressiveness, including Sol LeWitt's and Walter De Maria's use of specific units or Fibonacci numbers.

Venet soon began to present school mathematics, physics, chemistry and various kinds of industrial drawing. The hand-drawn or photographically reproduced graphs, meteorological charts, blown-up book pages, and economic diagrams that are the products of this effort were conceived as lessons whose goal it was to instill in their beholders a stringent way of reasoning.[12] The titles of these works (*Spectrum Calibration Diagram* [1967]; *Time Spectrum of Coincidences between Electron and Gamma Rays* [1967]; *Parabole de la function* $y = 2x^2 + 3x - 2$ [1966]) were meant to exclude any interpretation or description that would exceed the values demonstrated in the diagrams themselves. Venet thus claimed pure objectivity for his didactic presentations of blown-up mathematical equations: "I did not present Mathematics as Art, but Mathematics as such, for its own importance, for its own function."[13]

Only if the copied subject matter does not allude to anything outside itself can the idea behind the work truly be its sole focus, and the fact that this idea is not simply expressed becomes its content. Venet's didacticism differed in crucial ways from Rose's, for whom didactic art remained tied to Duchamp's idea that anything in the world, once it has been chosen for this task, can be experienced as art. Venet, on the other hand, did not lay claim to the Duchampian legacy in this way; his optimistic assumption was that, on the contrary, his use of diagrams would enable him to circumvent aesthetic experience altogether. His work of the mid-1960s establishes a kind of techno-artistic pedagogy that combines technical expertise with abstract knowledge. Crucially, if in one sense Venet's demonstrations of mathematical equations do not limit themselves to the purely instrumental aspects of technology—stressing its artistic possibilities instead—they also expose the gap that separates a mathematical notation from the

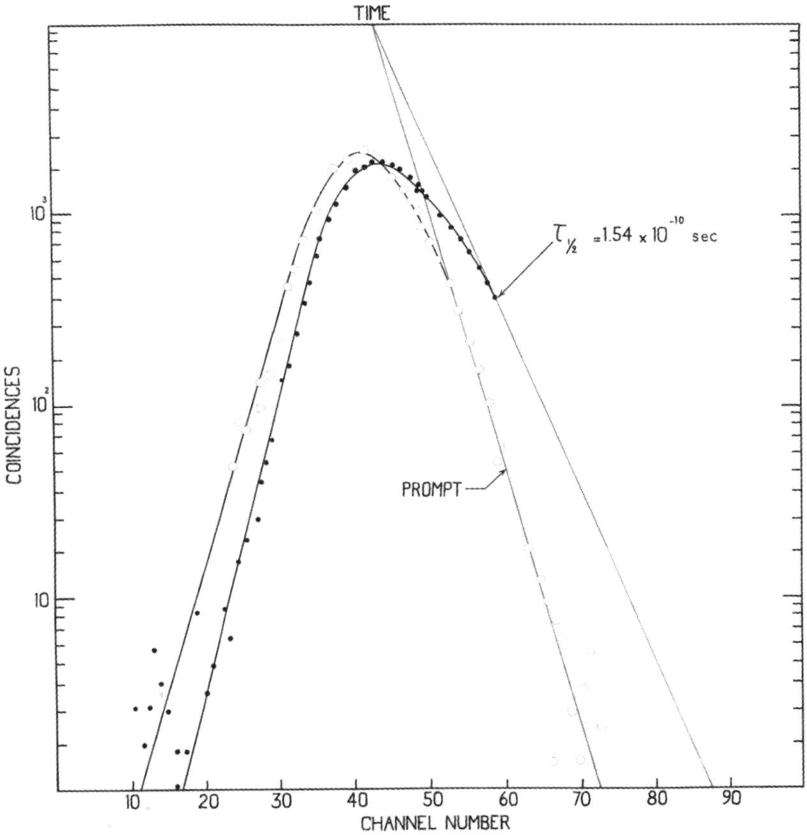

Figure 2.2 Bernar Venet, *Time Spectrum of Coincidences between Electrons and Gamma Rays*, 1967. Acrylic on canvas. Museum of Modern Art, New York, US. Photo credit: © Bernar Venet.

aesthetic experience we may attribute to it. In the last resort, it is such differentiation—between a thought process, its semiotic notation, and the latter's aesthetic qualities—that constitutes the didactic lesson of Venet's work from the mid-1960s.[14] His approach clearly differed from classical aesthetics, which had aimed for the convergence of beauty and truth, epitomized in the formula "the beauty of truth." As Dieter Mersch has argued, such thinking was grounded in mathematics or geometry, inasmuch as harmonious proportions and symmetry were thought to lend knowledge irrefutable credibility.[15] In his rejection of such thinking, Venet came close to Max Bense's efforts to base art production on mathematics and semiotics. Like Venet, Bense viewed aesthetic and semantic information as essentially separate, defining both pragmatically, through the way they were being used.[16]

While he acknowledged the importance of Duchamp for his work, Venet was careful to distinguish his approach from the readymade, with the didactic element as the chief point of difference. The information Venet borrows did not, in his view, function like a readymade inasmuch as he did not substitute—in the manner of the *Nouveaux réalistes*—a represented object with a real one; nor did he, in the way other conceptual artists tended to do, replace an object with a text. Furthermore, unlike the readymade, which, once transferred to the art context, became fully disconnected from the real-life environment in which it existed before, Venet's information pieces, fully readable and unaltered as they were, remained connected to the scientific discipline from which they hailed; instead of negating the use value of the borrowed item, as the readymade did, the artist's didactic demonstrations manifestly affirmed such value.[17]

Venet clearly did not claim for himself the status of an expert in any of the disciplines whose knowledge he demonstrated. Indeed we can read his practice, and didactic art of the 1960s more generally, as a critique of the figure of the expert that informed the Fordist postwar economic system, thus weakening the artist's separation from other areas of expertise.[18] Didactic artists also in this way went against one of the more repressive strategies of the existing education system, for, as Alain Badiou has argued, the separation of the sciences from the humanities that came under attack in 1968 was one of the most effective means for that system to maintain the status quo, separating "the 'pure' practice of theory (the sciences) from instruction in ideology (the arts) by summoning each individual to make a choice between the two based on the supposed 'gifts' the system took pains to detect. In the long run this 'choice' implies in fact the enslavement of science itself to the vague humanism . . . of liberal thought. Nothing is generally more oblivious to the critical powers of science than a scientist. Nothing is better prepared by the educational apparatus for political slavery than the 'expert.'"[19]

While also tentatively overcoming the separation between science and art, Venet's engagement with science contested a model of art production based on specialized technical skill, leading to the idea that the artist, rather than being an (art) expert, (re)connects with a more generalized understanding of (social, scientific, and also pedagogical) expertise.[20] I take my cue here from John Roberts's charge that the biggest provocation of post-World War II art lies not in the fact that it does not rely on the artist's skill, but rather in the fact that it opened the category of authorship to a whole panoply of non-art-related skills, including instruction: "As Duchamp's [calling the readymade a] '*rendezvous*' suggests, the superimposition and reorganization of extant forms and materials opens up the category of art to non-artistic technical skills from other cultural, cognitive, practical and theoretical domains: film, photography, architecture, literature, philosophy and science. Indeed, if art is a site of many different disciplines, materials, and theoretical frameworks, art can be made quite literally from *anything*."[21]

This indeed is the trajectory Bernar Venet follows in his work of the 1960s, combining the critique of the specialist that characterizes what Roberts calls the "post-Cartesian" artist with Burnham's interest in an expanded environment. Interestingly, post-Cartesian artists, in Roberts's view, are not defined exclusively by their loss of skill. Rather than continuing to fetishize technique by focusing on skill as being absent—as any vaunting theory of skillessness does—the post-Cartesian artist comes close to what Joseph Beuys and other cofounders of the Free International University declared in 1973: "Whereas the specialist's insulated point of view places the arts and other kinds of work in sharp opposition, it is in fact crucial that the structural, formal and thematic problems of the various work processes should be constantly compared with each other. The school does not discount the specialist, nor does it adopt an anti-technological stance. It does however reject the idea of experts and technicians being the sole arbiters in their respective fields."[22] In other words, the point is not the abolition of specialization but rather its integration into contexts where specialized knowledge can be compared with other forms of labor, a demand advanced already in the 1920s by the productivist art theorist Boris Arvatov.[23]

The copying from science and mathematics that became Venet's main strategy in 1966 was designed to enable such comparisons. Since his diagrams had been purged of any identifiable (art) content, Venet believed that they could be switched without loss from one medium to another. The artist approached his reproductions as a means to create a form that would be neither modernist in a Greenbergian fashion—focused on belaboring its own medium—nor representational. Instead, it is semiology that occupies him, at a time when the basic texts of this field of inquiry had barely been translated into English.[24] Expressly aligning his approach with the geometrical drawings that Soviet constructivist Aleksandr Rodchenko created with the help of compasses, rulers, and other instruments in the 1920s, Venet used the term "monosemy" to explain his interest in diagrammatical notation. The artist had found this term in Jacques Bertin's recently published *Semiology of Graphics* (1967), a key work for the heightened interest in diagrams and information design that marked the 1960s. For Bertin, who was especially interested in the mobility of visual information in different media, graphic representation in the form of maps, diagrams, and so on was "monosemic," differing in this respect from figurative representation (art, for example), which was, in his terminology, "polysemic" because it was open to different interpretations.[25]

Venet's own use of graphic information coincided both with the publication of Bertin's book and with the radical reforms of the mathematics curriculum at US schools in the mid-1960s (called "New Math"). The artist has pointed out that his works are monosemic only in the use they make of symbols: "The use of mathematics brings monosemy into play. . . . The picture is neither expressive nor aesthetic, because it is structured by a mathematical code which admits no other values, and which itself is valuable only as a function."[26] By contrast, when these same works are being relocated (i.e., by being moved to a gallery or museum), this change of context irrevocably alters the signs' univocity.[27]

Venet viewed his panels of the mid-1960s not as generalizations but, on the contrary, as utterly specific to the problems they spelled out (so specific, in fact, that no other notation would be possible).[28] And while they undoubtedly form part of the "diagrammatical turn" to which Lucy Lippard and John Chandler allude in their famous 1968 article "The Dematerialization of Art" where they discuss the "emphasis [in art of the 1960s] on diagrams and projects, on models and working drawings rather than on finished pieces,"[29] Venet did not regard his *tableaux* as sketches for future projects; nor did they serve, in his estimate, the way verbal instructions or descriptions often do in conceptual art, that is, as tautological affirmations of a work's self-referential qualities.[30]

Venet confidently referred to his approach as "rational art," simultaneously aligning himself with minimalism and seeking to distinguish himself from the new trend: "The work of these artists [the minimalists] is 'rational' because they obey the laws of deductively reasoned construction in which the system of production is rigorously coded beforehand."[31] Venet did feel an affinity for positions held by the minimalists (several of whom he befriended during his stay in New York)—their quest for specificity, opposition to interpretation, rejection of relational or anthropomorphic sculpture, and interest in presentness. Yet he pursued objective rather than phenomenologically grounded knowledge without thinking of his *tableaux* as objects, and without altering their shape in the vein of Frank Stella or Kenneth Noland. Venet's interest in signs and code as a means to create and transmit concrete knowledge, as opposed to the "word-objects" that so fascinated the minimalists, further increases his distance from the minimalist project.[32] As he explained: "My purpose was not to dematerialize art, but to stress . . . that the originality of my work was in its content, the knowledge it conveyed, and its symbolic system, and not in its material characteristics (or lack thereof). The essential element was its new content, the monosemic code, which offered me a large field of investigation and, eventually, positioned my art at the opposite pole of minimalist reduction."[33]

It did not escape Venet's critics that his assertion that his demonstrations successfully avoided aestheticization might be optimistic.[34] Of course, such optimism has its own history. For example, when in the 1920s the progressive philosopher and social scientist Otto Neurath developed his "pictorial statistics following the Vienna method"—combining pictorial symbols with numbers and words to convey social facts—as part of his association with the newly founded Viennese Museum of Society and Economy (1924), his explicit goal was to create an international graphic language capable of conveying facts more efficiently than emotion-laden words could. Neurath argued: "image-based pedagogy, especially pictorial statistics, has international relevance. Words carry more emotional elements within themselves than images based on quantities; . . . *words divide, images connect*. . . . Pictorial statistics is not only a question of school education but beyond that of the education of mankind."[35] However, while in Neurath's case, statistics-driven graphic images had a clearly defined practical function, in Venet's case, that function remained deliberately theoretical. The diagrams Venet copied mattered not because of how useful they were (they were not) but as proof that subject positions can be established without recourse to any forms of subjective expression.[36]

In 1967, Venet set up a working program that anticipated the systematic coverage of different areas of scientific inquiry from the natural and social sciences. As Lucy Lippard notes in *Six Years*,

> Bernar Venet decides to present during the next four years: Astrophysics, Nuclear Physics, Space Sciences, Mathematics by Computation, Meteorology, Stock Market, Meta-Mathematics, Psychophysics and Psychochronometry, Sociology and Politics, Mathematical Logic, etc. "For each discipline an authority advised me upon the subjects to be presented. . . . The question was not to make a new object, a new readymade out of mathematics. I attributed a didactic goal to their presentation. Scientific diagrams were painted, at first by hand, on large canvases; later some were accompanied by taped lectures and the 'paintings' became photographic blow ups of texts or diagrams directly from books."[37]

In his search for areas of cutting-edge science from which to copy, Venet soon began to consult with specialists on the scientific subjects to be represented based on their importance, so that any aesthetic consideration associated with his choice could be excluded. In January 1967, he met Jack Ullmann, a physicist at Columbia University who began advising him on his selection of scientific material based on its relevance and innovation[38]—excluding any aesthetic considerations—and who also showed him the Columbia Mathematics and Physics Library, where Venet would find much of the material he used for his demonstrations. That same year the artist began to create his "rational images" based on weather reports and material from astrophysics, as well as diagrams drawn from the social sciences and economics.[39] As he blew up the information copied from these various disciplines, Venet used a process of proportional scaling, whereby the functions of an image's different parts remained unchanged even as its overall size increased. The artist distinguished this technique from what he called "agrandissement," in which the image's enlargement affects its composition and style, which in its turn modifies its symbolic value. Venet associated this process of enlargement with the traditional artistic methods and genres that he aimed to avoid.[40]

Audio recordings became especially important to the artist.[41] During a meeting of the International Physics Society in 1967, he recorded a lecture by a young professor of theoretical physics on magnetic tape and then played that lecture to a group of his friends in his attic studio. The acousmatic framing Venet uses in this instance suppresses all visuality in the didactic process, concentrating instead on the voice alone; its bearer remains invisible. In this way, listeners were forced to concentrate their attention on the information conveyed, rather than being distracted by the visual aspects of its delivery. This is why Venet insisted that in this work, and in other, similar works, the point was to show that originality was not in the artwork's form or technical medium viewed as separate entities, but in its overall content: "It's evident that the means used are not considered in themselves, they are part of a whole and function in such a way that they valorize a specific theme whose informational properties are the only constitutive element."[42]

In 1968, Venet began to present live scientific lectures by his friend Ullmann, the physicist Martin Krieger, and the medical scientist Stanley Taub at the Judson Memorial Church Theater in Manhattan, whose director he had met a short while earlier. After a year of preparations, the lecture series finally started on May 27 and 28, 1968, spread over two evenings. The first talk was given by Krieger and concerned "Neutron Emission from Muon Capture in Ca^{40}," while the second event consisted of three simultaneous lectures by Krieger, Ullmann, and Edward Macagna before a black screen. Venet considered this second event the least persuasive part of his project because it reminded him too much of artistic formats such as collage.[43] The third lecture, delivered by Taub, was about the possibilities for the development an artificial human larynx. As part of his presentation,

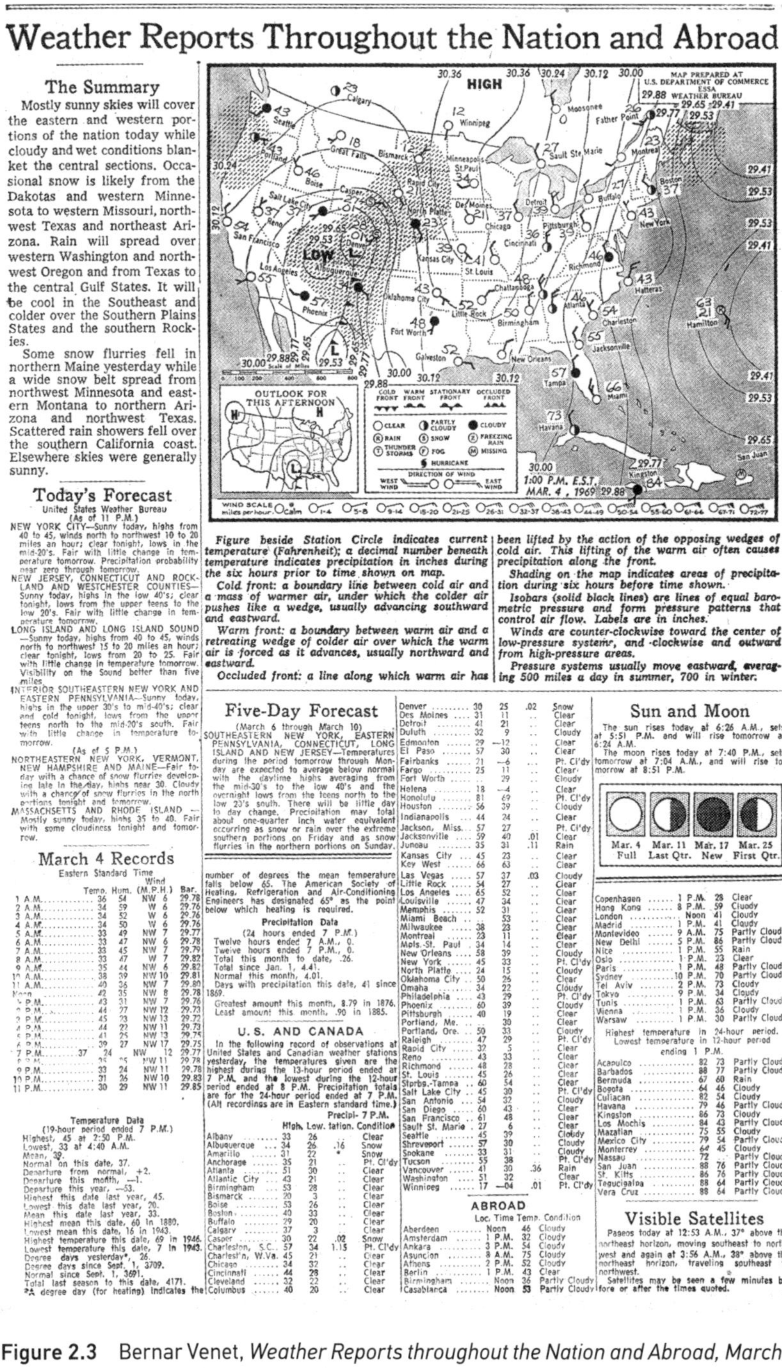

Weather Reports Throughout the Nation and Abroad

The Summary

Mostly sunny skies will cover the eastern and western portions of the nation today while cloudy and wet conditions blanket the central sections. Occasional snow is likely from the Dakotas and western Minnesota to western Missouri, northwest Texas and northeast Arizona. Rain will spread over western Washington and northwest Oregon and from Texas to the central Gulf States. It will be cool in the Southeast and colder over the Southern Plains States and the southern Rockies.

Some snow flurries fell in northern Maine yesterday while a wide snow belt spread from northwest Minnesota and eastern Montana to northern Arizona and northwest Texas. Scattered rain showers fell over the southern California coast. Elsewhere skies were generally sunny.

Today's Forecast

United States Weather Bureau
(As of 11 P.M.)

NEW YORK CITY—Sunny today, highs from 40 to 45, winds north to northwest 10 to 20 miles an hour; clear tonight, lows in the mid-20's. Fair with little change in temperature tomorrow. Precipitation probability near zero through tomorrow.

NEW JERSEY, CONNECTICUT AND ROCKLAND AND WESTCHESTER COUNTIES—Sunny today, highs in the low 40's; clear tonight, lows from the upper teens to the low 20's. Fair with little change in temperature tomorrow.

LONG ISLAND AND LONG ISLAND SOUND—Sunny today, highs from 40 to 45, winds north to northwest 15 to 20 miles an hour; clear tonight, lows from 20 to 25. Fair with little change in temperature tomorrow. Visibility on the Sound better than five miles.

INTERIOR SOUTHEASTERN NEW YORK AND EASTERN PENNSYLVANIA—Sunny today, highs in the upper 30's to mid-40's; clear and cold tonight, lows from the upper teens north to the mid-20's south. Fair with little change in temperature tomorrow.

(As of 5 P.M.)

NORTHEASTERN NEW YORK, VERMONT, NEW HAMPSHIRE AND MAINE—Fair today with a chance of snow flurries developing late in the day, highs near 30. Cloudy with a chance of snow flurries in the north portions tonight and tomorrow.

MASSACHSETTS AND RHODE ISLAND—Mostly sunny today, highs 35 to 40. Fair with some cloudiness tonight and tomorrow.

March 4 Records

Eastern Standard Time

	Temp.	Hum.	Wind (M.P.H.)	Bar.
1 A.M.	36	54	NW 6	29.78
2 A.M.	34	59	W 6	29.76
3 A.M.	34	52	W 6	29.76
4 A.M.	34	50	W 6	29.76
5 A.M.	33	49	NW 7	29.77
6 A.M.	33	47	NW 6	29.78
7 A.M.	33	45	NW 7	29.79
8 A.M.	33	47	W 7	29.82
9 A.M.	35	44	NW 6	29.82
10 A.M.	38	39	NW 10	29.81
11 A.M.	40	36	NW 7	29.80
Noon	42	35	NW 8	29.78
1 P.M.	43	31	NW 7	29.76
2 P.M.	44	27	NW 12	29.73
3 P.M.	45	23	NW 13	29.72
4 P.M.	44	22	NW 11	29.73
5 P.M.	41	25	NW 13	29.75
6 P.M.	39	27	NW 17	29.75
7 P.M.	37	24	NW 12	29.77
8 P.M.	35	25	NW 11	29.78
9 P.M.	33	24	NW 11	29.78
10 P.M.	31	26	NW 10	29.83
11 P.M.	30	29	NW 11	29.85

Temperature Data
(19-hour period ended 7 P.M.)

Highest, 45 at 2:50 P.M.
Lowest, 33 at 4:40 A.M.
Mean, 39.
Normal on this date, 37.
Departure from normal, +2.
Departure this month, —1.
Departure this year, —53.
Highest this date last year, 45.
Lowest this date last year, 20.
Mean this date last year, 33.
Highest mean this date, 60 in 1880.
Lowest mean this date, 16 in 1943.
Highest temperature this date, 69 in 1946.
Lowest temperature this date, 7 in 1943.
Degree days yesterday*, 26.
Degree days since Sept. 1, 3709.
Normal since Sept. 1, 3691.
Total last season to this date, 4171.
*A degree day (for heating) indicates the number of degrees the mean temperature falls below 65. The American Society of Heating, Refrigeration and Air-Conditioning Engineers has designated 65° as the point below which heating is required.

Precipitation Data
(24 hours ended 7 P.M.)

Twelve hours ended 7 A.M., 0.
Twelve hours ended 7 P.M., 0.
Total this month to date, .26.
Total since Jan. 1, 4.41.
Normal this month, 4.01.
Days with precipitation this date, 41 since 1869.
Greatest amount this month, 8.79 in 1876.
Least amount this month, .90 in 1885.

MAP PREPARED AT U.S. DEPARTMENT OF COMMERCE ESSA WEATHER BUREAU

OUTLOOK FOR THIS AFTERNOON

1:00 P.M. E.S.T. MAR. 4, 1969

Figure beside Station Circle indicates current temperature (Fahrenheit); a decimal number beneath temperature indicates precipitation in inches during the six hours prior to time shown on map.

Cold front: a boundary line between cold air and a mass of warmer air, under which the colder air pushes like a wedge, usually advancing southward and eastward.

Warm front: a boundary between warm air and a retreating wedge of colder air over which the warm air is forced as it advances, usually northward and eastward.

Occluded front: a line along which warm air has been lifted by the action of the opposing wedges of cold air. This lifting of the warm air often causes precipitation along the front.

Shading on the map indicates areas of precipitation during six hours before time shown.

Isobars (solid black lines) are lines of equal barometric pressure and form pressure patterns that control air flow. Labels are in inches.

Winds are counter-clockwise toward the center of low-pressure systems, and clockwise and outward from high-pressure areas.

Pressure systems usually move eastward, averaging 500 miles a day in summer, 700 in winter.

Five-Day Forecast

(March 6 through March 10)

SOUTHEASTERN NEW YORK, EASTERN PENNSYLVANIA, CONNECTICUT, LONG ISLAND AND NEW JERSEY—Temperatures during the period tomorrow through Monday are expected to average below normal with the daytime highs averaging from the mid-30's to the low 40's and the overnight lows from the teens north to the low 20's south. There will be little day to day change. Precipitation may total about one-quarter inch water equivalent occurring as snow or rain over the extreme southern portions on Friday and as snow flurries in the northern portions on Sunday.

U.S. AND CANADA

In the following record of observations at United States and Canadian weather stations yesterday, the temperatures given are the highest during the 13-hour period ended at 7 P.M. and the lowest during the 12-hour period ended at 8 P.M. Precipitation totals are for the 24-hour period ended at 7 P.M. (All recordings are in Eastern standard time.)

	High.	Low.	Precipitation.	7 P.M. Condition
Albany	33	26	..	Clear
Albuquerque	34	26	.16	Snow
Amarillo	31	22	*	Snow
Anchorage	35	21	..	Pt. Cl'dy
Atlanta	51	30	..	Clear
Atlantic City	43	21	..	Clear
Birmingham	53	28	..	Clear
Bismarck	20	3	..	Clear
Boise	53	26	..	Clear
Boston	40	33	..	Clear
Buffalo	29	20	..	Clear
Calgary	37	3	..	Clear
Casper	30	22	.02	Snow
Charleston, S.C.	57	34	1.15	Pt. Cl'dy
Charlest'n, W.Va.	45	21	..	Clear
Chicago	34	32	..	Clear
Cincinnati	44	28	..	Clear
Cleveland	32	22	..	Clear
Columbus	40	20	..	Clear
Denver	30	25	.02	Snow
Des Moines	31	11	..	Clear
Detroit	41	21	..	Clear
Duluth	32	9	..	Cloudy
Edmonton	29	—12	..	Clear
El Paso	57	30	..	Clear
Fairbanks	21	—6	...	Pt. Cl'dy
Fargo	25	11	..	Clear
Fort Worth	..	29	..	Cloudy
Helena	18	—4	..	Clear
Honolulu	81	69	..	Pt. Cl'dy
Houston	56	39	..	Cloudy
Indianapolis	44	24	..	Clear
Jackson, Miss.	57	27	..	Pt. Cl'dy
Jacksonville	59	40	.01	Clear
Juneau	35	31	.11	Rain
Kansas City	45	23	..	Clear
Key West	66	63	..	Clear
Las Vegas	57	37	.03	Cloudy
Little Rock	54	27	..	Clear
Los Angeles	65	52	..	Clear
Louisville	47	34	..	Clear
Memphis	52	31	..	Clear
Miami Beach	..	53	..	Clear
Milwaukee	38	23	..	Clear
Montreal	23	11	..	Clear
Mpls.-St. Paul	34	14	..	Clear
New Orleans	58	39	..	Cloudy
New York	45	33	..	Pt. Cl'dy
North Platte	24	15	..	Cloudy
Oklahoma City	50	26	..	Clear
Omaha	34	22	..	Cloudy
Philadelphia	43	29	..	Pt. Cl'dy
Phoenix	60	39	..	Cloudy
Pittsburgh	40	19	..	Clear
Portland, Me.	..	30	..	Clear
Portland, Ore.	50	33	..	Cloudy
Raleigh	47	29	..	Pt. Cl'dy
Rapid City	32	5	..	Clear
Reno	43	33	..	Clear
Richmond	48	28	..	Clear
St. Louis	45	26	..	Clear
Stprbg.-Tampa	60	54	..	Clear
Salt Lake City	45	30	..	Pt. Cl'dy
San Antonio	54	32	..	Cloudy
San Diego	60	43	..	Clear
San Francisco	61	48	..	Clear
Sault St. Marie	27	6	..	Clear
Seattle	45	39	..	Cloudy
Shreveport	57	30	..	Cloudy
Spokane	33	31	..	Cloudy
Tucson	55	38	..	Pt. Cl'dy
Vancouver	41	30	.36	Rain
Washington	51	32	..	Clear
Winnipeg	17	—04	.01	Pt. Cl'dy

ABROAD

	Loc. Time	Temp.	Condition
Aberdeen	Noon	46	Cloudy
Amsterdam	1 P.M.	32	Cloudy
Ankara	3 P.M.	54	Cloudy
Asuncion	8 A.M.	75	Cloudy
Athens	2 P.M.	52	Cloudy
Berlin	1 P.M.	43	Clear
Birmingham	Noon	36	Partly Cloudy
Casablanca	Noon	53	Partly Cloudy
Copenhagen	1 P.M.	28	Clear
Hong Kong	8 P.M.	59	Cloudy
London	Noon	41	Cloudy
Madrid	1 P.M.	41	Cloudy
Montevideo	9 A.M.	75	Partly Cloudy
New Delhi	5 P.M.	86	Partly Cloudy
Nice	1 P.M.	55	Rain
Oslo	1 P.M.	23	Clear
Paris	1 P.M.	48	Partly Cloudy
Sydney	10 P.M.	70	Partly Cloudy
Tel Aviv	2 P.M.	73	Cloudy
Tokyo	9 P.M.	34	Cloudy
Tunis	1 P.M.	63	Partly Cloudy
Vienna	1 P.M.	36	Cloudy
Warsaw	1 P.M.	30	Partly Cloudy

Highest temperature in 24-hour period. Lowest temperature in 12-hour period ending 1 P.M.

Acapulco	82	73	Partly Cloudy
Barbados	88	77	Partly Cloudy
Bermuda	67	60	Rain
Bogota	64	46	Cloudy
Culiacan	82	54	Cloudy
Havana	79	46	Partly Cloudy
Kingston	86	73	Cloudy
Los Mochis	84	43	Partly Cloudy
Mazatlan	75	55	Cloudy
Mexico City	79	54	Partly Cloudy
Monterrey	64	45	Cloudy
Nassau	72	..	Partly Cloudy
San Juan	88	76	Partly Cloudy
St. Kitts	86	76	Partly Cloudy
Tegucigalpa	88	64	Partly Cloudy
Vera Cruz	88	64	Partly Cloudy

Sun and Moon

The sun rises today at 6:26 A.M., sets at 5:51 P.M. and will rise tomorrow at 6:24 A.M.

The moon rises today at 7:40 P.M., sets tomorrow at 7:04 A.M., and will rise tomorrow at 8:51 P.M.

Mar. 4 Full — Mar. 11 Last Qtr. — Mar. 17 New — Mar. 25 First Qtr.

Visible Satellites

Pageos today at 12:53 A.M., 37° above the northeast horizon, moving southeast to northwest and again at 3:56 A.M., 38° above the northeast horizon, traveling southeast to northwest.

Satellites may be seen a few minutes before or after the times quoted.

Figure 2.3 Bernar Venet, *Weather Reports throughout the Nation and Abroad, March 14, 1969*. Photographic enlargement. Photo credit: © Bernar Venet.

Taub showed two instructional films. Venet's dissatisfaction with the three parallel lectures on the second evening is symptomatic of his fear that his "copied" lectures might be mistaken for performances rather than neutral demonstrations, and thus lose their monosemic character. Through 1969, Venet organized ten more lectures similar to these, all involving specialists delivering lectures either live or on tape.

In a slightly later work, *The Logic of Decision and Action* (1969), the artist presented a black-and-white panel with a blown-up photograph of the table of contents of a book of the same title, edited by historian of science and philosopher Nicholas Rescher, that had been published a couple of years earlier by the University of Pittsburgh Press. Dedicated to the theory and logic of "decision-making, problem solving, act analysis, and preference," the volume consists of four essays by different scholars who develop what the editor refers to as a "novel concept of heuristic power." A number of differences separate Venet's presentation of the *Logic of Decision and Action* table of contents from his earlier rational images. In his remarks on Venet in his book *The Structure of Art*, Burnham notes that the artist's "choice of the book *The Logic of Decision and Action* has a two-edged implication: for one, he is presenting a text which to some extent reveals the constancy of the structure of art-making; at the same time through the dialectical, and thus historical, progression of knowledge as an integral aspect of the human condition, he is subverting the historical-mythic structure behind all avant-garde art. Like Daniel Buren, Venet presents post-Duchampian art which questions present epistemological assumptions in as exacting a way."[44] Going beyond the diagrammatic logic of the artist's earlier panels which emphasized the neutral demonstration of scientific content, Burnham interprets *The Logic of Decision and Action* as a juxtaposition of two epistemological regimes, one artistic and transcendent/mythical (the avant-garde), and the other based on cutting-edge scientific research, inscribed into an area where progress is marked by the clash between older assumptions and the competing new hypotheses that come to replace them. Copying the table of contents from Rescher's book, Venet, Burnham argues,

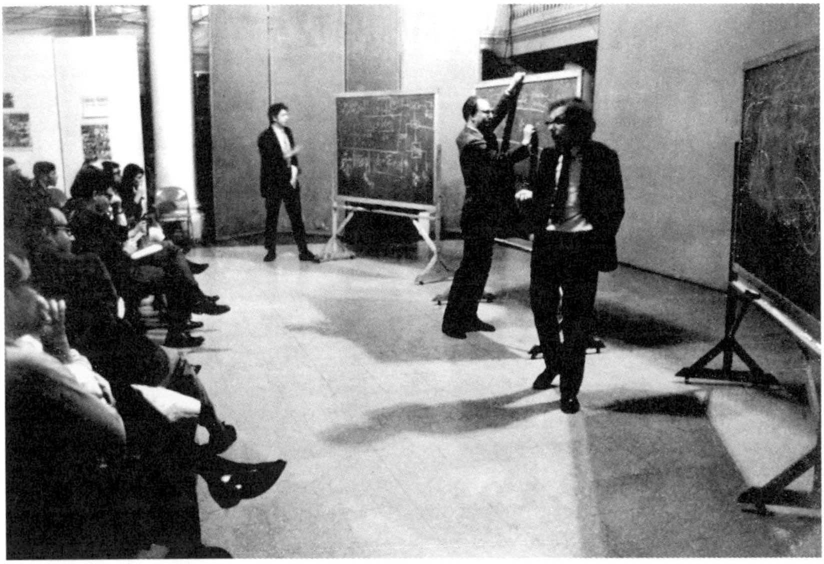

Figure 2.4 Bernar Venet, *Relativity's Track: Three Performances*, May 27–28, 1968, Judson Dance Theater, New York. Simultaneous performance-lectures by Jack Ullman, Edward Macagno, and Martin Krieger. Photo credit: © Bernar Venet.

endorses the dialectical logic that drives historical-scientific progress rather than the mythical cyclicity that is characteristic of modernism, or the seriality so often encountered in minimalist sculpture.[45]

In more ways than one, the expansive approach to didactic art adopted by Venet recalls the Situationists, who in the 1950s had espoused their opposition to formal innovation as the engine behind modernism, and who practiced *détournement*, in Guy Debord's words, as a form of "education for the proletariat."[46] To Debord and his friends, the appropriation of stolen fragments from existing films, texts, or images was a critical, even analytical, operation that both recalled a stolen fragment's host text or film *and* critiqued that text at the same time by inserting the stolen fragment into a new context. The critical practice Debord proposes rejects, as Venet does, any formal innovation or the kind of rationality associated with a metalanguage. Debord's experimental films, especially, are examples of *détournement*'s didacticism: they are not films per se but rather *demonstrations of films*, and what matters in them is not their technical innovation but the dialogue they enable. This is obvious, for instance, in the film *Hurlements en faveur de Sade* (1952), which included no images and which harbored Debord's conviction, arguably shared by Venet, that "negative" neo-avant-garde art is as much of a dead end as an art focused on objects, and that both need to be replaced with demonstrations designed to raise the stakes for communication and dialogic exchange.[47]

While it is often said that the 1960s nurtured a naive belief in the feasibility of authentic dialogue, at the same time, such optimism—especially where it ignored the boundaries of class and education—was subjected to a harsh critique. Theodor W. Adorno, for one, questioned the a priori assumption that ideas are transparent to each other and that they can become without further ado subject to intelligible conversation. For him, "the existence of some kind of *universitas literarum*—suggesting the a priori agreement that all intellects are capable of entering into communication with each other" was nothing if not an instance of conformism.[48]

Another artist whose interest in demonstration links him to the Situationists is Daniel Buren, whom Burnham mentions in connection with Venet in the passage cited above. Buren, whom Venet met in the mid-1960s, first created his *Wild Billboarding* (*Affichage sauvage*) in April 1968 by illegally covering two hundred billboards in Paris with white-and-green-striped paper.[49] This work is directly connected with his *Sandwich People* (1968), which had two men strolling around Paris carrying panels covered with the same striped paper.[50] It is as if between them Buren and Venet developed the two main prongs of the Situationists' pedagogical approach: on the one hand, the idea that spatial transfer and recontextualization are in and of themselves political acts (Buren); and, on the other, the assumption that only the reliance on borrowed or copied content can prevent art from sliding into spectacle (Venet). In Venet's conception, if the monosemic logic that governs mathematics and the precision of its symbolic notation can be carried over into the non-art sphere, communication quickly loses its alienated, inauthentic qualities.

Not unlike Venet, though from a different starting position, Buren additionally articulates a critique of a type of reception of the Duchampian readymade that was becoming more and more widespread in France at the end of the 1960s. In this view, Duchamp was seen as the avatar of an inconsequential and bourgeois individual freedom whose "magic touch" turned ordinary objects into art without any recourse to the political and ideological circuits along which these objects traveled.[51] Ignoring the broader implications of Duchamp's practice—which turns on the critical examination of art as/and institution and its discursive outlets—Buren's critique tended to pit the (rejected) art of heroic individual expression and innovative (abstract) form against an art focused on content and a more or less explicit (political) message. This position would be endorsed by the radical art students who in May 1968 turned the occupied École des Beaux-Arts into a workshop producing posters for protesters demonstrating in the street (the famous *Atelier populaire*).

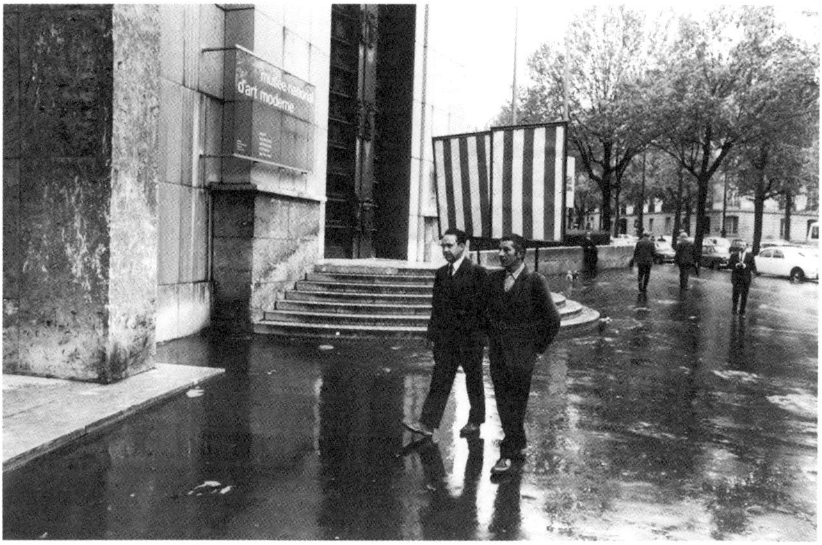

Figure 2.5 Daniel Buren, *Hommes/Sandwichs*, work in situ, Paris, April 1968. Detail. © DB-ADAGP Paris / Photo: Bernard Boyer.

Buren and Venet represent two related if distinct alternatives to this unforgiving critique of Duchamp. To begin with Buren: it is often pointed out that his practice—stripped as it is of any expressive content—radically questions the position of the author and their agency, shifting the burden of signification from expression to the work's urban, discursive, and institutional context. In this sense, we might argue, Buren takes his cue from the program of environmental didacticism outlined by Burnham. And yet, while such a move can clearly be read as political in the way it places art at the disposition of dialogue and discussion, it was manifestly not political in the way in which, say, the radicalized students on the streets of Paris may have imagined. As Sami Siegelbaum writes, "reading Daniel Buren's striped posters of April 1968 through the . . . *Atelier Populaire* suggests . . . that spatial appropriation trumped more specific communicative goals so that the medium—and most specifically the physical location of the work in the street, rather than its particular political content—became the message."[52] As Siegelbaum further notes, Buren's striped billboards from the late 1960s not only lacked any legible political message, they also remained "committed to a model of negation that refused any possibility of communication,"[53] putting the artist at odds with those among his colleagues—for example, the students in the *Atelier*—who advocated a more transparently political role for art.

Venet, for his part, certainly also sought neutrality, although he did so not by stripping the artwork of content but by citing instances of signification that exclude aesthetic mediation, all the while remaining open to communication. In this way, Buren's and Venet's works of the mid-1960s show art's didactic expansion, albeit in different, if complementary, directions. While Buren focused on the urban context in which his posters and billboards appear (or ambulate), for Venet, knowledge and its different symbolic notations replaced expressiveness and formal innovation, as art's reach expanded into the sciences and mathematics, areas with which art had until then seemed to have only implicit connections.

ADRIAN PIPER'S "FOOD FOR THE SPIRIT"

A few years after Venet began with his demonstrations, Adrian Piper—also in New York City—approached the problem of (impossible) neutrality from a radically different, autodidactic angle in her performance entitled *Food for the Spirit* (1971).[54] In preparation, the artist studied Immanuel Kant's *Critique of Practical Reason* (1787) during two months of complete self-isolation in her New York attic, in what amounted to an autodidactic lockdown. During the performance, she grappled with Kant's ideas and measured the effect these ideas had on her physically as well as psychologically. As Piper wrote in 1981, ten years after completing her performance,

> this piece was performed in my loft in NYC continually throughout the summer of 1971. I had become very interested in Kant's *Critique of Pure Reason*, had taken a graduate course on it at CUNY the preceding spring, and spent the summer doing nothing else but studying and writing a paper on it, doing yoga, and fasting. I didn't see other people at all and went out only to shop and take walks for exercise. . . . I would read certain passages that were so intensely affecting and deep that I would literally break out into a cold sweat.[55]

Although *Food for the Spirit* may seem isolationist and far removed from politics, Piper has argued that while her early art production may not qualify as a direct response to the (political) events of the late 1960s, it was nevertheless linked to these events through their didactic reflex. As Elizabeth Kaufmann notes, "rather than thinking of her artwork as a vehicle to effect political change directly, she [Piper] thought of it as a didactic tool."[56] In an autobiographical text from the early 1970s, the artist notes that after two art-specific transitions that defined her early career in the late 1960s, the first from painting to minimalism, and the second from minimalism to conceptual art, it was especially the central political events of the decade—Nixon's invasion of Cambodia, the women's movement, the Kent State and Jackson State police shootings, and the closure of City College where Piper had begun to study philosophy—that contributed to her increasingly intense questioning of the art world in which she had begun to operate, including its misogyny and racial bias.[57] During this time, according to her own testimony, Piper became not so much "political" as self-aware, realizing that one may be a necessary precondition for the other. (Self-)education played a vital role in this process.

In the way Piper controls her surroundings by limiting outside contact as she studies Kant's work, *Food for the Spirit* is reminiscent of a previous work by the artist, *Untitled Performance at Max's Kansas City* (1970), during which she walked blindfolded through the well-known diner filled with customers, her ears closed up with plugs, and gloves on her hands.[58] Piper's reduction of outside stimulation in both these performances can be seen as a response to Kant's assertion that our sense perceptions' ability to teach us (*lehren*) is inversely proportionate to the intensity with which they affect us: "The more the senses are *affected* in proportion with the influence exerted on them, the less they *instruct*. Conversely, if they are expected to instruct a lot, they need to produce moderate affect."[59] Like other philosophers, Kant distinguished between two different kinds of sensory affect, an outer one and an inner one, with the outer one being defined as our ability to perceive an exterior material object and be affected by it ("whereby the human body is affected by corporeal things"), and the inner one as a form of affect from within (*durchs Gemüt*).[60] In both *Untitled Performance at Max's Kansas City* and in *Food for the Spirit*, Piper's self-isolation suggests a desire to maximize the autodidactic potential of the situation in which she places herself by isolating herself, thus limiting the affect reaching her from her external surroundings in order to stimulate affect from within.

Despite the measures she takes to limit its perceptional impact, as Piper's 1981 commentary on *Food for the Spirit* explains, the *Critique* perennially threatens to mentally overwhelm the artist, compromising her methodical effort to teach herself, and confirming Kant's assumption that too much affect may limit the didactic benefits of an object we perceive: "My involvement in it [Kant's *Critique*] was so great that I thought I was losing my mind, in fact losing my sense of self completely."[61] In these moments, in order to prevent the further dissolution of her self, Piper interrupts her reading and steps in front of a mirror, "to peer at myself to make sure I was still there."[62] She rigs the mirror with a camera and a tape recorder, "so that every time the fear of losing myself overtook me and drove me to the 'reality check' of the mirror, I was able both to record my physical appearance objectively and also to record myself on tape repeating the passage in the *Critique* that was currently driving me to self-transcendence."[63] If Piper's reading of Kant's *Critique* as part of her performance initially creates a sense of transcendent vertigo, her periodic repetition of the phrases read in front of the mirror serves a different goal, namely to bend her reading back to the body, so that the *Critique* can once again figure as nothing but "a book with good ideas in it that I had chosen to study, and not the entrance into a transcendent reality of disembodied self-consciousness."[64]

What is reading? As a form of *studium*—derived from Latin for "painstaking application"—reading, we might say, is a form of mediation between self and otherness, between the objectivity of the text and the interiority of the reading subject. Apart from "painstaking application" (which Piper clearly practices in her performance), the Latin term *studium* can also mean "zeal," opening the possibility of a hidden element of passion in what otherwise appears to be a highly rational, measured process of assimilation. Piper's "disembodied self-transcendence" and self-demonstration in front of the mirror highlight not only this element of passion but also the more ritualistic and contemplative aspects implicit in the reading process, an activity Martin Heidegger, not coincidentally, viewed as reading's very essence: "What does reading [*Lesen*] mean? What carries and guides in the act of reading is an act of inner concentration [*Sammlung*]. In relation to what does such concentration collect? In relation to writing, to what is said in writing. Real reading is the contemplation/collection of what once already occupied our being unbeknownst to us."[65]

Heidegger's interpretation depends on the double meaning of the verb *lesen*; while in most contexts, the word means "to read," it has a secondary, less frequently invoked meaning: "collecting" or "selectively binding together" (as in the word *Weinlese*, meaning the seasonal collecting or harvesting of grapes for wine production). As such, it connects with *Sammlung*, which refers both to "collection" or "gathering together" and to a form of "spiritual concentration" or contemplation. Reading as a form of *Sammlung* has two crucial implications: first, it suggests that reading too can function as a form of contemplation or concentration, and as such, second, it is, to repeat Heidegger's words, "the contemplation/collection of what once already occupied our being unbeknownst to us." In other words, reading, in Heidegger's sense, is a form of (self-)reproduction or, to stay closer to his terminology, of (self-)re*collection*. Of course, on the face of it, this statement contradicts the general consensus that views reading as little more than the progressive decipherment of written words and sentences so that new information can become available as our eyes move from one line or page to the next. Such an understanding equates reading with a more or less mechanical transfer of information from the written text to the reader. By contrast, Heidegger's view of reading as self-reproduction and re-collection (*Sammlung*) places it in close relation to the reader's self: in order to "really" read a text, we need to discover and acknowledge its constitutive relation to our own self or being, as if the text were a partially blinded mirror in which we recognize ourselves.

It is in this sense that Heidegger's view of reading might be relevant for understanding Piper's work. To recapitulate, in 1981, the artist reported a double reaction to her reading of Kant: the first—holding the book, as it were, at arm's length—treating the *Critique* as a purely instrumental object ("a book with good ideas in it that I had chosen to study"); and the second using it as "the entrance into a transcendent reality of disembodied self-consciousness,"[66] to the detriment of the volume's instructional function. How might these two approaches—the purely didactic instrumentality of reading here, the complete loss of self in a nirvana of transcendence there—be avoided or integrated, so that a process of self-recollection (or self-recognition, in Heidegger's sense) might set in? I believe that the photographs Piper takes of herself in the mirror hold the answer. A process of reading is at work here, too: after all, Piper "reads" herself in the mirror, and she takes pictures of this very process, no doubt struggling to recognize anything in the semi-darkness. While most commentators follow the artist's interpretation that her snapshots are a mere prop designed to assure her that she is "still there," few acknowledge the fact that these "snapshots of a reader" (in a double sense) who has just left behind a book she has been engrossed in offer their own take on the idea of reading. In fact, Piper's placement of herself in front of the mirror, her taking pictures of herself over time, dramatizes the process of self-reproduction—implying the memory of a hidden part of ourselves—that Heidegger had identified as "real" reading. However, where for Heidegger the temporal parameters of this process of remembering had remained somewhat obscure, Piper's snapshots of herself in the mirror highlight, precisely, its unfolding over time. Furthermore, by moving over from her desk to stand in front of a full-size mirror, and by creating a *Sammlung*—a collection and a contemplation—of these snapshots, Piper extends to the body the element of self-reproduction that Heidegger associated with reading.

The idea of reading as a performative process that includes the body gained traction in the 1960s. In his influential study *Method and Truth* (originally published in German in 1960), Hans-Georg Gadamer illustrates the point that reading as a process of reproduction and recollection, as theorized by Heidegger, always has a somatic dimension, even when such reading is silent: "There is obviously no sharp differentiation between reciting and silent reading. Reading with understanding is always a kind of reproduction, performance, and interpretation. Emphasis, rhythmic ordering, and the like are part of wholly silent reading too. Meaning and the understanding of it are so closely connected with the corporeality of language that understanding always involves an inner speaking as well."[67] What is at stake here is not only that "the reader matters"—an assertion that formed the basis of reader response or "subjective" literary criticism from the late 1960s on[68]—but also the fact that even silent reading presupposes the possibility, even the necessity, that we physically reproduce ourselves in or through the text we are reading. It is this, we might say, structural prerequisite of "real" reading—reminiscent of Heidegger's view, but also going beyond him—that is dramatized and extended in Piper's mirror images, and that includes, crucially, the physical attributes of her race and gender. What these photographs illustrate, then, is the fact that successful reading always presupposes one's ability to hear oneself speak, to recognize oneself as having a body, with everything this entails (skin color, gender, etc.). And in this sense, we might argue, *Food for the Spirit* points toward a way of developing one's self in the most comprehensive sense of that term, integrating the mind with the more physical aspects of our being.

3

BURLESQUE LECTURE DEMONSTRATION (ROBERT MORRIS, WALTER BENJAMIN)

In this chapter, I examine two lecture performances—Robert Morris's *21.3* (1964/1994) and Walter Benjamin's *Mondrian Lecture* (1986)—as a way of questioning academic lectures and their truth claims.[1] Both performances raise the problem of how we communicate knowledge in an academic setting and where we obtain the authority to do so, and both deploy elements of humor and the burlesque—especially impersonation and parody—to question widely held assumptions behind established forms of knowledge production and transmission, and how these assumptions privilege continuity, linear progression, and relations of cause and effect.

Demonstration is central to lecturing, which we can define as a form of ritualized speech in which an authorized speaker presents ideas, often using written notes. To this end, they may use different forms of communication including verbal language, gestures (using the lecturer's body), diagrams, and other visualizations. Also central to a lecture is the lecturer's personal engagement with what they set out to demonstrate, and whose reproduction during their lecture may affect lecturer and audience alike. The term "lecture" derives from the Latin *legere* (to read; in German *Vorlesung*, which has its roots in *lesen*, read). In the Middle Ages, lectures were often literally readings, as the lecturer held a book in their hands from which they read, suggesting that such lectures—ultimately a form of loud reading—played a mediating role between the printed book and speaking before a live audience.

The 1960s subjected the academic lecture format and its assumption of a felicitous rapport between the lecturer and their audience to a withering critique. When in July 1966 the Greek-German writer Vagelis Tsakiridis performed an action lecture (*Aktionslesung*) at Galerie Aachen,[2] he first played his lecture from a tape through a loudspeaker, and then proceeded to fast-forward the tape, stopping for random passages. Only after this did the artist appear, dressed in black, before the audience and began to deliver his lecture live, with its text projected on the wall behind him by an epidiascope after he was done.[3] On the one hand, Tsakiridis's puzzling remediation of an academic lecture situation seems to be instrumentally designed to enhance the listener's attention—all too often, lectures fail to sustain our ability to listen attentively for an extended period of time—reminding us, in the process, of the critical influence various recording media, such as a tape recorder, may have on how we process information. In this way, we might say, the artist's critique has a decidedly constructive, optimistic character that affirms the possibility of dialogue, at least under the right technical conditions. Yet on the other hand, by exposing his lecture to a process of gradual disintegration—cutting, forwarding, and repeating its content randomly—the artist also undermines the optimism implicit in the assumption, widespread especially in academia, that lecturing produces "dialogue" between speaker and listeners.

Less than a year after Tsakiridis, in 1967, Lacan also critiqued the idea of lecturing-as-felicitous-dialogue in two public lectures. Instead of delving—as he was expected to do—into an explanation of psychoanalysis, Lacan bluntly admits that he has "prepared nothing that is especially intended for you," and then focuses on the genre of lecturing itself, insisting that the assumption that a lecture be considered a form of dialogue is mostly designed to free us from the necessity to think: "Being in dialogue is one of the most enormous pretensions of our times. Have you ever seen people in dialogue? Occasions when we speak of dialogue are always a little bit like domestic quarrels."[4] In another 1967 lecture, Lacan argues that "in truth, the 'lecture' genre presupposes a postulate that is essential to the very name 'university': there is such a thing as a universe, by which I mean a universe of discourse. . . . It takes only a quick look at history to contradict the idea that the strata that have been laid down throughout history . . . come together to create that university—the University of Letters, the *Universitas Litterarum* that is basic to the teaching that bears the name."[5] Insisting, perhaps counterintuitively, that lecturing is an activity that must not pretend to "sow knowledge,"[6] Lacan insists that "my teaching is in fact quite simply language, and absolutely nothing else."[7]

The tension Tsakiridis and Lacan allow us to theorize—between the rational affirmation of demonstration as lecture and universal discourse, on the one hand, and a focus on the traumatic core of such optimism, the possibility that all dialogue may be a fantasy, on the other—structures demonstration-based artworks during the expanded 1960s like little else. What comes to the fore in these works is less the communication of facts than the process of their discovery by the speaker, including their articulation as part of a lecture. In an article about the production of self-evidence (*Evidenz*) in academic lecturing, Sibylle Peters has provided a genealogy of our understanding of lecturing as a form of demonstration. As Peters notes, in the early nineteenth century, an "art of lecturing" (*Kunst der Vorlesung*) began to emerge whose focus was less the transfer of knowledge than the demonstration of a process of fact-finding. In the way they demonstrate truth rather than simply stating it, lectures enable what Immanuel Kant referred to as "intellektuelle Anschauung" (intellectual contemplation). Peters credits Kant's questioning the convergence of concept and image as foundational for the modern view that what is self-evident is the result of the demonstration of the process of its discovery, and as such is subject to continuous performative renewal. In other words, the production of facts as part of a lecture entails not merely one's ability to identify a problem, but also the keen awareness of the methods used for solving it, since in

Peters's words, "we know because we are doing it."[8] This is precisely what Friedrich Schleiermacher, one of the chief theorists of the early nineteenth-century art of lecturing, argued when he wrote in 1808 that "the teacher has to let everything he says to his listeners emerge before them; he should not just tell them what he knows but instead reproduce his own process of cognition, the act itself, so that the listeners continuously do not merely gather knowledge but immediately observe the activity of the cognizing mind and, in doing so, emulate that process."[9]

The key to Schleiermacher's remark is what he refers to as emergence ("let everything he says to his listeners emerge before them"), a process that is also central to demonstration itself. In the nineteenth-century art of lecturing, the emergence of facts rather than these facts themselves became the focus of attention, with the express goal of inspiring listeners to imitate the methods used for their discovery.[10] In this sense, lectures are "exemplary" in Benjamin's understanding of the term, and as such they have a distinctly demonstrational function: they do not represent what is factual; instead, they demonstrate how certain facts were discovered.

Such exemplary production of knowledge also animates the first lecture performance I want to discuss in this chapter. In February 1964—before Bernar Venet presented his lecture at the Judson Theater—Robert Morris walked up to a lectern placed at the center of a stage at the Surplus Dance Theater in New York City.[11] Dressed like a college professor, in a suit and an ill-fitting tie, the artist began to deliver a twelve-minute live lecture. Rosalind Krauss has pointed to the burlesque, clownlike element in the artist's attire, and indeed Morris's costume and his "professorial" gestures strike us as faintly reminiscent of Dada's didactic counterpedagogy.[12]

Morris's appearance was accompanied by his recording of a passage from art historian Erwin Panofsky's book *Studies in Iconology* (1939), which was simultaneously being fed into the room by two loudspeakers so that it appeared as if Morris was delivering the art historian's text. Panofsky's groundbreaking contribution to art historical scholarship consisted of the

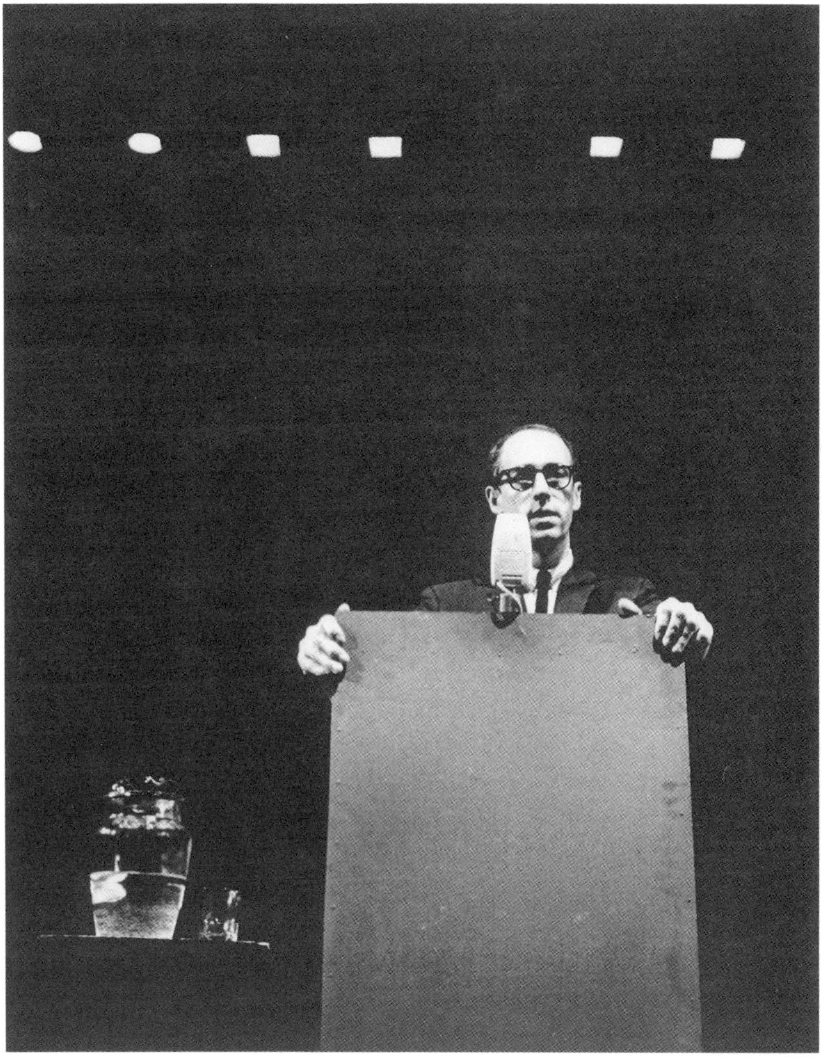

Figure 3.1 Robert Morris, *21.3*, 1964. © 2024 The Estate of Robert Morris / Artists Rights Society (ARS), New York. Image courtesy of Castelli Gallery, New York.

development of a methodology—called iconology—designed to help researchers progress from an artwork's "natural" theme to what Panofsky referred to as its "intrinsic meaning." This progress happens in a Hegel-inspired process of intensifying cultural contextualization whereby the scholar finds heteronomous meaning "in places where no one suspected there was any" and reconciles different cultural or artistic forms through increasing interpretive integration. Iconology thus enriches such forms with associative knowledge drawn from the fundus of the European humanist education. The following (famous) passage from *Studies in Iconology*, heard during *21.3*, illustrates Panofsky's approach:

> When an acquaintance greets me on the street by removing his hat, what I see from a formal point of view is nothing but a change of certain details within a configuration that forms part of the general pattern of color, lines, and volumes which constitute my world of vision. When I identify, as I automatically do, this as an event (hat-removing), I have already overstepped the limits of purely formal perception and entered a first sphere of subject matter or meaning.[13]

For Panofsky, "there is nothing less real than the present," and our perceptions are little more than mechanical registrations until our ability to articulate them with the help of iconology assigns to these perceptions an intellectually mediated pattern.[14] Such integration and its formulaic outcomes ("hat-removing") lend a sense of reality to the fleetingness of our perceptions, and this in turn is the true purpose of any instruction, since "even he who merely transmits knowledge or learning participates, in his modest way, in the process of shaping reality."[15]

While at first glance *21.3* follows Panofsky's lead—especially in its emphasis on lecturing as the gradual unfolding of a thought process that "participates in the process of shaping reality"—the thrust and purpose of Morris's demonstration ultimately contests Panofsky's method, especially with regard to the latter's assumption that the particulars of a formal perception can congeal into the overall *Gestalt* of a fully integrated interpretation. However, rather than stating his differences with Panofsky in constative terms—through explanations—Morris demonstrates them. At the center of his demonstration is an element central to any lecture's ambition to point to knowledge: the lecturer's body. For example, during a lecture, a speaker might use physical gestures for pointing out or emphasizing certain pieces of evidence, in this way allowing the audience to identify these gestures with the spoken words. It is precisely at this level, the level where a lecture demonstration felicitously integrates bodily gestures with their interpretation, that Morris intervenes by partially dissociating his own gestures from the words spoken.

How does this happen? After the first few moments when gestures and sounds are in sync, Morris's physical motions (pouring water, coughing, etc.) and the audible sound that corresponds to them (the sound of water being poured, the cough, etc.) begin to be subtly but noticeably out of sync with each other so that viewers become increasingly aware of the fact that the sounds they are hearing are nondiegetic and that there is a separate soundtrack—the recorded sound from the tape—that doesn't fully coincide with the lecturer's physical gestures (or words).[16] This increasing nonsynchronicity of Morris's lecture is not only slightly comical, it also calls into question the integration that Panofsky's method promises, together with its claim to proceed from the particular to the general.

By punctuating his performance with carefully scripted, nonspontaneous gestures that visibly interrupt the flow of his speech—and by thus making these gestures noticeable as such—Morris confronts the *Gestalt* of his lecture with the deadpan contingencies of its physical delivery. *21.3* thus preempts Krauss's view of Morris's sculptures where, she argues, the artist is interested in the difference between the phenomenological conditions for the perception of objects captured in their ideal *Gestalt*, on the one hand, and the differences noted by a viewer who views the same object in real space and time, on the other. Indeed, through his nonsynchronous delivery, the speaker's movements become separated from their mimetic context, cancelling in the process the impression that the lecture consists of ideas that precede their enunciation, and precluding the kind of linear continuity we ordinarily associate with an academic demonstration.

Through its emphasis on nonsynchronicity and nonlineraity, *21.3* establishes a dialogue with, among others, John Cage, with whose work Morris had been grappling at around the time he composed his lecture.[17] In the late 1940s, Cage had begun his *Lecture on Nothing* at the Eighth Street Artists' Club in New York City with the memorable words: "I am here, and there is Nothing to say."[18] As Branden W. Joseph has noted, when Morris, still in San Francisco, corresponded with Cage in 1960, they discussed among other things the role of linearity or continuity in music: "According to Cage, continuity—which refers to the note-to-note progression in a piece of music and by extension of a succession of events—invariably is received as the mark of subjective expression."[19] While, in traditional music, it is the interchange of persistence and modulation (change) that produces expression, Cage frequently sought to eliminate continuity and predictability from his works, on occasion with the help of tapes. For instance, in 1952, the composer created *Williams Mix*, a piece for eight simultaneously played tracks of single-track or four double-track tapes (it was the first time Cage used a tape recorder in his work). The piece's raw material consisted of 600 magnetic tape recordings, with the sounds "roughly grouped into six categories (city sounds, country sounds, electronic sounds, manually produced sounds, wind produced sounds and small sounds requiring amplification) and three modes of constancy/unpredictability (frequency, overtone structure, amplitude)."[20] In a labor-intensive process that took about one year, these tape bits were cut, prepared, and spliced according to the graphic disposition of the 192-page score.

As Morris's gestures in *21.3* develop a life of their own, it is as if he were reacting to the sounds in the room the way a dancer (re-)acts to the music as part of a dance performance. This allusion to dance is not a gratuitous coincidence in this context: ever since the mid-1950s, Morris had become more and more interested in modern dance, and he conceived *21.3* as a dance piece. As Anael Lejeune has written, it was the artist's interest in documenting the artistic work process (which he believed was often neglected in favor of the finished work) that led Morris to modern dance, where—in contrast to classical ballet with its result-oriented form of movement—the process itself was considered the result.[21] This focus may seem to place Morris in the context of the kind of experiments undertaken at the time by Cage and his associate, the choreographer Merce Cunningham. In his choreography, Cunningham sought to wrest the dancing body away from expression or narrative, and while Morris's syncopal, spaced-out *21.3* lecture aims in a similar way at the evacuation of expression and intentional meaning, there are also important differences between him and Cunningham or Cage. For the later Cage, the collapse of art into life resulted in the full "blanching" of consciousness so that neither memory nor intention might interfere with one's immersion in the world. But for Morris, such a state of affairs—an extended present cut off from any past or future—was no more achievable than the integration of contingency in a comprehensive hermeneutic horizon promised by Panofsky: despite all of the attention paid to Morris's "accidental" gestures disconnected from their hermeneutic moorings, these gestures do after all remain dependent on Panofsky's text playing in the background. Indeed, we might say that it is precisely the presence of this text and its continued (if also challenged) authority that separates *21.3* most decisively from the ideas of Cage and Cunningham. And this difference, I want to suggest, amounts to much more than a marginal detail.

For Cage, it was important that music and dance not express anything; he understood his work with Cunningham as a form of "pure doing" whose meaning completely depended on its observer. The complete collapse of art into life that was the composer's stated goal could occur only once consciousness, or indeed any form of expression, could be fully eliminated.[22] As Cage writes in a commentary that was included in his book *Silence*: "We are not, in these dances and music, saying something. We are simple-minded enough to think that if we were saying something we would use words. We are rather doing something. The meaning of what we do is determined by each one who sees and hears it."[23] By contrast, Morris, despite also clearly wanting to emphasize the importance of process and "doing," still remained interested in words and in the difference between heteronomous meaning, on the one hand, and process and enactment, on the other. How to further account for this difference? For Morris, we might say, the reference point is not "life as such," as was the case for Cage. While the latter's focus is the present moment isolated from both past and present, in Morris's lecture, for all its emphasis on the present moment, he does not view that present as cut off from past knowledge. As Joseph has usefully pointed out, "although Morris . . . was no more interested in self-expression than Cage, he would assert on the contrary that 'all of what does happen is in everybody's mind.'"[24] The difference between the two positions—the blanching of consciousness (Cage); the acknowledgment that past knowledge cannot be fully erased (Morris)—is crucial in this context. To allude to Allan Kaprow's famous phrase, for Morris there is no "un-educating" of the artist because for him the problem is not how to say "Nothing" or make consciousness fade (as in Cage's *Lecture on Nothing*) but rather what we can do with words and ideas that already exist (such as Panofsky's) and that he, Morris, "brought along anyway." By addressing his viewers in a dance-lecture, then, Morris's college professor does not simply aim to leave existing ideas behind, as if to acknowledge that the leap into a realm of purely constative statements may be as difficult to achieve as the jump into the complete absence of expression that was so important to Cage.

These concerns are not only congruent with Morris's interests as a sculptor at the time, but also with the way in which artists close to him, such as Yvonne Rainer and Simone Forti, among others, would rewrite the history of dance in the years to come.[25] In a 1965 article "On Dance," in which he seems to distance himself from Cage, Morris explained:

> While dance technique and chance methods were both irrelevant to me, I would never have denied the value, necessity

> even, of perpetuating structural systems. But for my purposes the need for such systems was for syntactical rather than methodological bases. My efforts were *bound up with the didactic and demonstrative* and were not concerned with the establishment of a set of tools by which works could be generated.[26]

While for Cage, the role of chance in music was primarily to allow for the generation of sound that would not be reliant on prolepsis, Morris, by his own admission, is not interested in chance as a generating tool ("chance methods") but in "syntactical" principles of construction that reveal the way a piece is put together or coded. In an article on the new dance in the United States published in 1974, Annette Michelson referred to the presence of such syntactical elements in contemporary dance as "parataxis," a term commonly defined as the placing of words or phrases in succession without the inclusion of any words that might regulate their coordination or subordination. Michelson has in mind the way that modern dance eschewed predetermined rhythmic or rhetorical patterns in favor of a kind of horizontal accumulation: "The vocabulary of movement was revised through a rethinking of the problem of energy release, and the accumulation of new materials generated paratactic structures."[27]

Michelson's approach captures the neoconstructivist thrust of Morris's lecture. It is telling, however, that in the passage cited above Morris places the emphasis not on generative tools but on demonstration and didacticism ("my efforts were bound up with the didactic and demonstrative"), as if to say that while tools for the production of art such as chance may usefully exist, his interest as an artist is on the side of showing and pointing rather than structures and methods. More generally, Morris breaks with the idea that knowledge and its production can be construed as a universal that either precedes its own enunciation or can be subtracted from the body of that enunciation, hinting at the process-bound, affective nature of the search for truth: not readymade, universal knowledge conventionally accepted by everyone, nor a present "rescued" by thought, as Panofsky would have it, but rather the sustained attention to clues and an acceptance that perfect synchronicity may be neither attainable nor desirable—in short, a perfect illustration of what Adorno referred to as "aesthetic education."

Like a Barthian *punctum*, Morris's inaudible words move us to establish a connection between a knowledge (Panofsky's) to whose presence they testify despite being—or because they are—mute. The medium for this establishment of a connection is Morris's dance performance itself. In his 2001 *L'Université sans condition* (The university without condition), Jacques Derrida stressed the importance of performance to lecturing by raising the question of what enables a professor to lecture with authority. According to Derrida, implicitly or explicitly, professors legitimize their lecturing through a (performative) promise to express themselves on this or that subject in the capacity of an expert. Lecturing is, in other words, authorized not simply by the professor *being* an expert but by an act of confession that he or she be considered such for as long as the lecture lasts: "Professing [*faire profession de*] means solemnly declaring what you are, what you believe, what you want to be by asking the other to believe that declaration by taking your word for it."[28] Derrida's point is that, in a lecture, constative elements (the professor is an expert) and performative elements (the professor asks their audience to consider them an expert for as long as the lecture lasts) go hand in hand with each other. What this suggests in turn, however, is that for constative academic speech to be authoritative, it always depends on an illocutionary act ("I profess") that precedes it since "to profess consists always of a performative speech act, even if the knowledge, the object, the content of what one professes, of what one teaches or practices, remains within the order of theory or constative."[29] Derrida's point is not to say that the authority invested in academic lectures is a fiction, or otherwise illegitimate. Rather, he is concerned with the conditions under which we grant an individual the power to speak with authority.

Pivoting back to Morris, it's as if in his lecture-dance, the constative and the performative, which Derrida interlaces in his argument, are kept separate from each other, with the lecture's academic content—the barely audible art historical argument—remaining firmly on the side of Panofsky, while the performative—the confession, in Derrida's terms—is located on the side of the artist. For Morris's lecturing professor doesn't speak as a specialist; as we notice as soon as his lip-syncing becomes out of step with the audible words, he literally does not have anything to say that wouldn't trail Panofsky's words. Any expertise or special knowledge we may be inclined to accord him, then, is located not in art historical theory but purely in his ability to perform and to embody without laying claim to any expertise other than that of the performance itself.

WALTER BENJAMIN'S RETELLING OF MODERNISM

Burlesque lecture performances that investigate the grounds for the authority to speak with humor and parody can be traced to Duchamp's efforts to establish art making as a parascience and, more generally, to Dada's "antipedagogical didacticism." Indeed, the Dadaists were as didactic in their verdicts and pronouncements as they were disdainful of all pedagogy.[30] Nowhere is this more apparent than in one of the earliest examples of an artist adopting the format of an academic lecture and then proceeding to negate the expectations that come with it, Tristan Tzara's *Lecture on Dada* (1922). Tzara—anticipating Lacan's refusal to lecture some thirty years later—eagerly sought to dispel his listeners' expectations that he might explain what Dada is: "I know that you have come here today to hear explanations. Well, do not expect to hear any explanations about Dada. You explain to me why you exist."[31] Not only does Tzara refuse to transmit knowledge about Dada, his gesture actually becomes the lecture's subject matter, as he suggests that lectures and their trust in rationality and intelligence are separated by an unbridgeable gulf from life itself: "Intelligence is an organization like any other, the organization of society, the organization of a bank, the organization of chit-chat. . . . It serves to . . . separate questions of a material order from those of a cerebral order, but to take the former very seriously. Intelligence is the triumph of sound education and pragmatism. Fortunately, life is something else and its pleasures are innumerable."[32]

A Dada impulse to use instructional forms to question Enlightenment takes on progress and rationality is also in evidence in my second example of a burlesque lecture performance involving, once again, a parody of an academic lecture, Walter Benjamin's *Mondrian Lecture*, which was performed live (in Slovenian) in 1986 at Cankarjev dom in the Slovene capital of Ljubljana, in what was then Yugoslavia.[33] In the performance, Walter Benjamin appears in the guise of an academic who lectures about a series of paintings that are initially presented as being by the modernist painter Piet Mondrian. At the beginning, the lecturer comes to the podium, positioning himself in front of a blackboard that serves as background to six paintings that look like works by Mondrian. After a brief introduction, Benjamin proceeds to read a lengthy passage from Mondrian's writings about the evolution of the artist's method of painterly abstraction, and then examines the signatures on the paintings themselves.

To his apparent consternation, the lecturer finds that the paintings are dated 1963, 1979, 1983, 1992, and 1996; they must therefore have been created after Mondrian's death. This startling finding—the alleged "Mondrians" are mere *copies* of Mondrians—instantly changes the tone of the lecture as Benjamin pivots from an analysis of the artist's style and method to a tongue-in-cheek inquiry into why anyone would have an interest in copying Mondrian and, more generally, what distinguishes a copy from an original.

In Benjamin's argument, which he also lays out in an article entitled "On Copy," he places less emphasis on the mechanical reproduction of art—art's technical reproduction being at the core of the historical Walter Benjamin's *Kunstwerk* essay from 1935/1939—than on the problem of reproduction by hand, a phenomenon that the historical Benjamin had cited mostly as an antecedent of mechanical reproduction: "In principle, the work of art has always been reproducible. Objects made by humans could always be

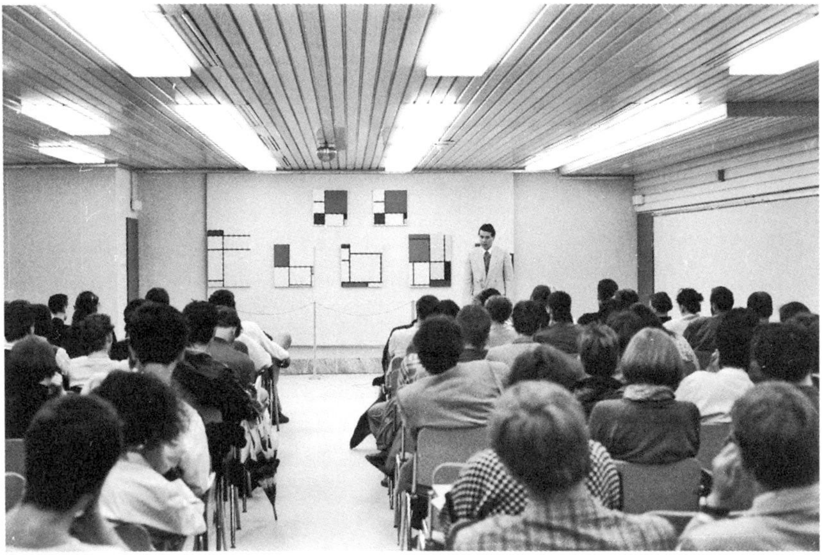

Figure 3.2 Walter Benjamin, *Mondrian Lecture*, Cankarjev dom, Ljubljana, 1986. Slide.

copied by humans. Replicas were made by pupils in practicing for their craft, by masters in disseminating their works, and, finally, by third parties in pursuit of profit."[34] For the historical Benjamin, while mechanical reproduction threatens the artwork's aura, this is not the case with reproduction by hand because then the reproduced work, once it has been examined by experts, can still be identified as a forgery: "But whereas the authentic work retains its full authority in the face of a reproduction made by hand, which it brands a forgery, this is not the case with technological reproduction."[35]

The historical Benjamin's insight is the departure point for Walter Benjamin's lecture performance at Cankarjev dom in 1986. In this lecture, as in his article "On Copy," the lecturer Walter Benjamin argues that there is a crucial difference between the forgery of a painting and its copy: while a forgery seeks to conceal the fact that it is an imitation, copies, in his understanding, tend to flaunt their status as reproductions in that they can only be understood as copies against the background of their original. The lecturing Benjamin is thus less interested in the semantic difference between an original and its copies than in their syntactical homology. By way of an example, he suggests that a copy of an abstract painting is still, in a sense, a realist painting:

> By definition, both an original and a copy are undistinguishable on the level of syntax. Semantically, they could be very different. For example: Is a copy of an abstract painting, an abstract painting, or not? In the copy we still see the original, thus it should be an abstract painting; on the other hand, being a faithful reproduction of another painting (object), it should be also a realistic painting. This ambiguity shows how a simple copy of an abstract painting could transform something "known" into something "unknown," turning the entire modernistic paradigm upside-down, and revealing that our idyllic backyard could be a minefield, too.[36]

As a painting of another painting, the copy of an abstract painting, Benjamin argues, may be considered a realist painting even if it does not look like one. Yet he goes even further than this by suggesting, in the course of his lecture, that since copies of abstract art may be produced for different reasons than their originals were, they therefore may be richer in meaning than even the originals themselves: "A copy will become more important than the original when the narrative (the story or play) it belongs to becomes more important than the narrative of the original."[37]

The fact that the lecturing Walter Benjamin focuses on Piet Mondrian for his demonstration is not a coincidence, of course: with Mondrian's career moving in a linear fashion from figuration to abstraction—even as he claimed that he always remained a landscape painter—the artist is a modernist par excellence. Mondrian's ambition, which the lecturer alludes to when he reads aloud a lengthy passage from Mondrian's writings, was to eliminate the difference between figure and ground—the basis for all figurative painting—which makes him a showcase for the effort to place art making on a solid epistemological foundation. Mondrian's total "ground," which no longer allows for a reliable distinction between background and foreground, is in a way the foundation of modernism itself, the basis for its universal (self-)knowledge.

Walter Benjamin critiques Mondrian's "grounded" modernism not by creating a new theory, but by reversing the steps that led Mondrian from realism to abstraction—we are being led back from abstraction to realism—as a way of questioning the linear art historical narrative that discards realism in favor of modernism (abstraction). In an argument reminiscent of Derrida's ideas on the nature of the sign, the lecturer argues that by reproducing an abstract painting we are inserting it into a bigger picture, a picture that includes both realism and abstraction at the same time. As a result, abstraction can no longer be conceived as painting's point zero (a flat surface that is a pure ground); instead, it turns out to be *only one possible way of painting among others*. With his demonstration—and unlike Mondrian, for whom the departure from realism was absolute and irreversible—the lecturer Walter Benjamin keeps both realism and abstraction in the balance. It is as if the copy and the original, realism and abstraction, now existed side by side, and did so out of necessity, since our understanding of the copied image *as a copy* depends on their continued juxtaposition (otherwise, we could not tell the copy from its original).

The copies of Mondrian in the lecture then represent a reformulation rather than a simple negation of modernism's claim to transparent language and universal, "grounded" truth—the kind of truth underwritten, in Morris's case, by a Panofskian faith in science and the humanities. In this way, the natural hegemony of abstraction as the new and solitary foundation for modern art—an absolute departure point—gives way to an "edifying" instead of a foundational approach that, rather than passing through styles and periods of art making in a linear fashion, keeps them in the balance in a manner akin to Richard Rorty's thoughts on postmodern edification.[38]

The lecturer Walter Benjamin's demonstrative critique of modernism is not a reversal based on nostalgia for realism; rather, it aims at a point where abstraction is relieved of its burdensome task of founding an unquestionable truth steeped in linear historical progress. Rather than simply declaring modernism and its truth claims invalid or outmoded, the lecturer argues that we may need to concede that realism can be used to create alternatives to modernism that have equal rights to being viewed as valid descriptions of the world. Again, the realism of the copied Mondrians as edifying alternatives to the grounded modernism of their originals is not dependent on the creation of a new formal language, the gold standard for any modernist innovation. After all, if a new formal language of abstraction to rival Mondrian's were created, we would simply be dealing with another round of modernism's promise of continuously renewed progress. What we are dealing with instead looks more like a relativization of the language of abstraction by inserting that language into a bigger picture.

From this angle, we can refer to Benjamin's demonstration as what Derrida called a "double narration," an effort to reinscribe the familiar tale that is modernism into a different narrative without aiming to replace it.

According to Derrida, double narration involves techniques that are "resistant to the point where it is no longer possible to separate 'false' (nominal and semantic) and original features, and thus they can no longer be included in the binary philosophical oppositions that they resist and disorganize, without attempting to create a third meaning."[39] To revert to the terms of classical rhetoric, we might say that double narration represents an instance of ethos losing its authoritative ground not by being directly challenged, but by being embedded in a pathos that belongs to another, syntactically indistinguishable ethical position.

This type of critique—one that avoids reinscribing itself into what it seeks to historicize—is especially significant in a country such as the former Yugoslavia, where after the Second World War modernism had gained the upper hand—resulting in what has been termed "nonaligned modernism"[40]—while in the countries of the Eastern Bloc it did not, or at least not to the same degree. The copies of Mondrian in Benjamin's lecture represent not only a reformulation (rather than the negation) of modernism with its claim to transparent language and universal, grounded truth; they also intervene in a certain understanding of Socialist Realism in Yugoslavia. This style enjoyed only a short lifespan in that country, and subsequently gave way to a renewed commitment to modernism. (Yugoslav writer Miroslav Krleža's speech denouncing dogmatic Socialist Realism was delivered in 1952 in Ljubljana, the same place where Benjamin delivered his lecture.) Extending the logic of Walter Benjamin's lecture performance to Socialist Realism, I argue that the latter is itself a kind of realist copy—a copy of the abstractions painted by members of the historical avant-garde. In that sense, and understood as a form of pedagogy, Socialist Realism functions as an edifying reformulation of an existing way of speaking (avant-garde abstraction), rather than a new discourse with a claim to absolute validity.[41]

4

FILM AS OPERATION (HARUN FAROCKI, PAWEŁ KWIEK)

Radical left-wing students and intellectuals in West Germany during the 1960s were keenly aware of the need to reeducate the public in order to have their message understood. To this end, filmmakers such as West Berlin-based Harun Farocki gestured toward a theory and practice of an agitational cinema that would take its cue from contemporary didactics and pedagogy.[1] Farocki's engagement during the late 1960s was based in the Marxist belief that nothing short of a radical change in ownership of the means of film and TV production—taking film out of the hands of private individuals, and public TV from liberal bureaucrats—could help film once again become a medium of enlightenment (*Aufklärung*), as it had been when directors such as Dziga Vertov used the medium to teach the Soviet people the new postrevolutionary ways.[2] The filmmaker's point was that cinema "belongs not to those who make it but to those who watch it."[3] Based on these assumptions, Farocki developed a theory of agitprop cinema whose foremost function was to demonstrate and to teach. To do this effectively, he wanted filmmakers to learn from the latest pedagogical theories that had, in his words, "suspended the hierarchical flow of information between teacher and student" and had, as such, found fertile ground among university students.[4] With the help of these ideas, film would become a form of politics, "analysis, demonstrations, actions, and, in between, films."[5]

As an early example, we might cite Farocki's 1969 anti-Vietnam War short film *Nicht löschbares Feuer* (*Inextinguishable Fire*). Produced a year after the filmmaker was expelled from the German Film and Television Academy (dffb) for revolutionary activities, the film starts by discussing the production of napalm by Dow Chemical for use in the Vietnam War and ends as an inquiry into the nature of film as a means to demonstrate. It begins with a speech by Farocki during which he reads the first-person account of a napalm victim and then addresses the difficulty of demonstrating the gruesome effects of napalm to a Western audience in such a way that they will not look away. It turns out that overcoming viewers' resistance by simply showing them napalm's effects is trickier than expected; we have difficulty watching Farocki extinguish a cigarette butt on his lower arm. He concludes that the only way out is to confront viewers with their own complicity in the agent's production:

> A cigarette burns at about 400 degrees. Napalm burns at about 3000 degrees of heat. If viewers do not want to have anything to do with the consequences of napalm attacks, then we have to examine what they have to do with the reasons for these attacks. . . . Once napalm has started to burn, it's too late to extinguish it. You have to battle the blaze where it is being produced: in the industrial plants.[6]

A central characteristic of Farocki's agitational style, and of the expanded 1960s more generally, is its connection of what is far away—for example, in Vietnam—with what occurs close by—in West Berlin—and in a style that seeks to foreclose the possibility of evading responsibility for one's complicity in what occurs in distant corners of the world.[7] Once his film's lesson has been understood by his audience, so Farocki's reasoning

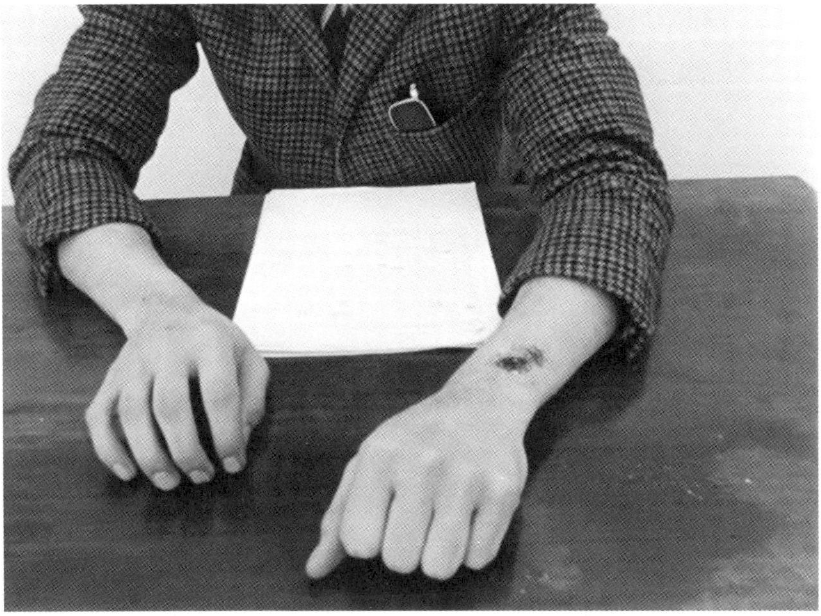

Figure 4.1 Harun Farocki, *Inextinguishable Fire (Nicht löschbares Feuer)*, 1969. Video still. © Harun Farocki GbR.

went, it would become impossible not to draw the right consequences from its insights.

Farocki referred to some of his short films of the late 1960s as "flyer films" (*Flugblattfilme*)[8] because they aimed to transfer a political flyer's major characteristics—brevity, succinctness, the direct address to a mass audience, but above all the ability to adapt to specific social and political circumstances—to the medium of film, thus also encouraging a form of reception that would be congruent with that of the flyer (or the newspaper, for that matter): fast, noncontemplative, concentrated.[9] Agitational flyer films can be described as a form of demonstration. In his radical short film *Instructions on How to Pull Off Police Helmets* (1969), Farocki uses extradiegetic arrows to point to weak spots in a policeman's uniform and body, with a special focus on how a demonstrator might push the helmet off the officer's head from behind.[10] His instructional film was accompanied by handwritten captions that ironically commented on what was being shown ("One weak spot" / "Many weak spots").

If on the one hand *Instructions on How to Pull Off Police Helmets* provided shockingly direct, antihumanist instructions on how protesting students in West Berlin might push back against the police, on the other hand, its diagrammatic form of presentation (the arrows) vividly illustrated how modern political education also had to rely on a new kind of instructional filmmaking in order to mobilize its audience.

Crucially, Farocki sought for his agitational films the same mobility that a flyer or a newspaper have as they react to their respective local audiences, and which conventional film lacks because it can only be screened in cinemas and cannot easily adapt to the specific situations in which it is shown. Newspapers were a crucial part of 1960s demonstration culture, both as the target of student protests—for example, the student protests in West Berlin against the right-wing Axel Springer press, especially the notorious *Bild Zeitung*—and as an outlet for demonstrators (artists and otherwise) producing their own newspapers. West Berlin students' radicalization progressed apace after student leader Rudi Dutschke was shot in 1968

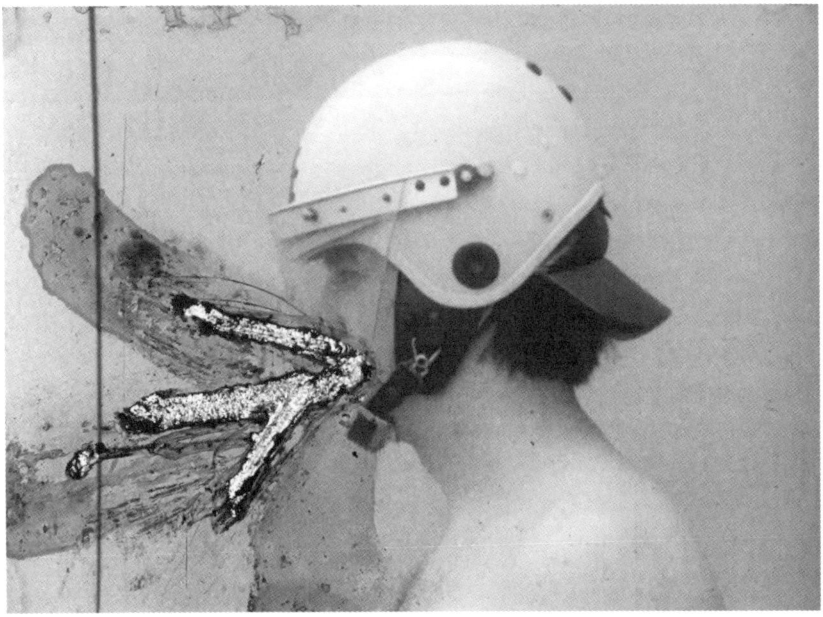

Figure 4.2 Harun Farocki, *Instructions on How to Pull Off Police Helmets* (*Anleitung, Polizisten den Helm abzureissen*), 1969. Video still. © Harun Farocki GbR.

by a man who was rumored to have had the *Bild Zeitung* in his back pocket. Earlier, in 1963, Thomas Bayrle, Bernhard Jäger, and Bazon Brock created what they called *Bloom Zeitung* (Bloom daily), a title reminiscent of the *Bild Zeitung*. While the name "Bloom" was invented (and may or may not be a literary allusion to James Joyce's character in *Ulysses*), the *Bloom Zeitung* was a precise copy of the *Bild Zeitung* of April 8, 1963, yet modified in such a way that all names were replaced with the name Bloom, beginning with the paper's title, and including advertisements and the main headline, "Bloom Wants to Remain Chancellor!" The artists distributed their paper for free in Frankfurt, with the hope that it might inspire passersby to reflect on the differences between its two versions (the regular *Bild Zeitung* versus the collaged *Bloom Zeitung*). Once the reading process had been freed from its subliminal moorings, the boundary separating consumption from production, and reading from acting, would, they hoped, become porous as both parts of the equation became dialectically intertwined, with reading now being an active engagement rather than an instance of passive consumption.

These ideas have a pedigree. Lenin had regarded the central organ of the Russian Social Democratic Labor Party *Iskra* (of which he was the editor between 1902 and 1903) as a crucial tool for the formation of a militant revolutionary movement, offering a primer in specific instances of oppression in the present:

> The question arises, what should political education consist in? Can it be confined to the propaganda of working-class hostility to the autocracy? Of course not. It is *not enough to explain* to the workers that they are politically oppressed (any more than it is to explain to them that their interests are antagonistic to the interests of the employers). Agitation must be conducted with regard to every concrete example of *this* oppression (as we have begun to carry on agitation around concrete examples of economic oppression).[11]

Lenin's contrasting juxtaposition of agitation with the help of the newspaper, on the one hand, and "explanation," on the other, distinguishes between the propagandist as the bearer of an explanatory framework that operates independently from concrete instances of oppression ("working-class hostility to the autocracy") and the agitator, who is focused on precisely these instances ("every concrete example of *this* oppression"). Where explanation draws on the macroanalysis of social relations (the workers' interests being "antagonistic to the interests of the employers," etc.), agitation focuses on the particularities of the present ("*this* oppression"). Only by means of agitation, Lenin contends, can revolutionary leaders teach the masses how to create a revolutionary organization with the necessary commitment to practice, "an organization ready at any time to support every protest and every outbreak."[12]

A related commitment to the newspaper as the linchpin of the dialectical resolution of the opposition between instruction (explanation) and practice, science and art, education and politics can be observed in Walter Benjamin's idea that with the rise of newspapers, the bourgeois emphasis on canonical expertise (*Bildung*) was being replaced with the ever-intensifying mobilization of the reader who thus advanced from passive consumer to active producer and participant.[13] Few ideas held greater sway over progressive art of the expanded 1960s than this one, especially in the way they redefined the artist's competence and specialization, with instruction being viewed as an exemplary form of deskilling: the more artists practice advanced techniques that exceed the limitations of their acquired skills, the more they would be able to learn from other (non-) specialists, and lead others by example.

Farocki's work with film-as-a-newspaper is a case in point. Like Lenin and Benjamin, Farocki was resistant to general theorization and insisted, as Lenin did, that revolutionary change required an intimate understanding of concrete instances of oppression. Only in this way, he assumed, could such examples become meaningful for understanding cases of injustice and oppression elsewhere. In an effort to distribute his film-flyers across the whole city, the filmmaker proposed switching their screenings between different venues, each time eliciting different audience responses, depending on the new context. He wrote: "What is the influence that the place of the screening and its situation have on a film's reception? Sometimes we showed the film in a meeting room before the event. In that case, the students took the hierarchically flowing information from the screen the same way they would accept it from a professor. If on the other hand we placed the devices outside, for example in front of the dining hall, then the students were encouraged to become active themselves . . . they disrupted the presentation or refused to be disturbed by the presentation."[14] The crucial point was the (optimistic) idea that a film can provide whatever viewers need in order to become conscious of their own situation, to analyze and ultimately change it. After the Second World War, this pedagogy had several German inflections, one of which Farocki references in his writings as "exemplarisches Lernen" (learning through examples). This theory, which usually goes by the name *exemplarisches Lehren* (teaching by example) is associated with two West German academics, Martin Wagenschein—an expert in the didactics of physics and mathematics at secondary schools—and Wolfgang Klafki, whose research focused on didacticism more generally.[15] A basic premise of Wagenschein's classic 1968 book *Teaching How to Understand* was the idea that instead of covering everything—an impossibility at a time when the availability, if not the mastery, of information was increasing exponentially in the developed world—teaching should devote itself to the extended treatment of specific problems rather than to systematic coverage. The hope was that students would be genuinely affected by the material they were taught, and that comprehensive understanding would replace rote knowledge, or what Wagenschein calls *Verwertungswissen* (recycled knowledge). Other key terms in his approach are *Erfahren* and *Erleben*, both of which roughly translate into English as "experience," hinting at the fact that in Wagenschein's scheme, learning is thought of as an affect rather than a purely cognitive function.

For Farocki, film was a means to foster a similar kind of assimilation, one based not on passive consumption but on active assimilation and interactive experience, since "what agitation says is not true in and of itself; it is true from someone to someone."[16] At the same time, the filmmaker was adamant that leftist agitational film should not simply adopt existing pedagogical models (including Wagenschein's) readymade, especially given how deeply they were imbricated in the capitalist process of production; instead, such film had to transform and modify the models, adapting them to its needs.[17] It was therefore crucial that theory, which Farocki, like so many other experimental filmmakers at the time, saw as an inalienable part of film practice ("agitation can use the theory of teaching"), not limit itself to what film shows, instead extending its reach to the social composition of its audiences and to its screening locations, techniques, and political objectives. Alluding to Soviet literary and film theorist Sergei Tretyakov's distinction between "descriptive" and "informative" literary texts, Farocki viewed agitational film as "operational." By "operational," he means, following Tretyakov, that film is part of the political operation on which it focuses, not least in the way it combines political with didactic theory: "An operational film about a demonstration decides for itself; it is part of the operation that consists in organizing a social class . . . the theory of the operational film and the theory of the operation are linked to each other."[18] As Volker Pantenburg has shown, film's operational side was a key category in Farocki's understanding of its political efficacy throughout his career.[19]

In another agitational film from the late 1960s, *Ihre Zeitungen* (Their newspapers, 1967), Farocki further elaborated his ideas on film's didactic operations. The short—its subtitle, dryly reminiscent of a college term paper, was "Problems of Anti-Authoritarian and Anti-Imperialist Struggle in Metro-Areas, on the Example of West Berlin"—begins with an anonymous reader of the Springer tabloid *B.Z.* (*Berliner Zeitung*) picking up his morning paper and walking through the streets of West Berlin, the large paper opened in front of him, while an accented voice uncannily similar to that of Nazi propaganda minister Josef Goebbels comments acerbically on the current American offensive in South Vietnam ("As a news item, a maimed news item, Vietnam comes to Berlin").

Suddenly, horrifying reports about acts of gruesome domestic violence in Berlin—a baby being killed in a bathtub, a husband punishing his wife for an alleged affair by extinguishing glowing cigarette butts on her body—supplement the news from distant Vietnam and crowd the *B.Z.* reader's consciousness. Then, as he waits for his bus at the local bus stop, the tabloid reader recognizes that the victim of domestic violence in West Berlin is a North Vietnamese rice farmer, inadvertently connecting two seemingly unrelated incidents of violence, one distant and one in his immediate vicinity. At this point, the protagonist's brainwashing by the Springer-generated right-wing propaganda is reversed, not because he has been told what to think, but because he was able to grasp independently that what happens far away is linked to what happens at his doorstep. Subsequently, the *B.Z.* reader starts asking himself questions that appear to be inspired directly by Wagenschein's *Exemplarisches Lernen* ("What is the difference between Berlin and Vietnam?"), and begins his transformation from passive consumer to militant activist and reader of Marcuse and Che Guevara. He then duly burns a *Bild Zeitung* on a West Berlin sidewalk, starts posting billboards with leftist political messages, and joins a collective of young militants who fight oppression with the help of their own newspaper, which now does double duty as a weapon by serving as a wrapper for stones during street demonstrations ("No stone without paper, no paper without a stone!").

The dialectical sublation on which the tabloid reader's conversion is based—with film serving as its vehicle—is a paradox: without reading the *B.Z.* propaganda, the young Berliner would clearly not have had his moment of epiphany. The tabloid thus becomes the stepping stone for his realization that West Berlin and Vietnam, the capitalist North and the global South, are linked by repressive politicians, brutal police, and corrupt media, and that it is therefore necessary to join the struggle against

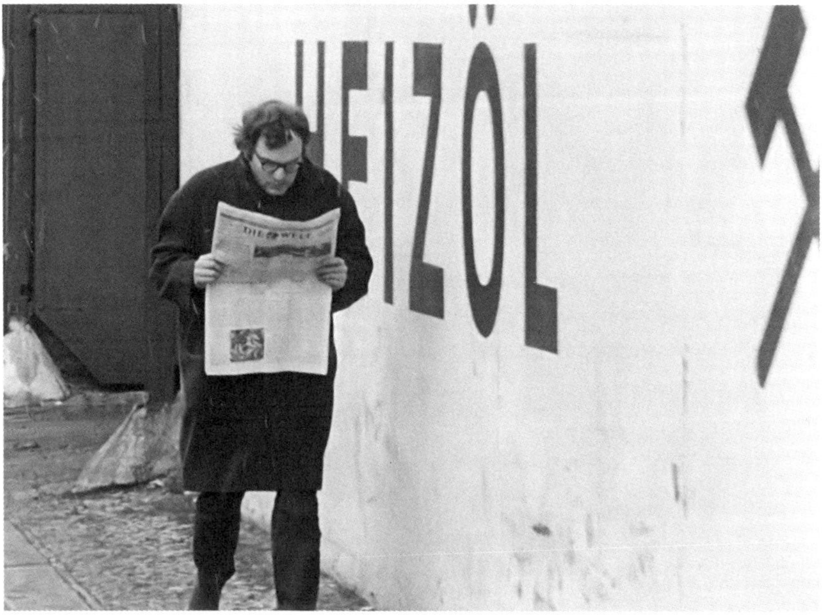

Figure 4.3 Harun Farocki, *Their Newspapers* (*Ihre Zeitungen*), 1967. Video still. © Harun Farocki GbR.

violence, imperialism, and neocolonialism all over the world. Such reasoning, which established parallels from the First World to the so-called Third World, was common among activists at the time. Dutschke, for example, translated Che Guevara's writing into German. As he wrote in 1968, the students' opposition to the war in Vietnam and their support for the liberation war of the Vietnamese people, which became more and more pronounced from the mid-1960s onward, lost much of their "abstract quality" once they were seen in conjunction with the students' own fight against the authoritarianism of their university bureaucracy.[20]

To be sure, the unproblematic way in which Farocki's film, and leftist political discourse during the 1960s more generally, unravels the problem of otherness by subsuming it under a general and generally *Western* notion of universal empathy and solidarity may seem to us today to be too focused on assimilability and the sublation of difference. Still, its approach to art as a form of political understanding—in a time when the idea of universal values had not yet been interrogated—is a lesson worth contemplating. That lesson is charismatic, not pedagogical in a traditional sense: no ideological master discourse, no series of explanations or rationalizations, and no preformulated political lesson led the young West Berliner in *Their Newspapers* to his epiphanous moment of empathy with a person thousands of miles away in Vietnam, and hence no prefabricated knowledge or "tendency" (to use Walter Benjamin's phrase) can ultimately explain his almost Pauline conversion from passive consumer to militant anti-imperialist.

Another of Farocki's agitprop flyer films from the same period deepens the lesson of exemplary learning and teaching: this was *The Words of the Chairman* (1967), created with fellow dffb student Holger Meins, a future member of the Rote Armee Fraktion. At the time, fascination with China's Great Proletarian Cultural Revolution was at a high point among the radical students. The same year marked a turning point in the history of the West German student movement when student Benno Ohnesorg was killed by police during a violent demonstration against a state visit to the German capital by the shah of Iran, Reza Pahlevi.[21] Farocki's short begins with a person reading behind a desk, leafing through *The Quotations of Chairman Mao Tse-Tung* (then affectionately known as the "Little Red Book") and running his finger under the lines as he reads. Meanwhile a voiceover, interrupted by propaganda choirs, intones: "Listen to his words and act based on his commands. . . . Mao Zedong has taken Marxism-Leninism to a completely new level. We have to take his words to a completely new level again! We have to supplement them based on historical experience. We have to boldly transform them. In our hands they have to become weapons that surprise the enemy."

After arriving at the chapter "On the Relations Between the Army and the People" in the Little Red Book, the film shows a hand tearing out pages from the book as its fingers—their function before had been limited to pointing and underlining Mao's words—begin to fold a torn-out page into a small paper airplane that looks like a fighter jet. The paper jet literally becomes a "flyer" like the ones handed out at numerous student demonstrations, by being "sent flying" through the air straight into the candlelight dinner of two people identifiable as the shah of Iran and his wife.[22] The paper plane crashes into the soup in front of the shah, splattering the monarch with dark liquid.

The Words of the Chairman pivots from a more formally defined process of demonstration (the finger moving along the lines of Mao quotes in the Little Red Book) to a more practical one (the flyers/airplanes that demonstrate against imperialism by targeting the shah and his wife), and the film's operational field is, in a sense, the space between the two, the transition from formal demonstration to political action—from education to reality-changing practice—based on the ideas of *exemplarisches Lernen*. The Iranian royal couple's visit to the West German capital Bonn and West Berlin had been preceded by weeks of enthusiastic reporting in the Springer newspaper, including *B.Z.* and *Bild Zeitung*, about the shah and his exuberant lifestyle. Meanwhile, exiled Iranians in West Germany and West Berlin were telling German student representatives about the dire political and social situation in Iran, especially through Bahman Nirumand's

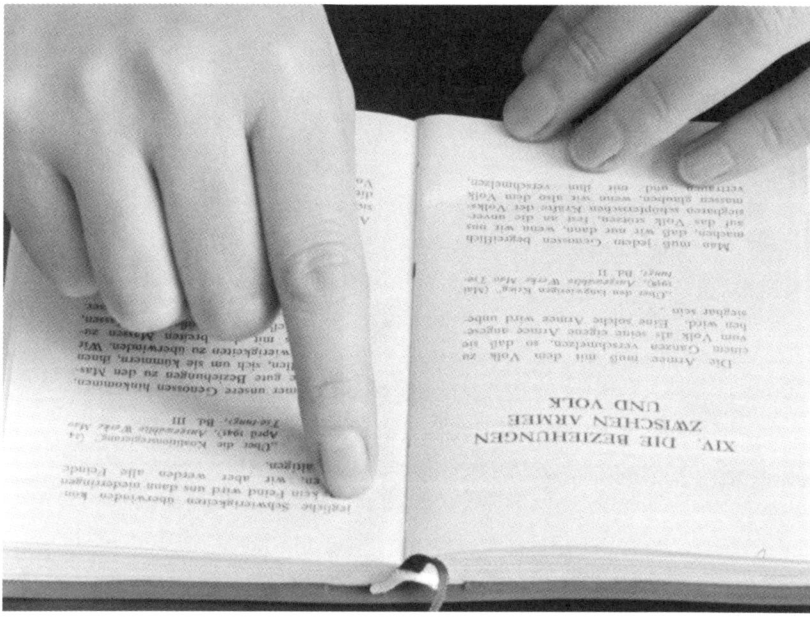

Figure 4.4 Harun Farocki, *The Words of the Chairman* (*Die Worte des Vorsitzenden*), 1967. Video still. © Harun Farocki GbR.

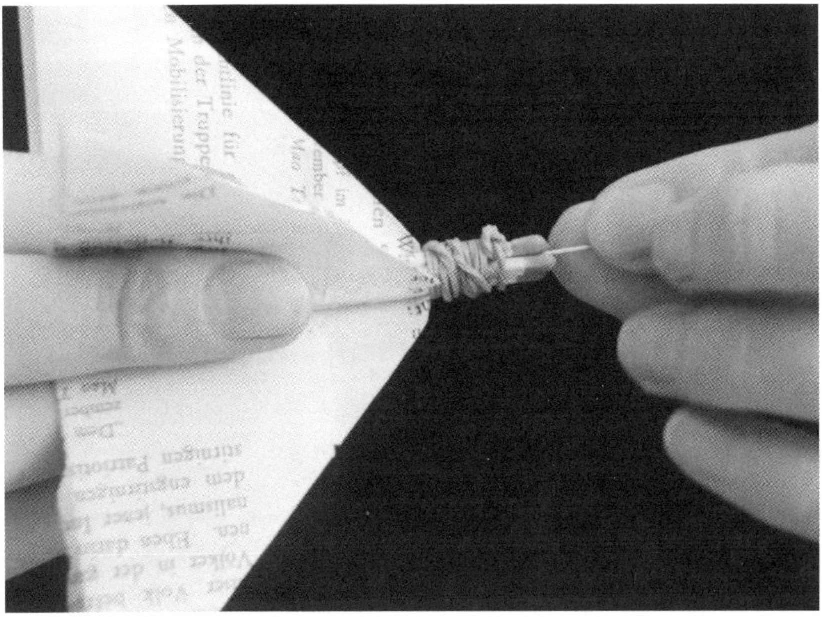

Figure 4.5 Harun Farocki, *The Words of the Chairman* (*Die Worte des Vorsitzenden*), 1967. Video still. © Harun Farocki GbR.

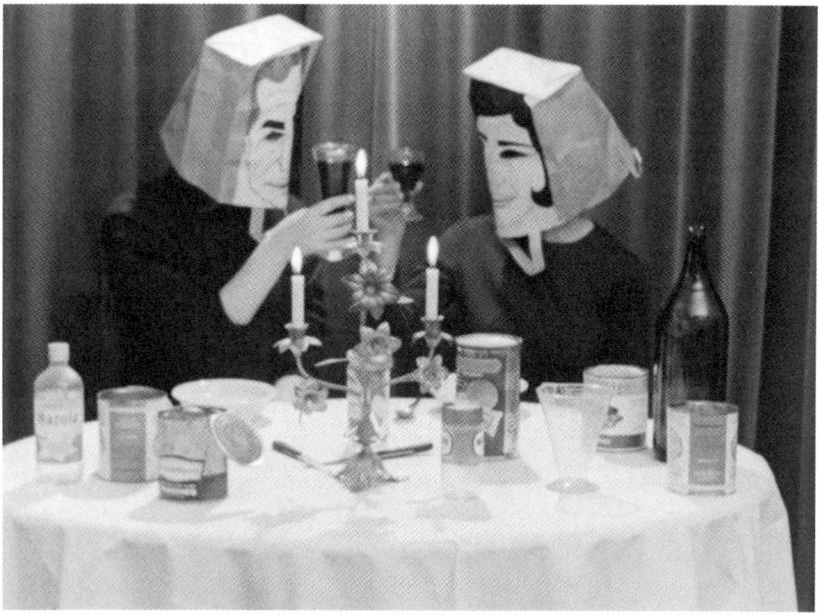

Figure 4.6 Harun Farocki, *The Words of the Chairman* (*Die Worte des Vorsitzenden*), 1967. Video still. © Harun Farocki GbR.

leftist Confederation of Iranian Students (1960) and his book *Persien. Modell eines Entwicklungslandes, oder die Diktatur der freien Welt* (Persia: model of a developing country, or the dictatorship of the free world, 1967).[23] Like Dutschke, Benno Ohnesorg had read Nirumand's book and decided as a result to participate in the legally announced anti-shah demonstration in front of the opera in West Berlin. At a meeting on the eve of the demonstration, on June 1, 1967, Dutschke had linked the fight for social justice in Iran to the students' primary concern, the fight against the war in Vietnam, and a flyer in the form of a "Wanted" poster was handed out that described the shah as a thief and murderer.[24]

Words of the Chairman does not directly participate in the information wars between the right-wing press and the left-leaning Iranian student movement, nor does it directly intervene in the struggle around the shah's visit. While it is true that the film's argument takes its departure from Mao's words, it is the transformation of these words, the possibility of their adaptation for political struggle, and the importance of rhetoric and reading that are the film's main concerns. What kind of transfer is necessary for words to be transformed into political action, and how do they become "weapons"? In rhetoric, such transfers "from one level to another"—to paraphrase the voiceover in Farocki's film—are called metaphors ("carrying over"), a connection of which Farocki is highly conscious. As he writes years later, the idea for the film came to him during a trip to South America: "I was on a ship—this sounds like a novel: I had just embarked for Venezuela on June 2, 1967, as the shah of Iran was arriving in West Berlin. There were protests, a student was shot, and a new form of opposition movement came into existence. The idea for this film came to me while I was still aboard the ship. The film is structured like a commercial. The film takes a metaphor literally: words can become weapons. However, it also shows that these weapons are made of paper."[25] The multiple double-bind alluded to here—a leftist agitprop film being structured like a commercial; words written on paper that become weapons—is crucial for my argument since it reinforces the filmmaker's dialectical take on revolutionary struggle, one that presumes that successful agitation departs from an analysis of the local situation rather than focusing on a distant goal. Whether a word can become a weapon or not is thus decided by its operational context, not by the good intentions of the filmmaker. As was customary for him at the time, Farocki is particularly concerned with the effect his film might have on its audience and with the way this effect may change over time. As he writes in his autobiography, "when I showed this film to audiences in the late Sixties, it was highly praised. I think people understood then that over-obviousness is also a form of irony. This capacity was lost a few years later. I think it's coming back today."[26] His embrace of irony clearly distinguishes Farocki's approach from that of, say, Holger Meins, whose notorious short film *How to Build a Molotov Cocktail* (1968) displays nothing but disdain for rhetorical tropes such as metaphor or irony.[27]

For Farocki, the problem of agitation is first and foremost a way of asking the question of how demonstration—and, with it, political education more generally—can become effective in the first place, and what role film can play in this effort. Nowhere is this question posed more poignantly than in the above-mentioned film *Inextinguishable Fire*. Combining dramatized scenes with newsreel footage—the former subjected to distancing (*Verfremdung*) through the actors' wooden, objectifying way of speaking—the film is less a protest against the horror of napalm than a lesson showing why the dire effects of napalm have so little effect on those who consume such images, and how a more effective demonstration could be mounted.[28]

Student protests against the use of napalm and the Vietnam War more generally had occurred first at the University of California, Berkeley, in 1966 and at Wayne State University in Michigan, but soon spread to many other colleges and universities across the US.

In many cases, protesters held up banners and signs that carried some of the horrific photographs of Vietnamese victims of napalm that could be found in the press. For his part, Farocki undercuts any effort to base political demonstrations on a purely representational strategy. In fact, where *Inextinguishable Fire* does show such effects—for example on the body of

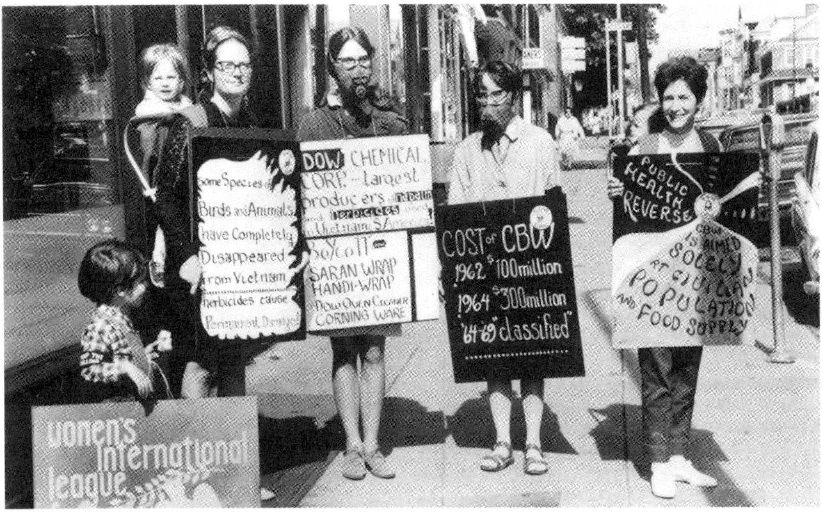

Figure 4.7 Dow protest, 1967. Image courtesy of Wisconsin Historical Society, WHI-100732.

a dead animal that is on fire—it combines the images throughout with a deadbeat, almost machine-like commentary that oscillates between a scientific demonstration and a sales pitch, which is not surprising given that the US government had entrusted napalm's production to a private company.

The reason, then, that images of the horrifying effects of napalm are not the basis of Farocki's didactic strategy for his film is the fact that this strategy itself is under investigation in *Inextinguishable Fire*. The filmmaker argues that the only way to make Western viewers aware of their own complicity in the US war in Vietnam is to analyze not merely the effects of napalm but the conditions under which it is being produced. It must be remembered in this context that Dow Chemical did not manufacture only napalm; most of its production was geared toward chemical agents with no combat use whatsoever. Only the smallest fraction of its workforce was even aware that napalm was being made on their plant's premises.

Farocki believes that it was this fact that made the production of napalm possible in the first place. Dow's management had made the conscious decision to adopt the government's line that napalm "saves lives" and that therefore any resistance from within the company must be repressed. Dissent among the employees was kept to a relatively low level because the chemical components of napalm, even if they are poisonous, could all potentially be used for different purposes ("Dow produces useful poisons and harmful poisons"), and Dow scientists were focused on developing these isolated components rather than making "napalm" per se. As the film demonstrates, individual engineers at Dow Chemical who were doing research involving napalm's individual component parts were not aware of their eventual use, which differed dramatically between the First and the Third World: "Dow insecticides help increase the harvest in Europe and the US; Dow herbacides kill crops in the Third World."[29]

Farocki's approach to his material in *Inextinguishable Fire* treats Dow's operations like a language, with the company's products acting like signifiers without stable referents. This structural approach in turn becomes the

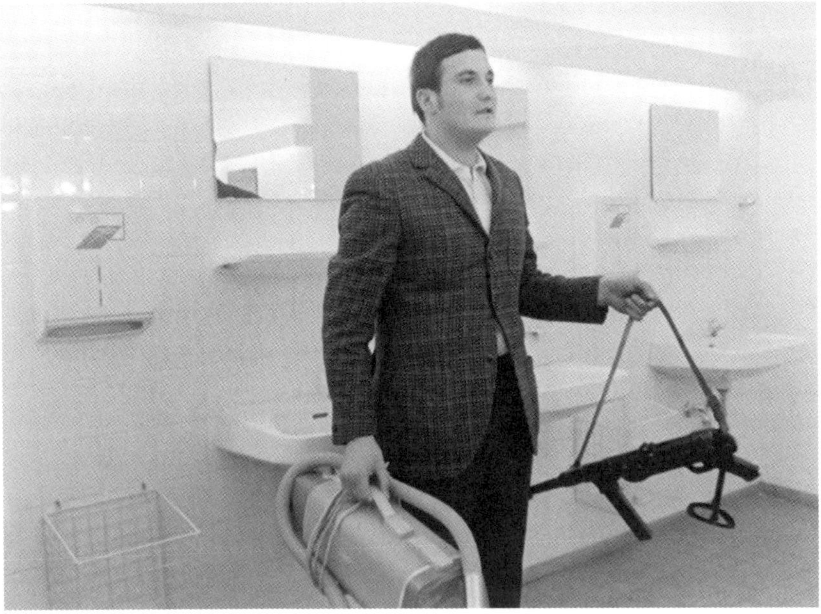

Figure 4.8 Harun Farocki, *Inextinguishable Fire* (*Nicht löschbares Feuer*), 1969. Video still. © Harun Farocki GbR.

mechanism whereby we understand why only a few inside the company questioned the production of napalm: because, as far as most employees were concerned, it simply did not exist. This, indeed, is the film's punchline: that the "intensified" (*verschärfte*) division of labor that characterizes production at Dow Chemical is the key to any didactically successful demonstration of napalm's effects, because it is the only way to show that we, the film's audience, may all be implicated, indeed responsible, for events and occurrences that happen far away from us, even if we have no primary knowledge of either those events or our implication in them. Film's function here is not to teach the correct way of thinking but to offer a lesson in the structural basis for our collective lack of consciousness, and hence our inability to act on it effectively.

The foundation for Farocki's approach is the realization that the difference between, say, a weapon and a household appliance should not be sought in abstract definitions or a political imaginary unhinged from its material context. This idea is encapsulated by the following remarkable monologue at the end of *Inextinguishable Fire*:

> I'm a worker and I work in a factory that makes vacuum cleaners. My wife could use a vacuum cleaner. That's why every day I take home one component part of a vacuum cleaner. At home I want to assemble the vacuum cleaner. But no matter what I do, it always turns into a submachine gun.
>
> I'm a student. Currently I work in a factory that makes vacuum cleaners. However, I think the factory produces submachine guns for Portugal. We could benefit from proving this. That's why I take home a component part every day. At home I want to assemble the submachine gun. But no matter what I do, it always turns into a vacuum cleaner.
>
> I'm an engineer and I work in an electrical plant. The workers believe that we produce vacuum cleaners. The students believe we produce submachine guns. This vacuum cleaner can

> become a useful weapon. This submachine gun can become a useful household appliance. What we produce depends on the workers, students, and engineers.[30]

The worker's and the student's assemblage projects fail because while they may have the right political instincts ("I think the factory produces submachine guns for Portugal"), they lack insight into the fact that a product's ontological status (what the product "is" or is meant to be a priori) may be less relevant than the operational use to which it is put by those who produce or acquire it. And in this sense, a vacuum cleaner (or napalm, as we saw) can indeed become either a weapon or a household appliance, depending on the intentions and goals of those who control it. Didactic film's role in this context is to demonstrate the structural necessity for workers and students to not only better grasp this mechanism, but also to acquire the political awareness necessary to turn words, images, and vacuum cleaners into weapons as part of the collective struggle against inequality and oppression, both at home and in the world at large.

PAWEŁ KWIEK: A FILM OPERATOR'S DEMONSTRATION

In Eastern Europe, Farocki's focus on the analysis of capitalist production as a prerequisite for successful political resistance had no traction. That, however, does not mean that experimental filmmakers on the Eastern side of the Berlin Wall were not interested in film's instructional qualities. A good example is Polish filmmaker Paweł Kwiek, whose 1972 *1, 2, 3 . . . ćwiczenie operatorskie* (*1, 2, 3 . . . A Cinematographer's Exercise*) carries a reference to (auto-)didactics ("exercise") already in its title.[31] The film presents a bricolage of disparate elements, from found footage to unscripted improvisations, sequenced in such a way that the viewer's attention is continuously redirected from the images' content to their formal arrangement. This happens, among other ways, through the syncopated repetition of key sequences, reminiscent of the repeated chants we hear during street demonstrations, or through allusive gestures such as the repeated motif of a person trying to scale a wall.

The phrase *ćwiczenie operatorskie*—the latter term derived from the Polish word for "cameraman" or "cinematographer" (*operator filmowy*)—in the film's title refers, on the one hand, to the filmmaker's view of his film as part of an ongoing learning process. Yet, in a broader sense, it implies the same expanded understanding of filmmaking we encounter in Farocki, of the filmmaker as someone who intervenes in social life as an operator, for whom, as Farocki had it, "the theory of the operational film and the theory of the operation are linked to each other."[32] That being said, while for Farocki the operational aspects of a film were closely tied up with its ability to analyze and organize, following the precepts of a pointed Marxist critique, for Kwiek they were focused more on showing the formal conditions under which such organization might proceed, without the explicit endorsement of one specific ideological position over another. As the art historian Łukasz Ronduda has observed, "this approach to the film's structure allowed for elements with political connotations to be interpreted in any possible way, depending on the context they were put into. It was not unequivocally clear whether the film supported or criticized a given symbol. . . . Kwiek's film was structurally incapable of promoting the dominant ideology of the time; its basic principle was interpretative openness and a deliberate indeterminacy of meaning."[33] In this sense, *1, 2, 3 . . . ćwiczenie operatorskie* and Kwiek's films in general subscribe to the same strategy of didactic recontextualization and semantic openness that is characteristic of Eastern European art in more general terms. Politically, this strategy subscribes to a broadly conceived humanism that by is no means simply apolitical and that doesn't as such exclude or avoid references to political figures or symbols (for example, in the case of Kwiek, to images of Lenin), yet without the kind of unequivocal political side-taking we find in Farocki.

If the *ćwiczenie* or "exercise" in the title of Kwiek's film refers us to the filmmaker's (auto-)didactic attitude toward his own film (he learns from making it), it might equally allude to Kwiek's audience, for whom watching the short amounts to a learning process in its own right, an exercise for which the film constitutes the manual. By teaching viewers how to comprehend its own complex language, *1, 2, 3 . . . ćwiczenie operatorskie* thus stakes out a terrain that allows the filmmaker to take back the right to show and to demonstrate, a right over which, in Poland, the state exercised a near total monopoly.

Not coincidentally, images of pointing, showing, and demonstrating constitute the visual backbone of the footage collaged in the film, from official demonstrations in the Soviet Union to a Workers' Day March and images of Lenin to having an index finger point to drawn images with text underneath. However, Kwiek's focus in refilming, coloring, and variously recontextualizing this footage is not the conventional totalizing perspective on the masses familiar from state TV, but rather is on the individual and their agency to show—*themselves*, among other things—and to demonstrate: in short, to control their own visibility.

The right to show (oneself) is also at the heart of *Sytuacja studia* (Studio situation), or *Video A*, a live performance involving the use of TV cameras which Kwiek created in 1974 as part of a Polish state television program devoted to experimental film.[34] Kwiek observed that as a media technology, television—over which the state had complete control in Communist Poland—is remarkable because every take produced by the TV camera immediately becomes visible. As he notes, "what fascinated me about television was the simultaneity in observing the effect and the working cause. So that one could create model situations in which the effect of an action was instantaneous, and in which one could observe and turn that observation into another object of cognition to be manipulated in turn."[35] Kwiek is referring to the simultaneity with which an image on live TV, unlike a film image, is created and broadcast at virtually the same time. As part of his own live TV experiment, Kwiek recreated this effect by positioning himself in the middle of a studio among three TV cameras that he identifies for the viewer, pointing to each of them based on what the viewer has most recently seen on the screen (the director's face, the studio, the other

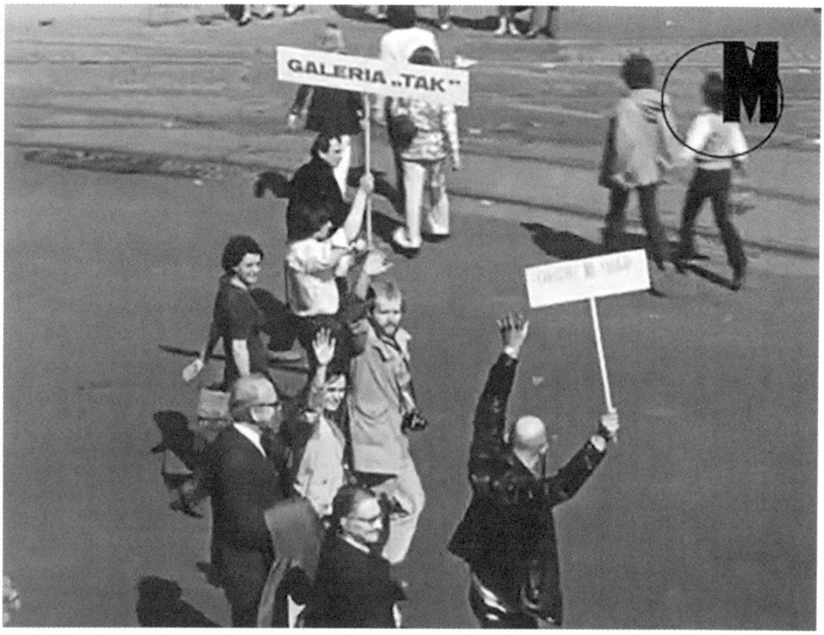

Figure 4.9 Paweł Kwiek, *1,2,3 . . . A Cinematographer's Exercise* (*1,2,3 . . . ćwiczenie operatorskie*), 1972. Video still. Image courtesy of Cyprian Kwiek.

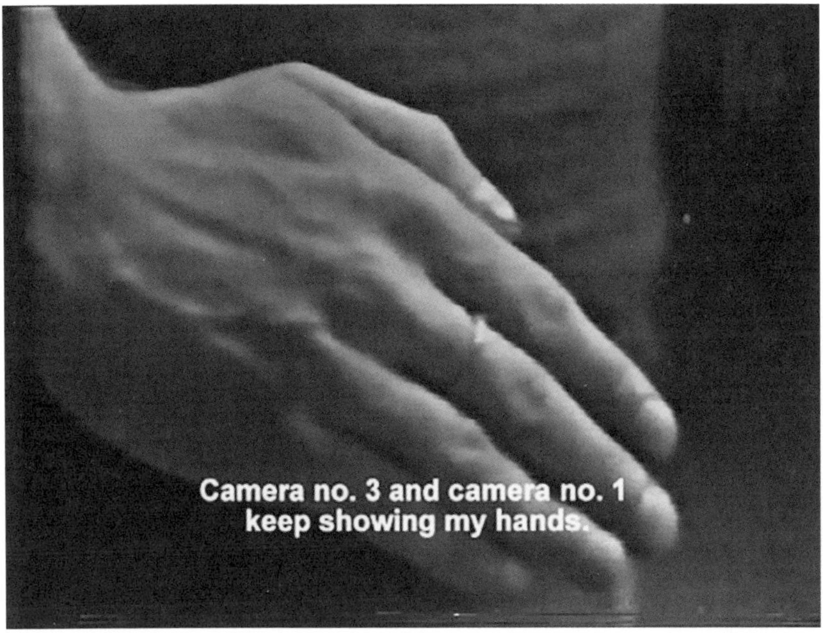

Figure 4.10 Paweł Kwiek, *Sytuacja studia* (*Video A*), 1974. Video still. Image courtesy of Cyprian Kwiek.

cameras, etc.). He then starts by directing camera #3 to pan on the right to his left hand in a close-up, while camera #1 is directed to focus on his right hand, using a long lens. After this, Kwiek directs cameras #1 and #3—both focused on his hands—to become activated in ever more rapid succession based on his shouted commands, so that we see alternating images of his left and right hands, depending on which camera is being activated.

The key to understanding this sequence of images is the fact that the cameras directed by Kwiek form a system whose component parts function in concert with each other and respond as such to the decisions made by its operator. Kwiek doesn't so much represent this system as he demonstrates its operation, and in this sense he shows a clear affinity with Farocki's operational approach. Formal analysis in *Sytuacja studia* functions as a stepping stone for a more thorough look at the conditions for image production and what licenses it, including the importance of the operator's decisions for what we see. Crucially, however, that operator (Kwiek himself), whose hands and face the TV images incessantly reproduce, is part of the same system he directs. Thus, the situation he creates in the TV studio has for Kwiek the character of a model: "And when one adds to this the structure of live intellect that enters this system, the model of reality created by television, the opportunity for the penetration of reality becomes doubled: a human being resides in the reality which is a model, and simultaneously this model becomes the reality inhabited by that human being. . . . Models . . . give one the opportunity to observe what is over the horizon of everyday life, what is at the limits of cognition."[36] The model situation allows us to understand that the manipulation of TV images and the reality they construct are beyond the horizon of ordinary cognition because their operator, and we as the audience, inhabit the very same reality. Only (film) art, with its power to create models for demonstration, may give us the opportunity "to observe what is over the horizon of everyday life."[37]

5

TAKING IT TO THE STREET: EASTERN EUROPEAN ART DEMONSTRATIONS (MILAN KNÍŽÁK, JIŘÍ KOVANDA, ENDRE TÓT, MLADEN MILJANOVIĆ, CIPRIAN HOMORODEAN)

On May 1, 1972, during the year of Documenta 5, Joseph Beuys—who routinely referred to his own work as demonstration—started his action *Clean-Up with a Broom* (*Ausfegen*) on Karl-Marx-Platz in West Berlin's Neukölln district after the end of the May Day demonstrations. His point was to exorcise not only the existing political system but even its detractors: the artist wanted to show that "even the ideology-fixated orientation of the students has to be swept away. That is to say, what was announced on the banners as the dictatorship of the proletariat."[1]

In a biting critical response to Beuys's sweeping appeal, painter Jörg Immendorff, a former Beuys student and cofounder of the professor-free LIDL Academy, in 1973 criticized his former teacher's neo-romantic take on revolution by creating a painting in the style of a didactic panel—titled *"Art Action"—Wait a Minute!* (*Eine "Kunstaktion"—Halt mal!*) whose left side shows two drawings depicting Beuys's *Ausfegen* action with the handwritten caption "Art Action" (*Eine Kunstaktion*), while below this the panel displays a painting in the style of another Beuys student, Blinky Palermo. On the right, under the handwritten words "Halte mal!" (Wait a minute!) in large letters, we see the monumental faces of a crowd of demonstrators pointing their fingers at Beuys's and Palermo's artworks to their left, while

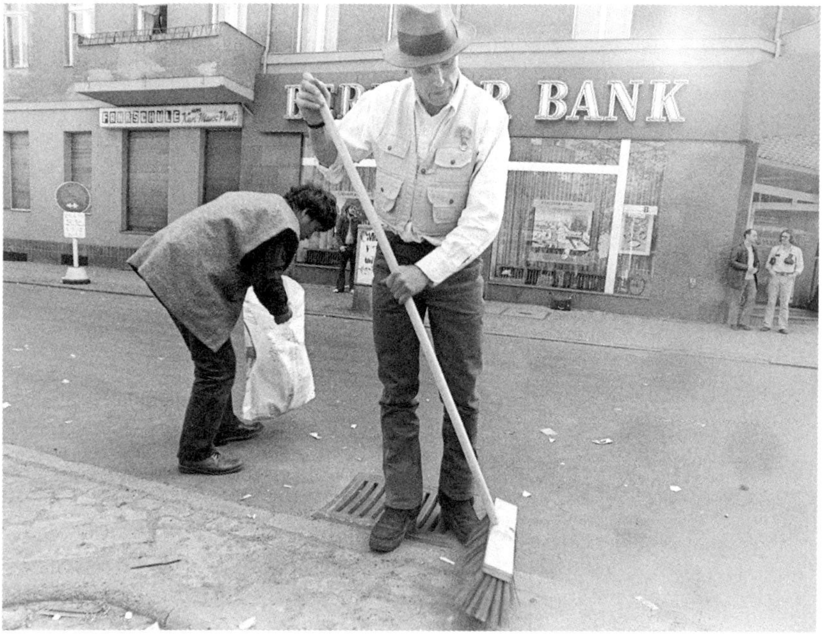

Figure 5.1 Joseph Beuys, *Ausfegen*, 1972. © 2024 Artists Rights Society (ARS), New York / VG Bild-Kunst, Bonn.

the handwritten caption renders the workers' thoughts and demands in a long litany of questions and slogans ("For whom do these artists produce their works? For whom is it useful when on May 1, the day of the social and political liberation of working people, Beuys cooks his art soup? . . . This kind of art only helps minimize the contradictions in capitalist society"). *"Art Action"—Wait a Minute!* registers Immendorff's protest against Beuys's confusion of radical art with radical politics, arguing instead for an art practice more openly committed to leftist ideals ("Create the basis for an art that serves the people by actively participating in the fight against imperialism, exploitation, and oppression!").

In a commentary on Immendorff's demonstration, Eckhart Gillen has argued that by adding captions that effectively limit the ways in which his work can be interpreted, Immendorff was eager "to disable the ambivalence and seductiveness of images."[2]

It's worth noting that in cold war Eastern Europe, Immendorff's demonstration would have been unthinkable because here the fight against "the ambivalence and seductiveness of images"—from an arguably leftist, state Communist position—was already the official (and only) possible position for official propaganda; as a result, the jargon of the radical New Left in Western Europe presented nonconformist Eastern European artists with considerable problems. As Václav Havel famously wrote, "a citizen of our country simply starts to yawn whenever he hears the word peace."[3] That does not mean, however, that (art) demonstrations had no purchase in the countries of Eastern Europe; on the contrary. Artists from the region used the technique less to "disable the ambivalence . . . of images" than, on the contrary, to *amplify* such ambivalence, in the hopes of unlocking its subversive potential in this way. For example, when the GDR-based artist Carlfriedrich Claus, who had virtually no opportunities for exhibiting his work inside his home country, gave his nonfigurative graphic works from the 1960s titles such as *Function of a Revolutionary Struggle* (1962), *Long-Distance Effect of the Russian October* (1963), or *Psychic Engine: Homage to Ho Chí Minh* (1970–1971), these titles deliberately presented a nonjargony, syncretic mix

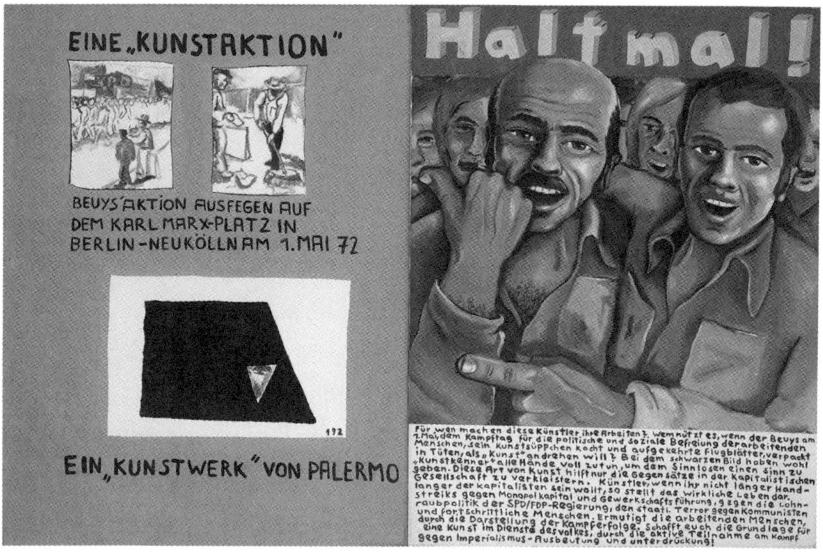

Figure 5.2 Jörg Immendorff, *"Art Action"—Wait a Minute!* (*Eine "Kunstaktion"—Halt mal!*), 1973. © The Estate of Jörg Immendorff. Photo: Museo Nacional Centro de Arte Reina Sofía.

of science, philosophy, and politics, while studiously avoiding any impression that they were imitating official propaganda pronouncements, or that the works thus named offered a straightforward illustration of these titles. Claus's works have a distinctly performative edge that seeks to combine a pointed leftist-Marxist political commitment with formal openness and expanded (rather than limited) ambiguity, a combination that would have been anathema to many of the radical protesters (and artists) in West Berlin.

Among the earliest and most significant examples of demonstration in art from Eastern Europe are the actions organized by Milan Knížák in the early 1960s in the Czechoslovak capital Prague.[4] In 1963, Knížák exhibited his *Demonstration of Objects* (*Demonstrace objektů*) on the street because the artist's apartment-cum-studio on Nový Svět was far too small for his purposes. In Pavlína Morganová's words, the artist "freed himself of well-worn artistic conventions and began to merely place a number of objects in the road (perhaps 'demonstrations of things' is a more apt description)."[5] The provocation of Knížák's intervention, as Morganová notes, lies not in the display of new artworks but in his demonstration of a new role for the artist. Rather than being a producer of images, the artist becomes the organizer, curator, and instructor whose activities purposefully disrupt the means-ends logic of daily existence by randomly exhibiting objects in a space clearly not designated for them. In 1964, after cofounding the group Aktual (Aktuální umění), Knížák carried out another series of mobile outdoor demonstrations in the streets of Prague: *The First Manifestation of Aktual Art* (*První manifestace Aktuálního umění*), which was accompanied by a written manifesto that functioned as a demonstration in its own right.[6] It was followed in the same year by *Individual Demonstration* (*Individuální demonstrace*), *Total Demonstration* (*Totální demonstrace*), and *Aktual Walk along Nový Svět—Demonstration for All the Senses* (*Aktuální procházka po Novém Světě—Demonstrace pro všechny smysly*), during which the artist led participants through a portion of Prague's Old Town. Every participant was given an article of daily use to carry around with them during the demonstration, from shoes to a teapot to articles of clothing. The participants' itinerary

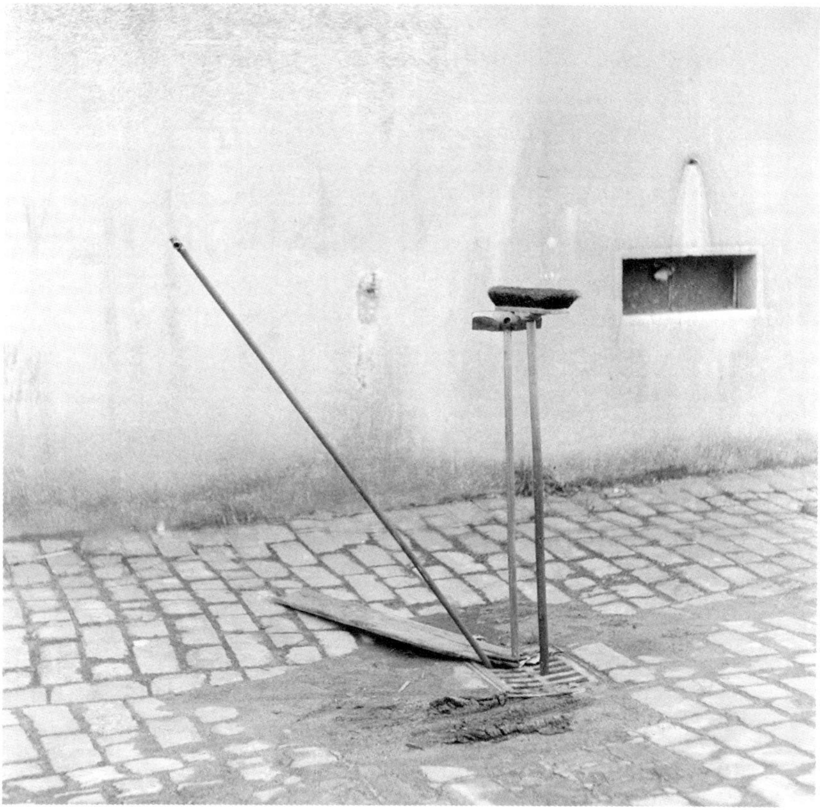

Figure 5.3 Milan Knížák, *Demonstration of Objects*, 1963. Image courtesy of Milan Knížák.

was interrupted at regular intervals by unexpected situations, such as being led into a small empty room where perfume had been spilled on the floor, a musician was playing the violin on his back, or, in Knížák's own words, "a chair comes down from above. *They look at it and point*. Then a man comes and puts the chair on a pedestal."[7] As is the case with the artist's other demonstrations, *Aktual Walk* can be described as both a rigorous disruption of the collective sensorial and aesthetic regime governing everyday life in the Czechoslovak capital, and as a school for learning how to demonstrate, albeit not in an explicitly political way. Indeed, Knížák's *Demonstrations* may count for being "antipolitical" in that they avoid declarative politics of the kind practiced by the government. This being said, in the way they marshal instruction, showing, and pointing, as well as in their ambition to radically change the participants' perception—both on a personal and a collective level—they clearly gesture toward new forms of politics.

Another action, *Demonstration for One* (*Demonstrace jednoho*, 1964), had Knížák kneeling on the ground in a colorful jacket with a safety pin attached to it while reading a book, with a handwritten sign next to him that asked passersby to "crow" as they went by. The demonstration was accompanied by the following written instruction:

> Stand still in a crowd, unfold a piece of paper, stand on it, take off your ordinary clothes and put on something unusual, e.g., a jacket half red, half green, with a tiny saw hanging from the lapel, a lace handkerchief pinned on the back. Display a poster on which is written: "I beg the passers-by if possible, while passing this place to crow." Lie down on the piece of paper, read a book, tear out the finished pages. Then stand up, crumple the paper, burn it, sweep up the ashes carefully, change your clothes, and leave.[8]

With its appeal to passersby to behave in ways that directly contradict the rational normativity of everyday life, *Demonstration for One*, as much as

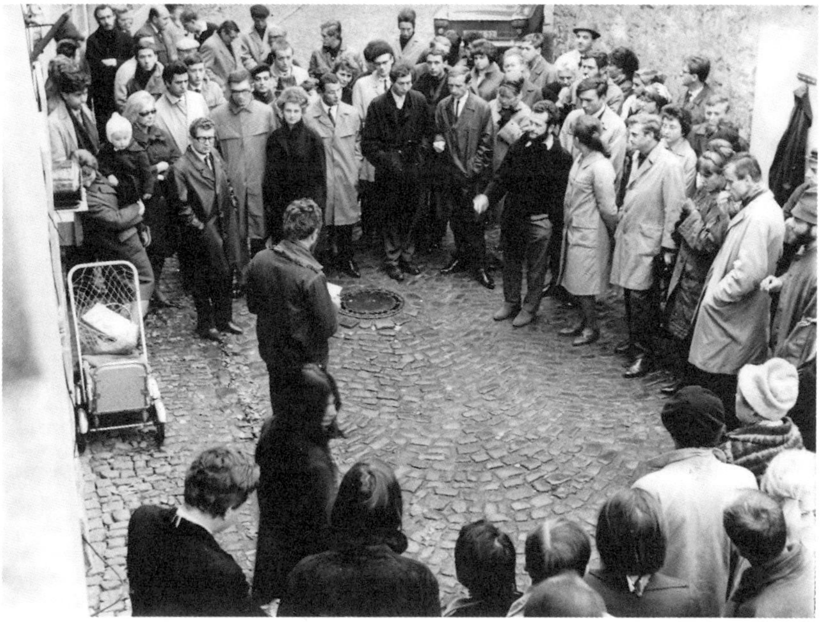

Figure 5.4 Milan Knížák, *First Manifestation of Aktual Art*, 1964. Image courtesy of Milan Knížák.

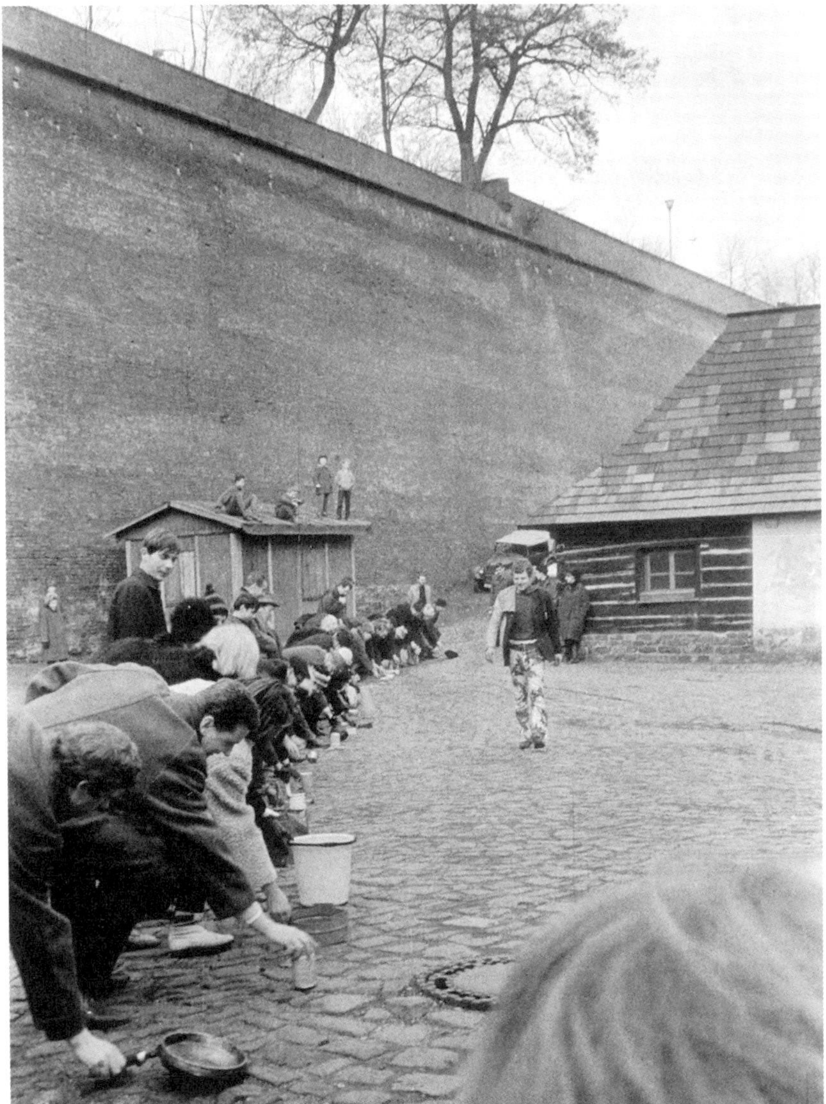

Figure 5.5 Milan Knížák, *Aktual Walk along Nový Svět—Demonstration for All the Senses*, 1964. Image courtesy of Milan Knížák.

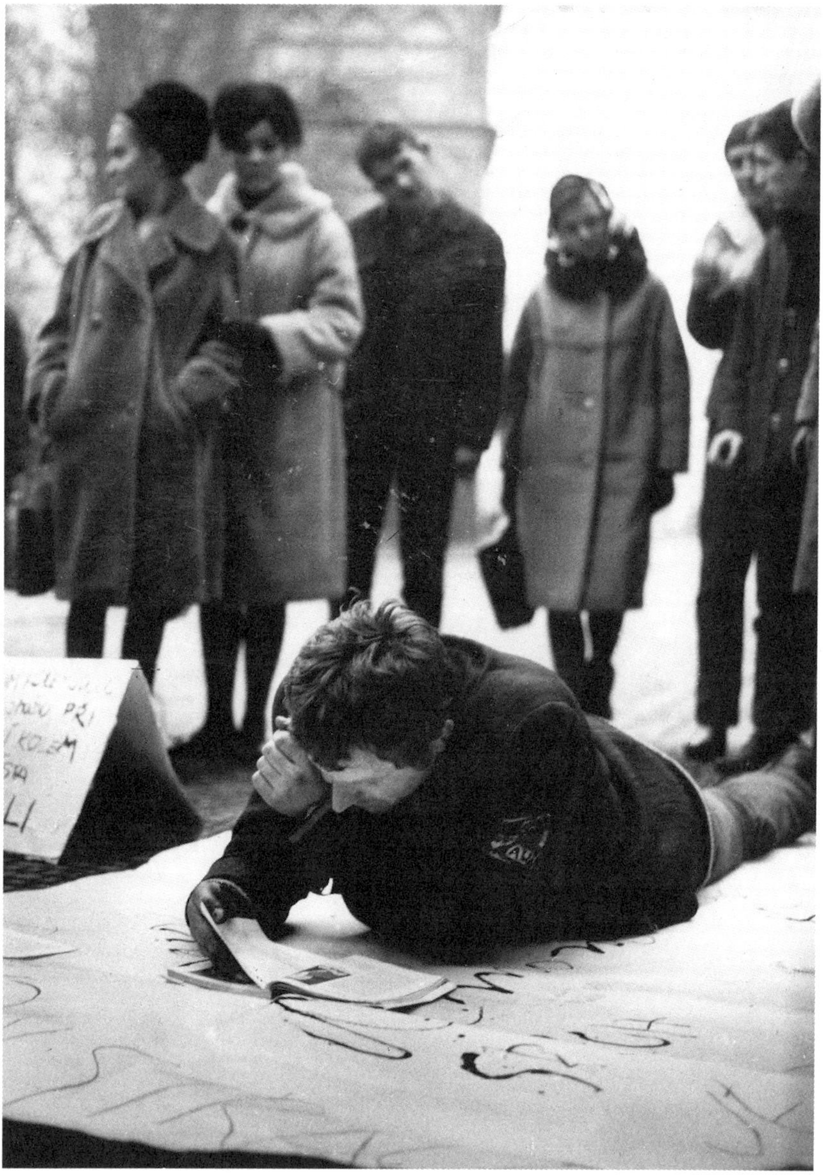

Figure 5.6 Milan Knížák, *Demonstration for One*. Image courtesy of Milan Knížák.

Knížák's other demonstrations from the early 1960s, promotes what Theodor W. Adorno claimed for dialectics—namely, an ability "to help the fool's truth become conscious of its own rationality."[9] In this spirit, with the help of demonstration, artists in Eastern Europe, too, developed their own alternative truth procedures, procedures that in time would, they hoped, lead to changes in consciousness.

In 1965, Knížák sent a large number of letters containing subversive instructions to random citizens whose addresses he found in the phone book. In the same year, in his *Lecture as Demonstration*, the artist asked, presumably rhetorically, "Does art mean to teach man how to live?"[10] The lecture serves as a powerful illustration of how art-as-demonstration may function as an effort to create an *event*. With Alain Badiou, we can define an event (*événement*) as something that cannot be deduced from what in a given situation seems probable, likely, or opportune; something, in other words, "which is purely hazardous, and which cannot be inferred from the situation, yet which is nevertheless a fixed multiple."[11] Knížák's *Demonstrations* can be understood as efforts to develop protocols that would allow him to integrate such events into normative reality, so that their alternative rationality—the fool's truth—can be recognized:

Walk without interruption for 24 hours on Národní Street in Prague!

Sleep with someone whom you love whom you do not love in the center of a busy city square and be just as perverse as you are when nobody can see you!

Burn every picture in your apartment and in their place hang up your soiled laundry!

Scribble obscene inscriptions on every street corner in the vicinity of your apartment!

Give your salary to the first nice person whom you meet!

Masturbate incessantly for 8 hours!

Burn every book on your bookshelf!

Masturbate in the presence of your mother father husband (wife) lover (mistress) son daughter friend!

Fall in love!

Drink 2 quarts of rum every day for 7 days!

Do not drink at all for 3 days!

Ask your wife (husband) to demolish your radio, television set, record-player, refrigerator!

Say hello to every person who passes you!

Commit suicide!

Live![12]

A similar didactic impetus—to explore the normative social and material environment of the Socialist city, injecting events into its aesthetic regime—can be seen in Bálint Szombathy's well-known demonstration *Lenin in Budapest* (1972). In this case, too, the clear antipolitical thrust of the action presents itself less as a fact than as an open question. After the official May Day parade on Dózsa György Road—including Communist leader János Kadár waving to the crowds from his tribune—Szombathy went to a city park to pick up one of the signs left behind by exhausted rally participants—a large, blown-up portrait of Lenin on a carrying stick—and started to walk through the streets and courtyards of the capital, with Lenin's portrait on his shoulder.[13] Of course, this was not a demonstration in the sense in which the students on the streets of Paris or West Berlin understood the term, that is, as a negation of the liberal state and the capitalist system that undergirds it. Instead of negation, Szombathy chooses to affirm, rather than denounce, the most iconic public image of the reigning ideology, Lenin's. The point to the artist's demonstration lies not in the way it denounces official truth procedures but rather in their multiplication. By this I mean that we do not really know how to interpret Szombathy's demonstration, what its goals or ambitions are, and so on. No flyers or other signs or commentary offer us any help in assigning it a clear message, as would normally be the case in a street demonstration, where slogans typically accompany images, assigning them value and meaning. In fact, I argue that it is precisely the inscrutability of Szombathy's attitude toward the Lenin portrait on his shoulder that represents the true scandal of his street demonstration, and that it is here that we must look for its political charge: Does the artist identify with Lenin, or does he display the Soviet leader's image indifferently? Is he proselytizing, trying to remind bystanders of the promises of the 1917 revolution? Or is he, on the contrary, making fun of this discarded piece of propaganda hardware? Or, yet another possibility, are we perhaps dealing with an instance of "overidentification" with the Bolshevik leader?[14]

Since *Lenin in Budapest* does not give us any clear-cut answers to these questions, Szombathy's action, like Knížák's demonstrations, promotes semantic openness rather than limiting the range of meanings we can assign to it. The artist forces us to relate the meaning of his action to the context in which it unfolds as he walks from street to street, and from courtyard to courtyard, exploring, in his own words, "the possible semantic situations of V.I. Lenin's image and the milieu in question where meanings of diverse authoritative messages occur."[15] By this, Szombathy seems to mean that any intervention in the aesthetic regime that governs the public sphere in Communist Hungary—where Lenin's portrait had a prominent if mostly ceremonial place—should concern itself less with that portrait's meaning than with the broad variety of ways in which it is seen and understood in different locales and circumstances.

With such an approach, Szombathy was certainly in good company. In his 1967 article on "Semiological Guerrilla Warfare," Umberto Eco had recommended a similar kind of tactic for anyone interested in asserting their freedom in the age of manipulative television and "total (mass) communication," an age when it may not be enough, according to Eco, to change the false or misleading messages that dominate the public sphere by seeking to control their source.[16] In a prescient argument, Eco notes that instead of concentrating on its "industrialized" source or the code in

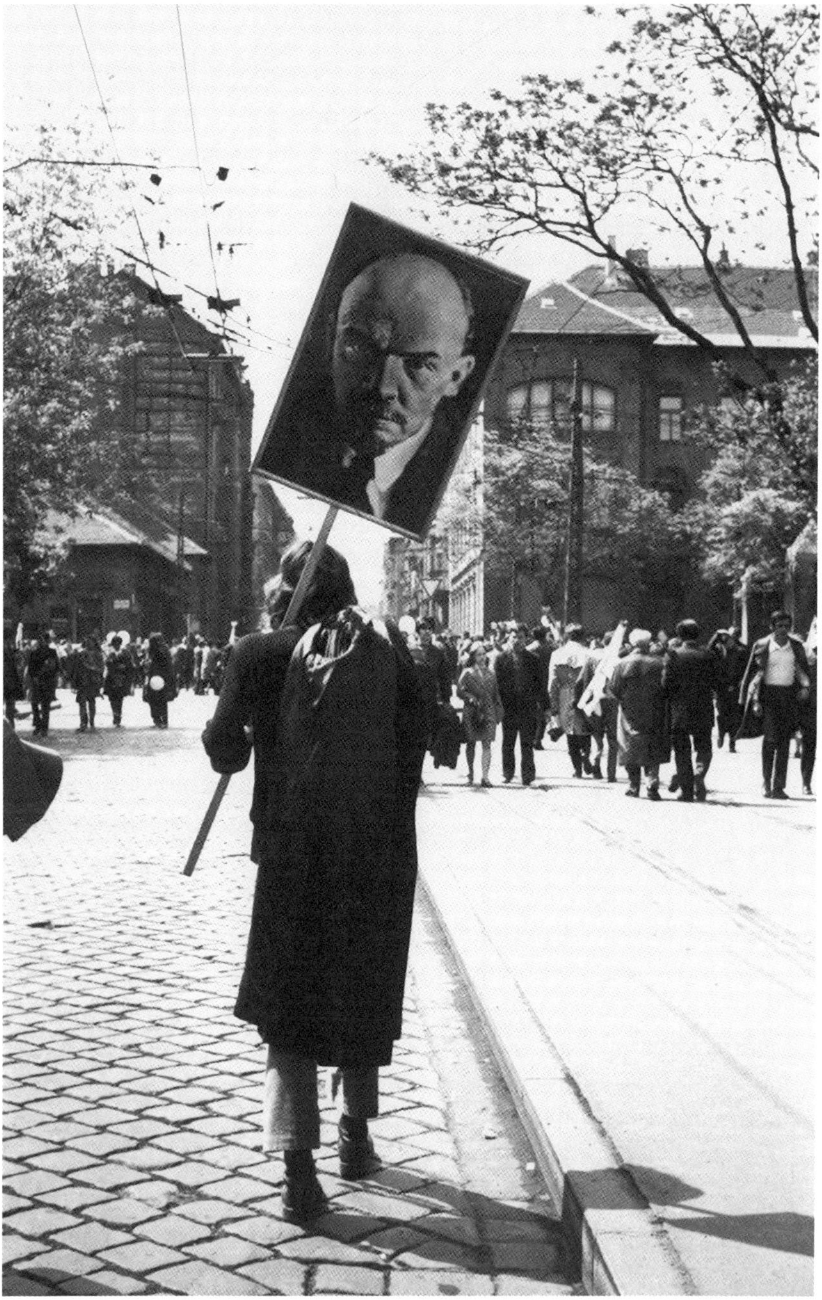

Figure 5.7 Bálint Szombathy, *Lenin in Budapest* (1972). Image courtesy of Bálint Szombathy.

which a message is sent, we should concentrate on educating its recipient so that they can adopt a more conscious attitude toward the message's decipherment: "We should be capable of imagining systems of complementary communication that allow us to reach every individual human group, every individual member of the universal audience, to discuss the arriving message in the light of the codes at the destination, comparing them with the codes at the source."[17]

Eco's argument amounts to a note of caution that it may not be enough to identify reactionary information sources and communication channels—such as the reporting practices of the right-wing Springer press in West Germany—with the goal of replacing these with new, more progressive ones. If such an approach sometimes trapped Western demonstrators in communicating their views, however just and reasonable they may have been, without much of a sense as to how their messages would be understood by their recipients, Eco believes the situation can be remedied only by a systematically developed focus on the many different ways in which messages are received by different audiences.

Artists, in particular, saw themselves as well equipped for taking such an approach, and Szombathy can serve as an example. Indeed, the artist's goal with *Lenin in Budapest* is akin to "semiological guerrilla warfare" (even though he likely had no knowledge of Eco's ideas) in the sense that while the artist cannot or does not want to simply negate, undo, or otherwise destroy or neutralize Lenin's portrait, what he can do is investigate, observe, or study its reception by taking the image to different parts of his city, to areas and audiences not generally included in the circuit of official rallies or demonstrations, and in a situation—the poster being carried by an artist, as part of an art action—very much unlike its habitual contexts.

This being said, while in the 1980s arguments such as Eco's became the basis for a new, postmodern semiology—a form of postmodern pluralization concerned not with facts but with the different ways we speak about them—postmodernism is manifestly not Szombathy's goal: he is not interested in different opinions about Lenin, or in claiming that Lenin did not exist, or that he was a semiotic effect. Instead, his goal is to establish artistic practice as instruction in a certain media literacy, a (perhaps overly optimistic) effort to start a conversation about the material conditions for critically evaluating images such as Lenin's portrait in different material and discursive contexts. This is also why, incidentally, we are not dealing, in Szombathy's case, with an instance of "overidentification" or with a form of Eastern European pop art. Of course, Warhol's work with fetishized images of celebrities such as Elizabeth Taylor, Elvis Presley, Jackie Kennedy, and Marilyn Monroe from the early 1960s onward, and his interest in the circulation of these images in the capitalist image sphere, bears some resemblance to Szombathy's appropriation of Lenin's picture, which was similarly iconic and ubiquitous in the countries behind the Iron Curtain.[18] And while Warhol's work with the images of celebrities (which even included Mao) may be close in some respects to Eco, it nevertheless remains concerned more or less exclusively with the communication channel, and with the different ways in which formal procedures such as reproduction and repetition affect the messages that travel through such channels. Warhol was manifestly not interested, though, in the effect or reception these images might have in different locations or social milieus. By contrast, the truly remarkable significance of art practices from Eastern European during the 1960s and '70s, including Szombathy's, lies in the fact that they took such differences very seriously. It is not for nothing that Szombathy leaves the Lenin image unaltered; the only thing that counts for him is its placement in different situations as he moves around with it, proving that the portrait's presentation as an exhibit in these contexts affects its perception and meaning.

Consider another demonstration by Szombathy, *Hammer and Sickle* (1974), which presents the artist in Florence, next to a house wall that shows the symbol of hammer and sickle, an emblem that was ubiquitous at the time not only in Italy but also in Communist Hungary and everywhere else in the Soviet sphere of influence. While *Lenin in Budapest* has the artist take Lenin's image around the city, here, it is Szombathy himself who recontextualizes the icon of Communism by posing next to it, again without any clear instructions as to what kind of connection the viewer is invited to draw between the artist, on the one hand, and the symbol, on the other. While it does appear as if the drawn symbol's elegantly curved line repeats the tilt of the artist's head and upper body, does this mean we should formally identify Szombathy with that symbol? Or, are we dealing with a mere accidental snapshot? And what does it mean for a Hungarian artist to place himself next to this icon of the international workers' movement, which is ubiquitous in Eastern Europe, in a Western country such as Italy?

Another Hungarian, Sándor Pinczehelyi, investigates the sickle and hammer using a similar approach to Szombathy's inasmuch as here again the symbol is not destroyed or neutralized but consciously adopted. By demonstrating with an *actual* hammer and sickle in his hands, however, Pinczehelyi seems to weaken the bond between the symbol and its ideological referent (the workers' movement, Communism), while at the same time, his way of holding both utensils also clearly recalls that same referent.

Demonstrations were a common way for artists to intervene in street life in the urban centers of parts of Eastern Europe and Yugoslavia, especially in the 1970s. In Poland, the experimental theater company Akademia ruchu, which was founded by director Wojciech Krukowski in 1973, organized hundreds of impromptu appearances in public space, using different forms of demonstration that avoided conventional theatrical means and narratives. Among the group's best-known performances, straddling the line between art and theater, there were also a few with explicitly didactic titles, such as *Lektoraty* (Lectures) in 1973 and *Lekcje* (Lessons) in 1976. In 1976, the year when workers in the city of Radom protested (and rioted) against unexpected price hikes for meat and other foods, in an action titled *Europa*, Akademia ruchu copied individual lines from Polish futurist Anatol Stern's 1925 poem "Europe" onto banners and displayed them after dark in busy Warsaw streets with increased pedestrian traffic, assembling an audience.[19] Some actors then ran with these banners into the headlights of specially positioned cars, while others threw the remaining banners in front of

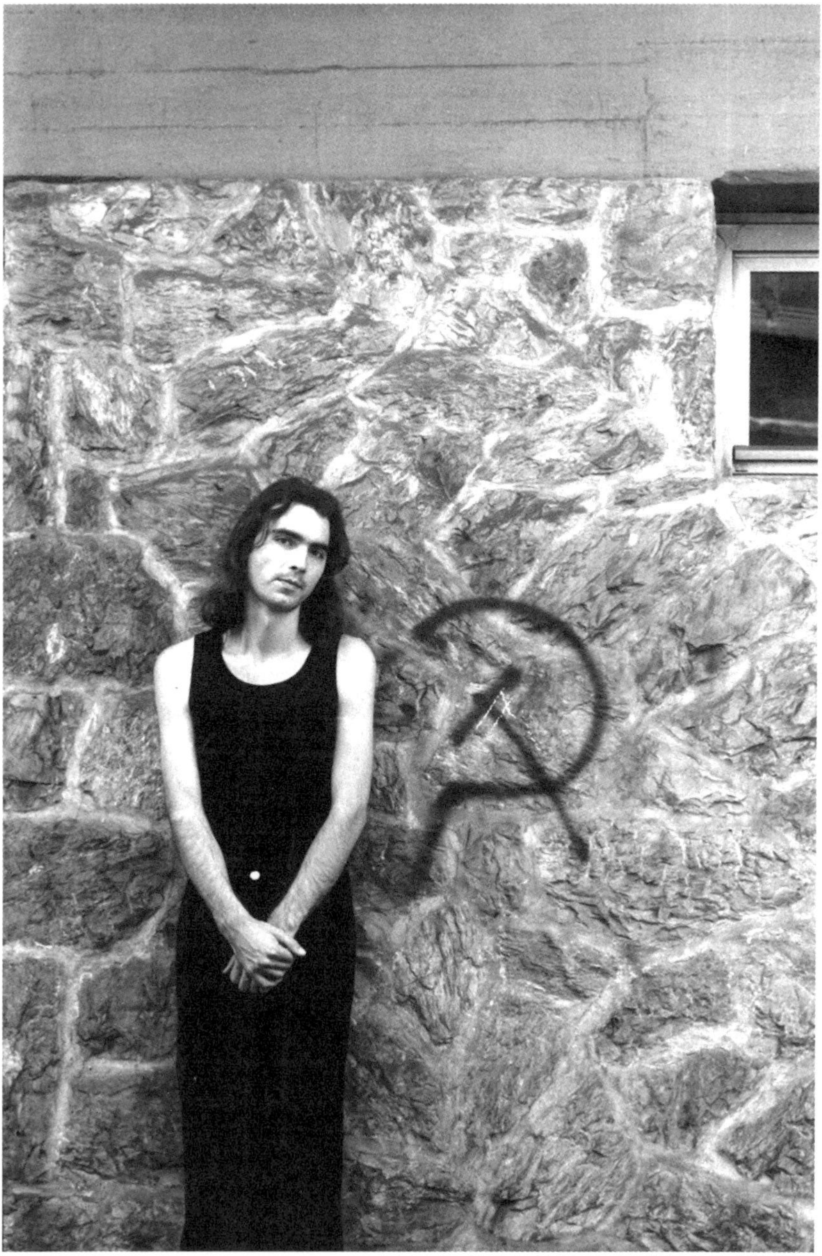

Figure 5.8 Bálint Szombathy, *Hammer and Sickle* (1974). Image courtesy of Bálint Szombathy.

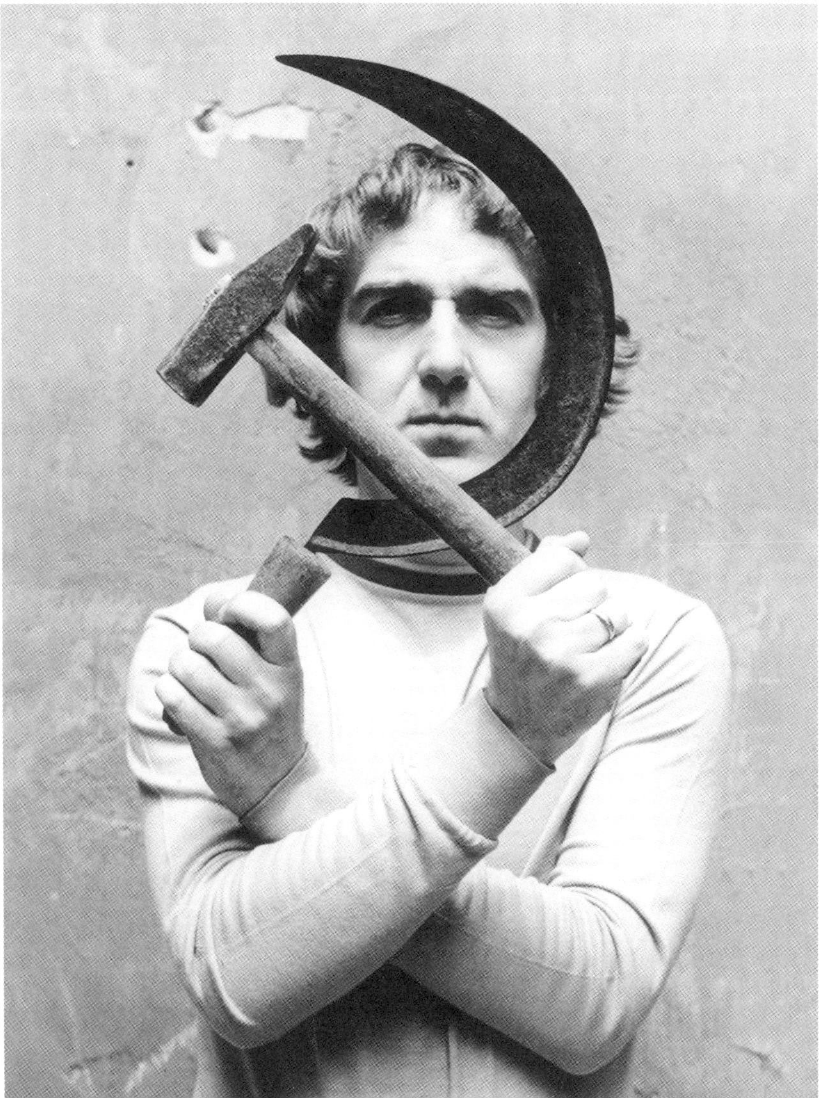

Figure 5.9 Sándor Pinczehelyi, *Sickle and Hammer I*, 1973. Ludwig Múzeum of Contemporary Art. Image courtesy of Sándor Pinczehelyi.

the audience, creating a tangle of words and lines whose chance combinations created new lines and new poems. After the end of the action, which was repeated in the cities of Gdańsk, Olsztyn, Bydgoszcz, Łódź, Kraków, Lublin, Poznań, and Wrocław, members of the audience would often pick up the banners, carry them around, or attach them to different surfaces around the city, in this way extending the life of the demonstration.[20]

While Akademia ruchu established no formal connection between its action and the Radom riots, and even though it functioned as cultural rather than social critique, the performance had profound political implications. Indeed, for anyone in the audience, the connection between *Europa*—the title referencing a continent of which most Poles at the time were only able to see a very limited part—and the events in Radom was not difficult to see, even though it was far from direct and the poetic ambivalence promoted by this demonstration allowed for a broad spectrum of interpretations.

In Czechoslovakia, Jiří Kovanda's elusive demonstrations charted a similar course in confronting the harsh reality of the post-1968 Czechoslovak Socialist Republic. The artist appeared on the streets of the capital, Prague, and started to engage in physical movements such as suddenly running away from a group of bystanders, standing on an escalator with his body facing in the wrong direction, or lifting his arms in the middle of the street. Like other, equally "invisible" street actions by artists in Eastern Europe at the time, Kovanda's actions barely cleared the level of noticeability, more or less eluding the attention of the public, who either did not notice the artist or preferred to give the impression that they did not. As was the case with Szombathy, these actions included no commentary of any kind when they occurred and were thus characterized by a distinct element of *Nachträglichkeit*: captured by an invisible photographer, they only became identifiable as demonstrations once the artist archived the photographs, adding captions and dates. Only at this stage do Kovanda's gestures reveal their true nature as (micro-)demonstrations and instructions, much as traumatic symptoms in Freud's elaboration point, like a diagram, in the direction of an accident they cannot recall or represent.

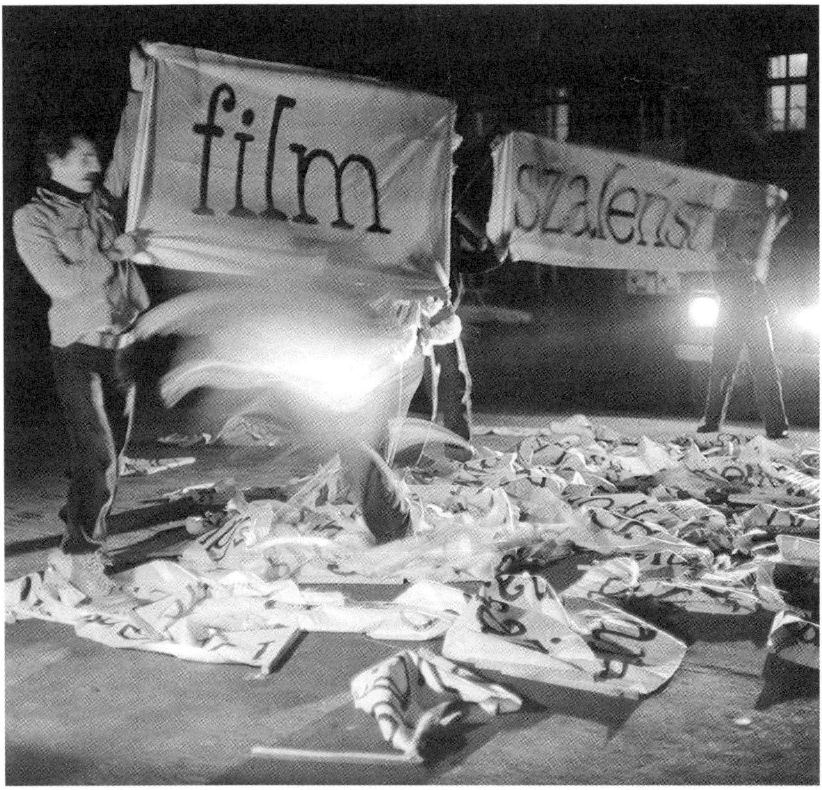

Figure 5.10 Theater Akademia Ruchu, *Europa*, Warsaw, 1976. © Stowarzyszenie Przyjaciół Akademii Ruchu. Photo: Stefan Okołowicz.

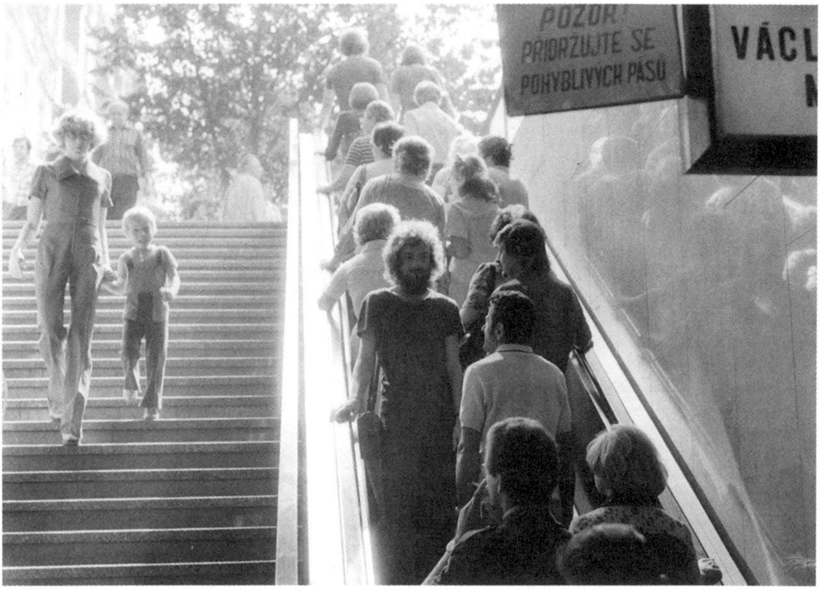

Figure 5.11 Jiří Kovanda, *Untitled (On an escalator . . . turning around, I look into the eyes of the person standing behind me . . .) (3 September 1977)*. Image courtesy of Jiří Kovanda.

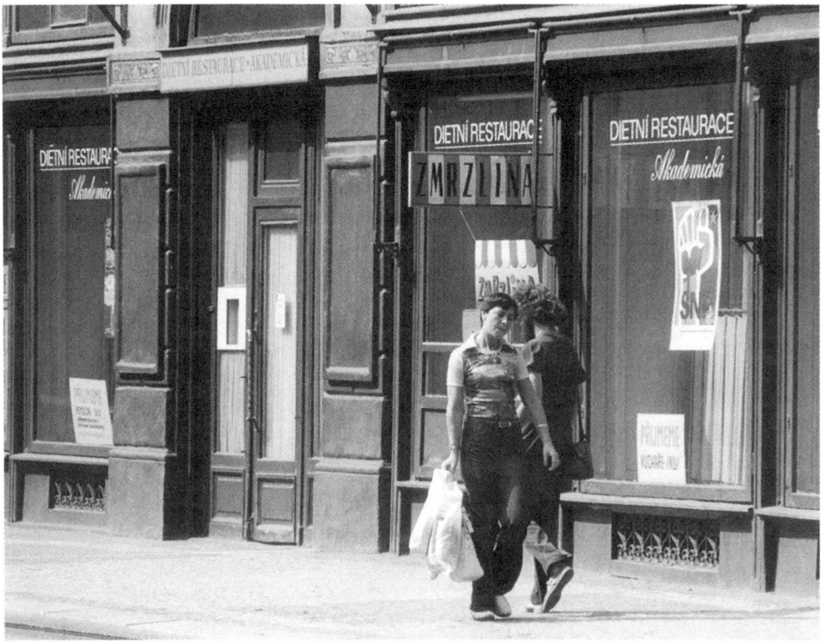

Figure 5.12 Jiří Kovanda, *Contact (3 September 1977)*, Prague, Spálená and Vodičkova streets. Image courtesy of Jiří Kovanda.

Kovanda's actions may be seen as a faint offshoot of a 1960s demonstration practice known as *Spaziergangsdemonstrationen* (strolling-as-demonstration) that was especially common in West Berlin. During a *Spaziergangsdemo*, student activists would mingle with passersby, avoiding any direct confrontation between themselves and the public, seeking to blend in with the crowd to such an extent that they became virtually invisible as demonstrators.[21] For example, around Christmastime 1966, members of the West Berlin-based Viva-Maria Group decided to infiltrate the city's busiest shopping street dressed up as ordinary shoppers, complete with packages and bags. Once they were part of the crowd, the demonstrators began to distribute leaflets and asked passersby questions about the need for a reformed police force, more free time, and condoms for police personnel.[22] While for the demonstrators the *Spaziergangsdemo* offered the invaluable advantage that they could quickly flee the scene as soon as the police arrived, bystanders could also become part of the action without being aware of it, often being arrested themselves.[23]

Where in an ordinary demonstration, the demonstration space—the slice of the city claimed by protesters for the duration of the manifestation—is more or less clearly circumscribed, a *Spaziergangsdemo* claims the entirety of urban space as its (potential) operational base. The same can be said for Kovanda as he injects himself into the crowds in different parts of the center of Prague as an invisible passerby/demonstrator. To be sure, much of what characterized the *Spaziergangsdemo* in the West, especially its more theatrical elements—street theater was frequently a part of the act—was hard or impossible to emulate in Czechoslovakia, and the artist is adamant that his actions not be understood outside of the framework of antipolitics. That being said, Kovanda's inadvertent appropriation of city space, his use of ordinary gestures in a context where the ostentatious nature of these gestures subtly but decisively undercut the public sphere's affective regime, and his conversion of passersby into unwitting co-demonstrators are all clearly reminiscent of *Spaziergangsdemos*.

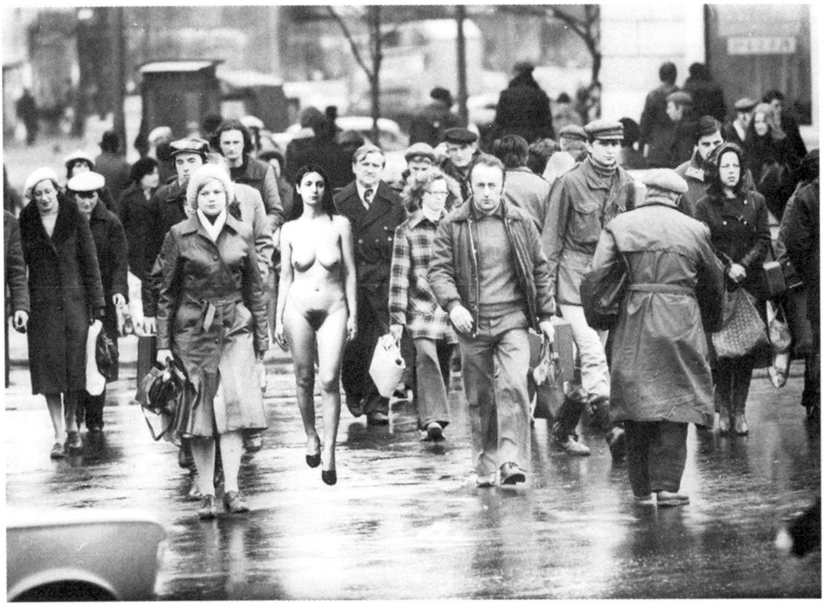

Figure 5.13 Ewa Partum, *Self-Identifications*, 1980–1989. © Ewa Partum, ARTUM Foundation, Museum Ewa Partum.

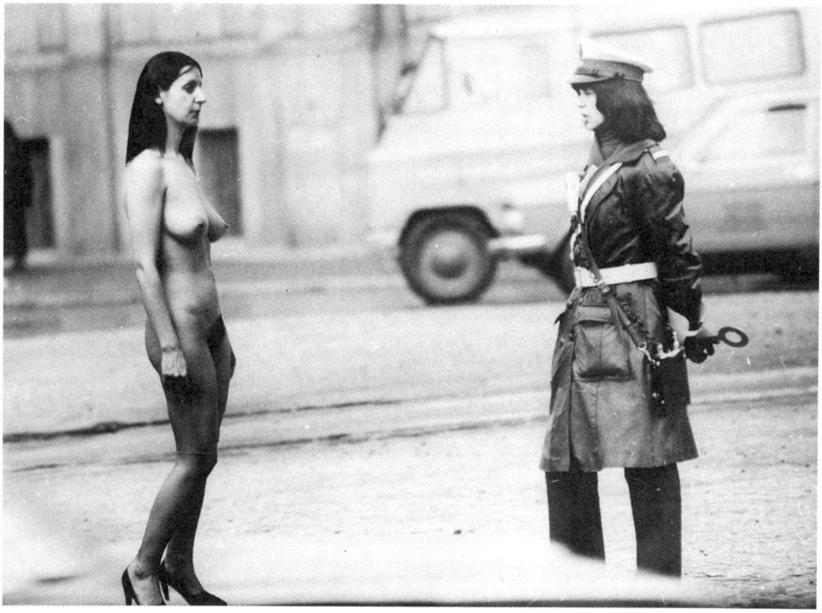

Figure 5.14 Ewa Partum, *Self-Identifications*, 1980–1989. © Ewa Partum, ARTUM Foundation, Museum Ewa Partum.

Nachträglichkeit also characterizes Ewa Partum's demonstrative series *Self-Identifications* (1980–1989), collaged photographs that include portraits of the artist herself, naked, among crowds of people in the busy center of Warsaw, in front of monuments, and in other urban spaces. In reality, such demonstrations could never have occurred, since public nudity of any kind was a taboo in Communist Poland. However, the scandal of Partum's demonstrations is not the artist's nakedness but the possibility that the female body, naked or otherwise, may become visible in the public sphere. Partum, too, creates an event; she discovers the photograph's ability to determine what can become visible in society, and what must remain obscure. While her collage remains circumscribed within the aesthetic limits of antipolitics, in Partum's imaginary encounter with the policewoman we can nevertheless glean the possibility for a real (feminist) politics, as antipolitical demonstrations always harbor that potentiality within their formal remit, hinting at an incision in the seamless order of the everyday.

In Eastern Europe, the decision of how to classify an art action (as political, artistic, etc.) was frequently made by the authorities after the fact, based on written reports by agents, informers, or the police themselves who intercepted or infiltrated art events and produced interpretations and (fictionalizing) accounts of these actions.[24] The art historian Kata Krasznahorkai reports that when Tamás Szentjóby performed an action reading in Budapest in 1972 on the occasion of Angela Davis's acquittal of murder charges in the United States—an event that Eastern Bloc governments hailed as the result of their publicity campaigns on her behalf—the secret police informant present in the audience described the event in his report as a "tacky demonstration" that purposefully abused the name of a US civil rights icon.[25] The agent had clearly come to the conclusion that Szentjóby's performance criticized not only the US and its justice system but the Socialist order as well.[26] A similar reaction followed another action by Szentjóby from the same year, called *Sit Out/Be Forbidden*, in which the artist sat outside the Intercontinental Hotel in Budapest, tied to a chair with a leather belt and his mouth gagged. Szentjóby seems to have been making a nonspecific allusion to Black Panther Bobby Seale, one of the "Chicago Eight" defendants who (alone among the defendants, the others of whom were white) was gagged and tied for days during their 1969 trial for conspiracy and inciting a riot after the 1968 Democratic National Convention in Chicago. All were sentenced to four years in prison by a white judge and an all-white jury.[27]

On the one hand, Szentjóby's demonstration sidesteps our expectation that nonofficial Eastern European artists do not criticize the West, since their critical attitude toward their own regimes implies their quasi-automatic embrace of liberal democracy and capitalism. On the other hand, given the artist's action's deliberate lack of a single referent—the reference to Searle ultimately remained unconfirmed—Szentjóby also expands his demonstration's operational remit beyond the West, to include Hungary itself (perhaps he was in fact referring to himself as tied and gagged). This became confirmed ex post facto when the Hungarian authorities classified the performance as a political demonstration that could only be interpreted as referencing the situation in Hungary itself.[28] Here again we can see how in Eastern Europe artists used techniques of amplification to expand the referential range of their demonstrations, whereas in the West, the limitation of ambiguity tended to be the demonstrators' primary goal.

In another example of art-as-demonstration in a Socialist country, the activist Grupa TOK, which was active between 1972 and 1973, staged regular demonstrations through the streets of Zagreb and Belgrade as well as, in 1973, in the Austrian city of Graz, with hand-held canvases displaying homemade abstract designs, stripes, dots, or grids in place of slogans or politicians' portraits. Referencing official demonstrations while at the same time distancing themselves from them through their nonreferential designs, the group promoted an expanded understanding of the environment as including both the natural and the human-built world.[29] Their demonstrations, as Maja Fowkes has argued, referenced both intra-Yugoslav cultural politics—especially the stirrings of nationalism in 1971—and the way that the Croatian nationalists' conflict with the left translated into rivalry between conservative figurative painting and abstraction.[30]

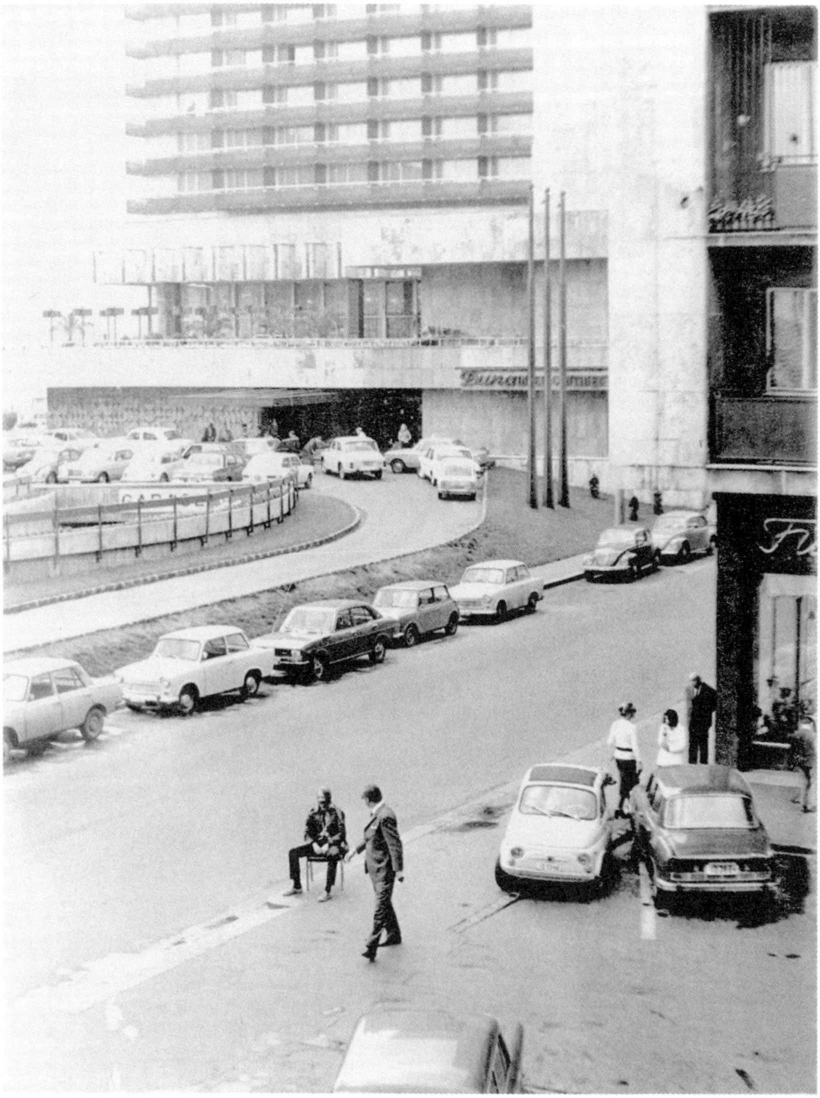

Figure 5.15 Tamás Szentjóby, *Sit Out/Be Forbidden* (action/demonstration), 1972. Image courtesy of Tamás Szentjóby.

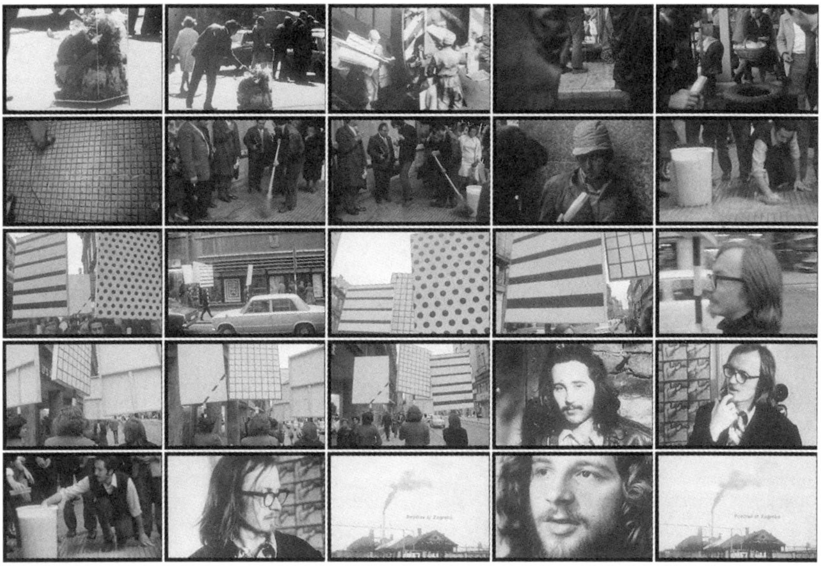

Figure 5.16 Grupa TOK, *Urban Guerrilla*, 1972. Video, color, sound, 01:34. Marinko Sudac Collection.

Art-as-demonstration was also practiced by artists from the region who left for the West. Starting in the late 1970s, when the authorities finally allowed him to leave Hungary to take up a scholarship in West Berlin, Endre Tót staged street demonstrations in various Western European urban centers (initially in West Germany), in which he walked through the streets, either alone or with a group of people, holding banners or signs.[31] Tót's demonstrations were much like any other street demonstration, except that what was written on the banners carried by participants was self-referential; instead of addressing a political demand or expressing an opinion, the banners and signs pointed to the act of demonstrating itself, hinting at the performative element in any demonstration, and making it the center of the action. For instance, one banner carried through the streets of Bonn, the West German capital, in 1979 read, "We Are Glad That We Can Demonstrate Here," while another, hanging around Tót's neck and practically covering him, says, "I Am Glad If This Can Hang Around My Neck." In the *Gladnesses* series, Tót shies away from any monoreferential political gestures and instead overtly overidentifies with the official Eastern European propaganda imperative to show joy and enthusiasm everywhere and at all times. However, the almost childlike sincerity of the feelings professed in the series is called into question by the absurdity and contradictoriness of the accompanying images. For example, *I'm Glad That I Can Read Lenin* (1976) shows Tót seated in a chair, hiding his face behind a book entitled *Lenin Is with Us.*[32] No active reading on Tót's part is necessarily implied; in fact, it seems as if the artist mostly uses the volume as a protective shield behind which to hide his face, a common defense mechanism during unpleasant encounters with official state organs such as the police.

Lenin and the state media make their appearance in other works of the series as well: *I Am Glad That I Can Read the Newspaper* (1973–1975) shows a newspaper with a big hole in the middle, while in *I Am Glad That I Can Stand Next to You* (1973–1975), the artist is positioned next to a giant Lenin statue and *You Are the One That Made Me Glad* (1975) has Tót's smiling face contrast with the swarthy somberness of Lenin's photo.[33] *Gaudeo Ergo Sum*

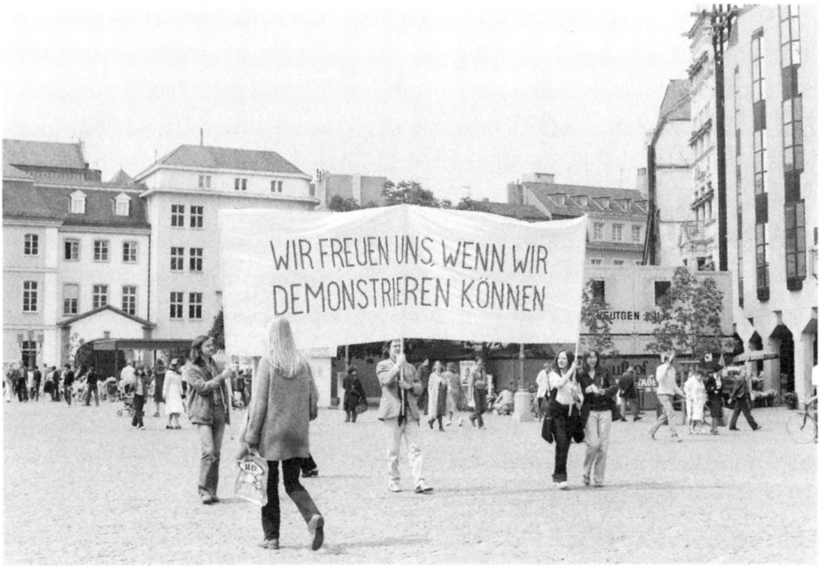

Figure 5.17 Endre Tót, *Wir freuen uns wenn wir demonstrieren können* (*We Are Happy We Can Demonstrate*), Bonn, 1979. Photo: Thomas Strauss. Image courtesy of Endre Tót.

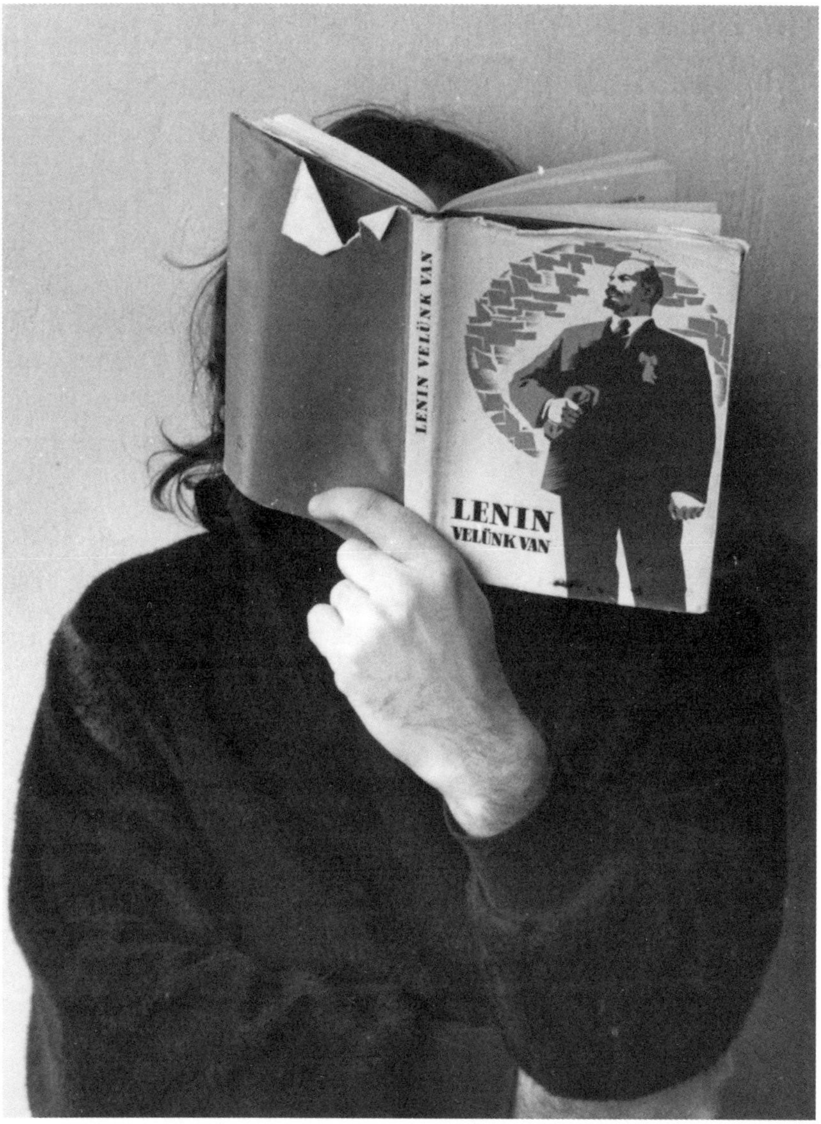

Figure 5.18 Endre Tót, *I'm Glad That I Can Read Lenin*, Middelburg, 1976. Photo: Peter van Beveren. Image courtesy of Endre Tót.

(1973–1975) combines "gladness" (*gaudeo*) with a reference to Descartes, in whose ontology a given truth—such as the existence of God—is viewed as self-evident to the degree that the demonstration that the sum of the angles of a triangle is equal to the sum of two right angles is considered self-evident. Descartes's "Cogito ergo sum" is also, in this sense, an excellent example of demonstration: if I am able to demonstrate that the sum of the angles of a triangle is equal to the sum of two right angles, then this must mean that I exist: "demonstro ergo sum." Tót's professions of joy in the *Gladnesses* series, avoiding any constative statements, are focused on the illocutionary utterance itself: the artist is glad that he can say, "I am glad to be saying that I am glad." Not unlike the professor in Derrida's understanding, Tót testifies to his joy in a speech act whose performative nature opens the possibility that it may be fiction, play, or irony.

The reception of the *Gladnesses* series differed dramatically between Western and Eastern Europe. In the countries of Eastern Europe, where Lenin was officially consecrated and hence mostly unread, mentioning his name in the gleeful terms chosen by Tót could only amount to sarcasm, while west of the Berlin Wall, the phrase "I Am Glad That I Can Read Lenin" played up to Slavoj Žižek's idea that Eastern Europe presents Western Europeans with their own ego ideal, an ideal generally focused on the desire for liberal democracy and capitalist enterprise: "Eastern Europe functions for the West as its Ego-Ideal [*Ich-Ideal*]: the point from which the West sees itself as a likeable, idealized form, worthy of love. The real object of fascination for the West is therefore the gaze, namely, the supposedly naïve gaze by means of which Eastern Europe stares back at the West, fascinated by its democracy."[34] Tót's publicly declared happiness about his newly gained right to engage in public demonstrations props up this kind of Western narcissism, even when what the Eastern European artist professes to be glad about (reading Lenin) is the direct opposite of what a Western audience expected from an artist from the Eastern half of the continent.[35]

In his *Outdoor Tests* (1980), Tót went out on various highways and public squares and held up signs as if in protest; however, this time the signs contained decidedly less gleeful statements than in the *Gladnesses* series, including "Where Am I Going?," "Where Am I?," "I Am Waiting for Nobody," or "I Am Looking for Nobody." While here again the performative aspects of demonstrating were clearly in evidence, the shift from professions of gladness to Tót's focus on a sense of loss or confusion could not be more striking: it is as if in the *Outdoor Tests* the artist displayed the reverse side of his glee to be demonstrating, by showing his audience the alienated confusion to which emigrants from Eastern Europe were prone once they arrived in the West. The *Outdoor Tests* in this way refute Descartes's ontological optimism ("demonstro, ergo sum"), which treated the demonstration of what we know to be true as the only possible confirmation of our existence. With his demonstrations, Tót seems to argue that in fact we can also confirm our existence by professing insecurity and a lack of orientation ("Where Am I?"), or by testifying to being unsure about where we are going and what we are doing. The legitimacy of Tót's process of (self-)questioning does not derive, as it does for Descartes, from merely affirming the sovereignty of reason and intellect.

HOW TO SURVIVE NEOLIBERALISM (MLADEN MILJANOVIĆ, CIPRIAN HOMORODEAN)

In more recent art from Eastern Europe, the fortunes of 1960s-style demonstration are partially being revived, albeit in a neoliberal economic and political environment where the hypertrophic and omnipresent rhetoric of "life-long learning" and self-development have finally succeeded in decoupling education from the disruptive, consciousness-altering agenda in which they were firmly anchored fifty years earlier. This being said, contemporary artists seem much less inclined to belabor the poetics of "antipolitics" than their Cold War predecessors were.

Mladen Miljanović created his *Didactic Wall* (*Didaktički zid*) in 2019 on the basis of training material originally issued by the Yugoslav People's Army before the breakup of Yugoslavia. *Didactic Wall* consists of a large

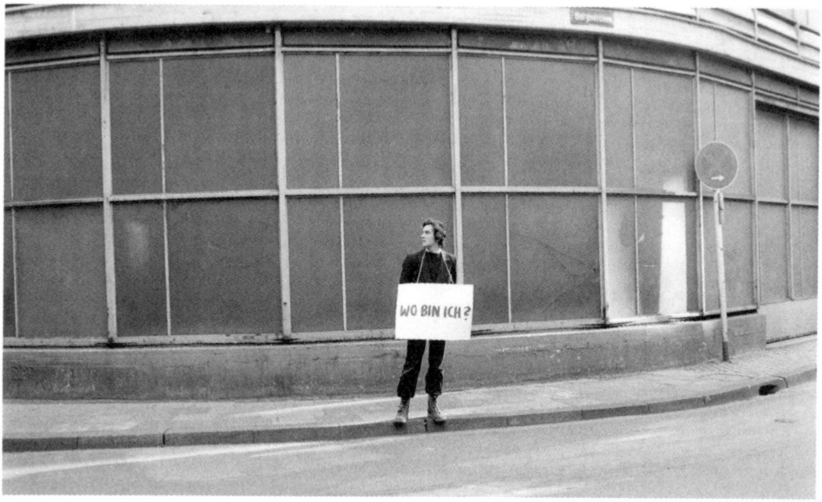

Figure 5.19 Endre Tót, *Outdoor Tests. Wo bin ich?* (Where am I?), 1980. Photo: Herta Paraschin. Image courtesy of Endre Tót.

slab of polished marble densely engraved with diagrams and captioned drawings in English, Arabic, Spanish, and Urdu that show soldiers who confront and ultimately master physical obstacles, hide from surveillance, orient themselves in unknown terrain, or establish their location. The basic function of *Didactic Wall*, which also exists in the form of a pocket-sized book and billboards posted in the town of Bihać, is to teach a lesson.

In the sense that the knowledge which *Didactic Wall* presents is not in itself new—since it was lifted from existing manuals—it resembles Bernar Venet's panels from the 1960s. What is different, however, is Miljanović's recontextualization and redeployment of this knowledge in a way that directs our attention toward the ongoing European refugee crisis and the discrimination, exclusion, and racism that lie at its foundation.

In 2012, the town of Bihać, situated in northern Bosnia, became a crucial waystation, indeed a point of no return, for thousands of refugees on their way to the European Union—more precisely to Slovenia, via Croatia—which is nowhere as close to Bosnia as at exactly this point. As soon as the Croatian authorities closed the border with Bosnia and Herzegovina, the migrants had nowhere to go and were literally stuck. As curator Irfan Hošić points out, "the Northern part of Bosnia is . . . a logical point for migrants' settling, gathering, regrouping and rethinking the rest of the travel through the well-protected borders of the European Union."[36] It is therefore not by coincidence that Miljanović positioned his wall precisely here, in Bihać, where it invites reflection on the borders that surround the European Union, and on how art might contribute toward overcoming them.

As a display of diagrams, Miljanović's wall has some affinity with Daniel Buren's *Wild Billboarding* (*Affichage sauvage*), yet it avoids the latter's abstractness; and while it borrows content from a non-art-related area of knowledge production (military science), at the same time, it does not strive for the artist's neutrality as Venet did. While *Didactic Wall* shares the aversion to expression and formal innovation that characterizes Venet's work of the 1960s in the way it redefines the artist's range of expertise and operation in

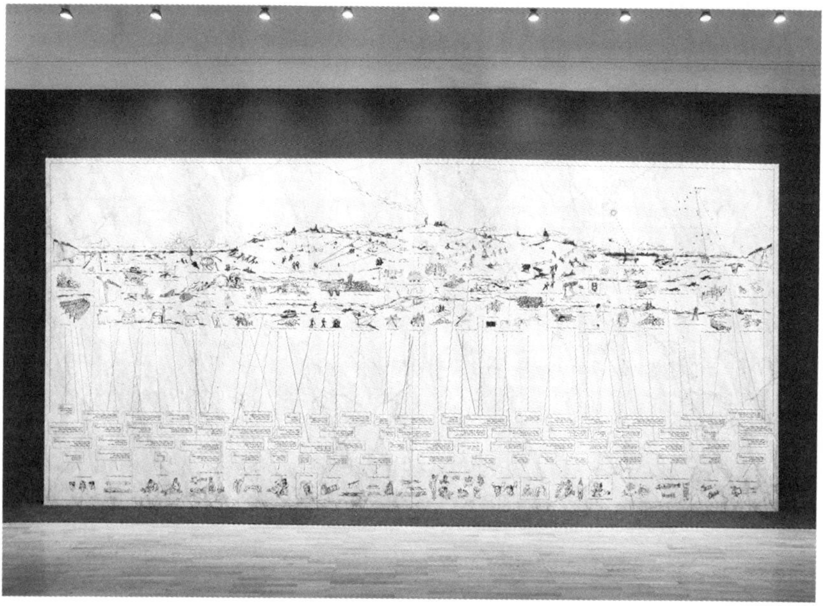

Figure 5.20 Mladen Miljanović, *Didactic Wall*. Engraved drawing on marble, installation view at Museum of Contemporary Art RS, Banja Luka, 2019. City Gallery Bihać, KRAK. Image courtesy of Mladen Miljanović.

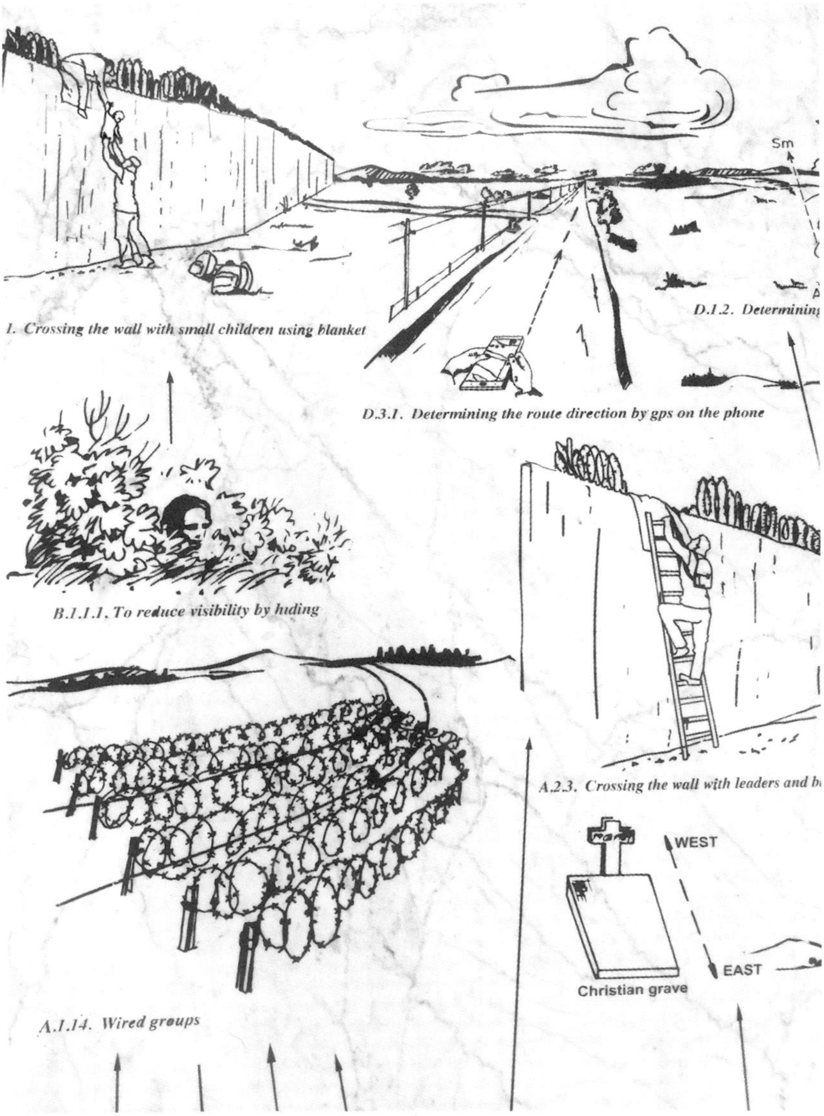

Figure 5.21 Mladen Miljanović, *Didactic Wall*. Engraved drawing on marble, installation view at Museum of Contemporary Art RS, Banja Luka, 2019. City Gallery Bihać, KRAK. Image courtesy of Mladen Miljanović.

the direction of instruction and didacticism, it does not view this redefinition in itself as already political and emancipatory. In other words, where the 1960s had tended to view the desire to instruct as a progressive position for an artist to take, Miljanović goes further by having his *Wall* intervene in a *specific* crisis situation of considerable proportions.

The fact that Miljanović's instructions are taken from military science is not coincidental, either; the artist had served in the Yugoslav army and argues that in tapping military knowledge, artists can learn to deploy their artworks in contexts not defined by art, which allows them to approach these contexts from strategic angles. As he writes, "working with different social contexts, every art project is necessarily a strategic project. Because if your work works towards the public, or within the public, it is inevitable that you need to develop the skills of tactical and strategic action, using all of the artistic arsenal you have."[37] Of course, the idea of the artist as a militant who redistributes knowledge that generally only serves the rich and powerful is also a crucial legacy of the 1960s.

Miljanović's lesson is neither academic nor simply self-reflexive, on the contrary; rather than making a "proposition about art," it's designed as an invitation to reflect on the political reality of post-1989 Europe, which is characterized, within the European Union, by a high degree of openness and borderlessness, yet at the expense of the many vulnerable populations outside of the EU's confines. Viewed in this light, Miljanović's point is less instruction in the concrete military maneuvers and techniques covered by the manual he appropriates—although it certainly can become useful in this way, too—than a reminder of the need to think of art operationally, and in a form that not coincidentally reminds viewers of the former Yugoslavia, a multiethnic state originally founded on principles of solidarity and tolerance.

Like Miljanović's *Didactic Wall*, Ciprian Homorodean's handmade book *Survival Strategies: Take the Book, Take the Money, Run* (2010)—my second example—was created in the wake of the global financial crisis (the artist labels it a "Crisis Special"), which hit Eastern Europe particularly hard.

As one report put it, "since September 2008, the global economic and financial crisis gained markedly in depth and intensity and waning foreign investor confidence in emerging markets dashed hopes of a decoupling of the CESEE [Central, Eastern, and South Eastern European] countries from the global financial crisis. As a result, the CESEE region was hit hard, in many respects even harder than other emerging market regions such as Latin America."[38] *Take the Book, Take the Money, Run* uses the didactic format to instruct viewers in how to survive the faltering economy and handle the tools necessary to steal from those who live comfortably, arguing that stealing is the only means those affected by the crisis have to overcome their economic and social disadvantage.[39] The handbook's dedication reads: "In a world dominated by materialistic values, stealing might be the most appropriate solution." As Homorodean contends in his preface: "This is a book about stealing your way out of the financial crisis. Get your basic necessities, keep your social standing, round up your annual income . . . Learn how to spot the ideal occasions for getting things without money, and practice how to do it without getting caught."[40]

Unlike Miljanović's *Didactic Wall*, Homorodean's manual does not reuse or retool existing educational material; instead, it presents a series of chapters with original drawings depicting different types of theft, burglary, or fraud in fictionalized situations, accompanied by handwritten text that explains these various stealing techniques and their benefits. The artist's tongue-in-cheek manual presents itself as an effort to systematize stealing in order to instruct and encourage others to do the same. Detailed drawings of specific locks and tools for various theft situations supplement the handbook, whose basic assumption is that theft is the only way to survive the crippling inequalities of an economic system based on wasteful consumption and profit maximization. In Homorodean's drawings, a thief might use a knife or razor blade to open the buttoned-down back pocket of a passerby in order to extract his wallet, or they might provoke a collision in order to take advantage of the victim's surprise by robbing her of her belongings. Other situations depicted range from a cleverly set-up car theft

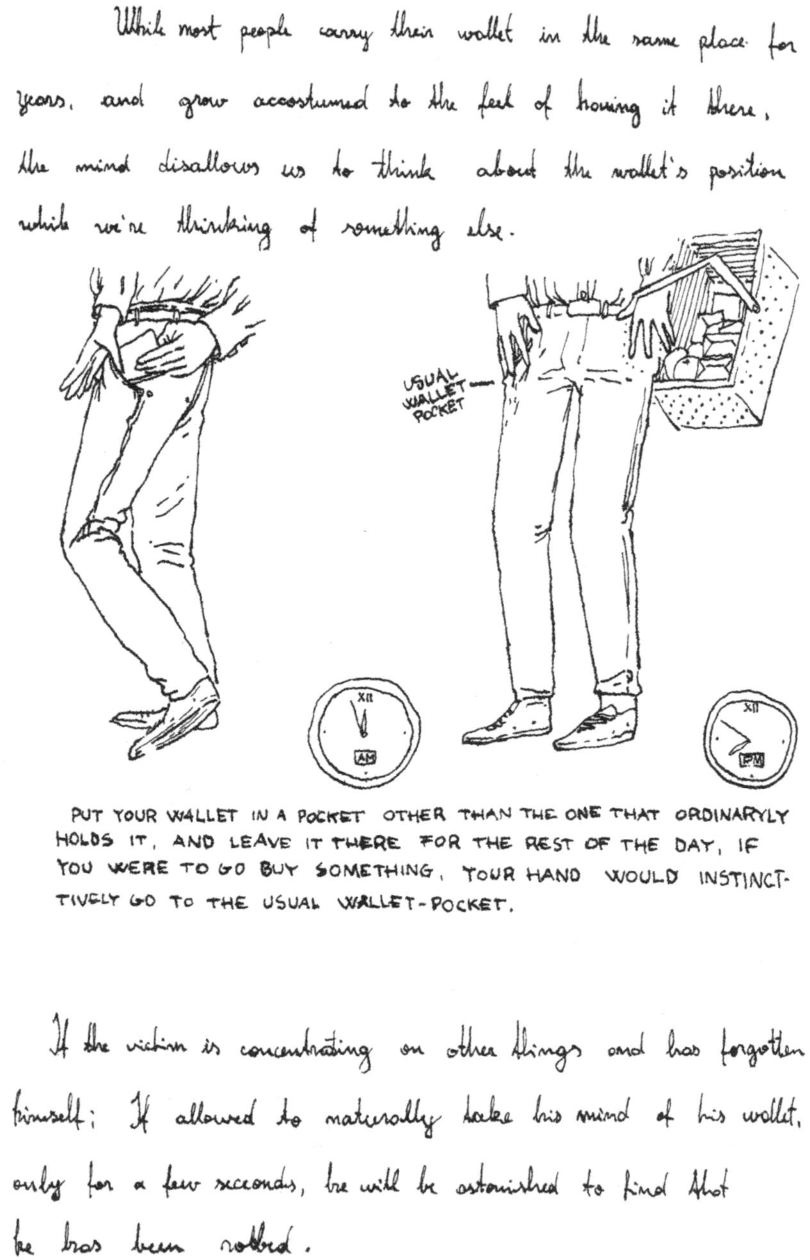

Figure 5.22 Ciprian Homorodean, *Take the Book, Take the Money, Run*, 2010. Image courtesy of Ciprian Homorodean.

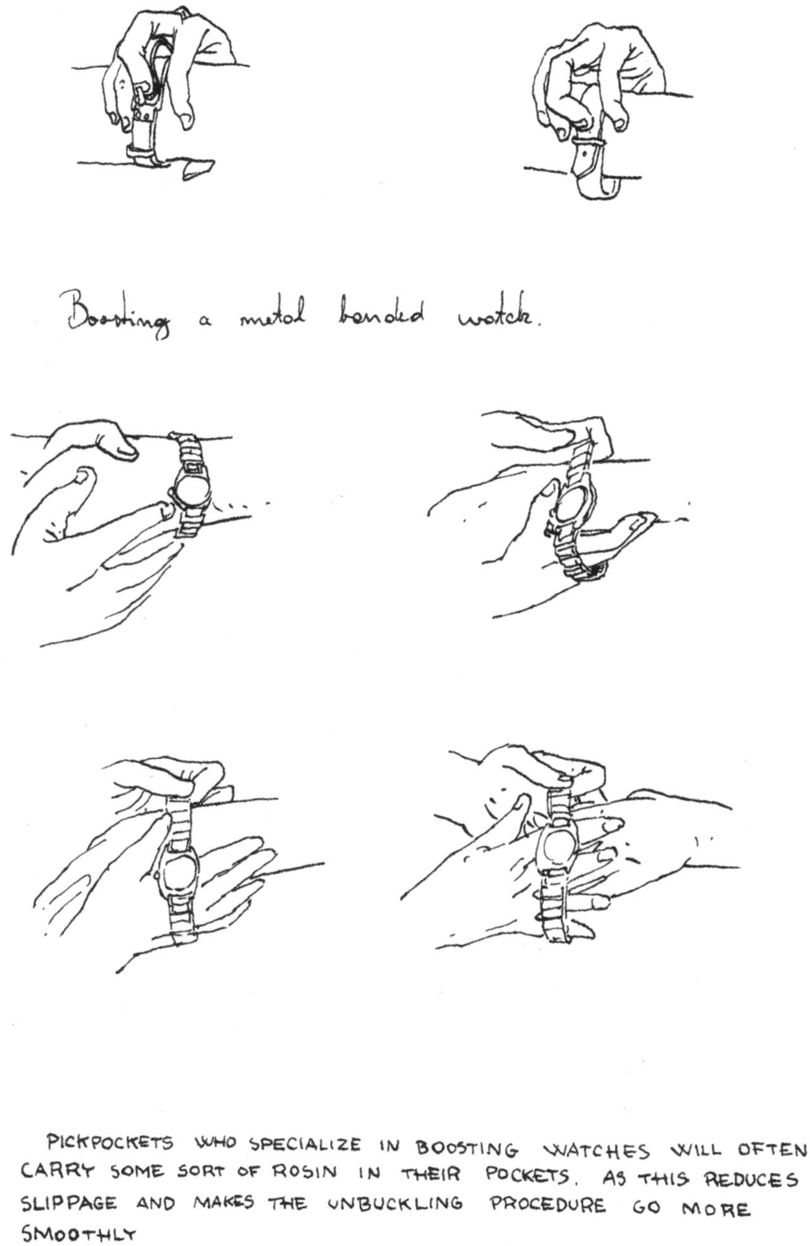

Figure 5.23 Ciprian Homorodean, *Take the Book, Take the Money, Run*, 2010. Image courtesy of Ciprian Homorodean.

followed by burglary to internet fraud ("Let Your Fingers Do Your Job"), posing as a "fake beggar" ("Kindness Pays"), bicycle theft ("Getting Your Free Wheels"), shoplifting ("Don't Shop. Lift"), and the theft of paintings from a gallery so that the stolen artworks may "regain their innocence, becoming pure affects of pleasure, priceless, free from the market and from the financial situation."[41]

As was the case with Miljanović, Homorodean's project must be seen as an effort to reexamine art's didactic commitments in the wake of the 1960s. On the one hand, with this project, Homorodean applies a double skill set both as a draftsman and an educator, suggesting that especially in times of crisis, artists have to also be instructors who intervene in reality by pointing to the inequalities and injustices that characterize life under global capitalism. Marked by conspicuous consumption, greed, and obliviousness to the plight of others, consumer capitalism in crisis pins the have-nots against members of the middle class. *Take the Book, Take the Money, Run* dispenses knowledge on how to address the problems that follow in the wake of this development ("This Crisis Special will get you acquainted with the essential vocabulary of unlawful appropriation techniques"). As the artist writes, "these chapters are particularly useful for the chronically unemployed, the hungry for work and the demanding consumers."[42] As a result, Homorodean's heroes steal and destroy luxury cars, rob wealthy home owners of their furniture, tour fancy neighborhoods collecting money for nonexistent social causes, or place cockroaches on the table of a starred restaurant halfway through a high-end meal so they don't have to pay: "Keep your head up in the material world even if you can't pay for it."[43]

Among the references Homorodean makes to 1960s underground culture, no other publication seems quite as relevant as Yippie cofounder Abbie Hoffman's legendary and controversial *Steal This Book* (1971). Designed as a survival and combat manual for the victims of capitalism, the book gives readers advice on how to live for free ("We cannot survive without learning to fight and that is the lesson in the second section"). In Hoffman's book, Proudhon's famous slogan "property is theft" is taken to its logical conclusion: if property is theft, theft is the only way for those who have nothing to take back what rightfully belongs to them. Hoffman, famous for wanting to combine the art of Andy Warhol with the politics of Fidel Castro, divided *Steal This Book* into three sections—"Survive!," "Fight!," "Liberate!"—that provide tips and strategies on how to survive in what he refers to as the "Pig Empire" ("Amerika is just another Latin Dictatorship"):

> The purpose of part two is not to fuck the system, but destroy it. . . . Be clever using section two: clever as a snake. Dig the spirit of the struggle. . . . Revolution is not about suicide, it is about life. . . . Become an internationalist and learn to respect all life. Make war on machines, and in particular the sterile machines of corporate death and the robots that guard them. The duty of a revolutionary is to make love and that means staying alive and free.[44]

Illustrated with captioned photographs and diagrams designed to teach specific survival techniques in a corporatized system where literally everything is subject to exchange, *Steal This Book*, much like Homorodean's manual, provides detailed text-based information on how to obtain goods and services without paying for them; practice shoplifting ("Steal Now, Pay Never"); dry clothes for free ("Wait in a laundromat. Tell someone with a light load that you'll watch the machine for them if you can stick your clothes in with theirs"); start an underground press or a guerrilla radio station; stage demonstrations; build homemade bombs ("The neat homemade bomb that really packs a wallop can be made from a regular aerosol can that is empty"); obtain political asylum in another country; and survive for free (and dodge the draft) in four large US cities ("FUCK NEW YORK"/"FUCK CHICAGO"/"FUCK LOS ANGELES"/"FUCK SAN FRANCISCO").

The tone adopted in *Steal This Book* is militant and confrontational—Hoffman calls street demonstrations a "form of warfare."[45] The book's view of instruction has none of the harmony-craving vision of information exchange espoused by the New Communalists and their worship of cybernetics, with its "notion of the globe as a single, interlinked pattern of information."[46] What makes Hoffman interesting to Homorodean—who lists *Steal This Book* in the bibliography ("References and Acknowledgments") that concludes *Take the Book, Take the Money, Run*—is, among other things, the suggestion that amateurism and ignorance may be the vigilante's biggest enemy. As an artist and instructor, Hoffman collects and systematizes a paramilitary counterknowledge whose goal is the revolutionary's successful camouflage: "Being a successful shoplifter requires the development of an outlaw mentality. . . . Camouflage is important. Be sure you dress the part by looking like an average customer."[47] To Hoffman, theft is born from the insight that we can survive life under capitalism only if we view it as a form of (irregular) combat. That being said, stealing is by the same token a revolutionary act, as it helps with the destruction of the hated system ("*Amerika*") and paves the way for its replacement with a different society: "The chapter headings spell out the demands for a free society. A community where the technology produces goods and services for whoever needs them."[48]

Homorodean's manual, created roughly forty years after *Steal This Book*, conspicuously sheds the revolutionary pathos that characterizes the earlier book. Where Hoffman dialectically demands that his students, the "Robin Hoods of Santa Barbara Forest," prepare for war ("It's ridiculous to talk about a revolution without a few words on guns") so that they can serve a higher moral law ("to steal from a brother or sister is evil. To not steal from the institutions that are the pillars of the Pig Empire is equally immoral"), Homorodean knows of no such appeals. His post-1989 thief is driven by nothing beyond the compulsion, dictated by the late capitalist system, to preserve his or her existence and to rob those who have. In the chapter devoted to illegal downloading as a way to obtain free music ("Let Your Fingers Do Your Job"), Homorodean writes:

> People didn't stop buying albums because they were philosophically opposed to how the rock business operated, and they didn't stop buying albums because the Internet is changing the relationship between capitalism and art. People stopped buying albums because they wanted the fucking money.[49]

In this sense, Homorodean dispenses with the last remnant of idealism in Hoffman's tract, the assumption that stealing serves a higher ethical imperative, or that its motivation could be anything other than the hope for material gain. Instead, the Romanian artist, having stolen Hoffman's book, goes on to update it for his own neoliberal moment.

6

LEARNING FROM THE SITUATION (ULRIKE MEINHOF, CLEMENS VON WEDEMEYER)

In German, the English word "education" unfolds into at least two related yet independent concepts, and each comes with a pedigree: *Lernen* or *Erziehung*, on the one hand, and *Bildung*, on the other. While *Lernen*, especially in our neoliberal era, is often associated with the assimilation of readily usable and monetized knowledge, *Erziehung* has a broader remit that refers to social reproduction by imparting knowledge to children in order to turn them into functioning members of society.

For its part, *Bildung* derived from *Bild* (image) and *bilden* (to form; to cultivate). While it includes the assimilatory aspects of *Erziehung*, *Bildung* also partially exceeds the limitations of that word by including the possibility of learning as an autodidactic process that avoids the hierarchical, power-driven relationship between teacher and student characterizing *Erziehung*. *Bildung* can be defined as a process of self-reproduction through the gradual accumulation of knowledge-as-experience, hence as a kind of life apprenticeship that is, not by coincidence, often allegorized as a journey. As a bourgeois ideal that passes for universal, *Bildung* is subject to overdetermination by class and other factors.

Philosophically, Western notions of *Bildung* have their roots in the Enlightenment idea—much criticized during the 1960s—that every young (typically male and white) individual disposes of an essential if undeveloped self that *Bildung* helps develop and manifest. One of the most-cited theorists of *Bildung*, the early nineteenth-century linguist and language philosopher Wilhelm von Humboldt ("Theory of Human *Bildung*," 1793/94), viewed a general course of *Bildung* that would include the classics (so-called *Allgemeinbildung*) as a gradual progression from simpler to more complex knowledge; he argued it was a prerequisite for anyone eager to form a socially connected and autonomous self, culminating in access to science or *Wissenschaft*.[1] Yet even here, *Bildung*'s political commitments are tenuously progressive at best. As Eva Borst notes, while Humboldt's theory of *Bildung* includes an element of (gradual) political change in the direction of republicanism and even a recognition of the problematic workings of capitalism, at the same time, it was designed to preclude that such change be brought about by violent revolution.[2]

During the 1968 student revolt in West Germany, *Bildung*, with its appeal to individual development without reference to its social situatedness, was being denounced as symptomatic of a society that had barely changed since the Nazi era and as a bastion of ultraconservative individualism with no regard for social life and its contradictions. Humboldt's understanding of *Bildung* too was now being criticized inasmuch as it seemed to shield the subject's interior from politics and economic life, thus isolating it within a fully autonomous zone of solipsistic introspection that was oblivious to questions of class and social production.[3]

Such critiques had an important precursor in Walter Benjamin, whose study of the intellectual's situation in the Soviet Union led him to the conclusion, in the early 1930s, that *Bildung*, and the specializing limitations it imposed on the art production of its bearers, prevented progressive Western artists from practicing true solidarity with the proletariat that went beyond representation.[4] In 1960s leftist circles, the critique of *Bildung* followed along similar lines, even in cases where Benjamin's class-conscious view of *Bildung*'s privileges was abandoned for a more broadly speaking humanist view. As Wolfgang Klafki wrote in an influential study published in 1963, "today *Bildung* can no longer be understood individualistically or with reference to the subject alone. Instead, it needs to be conceived from the beginning with reference to human togetherness, sociability and political existence."[5] Klafki also criticized traditional *Bildung* for its insistence that only those who have completed and assimilated its lessons have the right to act, as it appeared to bar young people without *Allgemeinbildung* or without access to it from active participation in society.[6] *Bildung*, in other words, was seen as a bulwark of conservatism and class privilege dispensed by authoritarian teachers and professors with no regard for their students as individuals.

It's true that not everyone on the left was ready to throw out *Bildung* wholesale. Already in the late 1950s, in a text titled "Theorie der Halbbildung" (Theory of semi-education), Adorno had argued that the crisis of postwar culture was the result less of *Bildung* per se—which Adorno continued to hold in high regard—than of its bastardized offspring, what he referred to as consciousness-dimming semi- or pseudo-education (*Halbbildung*).[7] For Adorno, *Halbbildung* was nurtured by the ever-increasing uncritical consumption of the mass media, especially television, and overall by the mass media's mechanical reproduction of reality. To blunt these effects, Adorno insisted that what was needed was increased media competency. In a radio discussion entitled "Radio and Television" (1963), he presciently insisted on the need to "teach . . . television" itself in order to enable viewers to see through its ideology, and urged the establishment of "educational television" as an antidote to conventional TV's deformation of consciousness.[8]

Other critics of *Bildung* during the 1960s who, like Adorno, were not willing to discard the concept altogether tended to stress its broad humanist appeal. In his influential 1960 study *Truth and Method*, the philosopher Hans-Georg Gadamer defined *Bildung* as "the properly human way of developing one's talents and capacities" in correspondence with an ideal

Bild (image) of what it means to be human, with art playing an important role in this process.[9] For Gadamer, *Bildung* is rooted in *Erfahrung* (experience) rather than in cognition, and as such represents a nondogmatic way of enriching our knowledge. Gadamer's ideas have some affinity with those of Friedrich Nietzsche, for whom the more formal aspects of *Bildung*, including the acquisition of academic knowledge, were little more than obstacles on the way to what he viewed as true *Bildung*, here understood as an act of liberation much closer to nature than to culture. Playing on the proximity of *Bildung* to *bilden* (to create), Nietzsche insisted on *Bildung* as a form of liberation from bourgeois culture:

> Your true educators and artists [*Bildner*] disclose to you the true and most original meaning [*Ursinn*] and substance of your being, something that is beyond education and image [*Unbildbares*], inaccessible, constrained, paralyzed: your educators cannot be anything other than your liberators. And this is the secret of all *Bildung*: that it doesn't afford us artificial limbs, waxen noses, or spectacles. All that these things can give us is merely the afterimage of true education. Rather, *Bildung* is liberation, the clearance of all weeds, debris, and vermin that want to tamper with the plant's tender seedlings. . . . *Bildung* is the imitation and adoration of nature, its completion. . . . Certainly, there may be other means for finding oneself, for coming to oneself out of the intoxication that usually envelops us like a dark cloud, but I know of no better remedy than to remember our teachers and those who sculpt us [*Bildner*].[10]

Nietzsche's anti-culture view of *Bildung* as a form of organic growth, together with his all-out hatred of academic knowledge and his powerful commitment to the educator-as-liberator, can help us unpack the multiple connections between art, radical activism, and opposition to traditional *Bildung* that mark the 1960s, including the decade's commitment to an alternative *Bildungsprogramm* that would privilege personal responsibility and political commitment over formal knowledge.

Alongside *Bildung*, the state-administered system entrusted with dispensing *Bildung* to the public, the so-called *Bildungssystem*—schools and universities—was equally viewed in the 1960s as being authoritarian, politically reactionary, and distant from real life. Students protested the fact that access to higher education was a privilege determined by social class, that academic knowledge production obscured its collusion with hegemonic power and authority, and that many professors were politically reactionary. The university was criticized as a place where knowledge and power conjoined to produce what Theodore Roszak in his seminal 1969 study *The Making of a Counter Culture* referred to as "technocracy," a term he used to pinpoint what was perceived as a concerted effort, on the part of academic, bureaucratic, and business elites, to fabricate false consciousness.[11] A slogan used in 1967 during a student demonstration in the city of Hamburg famously read, "Unter den Talaren—Muff von tausend Jahren," which roughly translates into "under the professors' regalia there's the stench of 1,000 years"—combining a commentary on the conservatism of the university faculty with a sarcastic reference to the Nazis' self-proclaimed "1,000-year *Reich*."

Despite all this, the university remained central to the students' emancipatory project, even as the creative responses to its "pedagogical technocracy" and its knowledge regimes—captured in the widespread slogan of "school as a factory"—varied, often culminating in rethinking the institution as a place where practice and activism trump the transmission of formal knowledge. This was sometimes based on the Mao-inspired assumption that the acquisition of knowledge does not require systematic study, a position that incidentally contradicted Marx, with whom protesting students in Western Europe tended at any rate to engage a great deal less actively than with Mao's Little Red Book.[12] This may also help explain the ever-growing number of anti-universities and anti-(art) schools founded by artists during the expanded 1960s, from Copenhagen's Ex-School (founded in 1961) to Rudi Dutschke's proposal for a counteruniversity (1967), London's Anti-University (1968), or Jörg Immendorff's aforementioned LIDL Academy inside the Düsseldorf Kunstakademie (1968) where, it was hoped, everyone would learn "to think rationally and autonomously."[13] In sum, the university retained its appeal for the students as a form of sociability capable of harnessing the imagination (*Phantasie*) to emancipatory politics. As Jürgen Habermas noted in 1967, "perhaps the process of petrification of our administered consciousness has progressed so far that today, the insensitivity to what in more naïve times philosophers called 'the good life' can only be broken through under the socio-psychologically exceptional conditions of university study."[14]

Ulrike Meinhof's film *Bambule: Juvenile Reform—for Whom?* (1970), which I will analyze below, is an excellent example of the way in which Marxist intellectuals during the 1960s battled both with the reactionary bourgeois championing of education (*Bildung*) and with its humanist critique from a position of pseudo-progressivism. Classified as a TV drama (*Fernsehspiel*), which ensured a late-night programming slot—and hence a smaller audience—*Bambule* was made inside Eichenhof (called Lindenhof, in the film) on Berlin's outskirts, a reform school (*Erziehungsheim)* that housed adolescent girls with difficult biographies, mostly with proletarian backgrounds, who had dropped out of the school system.[15]

Meinhof, a future RAF terrorist, began doing research for her only film in 1968 in the context of the so-called *Heimkampagne*, a campaign during which student activists agitated the residents of state-run reform schools for underprivileged adolescent youth in the state of Hesse, on the assumption that such agitation could be a radical tool for liberation and self-discovery. The film's title, *Bambule*, comes from German prison lingo, where it refers to noisy forms of protest ("*Bambule machen*"), typically by banging hard items against the cells' metal bars.[16] However, *Bambule* was not shown on German public television as scheduled, because ten days before it was slated to air, on May 14, 1970, Meinhof went underground and became one of Germany's most notorious terrorists.[17] This development has a prehistory:

the year 1968, when Meinhof wrote *Bambule*, saw the first violent acts committed from within the left-wing activist *außerparlamentarische Opposition* (APO) when two West Berlin department stores were firebombed by Meinhof's future comrades in arms, Andreas Baader and Gudrun Ensslin, among others. The attacks, known as *Kaufhausbrände* (department store fires), were carried out in retaliation for the police shooting, the year before, of the unarmed student Benno Ohnesorg during the demonstration discussed earlier against the visit by the shah of Iran and his wife, an event that radicalized parts of the formerly strictly pacifist student movement.[18] Baader and Ensslin were caught and put on trial. They did not hide their contempt for the court, stressing the global dimension of their actions (Ensslin: "I do not care about a few burnt mattresses, I am talking about burning children in Vietnam").[19]

In 1970—at the time when *Bambule* was supposed to air—Meinhof took part in the violent liberation of Baader during a spectacular commando raid, while he was visiting a public library under police escort. After this action, during which a library employee was seriously wounded, Meinhof, Baader, and Ensslin went on to found the Rote Armee Fraktion, which the right-wing West German media and the government called the "Baader-Meinhof gang." After training in a PLO-sponsored paramilitary camp in the Jordanian desert in 1970, the RAF committed a series of high-profile, bloody bombing attacks against representative figures and institutions in West Germany, including an assault on the US military headquarters in Heidelberg during which two soldiers were killed.[20] Arrested in 1972 and charged with four murders and numerous assaults with intent to kill, Meinhof and other members of the group, including Baader and Ensslin, were sentenced to life in prison in a lengthy trial that shook West German society like no other had before. In 1976, Ulrike Meinhof was found dead in her cell in the high-security area of the Stammheim prison near Stuttgart. The circumstances of her alleged suicide were never fully revealed.[21]

Meinhof's initial script for *Bambule*, based on her research, was edited by the film's director, Eberhard Itzenplitz, who finished producing it for

Meinhof; in the process, he altered her script to the point that calling *Bambule* Meinhof's film may be a stretch. In 2012, filmmaker Clemens von Wedemeyer found and published Itzenplitz's script as part of the research for his participation in that year's documenta.[22]

Bambule begins with the escape by Monika and her friend Irene over the fence surrounding Lindenhof, encouraged by other girls from inside a classroom where their helpless teacher is vainly trying to maintain discipline. While Irene goes to see her hard-working yet frustrated mother and grandmother—the grandmother, having lived through Nazism as an adult, is the only one who understands Irene's situation at the school—Monika is caught by Lindenhof staff and locked up inside the *Bunker*, an isolation cell whose graffiti-strewn walls, like so much at Lindenhof, recall a prison. There she has a long conversation with one of the teachers, Frau Lack, who is drawn to the girls but also serves the institution's sadistic director, Frau Turm.[23] Monika tells Frau Lack about her lifelong odyssey through Berlin's orphanages, among which one called "The Monastery" (*Das Kloster*) has left her with the most traumatizing memories, including the physical violence she endured from a nun called "Loving Mother."

At the Lindenhof, the adult pedagogues mostly communicate with the girls through prohibitions and orders issued in unaccented German, while the girls speak with a thick Berlin accent, highlighting their proletarian origins. On some level, the conflict between the girls and their minders, as depicted in the film, is a class war disguised as a struggle over authority. Yet class difference, which also manifests itself in the school's glaring exploitation of the girls' labor power, is not the only fault line dividing the juvenile residents from the staff; another is sexual preference. Irene has a relationship with Gisela, while Monika's flashbacks to her time at the Monastery reform school illustrate the violently repressive pedagogy of the resident nuns, who punish her for kissing another girl by cutting her hair in a brutal effort at desexualization. While homosexuality is a secondary concern in *Bambule* rather than the center of the film's attention (in Germany,

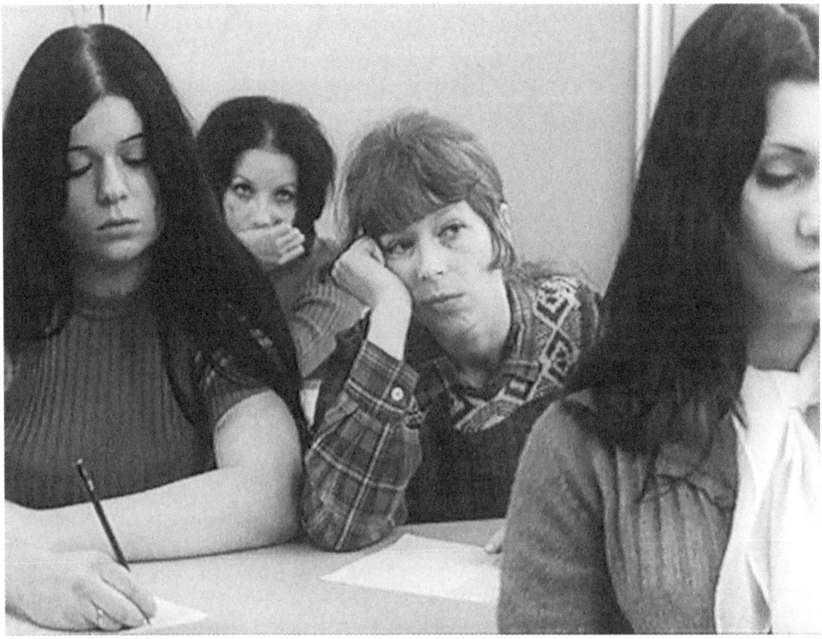

Figure 6.1 Ulrike Meinhof / Eberhard Itzenplitz. *Bambule*, 1970. Video still. © SWR.

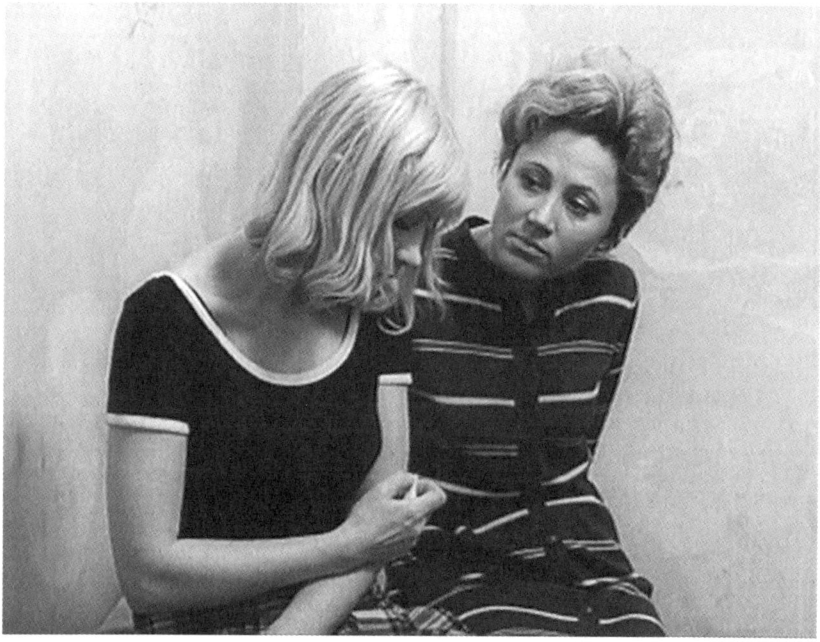

Figure 6.2 Ulrike Meinhof / Eberhard Itzenplitz. *Bambule*, 1970. Video still. © SWR.

organized instances of coming out and self-affirmation by homosexuals began slightly later, in 1970–1971),[24] it adds to the film's gloomy atmosphere. As was customary in the late 1960s, discrimination against women, authoritarian forms of pedagogy, the criminalization of homosexuality, and the deplorable conditions in state orphanages and juvenile halls of residence together constituted a gloomy picture filled with injustice and repression. Rather than being an issue in and of itself, the repression of sexuality is treated in *Bambule* as just one instance in a more general fight by those in power against all forms of enjoyment, while its surrogates, in the form of television and other types of inauthentic entertainment—or rather, their withdrawal—serve the powerful as weapons for enforcing compliant behavior.

The historic Eichenhof on which Lindenhof is based—the name, with its reference to *Eichen* (oak trees), evoked German folklore or clichéd romantic poetry—occupied the site of a Gestapo labor-education camp (*Arbeitserziehungslager*) that provided German firms with slave labor.[25] This prehistory is not coincidental or irrelevant; the APO movement's revolt in the late 1960s was motivated precisely by the continuities, on all levels of the state, between Nazism and postwar West German society, as countless West German officials were former Nazis.[26] With its portrayal of reform school education as an unrelenting system of control and surveillance, *Bambule* delivers a chilling, literal glimpse of what Adorno, in a famous 1966 radio address, invoked as "Education after Auschwitz." Adorno's phrase is generally understood to mean: "What can or should education after Auschwitz be like, how can education after Auschwitz prevent the Holocaust from repeating itself?"—a question Adorno answers with a pivot to the need to analyze the character of the subject-as-perpetrator, but also with the admission that the decisive factors in the rise of fascism may be situated outside of what is accessible to psychology and education.[27] For Adorno, who was famously pessimistic about civilization and other affirmative ideals as an antidote to the barbarity of Nazism, no modern pedagogical ideal—of which there were many during the 1960s—was productive unless it was preceded by a careful review of Nazi pedagogy so that the Holocaust might be prevented from repeating itself.

For its part, *Bambule* responds to Adorno's proposed "education after Auschwitz" in a decisive way: not with new ideas on how to prevent Auschwitz, but by demonstrating that in fact education *after* Auschwitz looks a lot like education *before* Auschwitz. In a sense, *Bambule* pushes Adorno's merciless critique of civilization and its values to new limits; where the theorist proposes to (psycho-)analyze the "manipulative character" in order to show the perpetrators the "mechanisms . . . that make human beings capable of such deeds . . . and seek to prevent that they become like that again by awakening a general consciousness of such mechanisms,"[28] Meinhof's film shows little confidence in the perpetrators' readiness to be reformed.

If in the 1960s school was frequently likened to a factory, in the case of Lindenhof it is more like a prison. While Monika is in the appropriately named *Bunker* with Frau Lack, she demonstratively writes a long number on her lower arm, as if she were in a concentration camp. The bureaucratic control over every aspect of the girls' regimented lives recalls a prison, as the Youth Welfare Department has a more intricate knowledge of their lives than they themselves do. Meanwhile, the brutal desexualization, drill, and open sadism of the nuns at the Monastery orphanage clearly recall Nazi pedagogy. As Jutta Ditfurth writes, "many West German and West Berlin reform schools, including Christian ones, were places where Nazi pedagogy survived as if in a cocoon. The pedagogical 'ideal' was to educate [*erziehen*] children and adolescents with socially precarious backgrounds into absolutely obedient, rightless, unfree, asexual creatures."[29] Crucially, the system that controls the girls encompasses their minders too: nowhere does this become more obvious than in Frau Lack, who is visibly torn between her sympathies for the girls and the need to perform her official duties as a member of the repressive *Heim* staff. The discussions she has with Lindenhof director Frau Turm over Monika's transfer to another institution (the notorious *Kloster* or Monastery) as a way of punishing Monika for her unwillingness to "redeem herself" (*sich bewähren*) further strengthen the impression that Lindenhof is a test case of what Adorno refers to as a "totally administered society":[30]

> We can talk about humanity's claustrophobia in the administered world, a feeling of being locked into a dense web of relations that has become naturalized [*vergesellschaftet*] through and through. The more densely woven the net, the more one wants to escape from it, while it is precisely its density that makes such an escape impossible. That intensifies the rage against civilization. The revolt against it is violent and irrational.[31]

In *Bambule*, the administered world comprises not only Lindenhof itself but also its outside, the "world beyond the fence," where capitalism reduces human beings to purveyors of labor power. When another student, Gisela, who leaves Lindenhof every day to go to her mind-numbing job in a department store, is confronted with Irene's fantasies about life outside, she tells Irene: "Just wait until you get out." The administered reality of the school is a totalized world that has no outside. It corresponds neatly to what Adorno and Horkheimer, in a radio broadcast from 1950, had referred to as "life that does not live."[32] Inside this world, as is the case with Louis Althusser's "state apparatuses"—of which school is one—repression and ideology interact to produce false consciousness and the mistaken assumption, crucial for maintaining the status quo, that "the School [is] a neutral environment purged of ideology" whose function is to impart to its students the universal values of civilization.[33]

In a Nazi labor camp such as the *Arbeitserziehungslager* that preceded the Eichenhof school, the selection and division of the camp's population based on a variety of criteria was a daily routine and part of the terror such camps unleashed on their inmates. At the Lindenhof, such selections continue as staff coerce the girls into work and punish their transgressions against the *Heim*'s written and unwritten rules with isolation or various forms of withdrawal. If these practices, together with its isolation cells and sadistic pedagogues, recall Nazi *Erziehung*, at one telling moment in the film, this perspective is supplemented by a glimpse at the situation in postwar Germany more generally.

That moment comes when Frau Turm scolds the girls for messing up their bedroom and tells them: "Everyone is guilty, those who have done it and the others, too [*Alle haben Schuld, die es getan haben und die anderen auch*]." On the one hand, Frau Turm's approach—punishing the whole group for the alleged wrongdoings of individuals within it—was a common practice in the Nazi camps, and so this statement once again reinforces a sense of continuity between the pedagogy practiced at Lindenhof and the preceding Nazi era, a pedagogy according to which fear of authority and readiness to obey were key social values. On the other hand, in the context of postwar West Germany—a society mired in fantasies of victimhood and collective amnesia regarding its own guilt and involvement in Nazism's crimes—the phrase "everyone is guilty, those who have done it and the others, too" has a different ring to it: it reads as a direct reversal of the collective tendency, widespread in West Germany at the time, to separate a narrow set of Nazi perpetrators from the population as a whole, and thus to dispel and reject any notion of collective guilt for Nazism's crimes (a comical version of this attitude is incapsulated in the phrase "I didn't do it, Hitler did!"). This attitude above all was the target of the APO, who pursued a radical program of desublimation and collective recall coupled with the (optimistic) belief in the possibility of raising the collective consciousness.[34] In a dialectical move highly characteristic of the didactic 1960s, then, Frau Turm's repressive gesture becomes the (necessary) prerequisite—as it were, the negative foil—before which the phrase "everyone is guilty, those who have done it and the others, too" can be read as an accurate description, against her best intentions, of the true conditions in postwar German society. In a situation where civilization—education, politics, the state—has itself become an instance of false consciousness, repression—"life that isn't lived"—becomes the only possible launch pad for a learning process that can offer a way out of its multiple alienations.

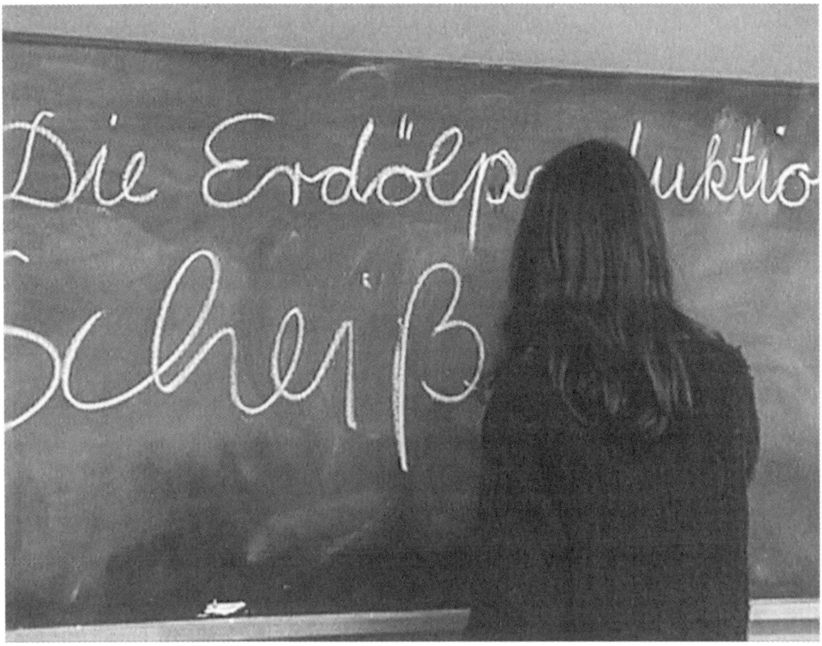

Figure 6.3 Ulrike Meinhof / Eberhard Itzenplitz. *Bambule*, 1970. Video still. © SWR.

The girls' revolt in *Bambule* against their administered world ("we are on strike") is, to use Adorno's words, "violent and irrational"—one of the girls simply writes "Scheiße Scheiße [shit shit]" on a classroom blackboard, just below the teacher's line, "Oil production in the USA." While their revolt is perhaps a rather helpless rebuttal of the oppressive pedagogy and coercive signification deployed by the reform school pedagogues (the imperative that things need to make sense, that they be logical, and so forth), the end of the film strikes a different tone.

When Irene turns herself in to the police after failed attempts to make money to buy a fake ID, she acknowledges that in the administered world in which she lives, Lindenhof is indeed her only home.[35] This insight is paradoxically intertwined with her heightened awareness of both her own situation and the need for further, more organized (and better theorized) struggle. Once she returns to Lindenhof, and as a result of her experiences in the outside world, Irene scolds her friend Iv for the lack of coordination and planning that characterized their spontaneous protest the day before ("If you don't know what you want, you cannot do anything"); she urges that their next revolt be accompanied by more discussion ("we need to talk more, much more, why we are doing this") and by a clearer articulation of their goals ("we need to write real stuff on the *Bunker* walls . . . not just that everything is shit"). As she now has a clearer idea of the bigger picture ("Reform schools [*Heime*] are prisons"), Irene knows that in order to find allies among the Lindenhof staff, they have to first define and defend their position rather than appealing to their educators' better instincts. If only they (the school's residents) "knew what we wanted, then Frau Lack could take the decision to be on our side."[36] In this way, if Irene's plan works out, the proletarian kids whom the juvenile "reform" system punishes by denying them a (higher) education and whom it forces into mind-numbing, underpaid jobs become, to quote Marx, those who "educate the educators." Adorno's question in "Education after Auschwitz" was: how can our knowledge of the educational mechanisms that made the perpetrators

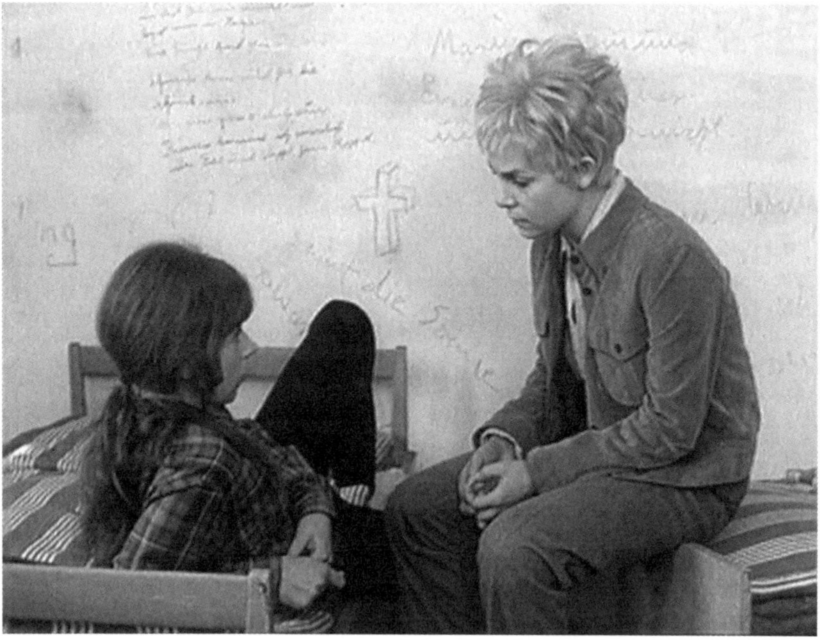

Figure 6.4 Ulrike Meinhof / Eberhard Itzenplitz. *Bambule*, 1970. Video still. © SWR.

commit their heinous crimes prevent them from committing such crimes a second time? The question in *Bambule*, which might also be considered an answer to Adorno's, is this: how can the victims of violence and oppression prevent themselves from being victimized again and again?

As I mentioned above, the filming of *Bambule* coincided with the tail end of the activist campaign against reform schools that targeted state-run reform institutions, including orphanages, and that denounced these institutions as neofascist prisons and "training camps for conformist capitalists," as one slogan went. During the summer of 1969, future RAF members Andreas Baader and Gudrun Ensslin also participated in this campaign, targeting a reformatory home for youth in the North Hess region of central Germany, where they posed as students of pedagogy wanting to test their theoretical knowledge in the practical realm. Baader and Ensslin were not really interested in exposing deficiencies in the system; rather than seeking reform, they "appealed to the residents to rebel against their administration and escape from the institution," appeals that several of the youth followed promptly, joining the revolutionary milieu.[37] As Bettina Röhl, Ulrike Meinhof's daughter, has commented recently, criticizing these efforts, "these adolescents were incited to revolution . . . , left to their own devices, drugs, and criminalization. . . . Many of the adolescents who followed their gurus and putative liberators Baader and Ensslin (themselves experimenting with drugs, from heroin to LSD) to their communes in Frankfurt later became terrorists."[38]

As a journalist, Meinhof made her own contributions to the *Heimkampagne*, among other ways in the form of radio features for stations all over West Germany that were based on interviews she made with girls from various institutions, material she then used for drafting *Bambule*.[39] In the commentaries that accompanied these radio features, Meinhof presents pointed analyses of the state of German juvenile reform, and of the way the education it dispenses serves to perpetuate the problems that in truth constitute its very nature. Juvenile reform education (*Fürsorgeerziehung*), in Meinhof's view, "has two functions for the proletarian family: to take the burden off the family; [and] to discipline the adolescent." As a form of discipline, *Fürsorgeerziehung* has a punitive character whose primary goal is to make the adolescent accept her situation and the system as a whole.[40] As Meinhof writes,

> what they do with the girls there is called care [*Fürsorge*]. . . . In their dossiers, we read: sexual promiscuity, homelessness, prostitution, change of work. Or: has contact with foreigners, wears miniskirts. . . . In their dossiers we read what speaks against these girls in the eyes of those who maintain these dossiers. They come from low-income families with many children, from overly small apartments and broken marriages. They ran [away] from home because they could no longer stand it there. They skipped school because school was awful. . . . Yet the failure of the school . . . is interpreted as their own stupidity.[41]

Rooted in the Marxist belief that we are the products of the material conditions in which we exist, Meinhof viewed reform school education as a means to perpetuate existing class distinctions and to shore up an anti-emancipatory, authoritarian education system: "Juvenile reform education serves the system, it's the stick that beats it into proletarian youth that it makes no sense for them to resist or to want anything other than to spend one's life in the factory, to work in an inferior position, to receive orders and to shut your face."[42] Such conditions were not an exception for Meinhof; on the contrary, they were the norm. As part of public education, reform schools were the place where "parents could no longer interfere, and so the State here acts in exactly the way it considers right."[43]

Much like the campaign against reform schools, the goal behind Meinhof's radio features—a crucial preparation for *Bambule*—was not to show the conditions in reform schools or to analyze the current state of the education system. Rather, the features were conceived as messages of active solidarity and pedagogical intervention, reflecting Meinhof's belief that once *Aufklärung* (enlightenment) has been dispensed and the victims' consciousness raised, they could not help but want to change the system that oppresses them.

Not surprisingly, Ulrike Meinhof's activist ambitions for her film were the biggest source of friction between her and director Itzenplitz, for whom politics entered art only in the most sublimated fashion, if at all.[44] As he remembered in a 2011 interview, "she [Meinhof] thought . . . this film, or film in general, was an appropriate, even altogether welcome means to change certain problems in society."[45] Whether or not she was able to sustain her belief in film is debatable, but what is certain is that Meinhof's ambition for *Bambule* was that her film would not just passively represent the shameful conditions under which the girls were kept at Eichenhof, but that she would instead involve them actively in the film's production. This in turn, Meinhof hoped, would liberate the school's residents from what oppressed them by inspiring them to try to escape from the institution that imprisoned them.[46] In this way, the film's production, together with the young women's realization that what was being filmed was in fact their life, amounts to a lesson close to Nietzsche's understanding of *Bildung*: not an accumulation of dead, formal knowledge but an act of lived emancipation, and a way of actively changing the direction of their lives. In other words, for Meinhof, *Bambule* was a means of demonstration, even agitation. As her biographer Jutta Ditfurth has written, "art and politics were connected for Meinhof."[47]

Taking all this into account, *Bambule*—with its production sandwiched, poignantly, between the arson attacks on the department stores in Berlin and the violent liberation of Andreas Baader, on the one hand, and Meinhof's turn toward terror and the underground, on the other—constitutes perhaps Ulrike Meinhof's last attempt to communicate from this side of terror. As such, the film expresses her hope that art, and more specifically film, might still be capable of binding the violence that the department store fires had unleashed to a process of (aesthetic) communication and education. *Bambule*, in other words, marks the turning point in Meinhof's life from respected left-wing journalist to most-wanted terrorist.

As Stefan Aust has argued, Meinhof's pedagogical ambitions for *Bambule*—her idea that the film could, didactically, help liberate the girls from their imprisonment—illustrate the wide gap that often separated calls for revolutionary action from reality during the 1960s, especially in the medium of film. Aust reports a telling exchange between Meinhof and her producer Dieter Waldmann during which Meinhof charged that members of the *Bambule* film team, including the professional actors themselves, did not care about the misery in which the Eichenhof girls lived. Reminding her that some of the actors in fact arranged for private meetings with the school's residents, and that one of the makeup artists offered professional help to one of the girls, Waldmann ends by asking Meinhof "if she really believed that the [film] team would stage a real revolution and put their job, family, everything at risk?"[48]

Precisely because she *did* believe this, Meinhof had initially wanted to avoid using professional actors, instead letting the Eichenhof girls play themselves. The idea of casting the reform school's students not with professionals but with its actual residents was essential for the didactic effect she hoped her film would have—not only on its eventual TV audience but, more importantly, on the cast itself, as its members—themselves victims of reform school pedagogy—would be witnesses to their own emancipation as part of a proletarian *Bildungserlebnis*, much like in a Brechtian *Lehrstück*. In a similar fashion, Meinhof refused to separate the production of *Bambule* as a film from the real-life context of its production, viewing the school's residents, even those not directly involved in the production, as active observers on whom the film would have a direct political effect.[49]

Yet as Meinhof went to the set almost daily to witness the production's progress—smoking or rolling a cigarette with no filters, as Itzenplitz reports—her unease about the project became more and more pronounced. Meinhof was convinced that *Bambule*, and perhaps film generally, did not—could not—live up to her ideas of how to change the girls' situation, and that agitating and organizing the school's residents, as Baader and Ensslin had done during their interventions in reform schools in North

Hesse, was politically much more effective than any work of art could ever be. As she wrote, "now it has become really clear to me that to create an uprising inside the school, to organize the students, is worth so much more than a billion films."[50] From this perspective, it is hardly surprising that Meinhof personally strove to influence the Eichenhof girls more directly by organizing classes at a local pub (to which no one came, to her surprise). She became close friends with at least one of the girls, Irene (who kept her name in the film as one of the main protagonists), and even went so far as to smuggle wire cutters into the Eichenhof building: expanded cinema.[51] As a result, during the film's shooting, several Eichenhof escapees, together with reform-home kids from Hesse who had been liberated by Baader and Ensslin, lived in Meinhof's apartment.[52] In a sense, the liberation of the girls, styled on Baader and Ensslin's actions in Hesse, was Meinhof's own *bambule*, a revolt not just against reform education and for the girls' emancipation, but also against the belief that film, art, and fiction were appropriate means to change anyone's circumstances.[53]

Unlike Itzenplitz, who considered the reform school residents a hapless, uneducated underclass stuck in an adverse system, for Meinhof such an analysis clearly fell short. Approaching her project from a principled point of view, she saw the Eichenhof girls as set back both by their proletarian origins and by the fact that they were women. Both facts made their incarceration at Eichenhof part of a much broader issue, the problem of how emancipation was possible for proletarian women under capitalism. As a journalist, Meinhof had always insisted that the emancipation of women could not be separated from the emancipation of the working class more generally, and vice versa. In 1968, when she was doing research for *Bambule*, Meinhof published a long article entitled "False Consciousness" in which she argued that "efforts by women [early in the last century] to emancipate themselves were fundamentally linked to those of the proletariat, and had also emerged with the latter."[54]

A frequent catchphrase of the New Left, "false consciousness" is typically understood as the proletariat's inability to properly conceive its own position in capitalist society due to ideological and economic constraints, so that a systematic and genuine understanding of its interests was impossible. In more general terms, "false consciousness" refers to our inability to recognize our situation for what it is, and to analyze the social and economic conditions responsible for this situation. While Marx himself never used the phrase, he did rethink consciousness, contra Hegel, as being dependent on the material relations of production in society and, as such, susceptible to control from without, including through education. Yet Marx was adamant that there could be no talk of a merely mechanical relationship between changes to the education system and changes in the consciousness of those whom it seeks to educate: "The materialist doctrine that humans are the products of circumstances and of education, and that therefore changed humans are the products of a different set of circumstances and changed education, forgets that circumstances are changed by people, and that educators themselves have to be educated. . . . The coincidence of changing circumstances and human activity can only be framed and rationally understood as revolutionary practice."[55] The phrase "educators themselves have to be educated" indicates that any lasting change in society is, according to Marx, part of a process whereby the positions of educators and students are variables rather than statically fixed, a viewpoint that was of great consequence for artists and activists alike during the late 1960s.

In her own article on the topic, Meinhof adopts a nuanced feminist position toward the idea of false consciousness. Distinguishing calls for equality—between the sexes, but also elsewhere in society—from demands for emancipation, she charges that while equality leaves existing social injustices intact and only seeks to distribute them more evenly, emancipation strikes at the heart of injustice by considering the social position and class, and not only the gender, of those in power. This leads her to conclude that while "equality is always achieved against men," demands for emancipation (of workers, women, etc.) target the social structure and the conditions of capitalist production itself. Crucially, this conclusion does not mean that she dismisses equality; rather, she sees in it a pragmatically necessary stepping stone toward emancipation. Meinhof connects middle-class women's demands for emancipation and increased access to higher education early in the twentieth century with the university's ever-increasing reshaping of knowledge production to fit anti-emancipatory causes:

> As the "logic of the heart" . . . that is usually associated with women was installed as a principle in the humanities, and as "intuition" became a cognitive organ, young women's access to the university was no longer capable of liberating them from the irrationality of the middle-class imagination, rather, it confirmed and solidified it. The desire of women to be emancipated . . . was now satisfied by their admission to an education system that was increasingly conditioned to fight against the emancipation of the proletariat, and hence also of women.[56]

While this argument cleverly implies that an increase in the emancipation of young middle-class women in the early twentieth century was linked to its very opposite—their access to education means they became part of a system entrenched in a fight against the emancipation of the so-called lower classes—in the case of proletarian women, access to (higher) education was simply denied.[57] This can be seen in *Bambule*, where the Lindenhof girls are either stuck in classroom lessons taught by incompetent teachers, or are forced to work menial "women's jobs" in the reform school laundry or, as in Gisela's case, as a store clerk. As Meinhof writes elsewhere, "middle-class youth are disciplined through their education. Proletarian adolescents, on the other hand, are punished and disciplined by denying them any education."[58]

Meinhof wrote her article about false consciousness in 1968 after she had drafted her film script, but before production began. At that moment, she was still reasonably optimistic about her *Bambule* project, even reconciling herself to the idea of using professional actors. As she wrote to Waldmann, "I have completely gone off the idea of using non-actors and of making a documentary. I think of non-actors as extras. Otherwise, I am for actors. The script simply isn't made for a documentary."[59] Yet Meinhof soon became impatient with what she perceived as the film's overly "cinematic" qualities, its realism, and the difficulty of agitating the student residents directly through the film's production.

To Itzenplitz, Meinhof's hope that the film would help to organize the reform school girls, making them aware of their class allegiances and framing their fight as a struggle for real emancipation, seemed unrealistic at best. Not coincidentally, after the first day of filming, when many of the Eichenhof girls had crowded the set, the director excluded all onlookers from the scene, a decision that set the stage for fundamental disagreements between him and Meinhof. Itzenplitz countered her ideas by insisting that the way to give the girls a voice was through the film itself, and by referring to his position as realism ("I had insisted on strict realism from the beginning").[60]

In his retrospective account of his collaboration with Meinhof from the mid-1980s, Itzenplitz mixes statements of chauvinism ("Ulrike Meinhof was not an attractive woman but she had . . . charisma") with skepticism about her idealism and lack of experience with filmmaking. His rhetoric casts Meinhof in the position of someone who is "searching" and whose deep humanism is always in danger of being hijacked by extremism and "ideology." Meinhof's desire to use her film as a means to agitate the girls and to raise their consciousness so that they might help themselves meets with Itzenplitz's outspoken disapproval. He rejected outright Meinhof's idea that the Eichenhof girls should play themselves on the grounds that, in his view, while untrained actors work well in supporting roles, they "fall short of themselves and . . . damage the film's ability to have a decisive effect" when they are asked to play lead roles.[61] More specifically, the director is convinced that nonprofessional (female) actors are not capable of convincing self-reflection: "However charismatic the effect of non-actors may be, we must not forget that . . . they are only convincing for as long as they can do in the film what they also do in life. But as soon as you ask them to . . . reflect upon themselves or define their intentions, they fail miserably."[62] For Itzenplitz, these "proletarian/trashy" (*prollig*) adolescents with their blatant "lack of intellectual preparation"[63] were capable of offering cinematically convincing instances of self-reflection only if these concerned their own concrete circumstances, while he believed only professional actors or acting students like the ones he ended up choosing for the main roles were capable of reflecting on situations other than their own:

> It always turned out authentic for as long as they let themselves be questioned about simple facts while participating in typical kinds of labor, such as working in the *Heim* laundry, the kitchen, or while they were eating. . . . They were always eating, and if you approached them during that time, then the resulting scene turned out absolutely authentic. But you were damned if during lunch you tried to involve them in theoretical disputes about the residents in general or about their custody [*Verwahrung*], or about basic political principles. This they could not do, even if you gave them the text to learn.[64]

Itzenplitz's comment reproduces a common stereotype of the time that women were un-self-conscious, "natural" creatures whose ability for abstract or theoretical (self-)reflection was underdeveloped. The director was particularly piqued by what he took to be Meinhof's criticism of his work on film, of which he charged she knew nothing ("It didn't become clear to her that . . . what this was about was the production of an artwork"), and he therefore questions her expertise ("The thing is that she lacked the experience . . . she had never made fictional films").[65] Itzenplitz charges that while Meinhof was initially on board with his filmic realism (he even quotes a letter in which she wrote that "the film [*Bambule*] is not fiction . . . [but] anchored in reality"), she gradually became more and more insistent that, in his words, the film needed to put its message across through every exchange between the protagonists. Indeed, as she visited the set on a daily basis, Meinhof often demanded that dialogue be changed in order to sharpen its political message, so that "the characters in the film . . . represent their current social position in the didactic [*lehrhaft*] fashion she desired, for the sake of the film's message."[66] In his recollections, adopting a position on the 1960s and on Meinhof that has since become canonical, Itzenplitz views her as a victim of her own "overwhelming idealism." As he writes, "it was the trauma of all those who are socially engaged, perhaps of all leftists in general, that paralyzed Ulrike and finally drove her to death. It is the ethical strength of the left to be driven by a strong idealism . . . but this also reveals their weakness. For where the necessary insight into the need to be modest and to help each other is missing, we often hear the hasty demand that those who 'don't get it' should be forced into what's good for them."[67] This assessment also explains the director's negative reaction to Meinhof's didacticism: his belief that it was neither realist nor realistic. He traces this back to what he perceived as Meinhof's (unrealistic) insistence that every piece of dialogue in *Bambule* contain the entire film's message in a nutshell, and to her work as a journalist: "The less emphasis there was on a linguistic confession that was being made at the time, the less weight she believed that confession carried."[68] The director believed that while in theory the effects of Meinhof's ideas were "impressive . . . they could hardly be spoken and therefore could likely not be acted on stage [*nicht spielbar*]."[69]

Vis-à-vis Meinhof, Itzenplitz adopts the position of a teacher, telling her, for example, that "the transmission of important social information must never in a film adopt the style of an opinion piece in a newspaper because in such a case, these characters would appear less than credible, even ridiculous."[70] Knowing this background, Meinhof's unease about Itzenplitz's conception for *Bambule*—steeped as it was in realism and in the conviction that while film may reflect or represent reality, it cannot itself be an agent of change—becomes plausible. Her purpose, clearly, was not to merely give the girls in the school a "text to learn" so they could "authentically embody" words that were not theirs, but to use film as a means to create a demonstration that would allow the Eichenhof residents to gain insight into what oppresses them. The film was not a work of art whose meaning is revealed only at the end of a conventionally realist narrative, but a didactic situation whose tentative merging of art and life—with the residents playing themselves and the "set" being their school—recalls the Situationist emphasis on collectivity and deliberate construction.[71] Tellingly, publisher Klaus Wagenbach recalls that Ulrike Meinhof was "not interested in getting closer to reality, but to the truth," and one would be hard put to find a better formula for what separated her from the two men—Itzenplitz and Waldmann—who ended up turning her ideas into a film.[72]

The ultimately fruitless discussions with Itzenplitz and Waldmann clearly wore Meinhof down, draining her initial enthusiasm for her film experiment and shattering her belief in film as an agent of social change. As she wrote, "while the intention may be correct, the means—a film—turned out to be wrong even as it was being made."[73] In 1970, shortly after filming had ended and around the time of Baader's liberation—an action that made Itzenplitz's fictions pale by comparison—she wrote to the director, "I do not want to be an author any more who elevates the problems of the base, for example of the proletarian youth, into the superstructure, where all that happens is that they are exhibited, that others delight in it, glorifying myself. I think the film is bullshit. That's my problem, really."[74]

CLEMENS VON WEDEMEYER, *BAMBULE* REPLAY: *RUSHES* (2012)

Ulrike Meinhof's project did not remain without its effects, even if these proved more belated than she anticipated. When Clemens von Wedemeyer created his synchronized three-channel HD film installation *Das Muster* (2012; the English title is *Rushes*), he sought to situate the production of *Bambule* within the broader continuity of twentieth-century German history. All of the three short films that make up *Das Muster* are set in Breitenau (Guxhagen), a former monastery near the city of Kassel that since the late nineteenth century had been used as an *Arbeitshaus* and a prison for beggars, vagabonds, and "lewd women."[75] Between 1933 and 1934, the site served the Nazis as what is considered their first concentration camp for political prisoners, and from 1940 to 1945 the Gestapo used it as a prison camp for German and foreign prisoners of war.[76] After the war, from 1952 on, the Breitenau complex—including the long-since-decommissioned former monastery church—became a locked reform school for adolescent girls. In 1973 the reform school was closed as a result of the efforts of the anti-reform-school campaign, and nowadays Breitenau serves as a home for psychiatric patients, as well as a memorial site (*Gedenkstätte*) for the Nazi crimes committed there, with a museum and other facilities.[77]

The three parts of *Rushes*, which its Documenta 13 installation presented on large screens arranged in a large triangle, are fictionalized twenty-seven-minute episodes from the history of Breitenau, focused on different periods in the history of the site, from its liberation by a US reconnaissance unit in 1945 to the filming of Meinhof's *Bambule* in the 1970s (here imagined to occur at Breitenau), and finally a visit to the contemporary museum by a German school group in 1990.[78] Teaching, and specifically demonstration, play a central role in the film, as becomes thematically explicit in the third segment, where a school teacher is at pains to explain the history of Breitenau to a group of school kids who lack any obvious connection or access to that past.

The film that is chronologically first in the triptych, centered on the capture of Breitenau by a US reconnaissance unit, sets the tone for the series as a whole in that it focuses on the problem of demonstration and the role played by the gestures of pointing and showing in our efforts to come to terms with the past. Throughout the episode, the US troops and especially the officer in charge, who speaks no German, need verbal translation and use multiple demonstrations and gestures of pointing in order to orient themselves in an enemy terrain with which they are not familiar, and which they do not understand. One of the vehicles for these mediations is film itself. Film is also instrumentalized by the liberated prisoners of the labor camp so they can tell their story to the world ("they are acting, you need to stop this," the US photographer complains at one point, referring to the German camp overseers).

Von Wedemeyer sets up the liberation of the camp as a dramatic reawakening of speech that takes the viewer from the silent destruction of documents and other evidence by the Germans at the beginning of the film to the Babylonic proliferation of languages after the liberation, when the camp inmates, who come from several European countries, begin to give testimony—each in their own tongue, which the others cannot understand—of what they have gone through.

At the same time, the film functions as a long series of verbal explanations and gestures of demonstration. These are not always immediately successful. "What is this place?" are the first words of the US officer in charge of the occupying unit after entering the site. When he asks his German-speaking interpreter what is going on in this former monastery, he is told that "they educate *Fremdarbeiter*, foreign workers [here]"—a reference to the Nazis' designation of Breitenau when in 1940 they reopened the site as an *Arbeitserziehungslager* (work-education camp). The officer clearly does not understand the euphemistic reference to education (*Erziehung*) in the context of a forced labor camp, and in his terse response, as a result, he simply omits that reference: "Slave labor?" (This scene unwittingly sets the tone for the next episode, focused on Meinhof's film *Bambule*, with its contention that, in Germany, education has *always* made slaves of its subjects, suggesting that from the standpoint of the late 1960s, the interpreter was indeed correct with his unintended insinuation that, at Breitenau, the Nazis acted as "educators" when they enslaved foreign prisoners of war.)

The interpreter's translation of what the Germans captured by the US troops say is one of several forms of mediation in this film; it is supplemented, in the next episode (centered on *Bambule*) by the mediating role of acting, and in the third by the efforts of the schoolteacher to instruct his students about the German past. The central instance of such mediation in the three episodes that make up von Wedemeyer's installation, however, is ostension, instances of explicit pointing and showing. In the first episode, because they all speak different languages, the protagonists have trouble understanding each other, and so nonverbal demonstration seems an appropriate way to communicate. At the beginning, one of the Breitenau staff offers to show the commanding US officer "everything," suggesting that "this is not a concentration camp," and that everything at Breitenau was "totally normal." However, a practical act of demonstration, this time by two of the liberated inmates themselves, soon proves him wrong: while searching the attic of the prison building in search of evidence, they recover a series of objects of everyday use that can easily be identified as belonging in a prison—a metal food plate, a prison blanket, an engraved spoon, prison and work IDs, a yellow Star of David, the camp's occupancy book—and hold these objects, in silence, in front of the camera. Like any demonstration, this series of gestures provides examples of something that for one reason or another eludes comprehension or definition, as if with their silent demonstration of objects directly connected to victims, and using the film camera as their imaginary witness, the inmates hope to provide the kind of illumination of the truth that words are unable to give.

Ostension can also function as a teaching method, but one that is closer to the teaching of Saint Paul, according to Badiou's account in *Saint Paul: The Foundation of Universalism* (1997), than to traditional pedagogy. According to Badiou, Saint Paul's instruction in the Gospel of Christ ("truth as universal singularity") has nothing prescriptive about it, nor does it try to persuade or enlighten anyone by offering proofs or established truths; instead, in order to spread the message of Christ, Paul "expressly rejects signs . . . as well as wisdom. . . . For Paul . . . it is precisely the absence of proof that . . . is constitutive of the Christian subject."[79] Similarly, demonstration, in *Rushes*, does not explain the events to which it makes reference; nor does it illustrate or even document them. In some cases in these films,

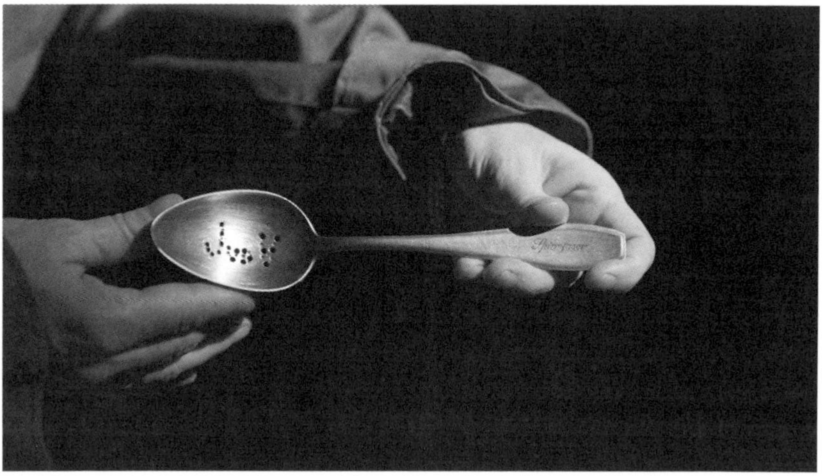

Figure 6.5 Clemens von Wedemeyer, *Muster (Rushes)*, 2012. Video still. KOW, Berlin & Galerie Jocelyn Wolff, Paris. Image courtesy of Clemens von Wedemeyer.

demonstration is not even understood by anyone other than the demonstrator himself. This is illustrated when the French prisoner René, deeply traumatized by the gruesome events he has witnessed, leads the US military photographer aside in order to demonstrate to her, using his hands and body, with a commentary in French she does not understand, the exact circumstances of the massacre the Gestapo committed among the prisoners shortly before the camp's liberation.

In another scene, René explains, again in French, Breitenau's prison architecture, using his finger to point at the various elements of a realistic model of the site, followed by more untranslated (German) commentary from von Wedemeyer and from another voice offering additional information about the camp in English. The punchline is that von Wedemeyer leaves these segments untranslated; here again, demonstration is ostensive without providing transparent proof or evidence; rather, it is the demonstrative gesture itself that is the focus of the director's concerns.

The second film in von Wedemeyer's installation recreates some elements of the production of *Bambule*, transferring the fictional events to Breitenau. The film begins with a rehearsal involving a film director (Eberhard Itzenplitz, in real life) and two young actresses (modeled on Irene and Iv in Meinhof's film) during a scene that reminds us of the events in the bunker (the "reflection room," or *Besinnungsraum*), after Irene has come back to Lindenhof to find Iv in solitary confinement. In von Wedemeyer's film, the director becomes increasingly short-tempered because the actresses do not seem to pay attention to his insistence on the technically correct pronunciation of certain parts of the dialogue. Correcting them repeatedly, he tells the young women that they should avoid speaking their lines "aus dem Bauch heraus" (from their stomachs). Where Meinhof had insisted that every word in a spoken line has equal importance, in *Rushes* the director tells the actresses that there is only *one* important word in every sentence. They become increasingly frustrated with these admonitions, arguing that what the director demands will make their lines sound unnatural and artificial, stray too far from the actual atmosphere in a reform school, and

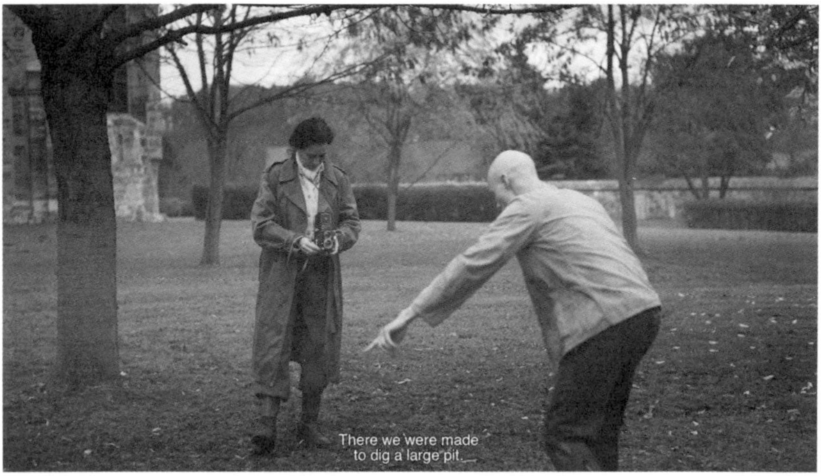

Figure 6.6 Clemens von Wedemeyer, *Muster* (*Rushes*), 2012. Video still. KOW, Berlin & Galerie Jocelyn Wolff, Paris. Image courtesy of Clemens von Wedemeyer.

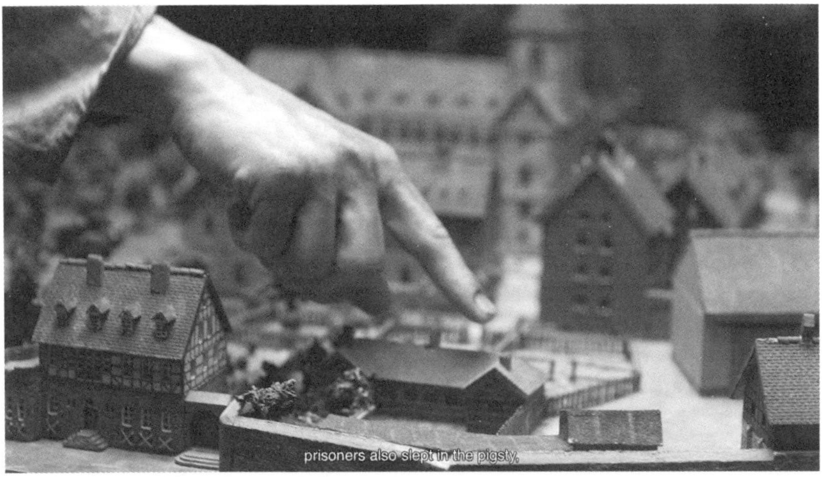

Figure 6.7 Clemens von Wedemeyer, *Muster* (*Rushes*), 2012. Video still. KOW, Berlin & Galerie Jocelyn Wolff, Paris. Image courtesy of Clemens von Wedemeyer.

make it difficult for them to decide whether their characters are meant to sound more ready to "revolt" or more like "resignation."

At one point, the conflict seems to escalate as the young actresses (literally) turn the table on the director and direct the film's lines ("If you give in, they're happy that they screwed you up") at him, as if they were staging their own internal *bambule*, and strengthening an impression one has from the scene's very beginning: namely, that von Wedemeyer is less interested in a simple restaging of the production of Meinhof's film than in the juxtaposition of two distinct conceptions of critical filmmaking, as represented by Itzenplitz and Meinhof, respectively. On the one hand, Itzenplitz insists on the need to use actors for the film's lead roles ("the characters would seem ridiculous if they spoke lines they are incapable of thinking themselves"). Itzenplitz also believes in the efficacy of technique and the kind of rational self-reflection that Jürgen Habermas advocated since the late 1960s, when he severely criticized the radical German student movement for its irrationality and proclivity for "immediate gratification," including in his critique of their rejection of history and symbolic mediation, which appeared self-defeating and irrational to Habermas.[80] When the director in von Wedemeyer's film insists that only one word in every spoken sentence carry meaning, he clearly displays the kind of faith in language's ability to be transparent to the ideas and intentions of its speaker that is fundamental to Habermas's critique as well.

In Ulrike Meinhof's case, on the other hand, her distrust of representation in film and elsewhere; her idea that only if the girls played themselves could other students in the school be inspired with the spark of revolt; and finally, her belief that *Bambule* should function as a form of agitation all testify to her frustration with the aesthetic mediations and faith in (self-) reflection favored by Itzenplitz. Meinhof's absence from the set and Irene and Iv's search for her ("Is she coming today?")—not least so she might give the actresses guidance on how to interpret their roles—is as much thematized by von Wedemeyer as the tensions between the film director and the absent Meinhof. At one point, the director (representing Itzenplitz) charges that "she [Meinhof] cannot reformulate everything [in the *Bambule* script] just because something comes up in the news. Film is all about separation"—a statement that pinpoints the differences between Meinhof and Itzenplitz as being rooted in a conflicting attitude toward the possibility of film inciting social revolt. For Meinhof, as was the case with Farocki and Holger Meins, film was an instrument designed to intervene directly in ongoing struggles, while for the director—whose chauvinism and condescension toward the lower classes are palpable in von Wedemeyer's film—only the mediation of aesthetic form can ensure that art rises above the vicissitudes of daily politics, a position Meinhof would no doubt have qualified as idealist.

The students' reaction seems to prove Meinhof right. During a visit to the school by local teenagers aspiring to become extras in the film, the resident girls, who want to play themselves, feel that they are being denied access to the buffet provided for the visitors. The girls start protesting against this, telling the visitors that "they also want a piece of the cake": "If our film in the reform school cannot even change that, then what is it good for?"

This rhetorical question accurately reflects Meinhof's (rather than Itzenplitz's) thinking, inasmuch as it was Meinhof, not Itzenplitz, who expected the filming of *Bambule* to function as a form of agitation, with direct emancipatory results for the school's residents. Shortly afterward, a girl talking to the actress playing Irene questions the actors' ability to portray the reform school residents accurately ("In a film you cannot speak the way we do in the reform school. That's why it sounds wrong even if it's correct"). She also wonders why it was necessary to make the film at all, other than "to increase [the participants'] glory," since it does not actually change anything in the lives of those inside the school.

In this second part of his installation, von Wedemeyer hints that the filmed revolt against the system of reform school education narrated in *Bambule* is itself enveloped by a repressive class system, and that questioning the education system cannot proceed without questioning that other

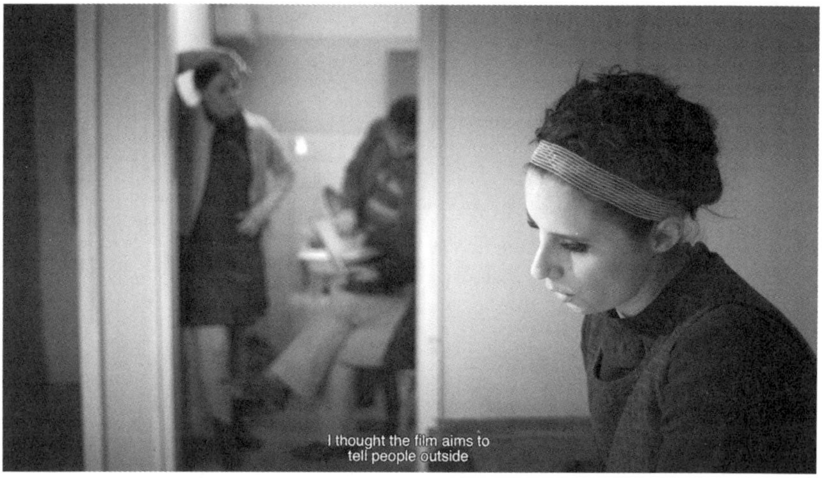

Figure 6.8 Clemens von Wedemeyer, *Muster* (*Rushes*), 2012. Video still. KOW, Berlin & Galerie Jocelyn Wolff, Paris. Image courtesy of Clemens von Wedemeyer.

system too, including the director's (Itzenplitz's) patriarchal authoritarianism, whose power remains intact as long as the two classes of girls—the school's residents on the one hand and the actors on the other—do not unite in solidarity. This unity, however, appears to occur at the end when, back at the school, the school resident and the actress who plays Irene restage the violent demolition of the dormitory, carrying their joint revolt to an unexpected end: breaking through the wall of the film set, they step into the space behind it, in the process demolishing the imaginary boundary that separated film from reality—an action very much in the spirit of Ulrike Meinhof.

The third episode of von Wedemeyer's triptych also begins with a lesson: it's 1994, the year when *Bambule* was finally shown on German television, and a teacher is in the process of showing his students Meinhof's film. His introduction focuses on Breitenau—its architecture and evolution from a nineteenth-century prison to the present-day psychiatric ward—and also touches on the campaign against reform schools (*Heimkampagne*) of the 1960s and on the trauma of (German) education more generally. And once again, this lesson, which the students follow distractedly ("Why are you here?" the teacher asks them), demonstrates more than anything the difficulties the youngsters have in understanding the past under the watchful eye of a teacher who seeks full control over it. Subsequently, as in part two, von Wedemeyer tells the story of the students' struggle to liberate themselves from their teacher's pedagogical regime, much as Meinhof had done in the late 1960s. At the beginning of the film, one of the students gets up from his seat and leans over the screen to watch *Bambule* with his head upside down, with the film's images mirrored on the surface of his eyeball. The scene not only recalls Bazon Brock's 1972 Aachen lecture given while standing on his head; it also has the effect of unshackling the young spectator, if only for a moment, from the teacher's control.

In another telling scene, one of the girls lies down on the wooden bench in the reflection room of the former reform school (where *Bambule* was filmed)—repeating Irene's gesture in Meinhof's film, and also the second

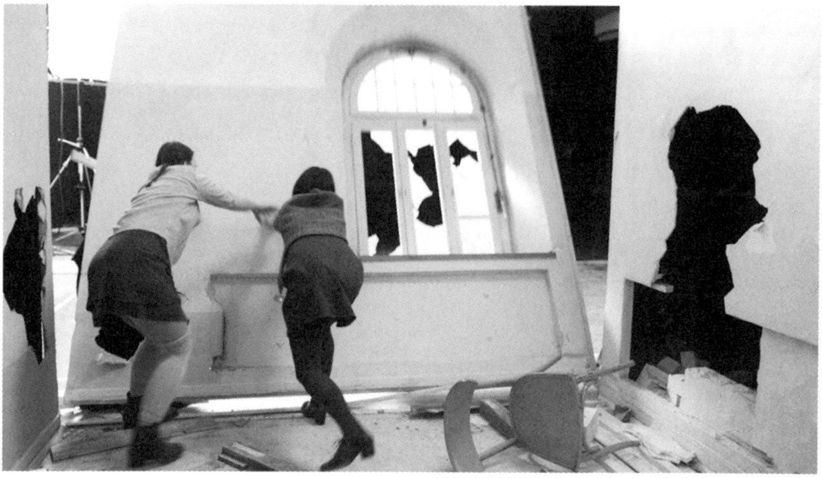

Figure 6.9 Clemens von Wedemeyer, *Muster* (*Rushes*), 2012. Video still. KOW, Berlin & Galerie Jocelyn Wolff, Paris. Image courtesy of Clemens von Wedemeyer.

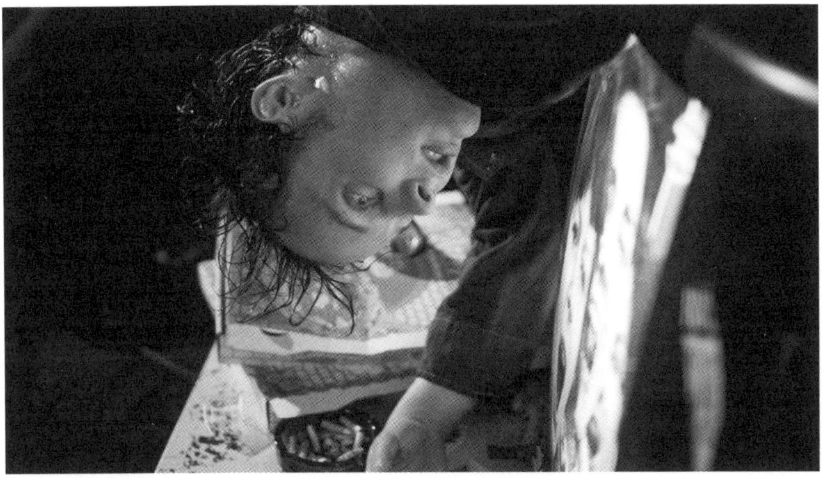

Figure 6.10 Clemens von Wedemeyer, *Muster* (*Rushes*), 2012. Video still. KOW, Berlin & Galerie Jocelyn Wolff, Paris. Image courtesy of Clemens von Wedemeyer.

part of *Rushes* when the actress playing Irene tries out the reflection room under the watchful eye of a pedagogue—only to be told sternly by her teacher that this is not the correct way of "making present" (*vergegenwärtigen*) the past. Yet the students in the third episode of the film develop their own way of researching history. In one scene, they run their fingers along the walls of one of the rooms in the former prison, moving their lips as they seek to decipher the illegible words ("der Führer"). Soon after that, one of them tells the teacher that they would never want to "become like you."

Rushes echoes Ulrike Meinhof's doubts about the possibility for art to act politically, and for revolutionary change more generally. At the same time, by adopting the perspective of the Holocaust victims (episode #1), the young actresses (episode #2), or the students (#3), von Wedemeyer also hints that maybe it is still possible to act politically, even as the horizon for these actions is no longer revolutionary change on a broad scale but smaller interventions in a neoliberal system immune to the more sweeping revolutionary goals of the expanded 1960s.

7

INSTRUCTIONS FOR SEEING (BAZON BROCK, WŁODZIMIERZ BOROWSKI)

With its educational turn during the 1960s, art routinely crossed the boundary with non-art, as teach-ins, action readings, political street theater, and so forth all functioned in a zone that included elements of both. A high-minded effort was under way to generate new forms of receptivity that would turn an art audience from reactive, unreflective consumers into actively conscious co-producers. Bazon Brock shared this ambition, as seen in his action lectures, public action teachings, and art demonstrations, but especially in his idea of instituting "art reception classes," culminating in his first Visitor School (*Besucherschule*) at the embattled Documenta 4 in 1968—the same year he suggested to Joseph Beuys that they cofound an anti-art academy.[1] A self-declared "artist without artworks," mercurial inventor of "agit pop," gratingly self-enlightened "instructor of the people" (*Volksaufklärer*), and early collaborator with Friedensreich Hundertwasser, Wolf Vostell, and Joseph Beuys, Brock developed a practice consisting of didactic actions that included the notorious "lectures standing on his head"—such as the one he performed at the 1964 Festival der Neuen Kunst in Aachen mentioned at the beginning of this book—that contributed greatly to the notoriety of happenings in the conservative West German press at the time.[2]

With his plans for the 1968 Visitor School—which, due to a lack of funds, could be realized only in a much-reduced form—Brock brushed against the grain of an exhibition of which he (and many others) was highly critical, not only for its refusal to include action art, Fluxus, and happenings, but also for casting a primarily retrospective, "documenting" eye on contemporary art production.[3] Instead, the *Besucherschule*—an initiative Brock would develop further at subsequent documentas in 1972, 1977, 1982, 1987, and 1992—focused on the exhibition's instructional aspects (*Vermittlung*), developing a (controversial) perspective on curatorship as inherently didactic, and arguing that the reception of contemporary art needs theory in order to be successful. While in 1968 such a position was irreconcilable with the more established view of documenta as a "temporary museum," in its next (1972) incarnation—Harald Szeemann's epochal Documenta 5—it would advance to being at the very core of the show's curatorial concept.[4]

Brock traces the history of the Documenta 4 Visitor School to the year 1959 when over two days, with Hundertwasser and Herbert Schuldt, he drew an endless bar in the form of a continuous line along the walls, doors, and windows of an artist studio at Hamburg's University of Fine Arts ("The Hamburg Line"), until the university administration forbade the action. Conceived as a kind of didactic happening somewhere between an academic seminar and museum pedagogy, the 1968 *Besucherschule*, similarly, "barred" Documenta 4 in an action that hovered somewhere between an alternative art academy and an information bureau. Brock's original plan had called for every visitor to be instructed individually by Brock himself, then by an actor, and finally by a psychiatrist before entering the exhibition. Once inside, so the original planning went, a walkie-talkie would allow visitors to continue to be in touch with Brock and his team, receiving more information that would help them process what they saw in the show. In the end, most of these ambitious plans went unrealized. And while in many ways Brock's ideas for the Visitor School preempted aspects of what today goes by the name of museum pedagogy, his ideas clearly went beyond teaching documenta visitors how to better understand the artworks they encountered in the show; Brock also—in a country without any serious art publications—wanted to enable the public to *judge* what they saw: "During the . . . Visitors School at Documenta 4 (Kassel 1968) I tried to . . . facilitate the visitors' marathon through the contemporary art scene by adding a few refreshing stops. One of them consisted in the invitation to respond to the following prompt when standing in front of a painting: 'This painting talks to me.'"[5] Brock would ask visitors questions about their attitude toward the exhibition, and what it reminded them of. Gesticulating and pointing to different artworks, the artist would then proceed to mention common clichés about contemporary art that he also presented on large pieces of cardboard or written on the walls of the classroom. Following this, he would criticize these clichés and continue the discussion by adding his own ideas.[6]

Understanding documenta literally—the word is derived from the Latin *docere* (to teach), and originally refers to a lesson or a written instruction—the 1968 *Besucherschule* set itself up as a kind of counterexhibition: not the stage for consumption and retrospective commemoration decried by progressive artists at the show's infamous press conference, but a training ground for tactile, active (hence critical) seeing.[7] As a didactic enterprise, the Visitor School was designed to show visitors how seeing, or indeed any form of art reception, might produce understanding, yet without preempting the results of that process. Brock did see the Visitor School as a school, yet without implying that what this school teaches is objectively true: "These are not schools where you learn what is objectively given but rather how to free yourself from the objective constrains of what is considered real [*das Vorgegebene*]."[8] In other words, while he was optimistic about Enlightenment ideals regarding the possibility (and the necessity) of understanding, Brock avoided any normative account of how such understanding might be achieved.

With his didactic approach to curating, Brock was in good company in the expanded 1960s. In progressive curatorship of the decade, efforts to activate the viewer often used reproductions accompanied by extensive notes and commentary, disrupting the reification of originals and the fetishization of art's objecthood. For example, in a series of "studio exhibitions" at the Staatliche Museen Preußischer Kulturbesitz in Berlin, Renato Guttuso's painting *The Banquet: Picasso and His Characters* (1973), a work that includes representations of various works by Picasso, was joined by framed reproductions of these works positioned next to Guttuso's canvas, a gesture designed to activate in the viewer a reading of Guttuso's and Picasso's work that didn't rest with passive contemplation.[9]

The idea of a didactic exhibition practice using reproductions to highlight the connections between seeing and learning, and encouraging the active disposition of visual perception over passive contemplation, has a predecessor in the famous *Didactic Exhibition* at the former Zagreb City Gallery of Contemporary Art, a traveling show (1957–1967) designed to teach the Yugoslav public about contemporary abstract art.

Didactic Exhibition was made up of ninety-two panels that demonstrated the history of abstract art using photographs, typescripts of art historical texts and quotations from writings by abstract artists, and reproductions from books and the press.[10] While the show serves as an early example of museum education that raised important questions related to canon formation, informed spectatorship, and the relationship between original and copy, it also redoubled, as Jasna Jakšić has noted, the didactic impulse implicit in modernism itself: "The didactic aim of modern art to win over and educate its public was often embedded in the works themselves."[11] Not coincidentally, *Didactic Exhibition* opened with a rendering of Alfred Barr's famous diagram of modern art, which is itself an eloquent reminder of the didactic nature of Barr's take on modernism, whose target was the educated art consumer.[12]

Like the curators of *Didactic Exhibition*, Brock conceived of the process of art reception as a form of labor, and hence as a process that was susceptible to correction and improvement; thus, the Visitor School could serve as an outlet for bringing about such correction.[13] Such thinking was

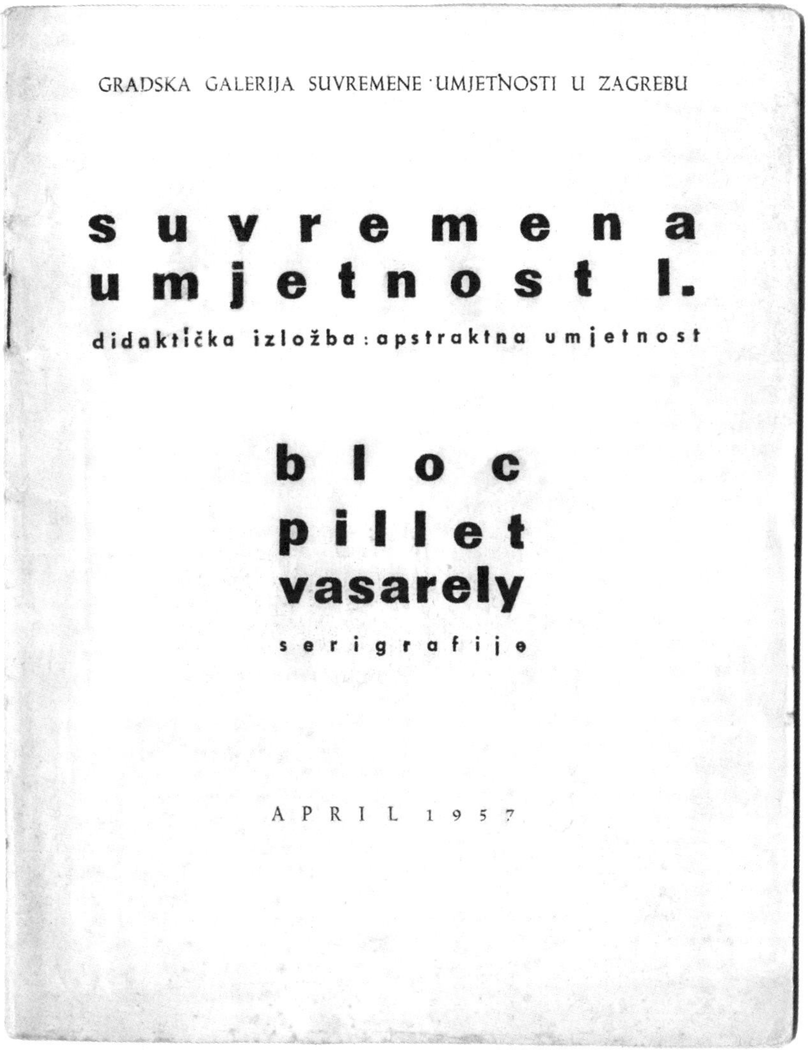

Figure 7.1 *Didactic Exhibition: Abstract Art* (Zagreb City Gallery of Contemporary Art, 1957), catalogue front cover. Photo courtesy of Marinko Sudac Collection.

broadly aligned with the materialist aesthetics of the New Left and, even more broadly, with Marx's conviction that lasting change is the product of a practice understood as a radical change of context. By conceiving of art reception as work, Brock takes labor out of the context of revolutionary politics and injects it into a subjective context where it mediates a private encounter with art. The point here was not, however, for viewers to simply reproduce or recreate the work of art for themselves, but rather to ask to what degree art and aesthetic theory can be transferred productively into the visitor's own life practice.

Brock produced an example of the kind of "seeing training" he had in mind in another project, his theatrical performance *The Theater as a Citizens' School, or "May I Explain This to You, Ma'am?"* (1968). At a theater in Frankfurt, the artist presented a lecture performance while the stage curtain behind him revealed the lower legs and feet of a group of people—both actors and spectators whom Brock had invited to stand on the stage—otherwise hidden from the audience's view. Viewers had to deduce what was happening on the stage from the position and movements of the feet—inferring what they could not see based on what was visible. In Brock's view, this process helped viewers develop a sense for the importance of actions and events that did not, as is normally the case in the theater, visibly occur at the center of the stage, which in turn helped reinforce the bond between seeing and thinking.[14]

The understanding of art reception as an active production process that alters both the role of the recipient—from passive consumer to co-producer—and a view of the artwork that stresses its open qualities as much as its malleability during its reception had already revolutionized the way literary scholars thought about reading a text.[15] In the mid-1960s, David Bleich developed what came to be known as subjective reader response criticism, which assumed that the reading process constitutes the text in the reader's mind and that this dynamic process can be analyzed through their subjective responses.[16] With their focus on pedagogy and the reader, Bleich's ideas are comparable to Brock's Visitor School, where documenta assumes the role of the text in Bleich's model, functioning as an experimental relay station for the viewers' responses and reactions as much as it functions, more fundamentally, as a school that helps them develop their ability to see. As Brock noted in his commentary on *Theater as a Citizens' School*,

> to train the public's receptiveness to art is not something we can ask of the producers, even though some artists have begun to develop their objects in such a way that they appear to be materializations of their process of reception. [However,] the majority of producers . . . remains stuck in a didacticism that tends to obstruct reception. Such didacticism is designed to facilitate the addressee's access to the production offered to him or her. . . . Unfortunately, art criticism, too, is for the most part beholden to an understanding of didacticism that considers playful assimilation the most appropriate form of reception. It criticizes exhibitions where reception is presumed to be an exhausting kind of labor. In truth, such assimilation can only proceed in analogy with the process of production.[17]

Brock makes a poignant distinction between successful and unsuccessful didacticism, arguing that successful exhibitions do not make the process of art reception easier but, on the contrary, make it more difficult by revealing the degree to which reception requires labor. Yet it is also true that, as Bernd Blaschke has argued, to view labor as the *only* form of art reception would mean to neglect other forms of receptivity not related to work: "Doesn't his [Brock's] insistence on meaning . . . and on reception as labor imply the restriction of aesthetic experience to a very limited part of what is aesthetically possible?"[18] Still, Brock's idea of a "complicating" didacticism that does not merely aim to make things easier for the exhibition visitor—instead training them to develop their abilities to understand and judge contemporary art—provides a fitting response to models of reception driven by expediency and ready consumption.

Since the early 1960s, Brock had referred to his practice as that of a *Vermittler*, a term that can mean both "mediator" (say, in a conflict) and "teacher" or "instructor" (as in *Sprachvermittler*, meaning "language instructor"). In Marxism, *Vermittlung*—derived from *Mitte*, meaning "center" or "medium"—functions as a crucial link between production and understanding. According to Marx, humans are capable of understanding reality only to the extent that they (re-)make and (re-)produce that reality in a process that mediates (*vermittelt*) between human history, on the one hand, and nature, on the other.[19] For Adorno, too, *Vermittlung* had a crucial role to play, mediating between human understanding and its object. As Brian O'Connor has argued, in Adorno's theory, we experience an (art) object in ever richer ways by discovering (but not ultimately uncovering) its complexities:

> Adorno describes the mediating (*vermittelnd*) role played by the subject as the "how," and by the object as the "what" in this relation. As the "how," the subject is in the business of articulating and conceptualizing the object, whereas the object, as the "what," is that to which the subject must adjust its concepts. Because of this process of articulation and adjustment, the relation of subject and object cannot conclude in the identity of the two. Adorno describes it as follows: subject and object "constitute one another as much as—by virtue of such constitution—they depart from each other."[20]

Adorno reminds us that *Vermittlung* changes dynamically with the object's perception, so that the latter's protocol has to be continuously adjusted as the object is being progressively discovered; this idea not only presumes that the object resists instant recognition by being "difficult"—preempting any lasting identificatory reconciliation—but in this way also blocks the progressive integration of cognition and object that had been a hallmark of Hegelian thought.

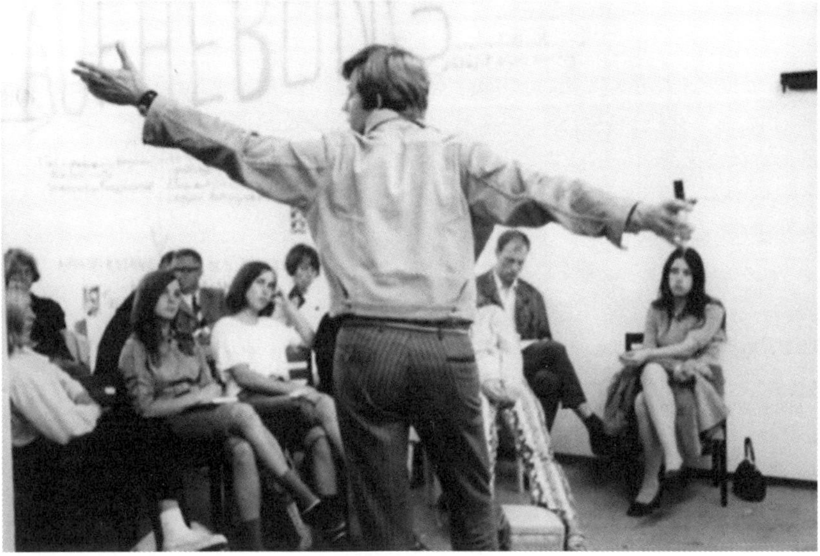

Figure 7.2 Bazon Brock, *Visitor School* (*Besucherschule*), Documenta 4, Kassel, 1968. Image courtesy of Bazon Brock. Photo: Estate of Hans Puttnies.

In the way that it creates a post-Hegelian context for making art reception difficult, Brock's *Besucherschule* functions as a clear antipode to radical theories of affect and spontaneity that cast scorn on *any* form of mediation. A case in point is the Situationist Raoul Vaneigem, who in his 1967 *The Revolution of Everyday Life* (*Traité de savoir-vivre à l'usage des jeunes générations*) advocated a kind of affect-driven spontaneity that denied *Vermittlung* any role in the creative process. In fact, Vaneigem associates *Vermittlung* with falsehood and ideology ("the communication of the inauthentic, the non-lived") and sharply distinguishes it from what he calls agitation, defining the latter as a use of signs that is poetic because it does not rely on difference. While for Vaneigem *Vermittlung* appears on the side of form, agitation is on the side of revolution (immediacy, authenticity). Vaneigem's model poet-agitator teaches affectively, and without any apparent recourse to mediation through sign use, including words: "Let our model be the agitator, who invests his words and signs so forcefully with living reality that all the others are pulled along in their wake: an exemplary repurposing of language."[21] Given his opposition to *Vermittlung*, Vaneigem had nothing but disdain for Lenin's didacticism ("The revolution as 'explained' by gunfire to the Kronstadt sailors . . . that too was Leninism. Not theory but ideology"),[22] and he did not share the idea of aesthetic experience as a form of prolepsis; instead, to Vaneigem, all mediation was by definition aligned with power. Only "spontaneous" poetry and theory could offer a way out: "Power is confirmed in its function of grand mediator. Spontaneous poetry is *antimediation* par excellence."[23] Vaneigem here invokes a totalized present from which all differentiation, temporal and otherwise, has vanished: "What I want is not a succession of instants but one huge moment. A totality that is lived in the innocence of duration."[24] Nothing could be further removed from the New Left's understanding of a world that is mediated through and through.

The second iteration of Brock's 1968 *Besucherschule*, at Documenta 5 (1972), was canceled as a live event due to a budget shortfall. The school was replaced with a programmable, modular image wall entitled *Audio-Visual*

Preface (*Audio-Visuelles Vorwort*), conceived by Karl Heinz Krings, an expert in didactic multimedia systems and Brock's colleague at the University of Fine Arts in Hamburg, where Brock held a professorship at the time. It consisted of twelve stacked standardized cubes, the screens measuring ninety by sixty centimeters. Each of these cubes was served by two electronically programmed slide projectors, so that two thousand slides could be shown at any one time, with the transitions manipulated to varying audiovisual effects. Apart from text and images, diagrams and symbols guided the visitor through the information presented, thus foregrounding the system's didactic functions. The looped slide presentation was supplemented, four times a day, by eighty-minute, live "mediations" (*Vermittlungsveranstaltungen*) during which Brock sought to explain Documenta 5's ambitions to a broader public in a format that wavered between deadpan academicism and Dadaist anti-art attitudes, with Brock incarnating a role somewhere between an overly zealous exhibition guide and a garrulous university professor.

Documenta 5 was the first documenta to operate based on a unifying theme—"Image Worlds Today—Questioning Reality."[25] In line with the third and final concept for the show that was drawn up in March 1971 by members of the "group of realizers" (*Realisatorengruppe*)—including Harald Szeemann, Brock, and Jean-Christophe Ammann[26]—the documenta combined the display of art objects with large numbers of non-art images. These non-art images were drawn from a series of what the organizers referred to as "image worlds" (*Bildwelten*), including press and propaganda imagery, religious images, and images created by the mentally ill; as Szeemann explained, all of them acted "as substitutes for all the images in the world."[27] Although Brock's own role in the conceptualization of Documenta 5 is often played down in comparison with Szeemann's, his input was not unimportant. Borrowing freely from Saussure, Adorno, and others, Brock argued that documenta needed to help visitors to sharpen their critical faculties so they could successfully grasp the different claims on reality represented by the images in the show. This repositioning couldn't have been more momentous: from a museum-style survey (Documenta 4) to a focus on *Vermittlung* and the analysis of the late-capitalist mediasphere (Documenta 5), moving past the 1960s obsession with false consciousness. The text that accompanied the *Audio-Visual Preface* in the catalogue—a heavy looseleaf tome resembling a seminar folder, with hundreds of pages—explained under the title "A New Image War" (*Bilderkrieg*) how images from different areas of the public sphere (film, advertising, etc.) relate (to) reality, based on the relationship between three categories referred to as the "reality of the image" (*Abbildwirklicheit*), the "representation of reality" (*Wirklichkeitsabbildung*), and "the identity or non-identity of image and representation" (*Identität und Nichtidentität von Abbildung und Abgebildetem*).[28] Fundamental to all three is the idea that in order to understand images and their impact, one has to account for the claims on reality made by the media technologies that produced them in the first place.

The organizers' original (unrealized) plans for the technological mediation of information at Documenta 5 had gone beyond the *Audio-Visual Preface*, and included a "kinetic catalogue" in the form of monitors at various points in the exhibition, as well as an electronic "Information Center" whose purpose would have been "viewer participation" (already a cliché at the time).[29] Brock himself had originally hoped to integrate his wall into what he referred to as an "automated teaching machine for large (visitor) groups" (*Großgruppenlehrautomat*), including an answering service. The idea for such an interactive teaching machine, functioning as a kind automated museum pedagogue, needs to be placed in the broader context of the discussions around the relations between technology and pedagogy during the 1960s, as well as the idea of "programmed" learning and the role of the computer in it.[30]

The primary task of the image wall in the *Preface* was, according to the catalogue, "to offer a generally accessible introduction to the theme of documenta 5" through the projected texts and images, which functioned as an automated didactic tool: "Automatic multi-projection slide screens are being used wherever information needs to be processed didactically and where that information is being taught [*vermittelt*] independently of time and without input from the user."[31]

The *Preface* slide show allowed viewers to see not only the works in the exhibition but also those that had not been chosen for inclusion; in this way, Brock argued, visitors were in a unique position to judge the show from the curator's perspective, since it's generally the curator's privilege to view an exhibition from the perspective of both what is present in the show and what has not been chosen to be exhibited.[32] Earlier, in connection with his 1968 *Besucherschule*, Brock had argued that only if they were able to compare what was on display in the exhibition with what had not been included in it would viewers be able to competently judge the show: "The viewer has to be able to judge how the show might have looked differently. In any case, the knowledge of the relationship of what is shown with what is not shown is the basis of all judgment."[33]

The relationship between what was shown and what was not shown in the exhibition was mediated effectively by the fact that the Visitor School presented all of its material—chosen and nonchosen artworks alike—exclusively in the form of slides. Brock felt that by remediating the documenta's artworks in this way—presenting everything in a fully standardized format—the images in the show would become homogenized to a degree where their visual or aesthetic attributes—individual style, technique, expression—would no longer be recognizable, or at least greatly diminished. Stripped of their differences in this way, the works would thus be left to function on a discursive level alone, with words and theory—the Visitor School itself—providing the commentary that would allow viewers to distinguish them from each other, attribute meaning to them, integrate them into art history, and so on.

The use of slides as part of art historical demonstrations goes back to Heinrich Wölfflin's early twentieth-century use of an electric magic lantern (sciopticon) for the double projection of slides during his lectures at Berlin University, and to art historian Hermann Grimm before him. Indeed, Wölfflin's use of black-and-white slides served a purpose similar to the one outlined by Brock for his Visitor School: to explain art by deemphasizing its visual attributes. The motivation behind this, as Dan Karlholm has noted, was that "in order to explain and highlight the element of art in art, art is insufficient. The art-less facsimile of the black-and-white photograph is better suited for this purpose, for it transforms the overwhelmingly nuanced and materially captivating art object into a flat binary system of formal contrasts."[34] Here the material attributes of the artwork are an obstacle to distilling its meaning as part of a didactic exercise. Zeynep Çelik Alexander has called Wölfflin's lectures "a dress rehearsal for Walter Benjamin's artwork essay as well as the Frankfurt School's famous critique of mass media."[35]

With its focus on the relationship between visible and invisible objects, Brock's automized *Preface* supplements the manifested show—the works exhibited—with a virtual dimension that allows viewers to contemplate Documenta 5's curatorial concept from a position deliberately distanced from the exhibition space itself.[36] From this argument flowed the idea, explained both in Marxist philosopher Hans-Heinz Holz's catalogue essay—a book-length treatise entitled "A Critical Theory of Aesthetic Signs"—and by Brock himself, that in the postformal age, art needs theory in order to be fully understood. As Holz maintains, without theory, seeing remains caught in phenomenological reductionism: "An exhibition program that views the commentary on what is being presented in the show as an integral part of the exhibition departs from the premise that the immediate presence of the work of art in our perception may not be sufficient for understanding what the work means."[37] Arguing that seeing needs to be transformed from being purely receptive and passive to becoming more dynamic and tactile, Holz notes that this can occur, both practically and theoretically, as part of a learning process (in line with the slogan "Learn How to See Better With Documenta"): "Seeing can be learnt, not only by doing but also and especially through enlightenment [*Aufklärung*]."[38] The key to such learning was the idea that theory was the discursive second wheel of the curatorial process. In a similar vein, Brock himself argued that only theory was capable of mediating between art and other areas of life: "art after documenta 5 means then: the dependency of art production and art reception on theory has become irrefutable. If you do not want to view contemporary art as a random assembly of meaningless fragments of a process that . . . cannot be explained, then you need to ask to what extent art production . . . as a technique of living . . . can be applied to other areas of life."[39] For Brock and Holz, only theory could help dissolve the bourgeois attachment to art as a form of solipsistic consumption, creating a critical public instead: "Without theory it will not work, if art is to be considered not as a private culinary experience but as part of the public . . . ; the artwork that . . . becomes an object of public viewing [*Anschauung*] . . . is from the beginning a res publica [*eine öffentliche Sache*]."[40] This may also explain why they chose for the *Preface* a form of presentation—the centralized image wall—that transformed the exhibition into a form of expanded cinema with a collective audience.

Brock's obsession with *Vermittlung* resulted in some differences with documenta's chief curator.[41] In his introductory remarks for the catalogue, Szeemann mentions two key positions he had to reconcile, one focused on artists and the autonomous presentation of their works, and the other on the didactic need to teach visitors "how to see," the latter identified with what Szeemann refers to as a "School for Seeing" (*Sehschule*):

> The beginning of the planning for [Documenta] 5 fell into a time when . . . the doubts about the art world became bigger and bigger. During the two years of preparation two extreme solutions were suggested, one of them oriented on the artist, the other on the exhibition visitor. Both were impractical in pure form. Creating a documenta-as-event [*Ereignisdocumenta*] only would have delivered the institution over to the whims of a few, while creating only a School of Seeing [*Sehschule*] would

> have implied creating a seminar that gives up on the originals as events [*Ereignishaftigkeit der Originale*].[42]

Well aware of the conventional expectations brought to Documenta 5 by the public and the artists alike, Szeemann was at pains to dispel any sense that his show might put theory above the artists. While he pointedly refers to it as a *Vermittlungsort*, Szeemann was careful not to overemphasize the didacticism in his show. As he commented in 2001, "if there had only been the didactic element in Documenta 5, we would probably not be here today if it had not at the same time also been an event for the senses."[43] This statement may remind us of the fact that in May 1972, a group of New York artists, buoyed by the recent formation of the Art Workers Coalition in the United States, had affirmed the right of artists to challenge the curator's ideas, threatening to boycott documenta if their work was "exhibited in a classification without the artist [sic] consent."[44]

It was with Brock's *Audio-Visual Preface* and Beuys's *Bureau for the Organization of Direct Democracy by Popular Vote* that the didactic element came to the fore most directly at Documenta 5.[45] Similar tendencies were gaining ground elsewhere, and by the mid-1970s progressive curators fully embraced the idea of didactic exhibitions.[46] When in 1976 the director of the public Kunstsammlung Nordrhein Westfalen in Düsseldorf, Werner Schmalenbach, curated an exhibition with ten recently acquired paintings by Pablo Picasso, he called it *10 x Picasso: A Didactic Exhibition to Better Understand His Art. Images, Photographs, Texts.* In the show and in the black-and-white catalogue that accompanied it, every original painting was accompanied by banners and display panels with information about the artwork "written in simple phrases that took a demonstrative second place to the art."[47] This didactic commentary deliberately—if temporarily—aimed to disrupt the visitor's process of seeing. As Schmalenbach wrote,

> It is not a matter primarily of aesthetic experience but of understanding, cognizing, and even learning. The visual perception

> of the originals . . . is being accompanied by reading, and this means: seeing is by no means only strengthened, it is also consciously being disrupted. To be sure, in art, what counts is seeing, and again seeing, and some kind of knowledge. However, in our time, the desire to be informed has increased to such a degree that we have to take this into account, at least in the form of temporary exhibitions. . . . Perhaps the best way to see is through learning.[48]

Schmalenbach emphasizes the need to be informed in order to fully understand art, based on the assumption that even the most immediate aesthetic experience is mediated, and that reading and seeing complement each other, even where the experience seems to be purely visual: "If we assume, as I do, that in front of a painting we should basically forget all knowledge, then we can infer from this that you can only forget what you have."[49]

For all the disruption caused by the inclusion of non-art imagery in Documenta 5, one thing the inclusion of these image worlds did not do, perhaps surprisingly, is to expand documenta's geographic reach, which remained firmly restricted to Western Europe and North America. In fact, while Holz acknowledges that "the shrinking of distances corresponds to the internationalization of artistic expression," he then unapologetically reduces this internationalism to a universal Western "cultural style," brandishing contemporary art in regions other than Western Europe, to the extent that it is not built on a domestic vernacular, as a misguided imitation. Holz's verdict on art from Eastern Europe is particularly revealing in this regard:

> For a while it appeared as if the Eastern European popular democracies might find new approaches in their national—including folkloristic—traditions, this expectation was not met. . . . The popular democracies have only paid attention to Western examples . . . [art] production remains imitative and

> dependent on its originals—a phase of catching up that operates with formal languages with the sole aim of mastering them, not in order to distil from them new, innovative possibilities. What comes from the countries of Eastern Europe remains provincial and in a certain measure belated.[50]

The selection of artists for Documenta 5 clearly bore the stamp of such Cold War-inspired reasoning; while the inclusion of Socialist Realism as a *Bildwelt* failed after years of trying to secure the cooperation of the Soviet bureaucracy, no other Eastern European artists were included in the show.[51]

As Documenta 5 made clear, already by the 1970s, the "1960s" had ossified into a (Western) image world that included popular iconic photographs of the Apollo mission, the Vietnam War and the protests against it, or the images of the street demonstrations against the shah of Iran in West Berlin. Consequently, the *Besucherschule* commentary looked at the preceding decade as a more or less closed era when "art and social consciousness" were in harmony with each other ("epochal uniformity," as Brock calls it) because both still arguably had the same understanding of which images counted as legitimate (progressive, nonmanipulated) representations of reality, and which did not. This view of the 1960s is complemented by a critique of pop art and its synthesizing transfer of commodities into the realm of high culture: "Mass culture, elevated to the level of high culture by artists . . . was used in its new incarnation as advertising. Industrially produced commodities which artists had integrated into art practice . . . became all the more desirable."[52] Such late-capitalist circularity occluded the possibility of critique occupying the neutral ground formerly occupied by (high) culture.

As Documenta 5 argued, by the 1970s the social and political consensus that characterized the 1960s was subjected to a thorough and irreversible process of fragmentation, resulting in the loss of any universally legitimizing narrative. This development was accompanied by continuous processes whereby society fragments "into many partial areas and systems. There is no meaning to life that would be applicable and relevant for all those different social areas. . . . Every area has to create for itself a foundation for life and action. Its formulation, however, cannot occur in words alone; it has to be understood as a new definition of what constitutes reality."[53] The postmodern pitch of this argument was designed to explain the relative independence of the various *Bildwelten* on display at Documenta 5, theorizing an age where images were not only becoming more and more pervasive, but where the relationship between them and the reality they purported to represent could no longer be taken for granted, calling for a new type of cognitive model. As Brock argued: "We have to learn how to think in images. At school we only learn the word-based languages. The image languages remain unexplored and are relegated to vague assumptions. That is all the more troubling given that already today we perceive our world more through images (television, film, newspaper, advertising, decoration, design) than through word-based languages. The Visitor School wants to make a contribution to the learning of image-based languages [*Bildsprachen*]."[54] Brock was presciently convinced that our ability to judge images based on objectifiable criteria—he called it "image literacy"—was an essential necessity in the modern world, suggesting that Documenta 5 needed to assume functions that reached beyond autonomous art display into image pedagogy.

WŁODZIMIERZ BOROWSKI: THE AUDIENCE AS FAILURE

I want to place Brock's Visitor Schools and his Documenta 5 *Preface*, which he saw as an artwork as much as an instrument for the relay of information, in dialogue with the more aporetic efforts by Polish artist Włodzimierz Borowski to use demonstration to engage with, and define, his elusive audience in the late 1960s. Artists in Eastern Europe clearly shared their Western colleagues' interest in defining the dynamic relationship between the various image worlds that defined the realities they lived in, even as these image worlds differed dramatically between East and West. In

Borowski's as much as in Brock's work, didactic demonstration plays a central role, even when the social and political contexts in which the artists operated were broadly speaking incompatible. Interested early on in international art tendencies, Borowski—as was common among experimental artists in Poland and elsewhere in Eastern Europe—engaged in various self-educational activities before he gave up painting in favor of a rigorous process of questioning the (art) object, connecting the Duchampian readymade with the pursuits of kinetic art. These activities resulted in, among other things, his *Artons*, small amorphous objects made of various materials (including plastic), some of which lit up and created the illusion of movement;[55] and, even more importantly, between 1966 and 1971, in a series of demonstrational performances (*Pokazy*, or "Showings") in which Borowski used various strategies of pointing to highlight the aporetic nature of his relations with his audience. The term *pokaz* roughly translates as "an instance of showing" (from the verb *pokazać*), and is, as such, different from *wystawa*, a word that lacks a direct reference to demonstration, and is used to refer more formally to an exhibition.[56] *Pokaz*, on the other hand, centers on the gesture of showing and its address to an audience. During the demonstration that took place in 1966 at BWA Gallery in Lublin (*I Pokaz synkretyczny*), Borowski set the tone for his subsequent demonstrations, combining a presentation of his *artons* and early paintings with mirrors all across the gallery, which created a correlative for the act of seeing. As the artist wrote in his "Mirror Manifesto" (1966):

> [The mirror] makes the object unreal, it makes an illusion real.
>
> It substitutes the art object with an object of experience.
>
> It eliminates the "background noise" which permanently accompanies the information conveyed by an image.
>
> All we are left with in the traditional image is the "background noise" that aspires to the rank of information.
>
> It softens the "background noise," making a pure reception of experience easier.[57]

As we can see, information understood in its relationship with noise is as crucial for Borowski as it was for Brock in his construction of the Visitor School. For the Polish artist, the use of mirrors creates information out of noise while at the same time reducing noise to information. Another crucial effect of the mirrors is that the spectators experience themselves as "objects of experience"—as being "shown"—rather than as extraneous observers; the demonstration transformed the space of the exhibition so that spectatorship was itself subject to being observed, in this way putting pressure on any effort to address the situation from without.

Like his contemporaries Yves Klein and Piero Manzoni, Borowski is focused on the critique of painting in its social context, including the problem of authorship and the relations between artist and audience. Manzoni and Klein pursued their inquiry into the specular politics of the image in developed capitalism and in an atmosphere dense with commodification and commodity exchange. Borowski, for his part, grapples with the politics of the image in a country whose public spheres look very different from the ones in Western countries, situating his critique at the intersection of demonstration, happening, and conceptual art.

The artist presented his *4th Syncretic Demonstration* (*IV Pokaz synkretyczny*), entitled *Offering of the Furnace* (*Ofiarowanie pieca*, 1966), in the context of the first Symposium of Artists and Scientists ("Art in the Changing World"), organized by the critic Jerzy Ludwiński at a municipal nitrogen plant in the city of Puławy.[58]

The Symposium of Artists and Scientists was not the only art festival to be hosted in an industrial space in Poland during the 1960s. The symposium sought to actively engage the plant's workers and engineers with the avant-garde artists Ludwiński had invited for a monthlong residency. Discarding the possibility of working on a project involving material objects, Borowski decided on a performative demonstration that would paradoxically offer the assembled audience of workers, engineers, and artists their own plant's gas-burning furnaces as a gift. Appearing before them in a tuxedo, he conducted his offering, accompanied by song, in an almost liturgic ritual:

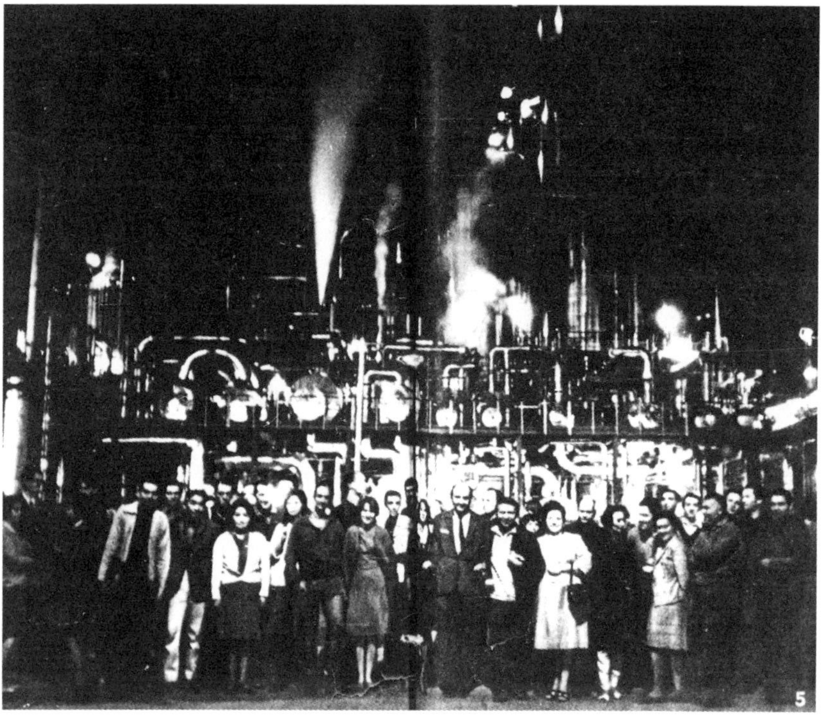

Figure 7.3 Włodzimierz Borowski, *Offering of the Furnace* (*Ofiarowanie pieca*), 1966. © Weronika Borowska. Image Courtesy of the Museum of Modern Art, Warsaw.

> Spotlights directed at the furnaces are illuminated . . . I am left alone in a small gallery, over a dozen meters above the ground. I begin speaking into the microphone. I say that, delighted with the beauty of the industrial landscape, I feel I can do little except treat the object from which I am speaking as a work of art and, as such, return it to the management of the Nitrogen Plant. At the same time, I ask that the object be treated with extraordinary care, as plates saying "explosive area" hang around it. In order to commemorate the moment, I begin to sing a song of my own composition with the lyrics "Urea, urea," pausing every now and then . . . to remind of the warning signs. At a certain moment my enthusiasm reaches its peak and the melody segues into the national anthem. I stop singing and descend the stairs . . . I feel my and their embarrassment, their outrage, and contempt for such a failed performance.[59]

By adopting an aesthetic attitude toward his surroundings ("delighted with the beauty of the industrial landscape, I feel I can do little except treat the object from which I am speaking as a work of art"), Borowski undercuts the symposium's official avant-gardist agenda with its assumption that as artists and engineers exchange ideas and discover what they have in common, art production and industrial production will become more aligned with each other. Additionally, by limiting himself to an act of demonstration without further commentary or explanation, Borowski hints that he lacks Bazon Brock's optimism about the possibility of teaching his audience how to see. Crucially, the key to the artist's "embarrassment" is not his ritualistic return of the furnaces to the plant's management but rather the audience's reaction to his demonstration, the impact it has or doesn't have on them. Indeed, it is on this level that Borowski considers his demonstration a resounding failure: "The spotlights are still pulsating. I approach the crowd, which hasn't disbanded yet. A couple of friends come up to congratulate or console. The rest seem not to notice me. . . . The management of the Plant is outraged."[60]

In some ways, Borowski's demonstrations of the mid-1960s recall Yves Klein's spectacular union of artist and audience in an almost mystical experience that combined postwar consumer culture with monochrome neo-avant-garde painting. Recall Klein's *Anthropometries* from the early 1960s, in which women painted with their naked bodies (as "living brushes"), following the artist's directions. However, Borowski's demonstrations lacked the element of specular exchange that animated Klein's work at the time. Instead, the Polish artist pegs his experiment to a rhetoric of failure ("failed performance") that recurs in several of his demonstrations. At the Puławy symposium, by "returning" the furnaces to the management after declaring them art, Borowski asserts that under the conditions of real existing Socialism, commodity exchange and art remain forever separated from each other.[61] And yet it is precisely his admission of failure that offers the artist a dialectical way out of the dilemma: even where his demonstration fails as a performance, it can after all still *succeed as failure*.

For Borowski, demonstrative failure is not only an aporia but also a form of creativity. Harald Szeemann had argued that "failure is a poetic dimension in art. I'm not talking about a protest against political relations, but about allowing a fiasco to actually take place."[62] In Borowski's work, too, failure is a productive, perhaps even poetic category. Nowhere is this more evident than in the demonstrative "anti-happening" *Pubes of Taint* (*Fubki tarb*, a wordplay on *tubki farb*, "paint tubes"). With the artist himself absent, the show took place in Ludwiński's Gallery Under the Mona Lisa (Galeria pod Moną Lisą) in Wrocław in 1967, and consisted of photographs of well-known figures from the Polish art scene, shown while they attended exhibitions at the same gallery. At the opening, a sealed envelope was opened and a text was taken out and then read aloud by Ludwiński.

In that text, its author (Borowski) states that the audience present in the gallery is the living material for the creation of his painting—they are its paint, as it were. Unlike Klein, however, Borowski addresses his

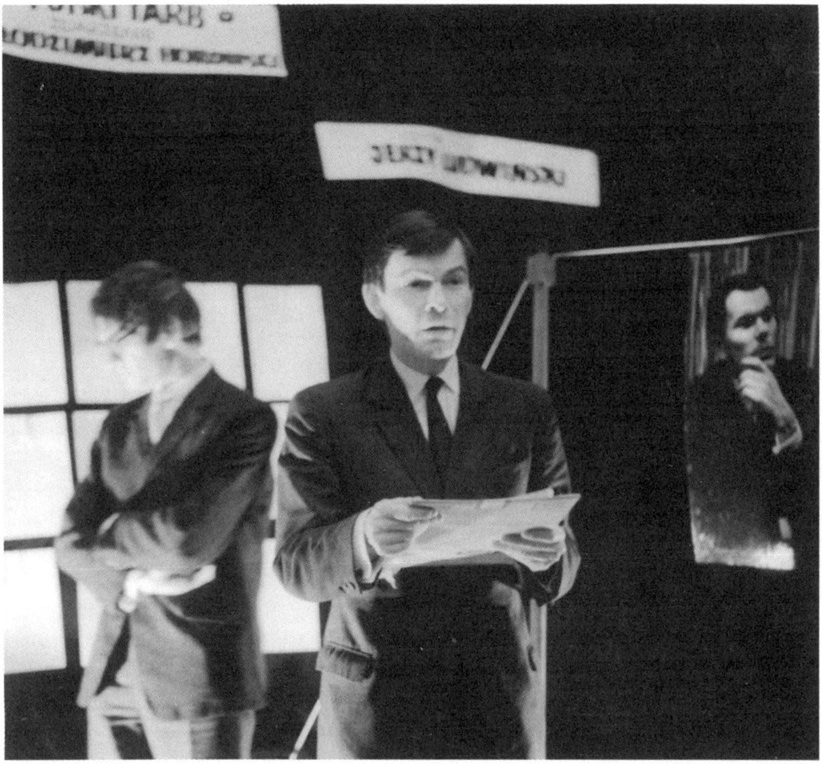

Figure 7.4 Włodzimierz Borowski, *Fubki tarb* (Jerzy Ludwiński, reading), 1967. © Weronika Borowska. Image Courtesy of the Museum of Modern Art, Warsaw.

"material" directly, suggesting that they, the audience, may strip naked, but then decides that they may not be suitable after all for creating the image he has in mind:

You are the co-authors and the material . . .

As co-authors you are sufficiently aware of the great risk of this experiment.

If the final effect of this artistic action is to fail—it is you who will take partial responsibility . . .

I accepted you as you are, as you want yourselves to be, as I imagine you to be. I took you wrapped.

In overcoats, or without, in suits and dresses, in stockings and pants, with purses and wallets or without . . .

You are standing or sitting, just as I wished . . .

The blood in your veins circulates just as I wished.

You breathe and think correctly.

But you could be unwrapped. I can feel your embarrassment. You are not prepared to do that. I did not notify you about that.

While before going to a party you take a bath, wash carefully and put on your clean and best underwear.

However, you did not come here to party. Your wrapping is of no interest to me. The wrapping does not necessarily testify to the quality of a product. Take off your coats . . . shoes . . . blouses . . . skirts . . . dresses . . . jackets . . . sweaters . . . slips . . . t-shirts . . . bras . . . pants . . . socks . . . underpants . . . stockings . . . socks . . . everything . . .

You are naked.

I know that not all of you have beautiful bodies. No shame about that. Paint squeezed out of a tube does not always look beautiful.

You are the material. The painting is not yet finished.

And what am I doing and why am I not amongst you? And perhaps I am here—in the Gallery?

Or I just dropped in for a moment and now I am strolling the streets . . . Preoccupied with that, perhaps I have forgotten about you completely.

I could as well drink out of desperation that the experiment ended in failure.

And perhaps I have decided to become the material of the experiment as well . . .

I am striving to create a great image.

I distance myself away from you more and more and I doubt the image will ever be big enough . . .

Please examine the photographs exhibited in the Gallery carefully. They advertise my material . . .

Production is in progress.[63]

As a demonstration of a project for creating a painting rather than its actual execution, *Pubes of Taint* develops a rhetoric of failure as part of the artist's imaginary address to his audience. At the center of this rhetoric is the (failed) merging of the artist with his audience, the very merger celebrated by Manzoni, who performatively designated people "art" by signing their bodies, thus establishing the value of this "material" as being reciprocal to his, the artist's, own labor (the act of signing).[64] In *Pubes of Taint*, too, Borowski designates his living "material" as art. However, Manzoni's unification of artist and audience in a spectacle of commodification—a procedure whose semiotic equivalent was described at the time by Roland Barthes in several texts as a kind of zero-sum exchange—is absent from Borowski's performance, much as the conspicuous consumerism and glamour that adorned Klein's performances were absent from Poland in the 1960s. Instead of performing art as a spectacle of exchange, the artist cannot make up his mind if his audience is even suitable for his project. Succumbing to doubt and uncertainty, he distances himself more and more from the audience, which, perhaps fittingly, is in fact the gallery visitors themselves: "I distance myself away from you more and more and I doubt the image will ever be big enough. . . . All of this is not enough for me. Or, I came to the conclusion that you make extremely miserable material."[65] In the end, Borowski abandons his project altogether: "Having discussed the text among my friends, I came to the conclusion that my statement is bad and gave up the idea of organizing the event."[66] The almost mythical merging of the artist in a spectacle of exchange—labor for art—in Manzoni and Klein is thus absent from Borowski's project, his autonomy ideally as untainted by the public and its expectations as by the institutional context of the symposium's official organizers.

For Borowski as much as for Brock, demonstration functions as a way to use didactics to interact with the public. Yet, while in Brock's case this happens through an institutional context dense with mediation—the Visitor School teaches the public that every aspect of our encounter with art, but especially the act of seeing itself, is mediated in one way or another—Borowski's experiment tentatively forgoes mediation and exchange in an ill-fated attempt to shore up the artist's autonomy to interact with reality on his terms. And where for Brock, the Visitor School is driven by an ultimately optimistic effort to harness seeing to knowledge, for Borowski, perhaps not coincidentally, this project—which assumes that our encounter with reality is best mediated by academic knowledge—is clearly at an impasse, leaving behind failure as its aesthetic detritus.

8

TEACHING WHAT DOES NOT EXIST (GNEZDO, ILYA KABAKOV)

In 1975, the three-member unofficial artist group Gnezdo (The Nest) created what they called a *School of Painting*, with the alternate name "Paint It Yourself!," in the apartment of one of the group's members, Mikhail Roshal, in Moscow's Dmitry Ulyanov Street.[1] Gnezdo's action constituted an unprecedented attempt by unofficial Soviet artists to engage with the public. As the group explained: "The idea was simple and funny. The beginner artist was offered black and white outlines of the masterpieces-of-the-world paintings, from Fragonard to Malevich and a paint palette. Using the latter, our subject had to colorize the available samples according to the originals. The idea turned out to be great fun, a collective creativity. Unfortunately, from the attained remakes only Cézanne and Fragonard survived."[2] The potential questions underlying the *School of Painting* are obvious enough: Who is an artist? and How are artists trained or taught? From a Western perspective, Gnezdo's action of enabling visitors to hand-color copies of masterpieces may seem like a throwback to pop art's infatuation with painting by numbers—albeit in a country where the kind of pop culture sustaining that infatuation did not exist—or it may resemble emancipatory discourses, familiar from the late 1960s, declaring that "everyone can be an artist." Beyond this, *School of Painting* performs a surprisingly accurate and unprecedented analysis of the situation of unofficial artists in the former Soviet Union.

These artists were isolated not only from the international art circuit but also, more generally, from the progression of Western (art) history, a history whose visual contours they knew only from reproductions. The two paintings to survive from Gnezdo's *School of Painting*—a "still-life by Cézanne" and "The Stolen Kiss by Fragonard"—represent the two antagonistic ends of that exclusion: modernist form (Cézanne), on the one hand, and painterly representation or expression (Fragonard), on the other. At either end of this spectrum, unofficial Soviet artists felt unable (or unwilling) to join the art historical process alongside their peers in the West. On the one hand, to base one's art making on representation (Fragonard) appeared impossible given that, as Ilya Kabakov once remarked, Soviet unofficial artists lived in a system where words had detached from semantics, and where any effort to avail oneself of existing means of expression—be they words or images—could only lead to inauthenticity and falsehood. On the other hand, formal innovation like Cézanne's, with its stress on problems related to the medium of painting itself, appeared equally unsuitable as a way of joining the process of art's history since the entire history of Western modernism, including Cézanne, was little known in the Soviet Union, a country where the victory of realist representation (Socialist Realism) had coincided with the near-complete suppression of modernism.

Three years after the *School of Painting*, in 1978, Gnezdo marched down Ulyanov Street for a few minutes with a red banner containing a rotated copy of Franz Kline's abstract composition *Accent Grave* (1955). The group's provocation, entitled *Art to the Masses*—the title reminiscent of Lenin's pronouncement that "art belongs to the people"—was remarkable not only for the fact that the group paraded abstract art down a public street in the Soviet capital, but also for being one of the exceedingly rare occasions when unofficial Moscow artists left the seclusion of their apartments to enter public space *as artists*. (During their next and last attempt to appear

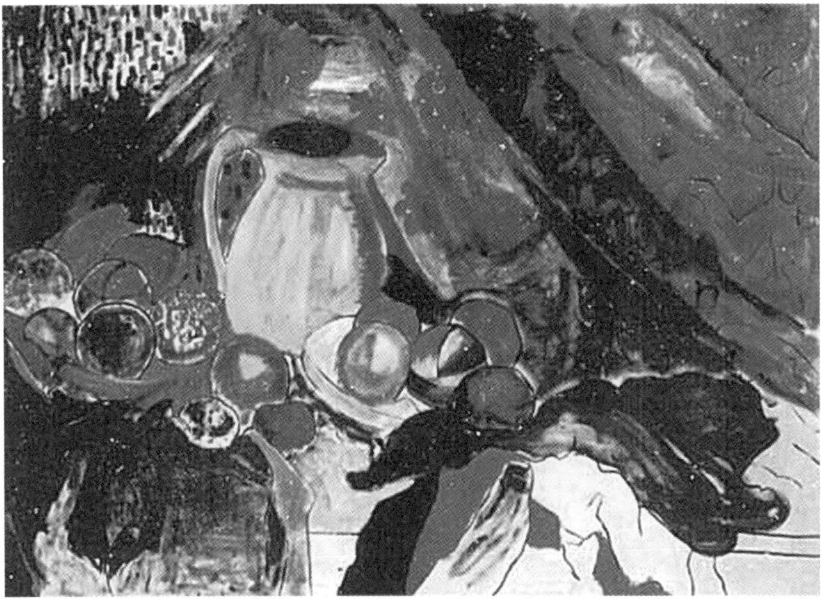

Figure 8.1 Gnezdo, *School of Painting: Paul Cézanne, Still Life*, 1976. Image courtesy of Viktor Skersis. Photographer unknown.

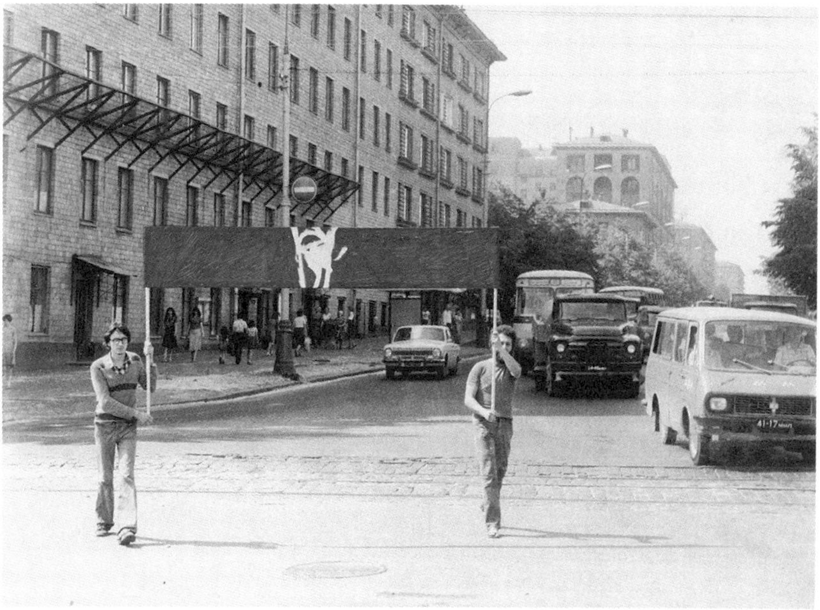

Figure 8.2 Gnezdo, *Art to the Masses*, 1978. Image courtesy of Viktor Skersis. Photo: Valentin Serov.

in public as artists, on the occasion of the famous Bulldozer Exhibition of 1974, the authorities brutally suppressed the event and destroyed many of the artworks.)[3] As a demonstration, Gnezdo's action presents a syncretic cross-section of positions, combining a banner with an abstract Western image with a title ("Art to the Masses") that seems culled from Soviet post-revolutionary (street) politics. Yet the artists are certainly not demonstrating for the freedom to become abstract painters; after all, the artwork they show is not their own, and the slogan "Art to the Masses" is as much a quotation as an educational program. If such a demonstration is didactic or pedagogical, it is so in a way that differs fundamentally both from late nineteenth-century Russian realism, with its efforts to use art as a means to educate the public, and from Soviet official art, with its focus on slogans as affirmations of hierarchic leadership. Gnezdo's demonstration is purged of any coherent representational program beyond the citation of a reproduced, scaled-down, and rotated abstract painting, plus a borrowed slogan. Its creativity lies not in authorial expression nor simply in its provocation (abstract art, let alone Western abstraction, was ostracized in the Soviet Union). And yet Gnezdo's demonstration has utopian potential precisely in the way in which it intervenes, for however brief a moment, in the official culture's totalizing image regime without at the same time imposing its own alternative. In this way, Gnezdo, whose members appear in the street *as themselves*, address themselves to an equally real, if admittedly elusive, public in order to begin an (equally elusive) dialogue with that audience.[4]

DEMONSTRATION IN ILYA KABAKOV'S WORK OF THE 1960S

Gnezdo's interventions, bold and unprecedented as they were, have a prehistory. Fifteen years before the group's actions, Stalin's death in March 1953 had ushered in the thaw period, introduced as part of a strategic effort to scale back the Soviet experiment and purge the system of the crimes of Stalinism. The thaw also resulted, among other things, in a series of spectacular international exhibitions held in Moscow, where nonfigurative painting from various countries in Western Europe and the United States was shown for the first time to unsuspecting Soviet audiences. Soviet unofficial artists began to address their isolation by assimilating, more or less playfully, the history of Western contemporary art, which they knew mostly from hearsay. For example, during the mid-1950s, Ilya Kabakov, then still a student, produced several hundred drawings in the style of abstract expressionism—a style then branded by the Soviet authorities as "formalist" and bourgeois. This autodidactic exercise was born from the artist's sense that the only way to join history (understood as Hegelian progress) was by mastering all of its successive stages.[5] As Yuri Sobolev, one of Kabakov's colleagues in the Moscow unofficial art circle, commented: "We decided that since entire cultural strata were virtually unknown to us, we would have to 'pass through' the whole history of contemporary art, starting around the 1930s. We would put out a still life or invite a model, then would become cubists, then Dadaists, then surrealists."[6]

From the beginning, efforts such as Kabakov's to "pass through" art history had a distinctly performative character, not least because, lacking any direct access to the originals, the material to be assimilated had to be reimagined or reproduced. As a result, Kabakov and his fellow artists soon discovered that their efforts to overcome their isolation by "mastering" (art) history were doomed. As Kabakov commented in the 1980s, "it goes without saying that there can be no such a connection with . . . History, least of all . . . with the history of art. The whole connection, this thin thread, existed only in the imagination. There, in this imagination . . . , 'bridges' were rebuilt and ideas, art currents were connected with each other. It's not necessary to point to the fact that this invented, 'reconstructed' history had little to do with the real one, the real processes."[7]

While their exclusion from (art) history thus remained unchanged, the efforts described by Kabakov were nevertheless highly productive: it's as if by constructing their own version of the history of an otherwise elusive modernism, unofficial artists not only sutured, in the register of the

Imaginary, the ruptures and missing links that separated them from Western art history ("There, in this imagination . . . , 'bridges' were rebuilt and ideas, art currents were connected with each other"), they also laid the foundations for their own independence from that history by "creating their own origins" in a (fictitious) history of modern art that would not exclude them.[8]

Before this background, the stark contrast between Kabakov's graphic work of the mid-1950s (and his elaboration of its relevance in the 1980s), on the one hand, and Gnezdo's mid-1970s *School of Painting* and *Art to the Masses*, on the other, is thrown into relief. In Kabakov's case, his project of *Bildung* focused on self-perfection and mastery and sought to lay the historical foundations for art production in an elaborate play of controlled fictionalization and historical recreation. In contrast, Gnezdo's more or less open address to a real audience outside of unofficial circles, complete with the exhortation "Paint It Yourself!," implied a crucial didactic shift from authority and control to a more open gesture toward dialogue and exchange—however rudimentary or factually inconsequential such a dialogue may have been, given the political conditions inside the Soviet Union at the time.

Sandwiched between the mid-1950s, the time of Kabakov's autodidactic exercises (the abstract expressionist drawings), on the one hand, and Gnezdo's two public demonstrations of the mid-1970s discussed above, lie the 1960s. Kabakov has described that decade as "a period of flowering for unofficial culture," by which he meant the close-knit community of artists, writers, musicians, and poets engaged in near-permanent exchange about their work, in more or less total isolation. Largely shielded from the international art circuit—though by no means without information about it—where pop, minimalism, and conceptual art were in the process of consolidating their grip on the decade, unofficial artists met and organized exhibitions in their own apartments, making up for the fact that they were all but invisible in Moscow's state-run art museums. And since there was no real audience for them, either, unofficial artists also doubled as their own public and—in the absence of any professional art criticism—critiqued each other's work. Some of their group, including Kabakov and his close friend Eric Bulatov, had attended the venerable Surikov Academy, which emphasized painterly realism and the national nineteenth-century tradition of the Wanderers (Peredvizhniki). But while Bulatov remained committed to painting even as he questioned some of its basic foundations, Kabakov soon turned to (painted) reliefs and panels.

The generation of *shestidesiatniki* ("those from the sixties"), born mostly in the high Stalinist 1930s, became a recognizable group among Soviet writers, artists, and intellectuals, a generation whose lives had been indelibly marked by the 1956 Twentieth Congress of the Communist Party of the Soviet Union, the Hungarian popular uprising and its suppression by Soviet troops during the same year, and the protests during the late 1950s in Poland. As Viktor Voronkov and Jan Wielgohs have noted, the thaw went hand in hand with fundamental changes to the pre-thaw (Stalinist) Soviet public sphere, culminating in the development of a hybrid "private-public sphere" where everything, including politics, could be discussed, and whose "ideal topographic locus was the kitchen."[9]

Before the momentous transition from monolithically repressive Stalinism to a more complex system of professionalized control and economic and social surveillance during the thaw, unofficial artists operated in an atmosphere seemingly far removed from the didacticism of official Soviet culture with its banners, mass demonstrations, and a mediascape designed to respond to the presumed malleability of the masses with a canonical diet of party-sponsored mass pedagogy. Yet this does not mean that these artists were themselves adverse to education and (auto-)didacticism, on the contrary. Because their unofficial circle came into being as a way of compensating for the absence of institutions where contemporary art would be taught or created, it functioned as an informal school where information, advice, and critique were shared, and especially knowledge that the Soviet educational system censored or excluded—from modern art to Freud. Thus were intellectual networks set up in which artists could move around freely, teaching each other without ever encountering anything Soviet.[10]

A vivid example of this didactic ambiance were the so-called seminars that took place in Kabakov's Moscow studio-attic during the 1970s. The artist would demonstrate his *Albums* to friends and visitors, holding them up and pointing at different volumes one leaf at a time, all the while reading aloud the accompanying text and giving explanations. By the early 1980s, these weekly seminars developed into "virtual research laboratories in which artistic positions were performed, discussed, and documented by a range of artists and writers."[11] It was out of this atmosphere that the so-called Moscow Conceptual School developed, complete with, in Matthew Jesse Jackson's words, "laboratory-like situations and didactic atmospheres."[12]

However, education and didacticism had formally affected Kabakov's work even during the 1960s, from the panels he filled with lists of neatly categorized verbal and pictorial information—diagrams reminiscent of the then-fashionable efforts to fuse cybernetics with pedagogy, a utopian "learning (with the) machine" that could not have escaped the artist's attention—to the statistical sampling of an (elusive) public's opinions in *Answers of the Experimental Group* (1971).[13]

Kabakov's interest in education here and elsewhere was a function of his ongoing and steadily developing effort to conceive (of) an audience for his work. In this regard, he was not alone. Barred from showing their work in state institutions, other unofficial artists also engaged in efforts to create a public for themselves, even though in some cases these efforts differed starkly from Kabakov's own. Take the painter Mikhail Shvartsman, who in 1970 formulated his concept of a "hieratic pedagogy" as part of a need to establish "spiritual contact" through art. The metaphysical pathos apparent in Shvartsman's ideas was highly fashionable among unofficial artists during the 1960s, and as such it was but the flip side of the didacticism of official culture. For Shvartsman and his colleagues, the painter was or needed to become a spiritual leader who handles the tools of his trade—paint,

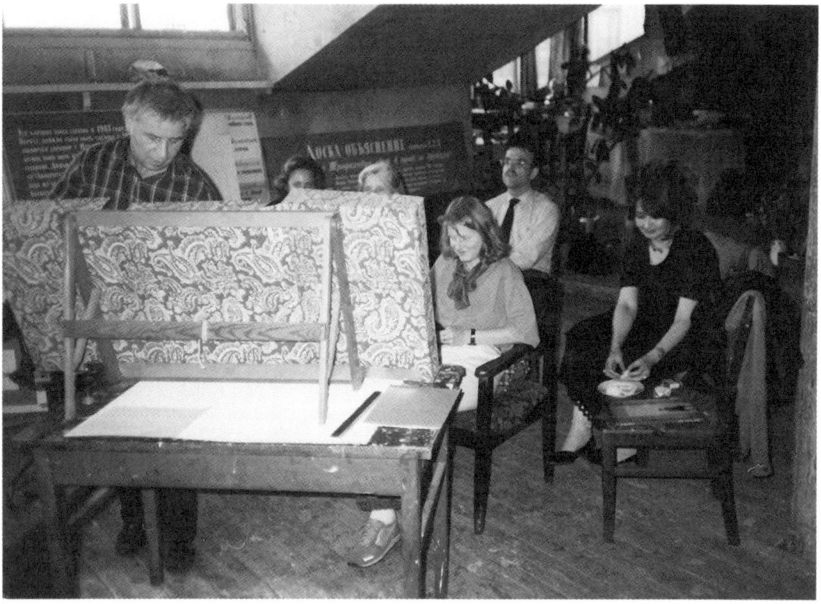

Figure 8.3 Ilya Kabakov showing his albums. Photo: Paul Jolles. Image courtesy of Emilia and Ilya Kabakov.

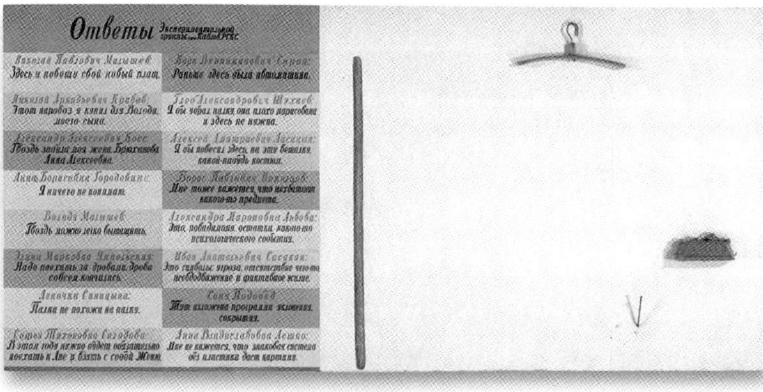

Figure 8.4 Ilya Kabakov, *Answers of the Experimental Group*, 1971, 2011. Private collection. Image courtesy of Emilia and Ilya Kabakov.

brush, and line—as instruments for uncovering an immaterial truth. As the artist commented, "know the pragmatism of things. . . . Be clear as a master, know the measure and the reckoning. Value a clear line, the magic of unforeseen curves, know the paint and the intoxication of color."[14] Shvartsman subsequently engaged in an agonizing effort to recruit followers for his truth-focused pedagogy, efforts that in 1974 culminated in the foundation of what he dubbed the Hieratic School of Painting at the studio of one of his students, Anatoly Chashinsky.

In their demonstration on a Moscow street, Gnezdo had aimed to give their (hypothetical) audience free reign to respond to the artists' call ("Paint It Yourself!")—thus embracing indeterminacy and unpredictability, a polyphony in which, as Mikhail Bakhtin described it, "no living word relates to its object in a *singular* way: between the word and its object, between the word and the speaking subject, there exists an elastic environment of other, alien words about the same object, about the same theme, and this is an environment that is often difficult to penetrate."[15] For the likes of Shvartsman, such polyphony—which he would likely have interpreted as a form of relativism—represented an insurmountable problem. In the context of "hieratic pedagogy," any disturbance of the firm bond between a sign and its single referent, any noise in the communication channel between the teacher and their disciples, was seen to represent a serious threat to the purity of the message about the (sacred) object, and indeed to the (art) object itself.

While he was certainly curious about the metaphysical pursuits of many of his artist friends, Kabakov sought to combine these pursuits during the 1960s with a more postmodern "polyphonic" approach that would connect different styles and methods in order to, again, "lay the historical foundations anew." The artist's work during the decade consequently alternated between flat drawings and oversized three-dimensional panels that combined a monochrome, mostly white, background with sectioned and/or painted everyday objects, such as a ball, fly, stick, or gun, thus freely mixing elements of figuration and abstraction with references to icons, modernism, and the historical avant-garde (constructivism, suprematism). And while, at first blush, works such as *Arm, and a Reproduction of a Ruisdael* (1965), *The Boy* (1965), *Couch Picture* (1965), *Pipe, Stick, Ball, and Fly* (1966), or *Machine Gun and Chicks* (1966) may seem to have something vaguely in common with Vladimir Tatlin's painted reliefs of 1914–1915, any such association is quickly dispelled: Kabakov's mixed-media works not only eschew the analytical take on materiality and constructedness that characterizes Tatlin's Culture of Materials, they are also conspicuously representational and plastic, as if they had fallen out of a colorful children's book. And while Kabakov's reference, in his memoirs, to these works as "absurdist" may recall Malevich's alogical pictures from 1914, his works owe little to Malevich's counterlogical program in paintings such as *Cow and Violin* (1913).[16]

Instead of establishing a language game or practicing transrational language (*zaum*) in the manner of Russian futurism (V. Khlebnikov), Kabakov's painted-object panels of the mid-1960s, I argue, need to be viewed as part of an ongoing investigation into the language of realism, a painterly tradition that was held in the highest regard at the Surikov Academy, where Kabakov had studied. In these works, the metaphysical quest for a space "beyond the picture plane" and the postmodern play with surfaces keep themselves in the balance. In a description of these panels from the 1980s, Kabakov elaborates on what I have in mind: the oscillation between the depiction of banal, everyday material objects, on the one hand, and a transcendent Otherness that exceeds them, on the other:

> When we represent something, we have an original such as a ball or a fly in front of us, and we copy it. When we imagine something "beyond reality," an "Other," then this basically cannot be represented, only experienced. However, the viewer, much like the artist, knows where it is to be found, where he has to look for it. The object, however . . . that has nothing to do either with real objects nor with "transcendent" reality

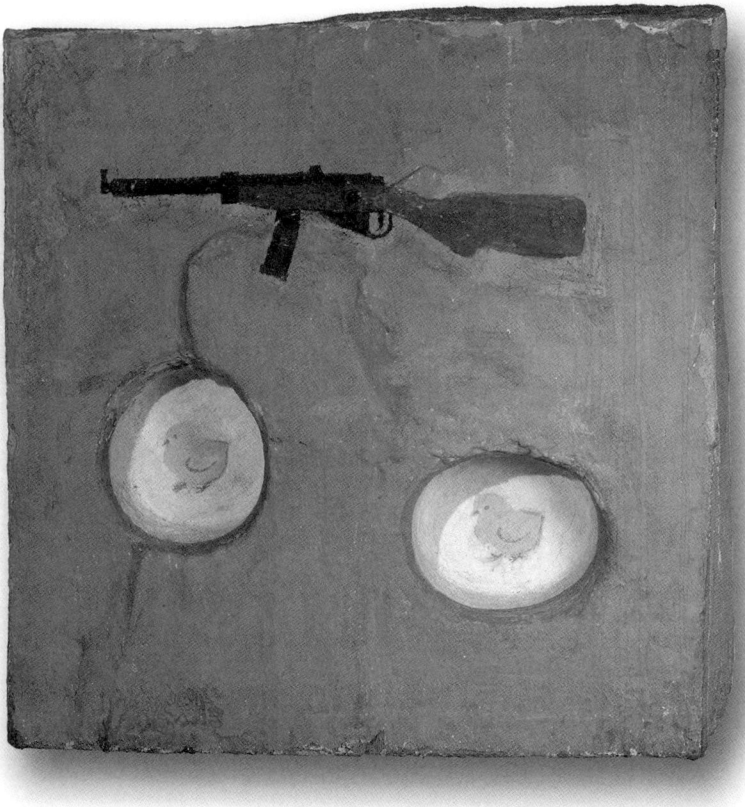

Figure 8.5 Ilya Kabakov. *Machine Gun and Chicks*, 1966. State Tretyakov Gallery, Moscow. Image courtesy of Emilia and Ilya Kabakov.

> remains hanging in the air like some total nonsense, literally like a bad joke.[17]

Kabakov's comment, in this passage, on the gap separating the (copying of) banal material objects ("total nonsense") from an Other that is "beyond reality" reads like an oblique commentary on what Roland Barthes, in a well-known essay published in 1968, termed the "reality effect." Barthes linked that effect to the presence, in realist fiction, of "insignificant details" that lack any explicit or implicit motivation for being included in the narrative, and that appear realistic to the degree that they overflow that narrative in a gesture of excess. The flip side of this mechanism, its precondition as it were, is the idea that the Real itself opposes or resists symbolic representation, so that representation remains in effect out of reach for (literary) technique: "The pure and simple 'representation' of the 'real,' the naked relation of 'what is' (or has been) thus appears as a resistance to meaning."[18] In this way, Barthes aligns the reality effect with the 1960s obsession with references to "the concrete" (insignificant details) as a weapon against meaning, "as if what is alive cannot not signify—and vice versa."[19]

In the Soviet Union, the bourgeois (consumer) object, which in Barthes's account organizes the distinction between what is significant and what is not, had no agency except as a kind of counterfetish, a thing whose only appeal was its shabbiness and dysfunctionality. As Jackson comments, in the Soviet Union, "commodities never lounged in shop windows, beckoning the entranced consumer. Objects, from apartments to automobiles to slabs of Masonite, were never unencumbered and new."[20] And as Kabakov himself remarked often, while Soviet unofficial artists recognized the overwhelming and inescapable presence of material objects in their daily lives during the 1960s, they also had to realize that these objects—which they experienced as "chaotic" and "ready to be thrown into the trash"—did not allow for any meaningful distinction, along Barthian lines, between what was significant and what was not, as everything seemed equally insignificant.

Kabakov's work of the 1960s reflects the difficulties he had in producing art that would provide a glimpse of the Real without sliding into either idealism (as in Shvartsman's metaphysical abstractions) or a state of utter, meaningless entropy. Even the lengthy didactic commentaries and explanations the artist habitually provided for visitors to his studio as he showed them his works cannot seem to provide a way out of this impasse. For example, in the artist's recollection, *Pipe, Stick, Ball, and Fly* was accompanied by the following explanation:

> Here there are as it were two lines that are not connected with each other. The first is a kind of joke about the objects in front of us: "The stick beats the ball, and the fly flies. OK, but what's the pipe there for? No idea, somehow, it's not working." Really a bad joke. But there is another connection as well, not between the individual objects but between the objects as a whole and the white base. They are all immersed, sunken into this white body, this white milk, and they exist for us only partially.[21]

In the absence of meaningful distinctions between what is significant and what is not, Kabakov's tongue-in-cheek mystification consists of the assumption that his didactic commentary, issued from a position ostensibly outside the fictional reality of the image, may successfully parse what is meaningful from what is not, allowing for the successful execution, finally, of a "masterwork" with some access to the transcendent Real. However, as the listless tone of the "interpretation" hints ("OK, but what's the pipe there for? No idea, somehow, it's not working"), the operation proves to be futile as the metacritical commentary reveals itself to be just as meaningless and "shabby" as the object on which it comments. As Kabakov writes: "And every time these explanations illuminated the object only insufficiently and one-sidedly, they could neither cover up nor justify the latter's idiocy."[22] In this situation, any kind of Barthesian reality effect—with its assumption of a differentiation between what has significance and what

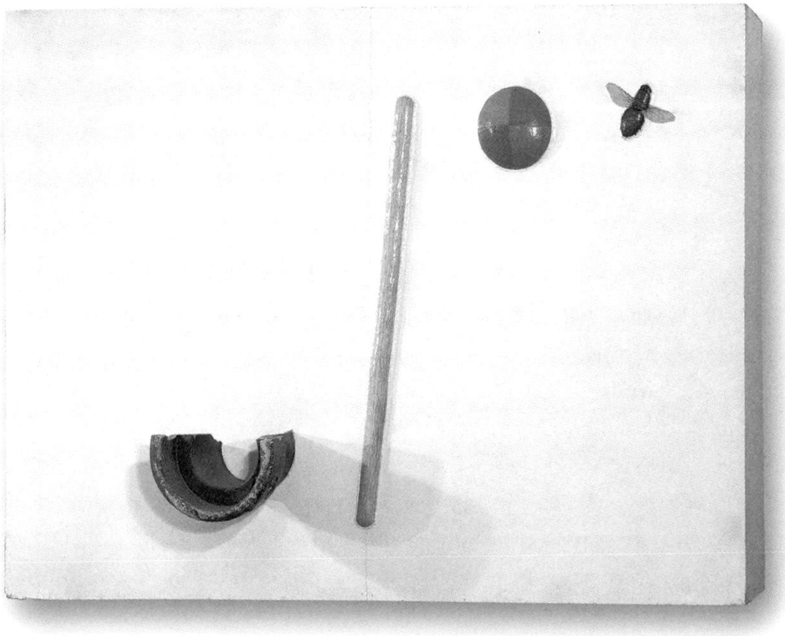

Figure 8.6 Ilya Kabakov, *Pipe, Stick, Ball, and Fly*, 1965. Ludwig Forum für Internationale Kunst, Aachen. Collection of Ilya and Emilia Kabakov. Image courtesy of Emilia and Ilya Kabakov.

does not—is clearly unworkable as there is no reliable position from which that distinction could be secured. Kabakov describes this effect as the object's "shimmering": "For a thing that is not secured in any way either by its status as an aesthetic object nor through its use value 'shimmers' as it were in our consciousness by making any categorization impossible, by pointing to all the possibilities of interpretation as equally plausible, and by rendering any choices made void in equal measure."[23]

Few works from the period embody such "shimmering" quite as memorably as *Arm and a Reproduction of a Ruysdael* (1965), consisting of a deep, white enamel plywood frame displaying a reproduction of Salomon van Ruysdael's painting *The Raid* (1656) and the flesh-colored papier-mâché copy of a human arm and hand whose opening is turned toward the observer. In one sense, the work sends us back to Sobolev's remark that unofficial artists need to unravel the history of art for themselves: it's as if between painterly figuration (the Ruysdael), Dada (the broken arm as a reference to the readymade, including Duchamp's *In Advance of a Broken Arm* of 1915), and suprematism (the off-white background on which the reproduction of the Ruysdael appears), *Arm and a Reproduction of a Ruysdael* confronts its viewer with an "instant" history of Western art, from classical representation to Malevich's post-object world. However, where the three art movements represented here might all be said to spar over the nature of representation—affirming it, as in Ruysdael's case, or rejecting/critiquing it, as in the case of suprematism or Dada—Kabakov does not appear to take sides, limiting himself instead to the demonstration of these approaches side by side. And if the way the artist strings up these different approaches is reminiscent of Joseph Kosuth's famous *One and Three Chairs*—which was created in the same year (1965), and of which Kabakov knew nothing at the time—the apparent incompatibility and randomness of the objects collected in *Arm and a Reproduction of a Ruysdael* makes it clear that Kabakov, unlike Kosuth, is not concerned with a structured inquiry into the nature of art (or language) per se.

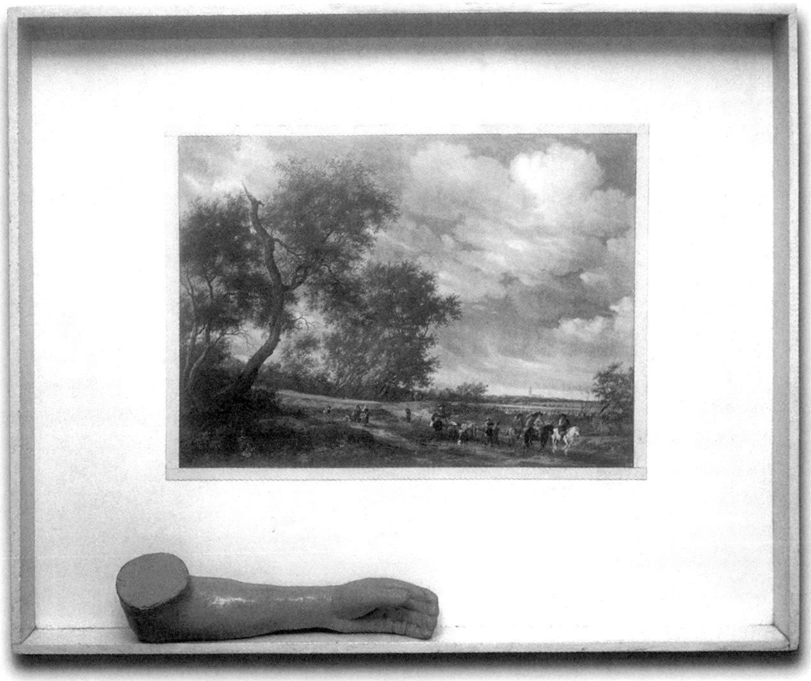

Figure 8.7 Ilya Kabakov, *Arm and a Reproduction of a Ruysdael*, 1965. Collection of Ilya and Emilia Kabakov. Image courtesy of Emilia and Ilya Kabakov.

Instead, I argue that Kabakov's interest, in this work as in others at the time, lies neither with representation nor with its critique but rather with the process of pointing itself, here designed to direct the viewer toward two fundamentally different perspectives on the work. The first, focused on the reproduced Ruysdael framed by the wooden enclosure, has the spectator fixated on that painting's represented space (the landscape with the village on the horizon) as if it gave access to a dimension *behind* the enclosure in which the shabby print is suspended, transcending the image's banality. This approach, which implicitly relegates the broken arm to a different level of representation outside the fictional space of the painted image, anticipates the investigations of the conventions of painterly realism carried out in the 1970s by Kabakov's friends, the painters Oleg Vasiliev and Eric Bulatov.[24]

The second perspective that the viewer is pointed toward appears diametrically opposed to the first. Here, any focus on the "deep space" of the picture is abandoned, and the broken arm is presumed to be located on the same level of reality as the Ruysdael reproduction. As a result, the Ruysdael image flattens, losing its painterly depth and its ability to transport us to a space behind the frame, turning into a flat, two-dimensional material object much like the arm itself. As a result, the frame around the panel holding the work now begins to look more like a box containing a shabby print and a papier-mâché arm.

In the way that it includes two images in one—two mutually exclusive readings, depending on what we as viewers choose to focus on—*Arm and a Reproduction of a Ruysdael* functions as what in German is called a *Vexierbild*, an "image that vexes" by including a hidden dimension, a different take or reading not immediately apparent to the naked eye.[25] As Franz Kafka wrote in his diary in 1911, "what is hidden in a *Vexierbild* is 'distinct and clear' for whoever has found what he was asked to look for; [but] invisible for [someone] who does not even know that there is something to look for."[26] In *Arm and a Reproduction of a Ruysdael*, it is the—to use Kabakov's own term again—shimmering oscillation between a metaphysical space behind the painting, on the one hand, and the relentless materialization of such a perspective—resulting in the banality and shabbiness of two random "trash" objects caught in a wooden box—on the other, that allows us to consider it a *Vexierbild*.

Crucially, with Kabakov, the double-dimensioned *Vexierbild*—which historically could involve a message whose overt display was not feasible or was otherwise inopportune—requires a didactic gesture of pointing that indicates that, to use Kafka's words, there is indeed "something to look for." Such a demonstration, a token of the *Vexierbild*'s performative side, can take many forms: from a commentary added to the work to the embodied position of the artist standing next to it, explaining the work or commenting on it, perhaps tilting it to one side or upside down so that its latent dimensions or perspectives may become visible to the unsuspecting viewer. Either possibility has a distinct place in Kabakov's work: as we saw, the artist routinely showed his works to visitors who came to his studio, often accompanying the display with a running commentary that before too long, in his *Albums*, actually became part of the work. It should by now be clear that these demonstrations are not an element added to the artist's work from without; they are, to the contrary, part of its core fabric. Nowhere does this become more apparent than in *Cubes* (1962), where much like in the later *Arm and a Reproduction of a Ruysdael*, the history of art appears to be distilled into the limited space of an oblong wooden support made up, like a Russian icon, of two painted wooden planks to which four horizontal rows of wooden blocks with painted "cubes" are affixed. The last row represents an oddity in that two of the cubes are painted directly on the wood panels—betraying the three-dimensionality that prevails elsewhere in the work—while two others contain two miniature landscapes, departing from the abstract design of the other rows.[27]

In the way it visually parses more or less explicit references to twentieth-century art history—from icons to constructivism (Tatlin's painted reliefs), painterly abstraction (the painted cubes can also be seen as individual color fields), and figuration (the painted landscapes as "windows" onto a space

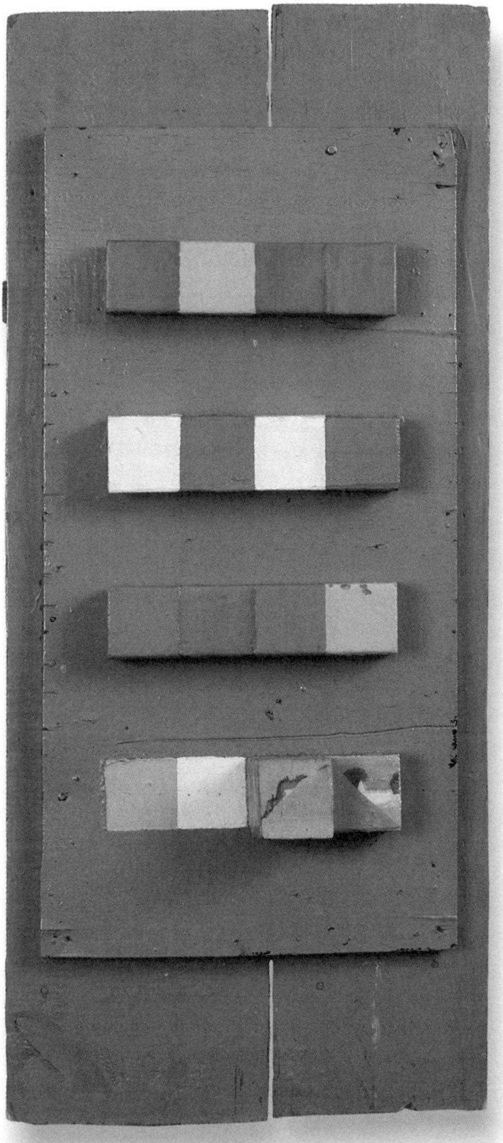

Figure 8.8 Ilya Kabakov, *Cubes*, 1962. The Norton and Nancy Dodge Collection of Nonconformist Art from the Soviet Union, Jane Voorhees Zimmerli Art Museum, Rutgers, The State University of New Jersey. Photo: Jack Abraham. Image courtesy Emilia and Ilya Kabakov.

behind the wooden support), *Cubes* may be compared with the didactic panels Kazimir Malevich—an artist who, not unlike Kabakov and his friends, had set up his own autodidactic passage through art history before arriving at suprematism—produced in Germany during the late 1920s in order to demonstrate the progression of twentieth-century art movements. Malevich explained this progression using a theory that he called the "additional element," by which he meant single graphic elements such as drawn curves—discussed by the artist in bacteriological terms—that would invade existing styles such as cubism and futurism like a virus, causing them to become part of an inevitable, natural process culminating in suprematism.[28] As Charlotte Lodder has argued, the demonstration panels Malevich produced to illustrate these ideas function as diagnostic tools designed to show the extent to which historical development is the result of mutation and infection, first by isolating the "additional elements" and then by demonstrating their effect on the artwork's "organism."[29]

It is interesting that in Kabakov's *Cubes*, too, an "additional element," extraneous to what appears to be the inexorable march of (art) history can be identified. As Jackson has pointed out, *Cubes* was initially called *A Mistake in the Row* (*Oshibka riada*), presumably a reference to the seemingly misplaced examples of figuration (the landscapes) in the last rows of unevenly positioned cubes.[30] However, where for Malevich the additional element dutifully executes its role as an instrumental (negative) part of Hegelian *Heilsgeschichte* whose inescapable culmination is the nonobjective world of suprematism—cancelling in the process any negativity with which the viral element may have been charged—in Kabakov's case, the "mistake," conspicuously placed in the last row of cubes and squares, remains unredeemed, as no final synthesis or stringent chronology can account for the random sampling of techniques and movements to which the panel refers.

If this may seem like a characteristic 1960s turn toward the introduction of the regulated production of chance and randomness into art, Kabakov—unlike, say, John Cage—does not elevate chance into a compositional principle. After all, the basis for Cage's work with chance, inspired as it was by

Schiller's program of aesthetic *Bildung*, was the artist's readiness to abandon control over his own work, a path manifestly not pursued by Kabakov.[31] In fact, *Cubes* quite literally has no natural support other than the artist himself: not obviously made for the wall, it's also not a sculpture, and so it is not immediately clear where it should be placed. As Jackson comments, "*Cubes* is not signed, nor does it hang on the wall or rest directly on the floor. Instead, Kabakov props it up to be photographed."[32] In the absence of any other suitable support, the artist becomes the sole "prop" for his work, and it is the work's photograph, which is all too often simply treated as an accidental accessory, that is in fact the only way we have of witnessing this fact.

However, there is more to the artist's propping up of *Cubes*. Like a *Vexierbild*, the work has a hidden visual dimension that does not reveal itself until the panel is seen from an oblique angle not immediately apparent to the viewer: "The angle of viewing . . . is important: the lowest rank of cubes yields a lopsided triangle, though only when viewed from the proper perspective. You have to lift and adjust this piece or squat and squint at it. Then the corny literalization hits you: here's Kabakov's Soviet 'Cubism.'"[33] In other words, without Kabakov holding his work or directing the viewer's gaze, its invisible side would remain inaccessible. And while this hints at the central importance of the artist "behind" the work, this does not mean that Kabakov operates vis-à-vis his work like an authority: rather, he functions like a demonstrator of its visual ambiguities, the "shimmering" and "flickering" between metaphysics and materiality that is the artist's answer to the grand (art) narrative Malevich's panels had visually charted. Meanwhile, the fact that this demonstrational dimension in *Cubes* should, as Jackson argues, strike us as "corny" rather than serious may only be logical, given Kabakov's operation in a universe—the Soviet one—where everything is equally insignificant and where no interpretation or viewpoint—not even the author's—can prevail over any other.

My insistence on the central importance of the artist as the one who "props up" his work for his audience in an act of didactic demonstration—without teaching anything in particular—goes, it must be said, against the

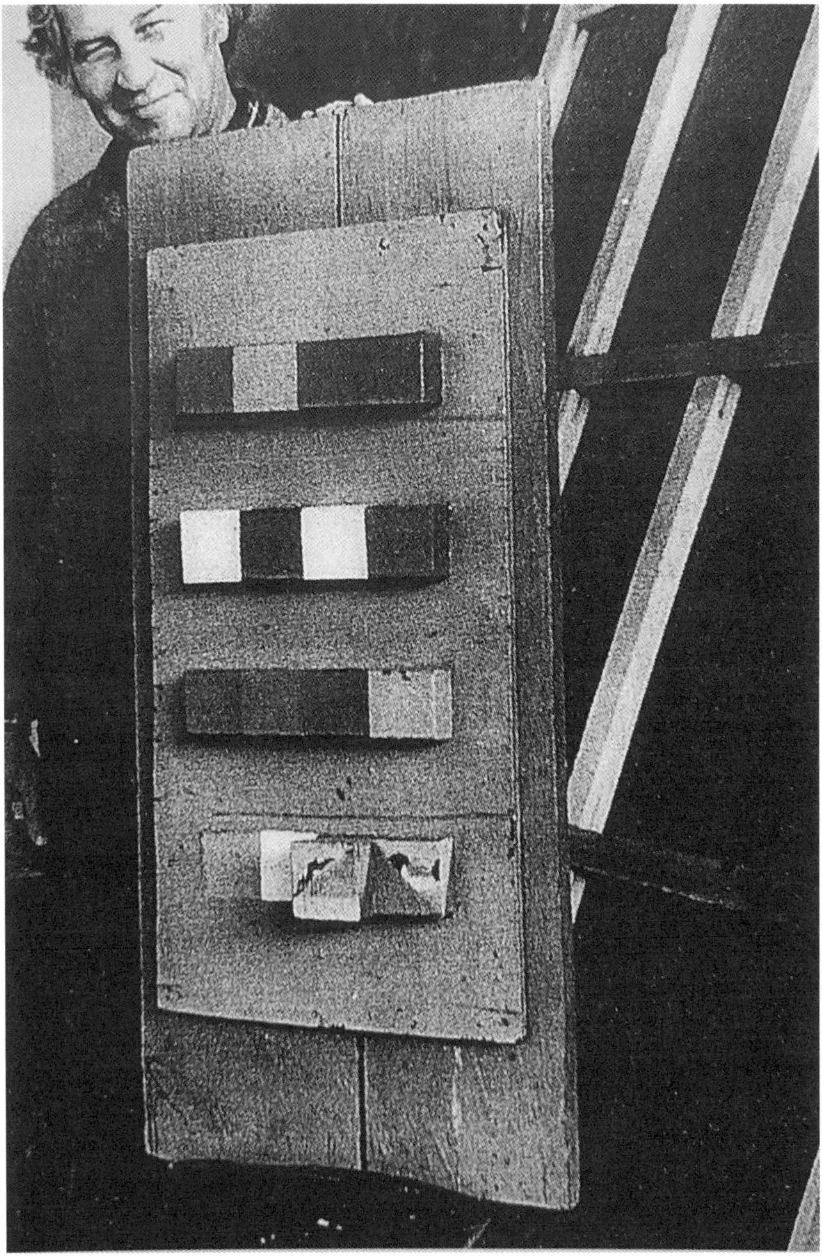

Figure 8.9 Ilya Kabakov with *Cubes*. Undated photograph.

grain of Kabakov scholarship, which tends to stress those aspects in his work that flatten the differences between the artist and his audience. The artist himself encourages such a view, insisting that his work of the 1960s was designed to establish an equal relationship with his viewers, one grounded not in hierarchy or social status but in dialogue. As Kabakov writes, "That is, unofficial art is addressed to a person who can enter into a dialogue with you on the same level. It does not engage in the well-known game: leader-crowd, teacher student, prophet adept, doctor-patient, and so on."[34] Such a dialogic and equal relationship between the artist and his audience as the basis of Kabakov's work is sometimes cast as the result of a heroic struggle with Otherness. Consider this assessment by Jackson, Kabakov's most astute critic: "The struggle throughout his art has been to overcome this Other ('the abstract viewer who does not exist'), to escape its ideological monitoring, whether it be the political gaze of the State, the pedagogical gaze of the Instructor, the professional gaze of the Editor, or the evaluative gaze of the Collector."[35] However, this viewpoint may give too much play to Kabakov's own mystification of his battle with such an Other, an idea that, like so many other statements by the artist, "flickers" between a performative and a constative register, between the register of a metapoetic statement and one that can be adequately understood only within the orbit of the work itself, as one idea or commentary among many.

By stressing the central presence of the author in his work of the 1960s—whether that presence be physical, symbolic, implicit, or explicit—I do not wish to undermine or negate the sincerity of Kabakov's struggle to "overcome the Other" or to level the gap that separates him from his viewers so that "dialogue" can ensue. Instead, I want to point out that the foundation for such dialogue is not the democratic, equalizing mode in which John Cage, say, invites his real-time audience to co-create his compositions, but rather a more stratified model. In this model, the artist, while duly implicating his own position in his work as one voice among others (and thus relativizing it), paradoxically still retains control over that work, while he conceives his public not, as was the case with Gnezdo, as unpredictable and present in real time (if invisible), but rather as a cacophony of voices and opinions selected and arranged by the artist himself (Kabakov), and over which he also retains control. If that sounds like a paradox, we may call this the paradox of "flickering authority," an authority veering back and forth between didactic monolingualism and Bakhtinian dialogue.

The many documentary photographs showing Kabakov next to or behind his works not only reveal the crucial role of the artist as the one who exposes the performative side of his painted objects so that they may not be confused with autonomous artworks that "speak for themselves" or formally belabor their own medium in a self-reflexive circle; the photographs also highlight his distance from the prevailing (Western) narratives regarding artists and their function. Where Cage's didactic strategy may have consisted of putting pressure on the hierarchies that separate a teacher from his or her students, the composer from the musician, or an audience from the performance, for Kabakov—and subsequently, for the Moscow conceptualists more generally—such leveling could not occur without the mediation and visible agency of the artist. And where Bernar Venet's goal was to reach, through his exposition of "pure" scientific knowledge, the kind of zero point of writing and interpretation that was so vital to the 1960s—effacing to the greatest extent possible his own authorial position—that position remained vital for Kabakov who, we might add, is less concerned with the "end of interpretation," with the pure notation Venet was chasing, or with the "death of the author" as declared by Roland Barthes in 1967. Where Barthes propagated the expansion of the text as a function of the author's vanishing, Kabakov proceeds, on the contrary, from the author's survival (or resurrection) inside the text: after all, in a world where everything is insignificant, the author's commentary does not escape from becoming insignificant, too, and survives as such.

9

DEMONSTRATION IN SOVIET AND POST-SOVIET SPACE (EXTRA-GOVERNMENTAL CONTROL COMMISSION, RADEK COMMUNITY, CHTO DELAT)

The engagement with demonstration by artist groups like Gnezdo and Ilya Kabakov's demonstrational gestures, for all their differences, respond in more or less explicit ways to the intensely demonstrative nature of (early) Soviet culture, with its pervasive emphasis on didacticism, agitation, and demonstration. As Devin Fore has argued, after 1917, "'everything was new, everything was for the first time,' [exposing] the incapacity of received language to address all of the unprecedented social, technical, and political formations."[1] According to Fore, in such a situation, what could not yet be named was instead being exemplified through demonstration: "Pointing towards exempla ostensively allows the subject, however provisionally, to cognize the present at a moment when the present has outpaced received routines of thought and categories of reason."[2] In the postrevolutionary Soviet Union, before the background of an overall pedagogization of society, life was quickly becoming unrecognizable for millions of people—and for many different reasons. Street demonstrations, posters, festivals, mass rallies, parades, and other such events and media often fulfilled an educational mission designed to instruct an unprepared population in the new life inside the Soviet Union.[3]

Demonstration was part of a revolutionary overhaul of the way that art was created and displayed, culminating, as Pamela Kachurin has shown, in the sweeping redefinition of the educational mission of existing art institutions, art schools, and museums.[4] Already in the early 1920s, members of the left futurist avant-garde used demonstration to exemplify types of art production which at that time lacked a meaningful nomenclature or an epistemological routine. The sculptural constructions that emerged from the laboratory phase of Soviet constructivism—famously displayed at the shows organized by the Society of Young Artists (OBMOKhU) in May 1921—functioned as demonstrations rather than exhibitions in the classic sense as they referred directly to the debates among the members of the Working Group of Constructivists regarding the relationship between construction and composition, and could not be understood without that background.[5] Or, consider filmmaker Dziga Vertov's documentary films from the same period, which also assumed a decidedly didactic quality, often with recourse to science, to prepare a largely unschooled population for its new life under Socialism. As Yuri Tsivian has commented, "the goal of divorcing film from literature which Vertov relentlessly pursued was complemented by no less manifest intentions to wed them to science. . . . Vertov's impetus to implant Marxism to film have one thing in common: each was, in effect, conceived as a brief public *lecture* of this kind, only delivered by means of silent film."[6] Alexander Gan, whose film *Long Live the Demonstration of Everyday Life* (1923) is another instance of art-as-demonstration in the early Soviet Union, depicted everyday life with cheaply produced, unscripted footage. Gan's filmic demonstration (the Russian word *demonstracija* is also used to refer to a film projection) functions as a form of agitation whose goal was to enable its addressee, the emerging Soviet public, to become an active co-producer, rather than being frozen into a position of static consumption.[7] The work of these early Soviet artists and filmmakers exemplifies how the new Soviet life and its art production necessitated equally innovative techniques for demonstration and display, including in the art museum. There can perhaps be no better illustration exemplifying this latter need than El Lissitzky's *Demonstration Rooms* (1926–1927) in Dresden and Hannover, which were designed to create an appropriate armature for displaying the new Soviet abstract art.[8]

Meanwhile, in the hands of Soviet leaders such as Lenin and Trotsky, demonstration was primarily a pedagogical instrument that showed the masses not only what was new—as the left-leaning artists did with their displays of the new (abstract) art—but also what they needed to know before the new could be fully embraced. Both leaders took a gradualist approach to the question of how to create an autonomous working-class culture in a country where the vast majority of the population was illiterate and unschooled, and both stressed the need for the proletarian vanguard to teach the proletariat what it might learn from the cultures of the preceding bourgeois era. As Trotsky wrote, "the main task of the proletarian intelligentsia in the immediate future is not the abstract formation of a new culture regardless of the absence of a basis for it, but definite culture-bearing, that is, a systematic, planful and, of course, critical imparting to the backward masses of the culture that already exists."[9] The basis for Trotsky's argument is the notion that the Russian working class had to take power at a point when it had not as yet been able to absorb (bourgeois) culture. There could not, Trotsky believed, be a genuine *Socialist* culture without a period of transitional apprenticeship during which the proletariat adopted elements of the old culture, while also transforming it in the process.[10]

By contrast, the proponents of another postrevolutionary artist faction of the 1920s, productivism, rejected both the left artists' idea of an original new art—on the grounds that it was necessary, in the words of one of productivism's premier theorists, Boris Arvatov, to "break . . . ties with any kind of 'pure art,' including that of the left"[11]—and Trotsky's "culture bearing" for pointing to things that were either dead or useless (such as bourgeois culture). Instead of focusing on aesthetic form, the productivists elaborated a theory of social art production, aiming to turn demonstration into a principle of construction for building the new life.[12] As Arvatov noted, "as the tendency of our epoch is that of industrial collectivism, society is given the opportunity to use its powerful and all-encompassing technique to consistently build its own life and, consequently, establish the concrete forms in which this life can be realized."[13]

In the early 1930s, the dynamic forms of demonstration elaborated by the avant-garde movements of the 1920s hardened into the mass pedagogy of Socialist Realism, the official art discourse introduced in the Soviet Union in 1932.[14] Its didactic iconography is saturated with emphatic references to teaching and demonstration, often with Lenin and Stalin cast as teachers of the masses, and with their command of different forms of ostensive communication designed to show that they have overcome the media-fragmentation cultivated by the historical avant-gardes.[15] Where in the 1920s, teaching and demonstration were conceived as a means to successfully embrace what was new in life after the revolution and to demand its preservation, in the 1930s, whatever potential for contestation was still left in demonstration turned into unconditional affirmation. The mass demonstrations depicted in Socialist Realist painting of the 1930s connote a world where the new has been drained of any sense of becoming; it has become an unquestioned reality. It's not a coincidence, therefore, that the slogans on the red banners held by the demonstrating masses in these paintings are often barely legible, or that they even seem to have no visible inscriptions at all.

DEMONSTRATIONS AS TRIPS OUT OF TOWN: COLLECTIVE ACTIONS

After World War II, art demonstrations pivoted away from city streets with their mass rallies to peripheral areas, a shift that became exemplary in *Trips Out of Town* by the Moscow-based group Collective Actions. Since the mid-1970s, the group's organizers have invited participants to travel by public transport to the urban periphery to observe minimal events and to register their own reactions in a zone the group refers to as a "demonstration field." The demonstration field is defined as an area of openness that combines a number of layers, relating to different temporal dimensions of the observed action. As the group's founder and chief theorist, Andrei Monastyrski, has written, "Here we can give a preliminary definition of the demonstrational field as the total of the psychological, visual, and empirical fields, which includes—it is important to note—both the experiences and events preceding the action itself as well as those continuing after the action's conclusion."[16]

Trips Out of Town aim to create an atmosphere of unanimity among participants, acting as a vehicle for directing consciousness outside of the boundaries of the intellect. Monastyrski makes a basic distinction between what happens in the demonstration field—the action's physical location—and the interior (psychological) experience of that event by the invited participants both before, during, and after its occurrence. Already before an action begins, the demonstration field expands to include a field of anticipation, during which the participants wait on the edge of the field for what is to come. Their anticipation—a loaded category in Soviet society, which was built on the anticipation or promise of Communism—itself becomes an experiential category, a kind of demonstration field in its own right for an action that hasn't occurred (yet).[17]

While the consciousness-raising efforts by demonstrators in Western Berlin and other places in the West were focused on the dialectical sublation of what is close by (at home) with what is far away, what is private with what is social, and so on, Collective Actions' goal was to immobilize that dialectic. In their understanding, the demonstration field can accommodate the most heterogeneous experiences and impressions at one and the same time and without resolving their differences, a situation that is much better suited to the posthistorical realm that was the postwar Soviet Union, where the vector of history no longer seemed to be pointing into the future.

The action entitled *Lozung* (*The Slogan*), which took place on January 26, 1977,[18] is one in a series of works where Collective Actions has used slogans

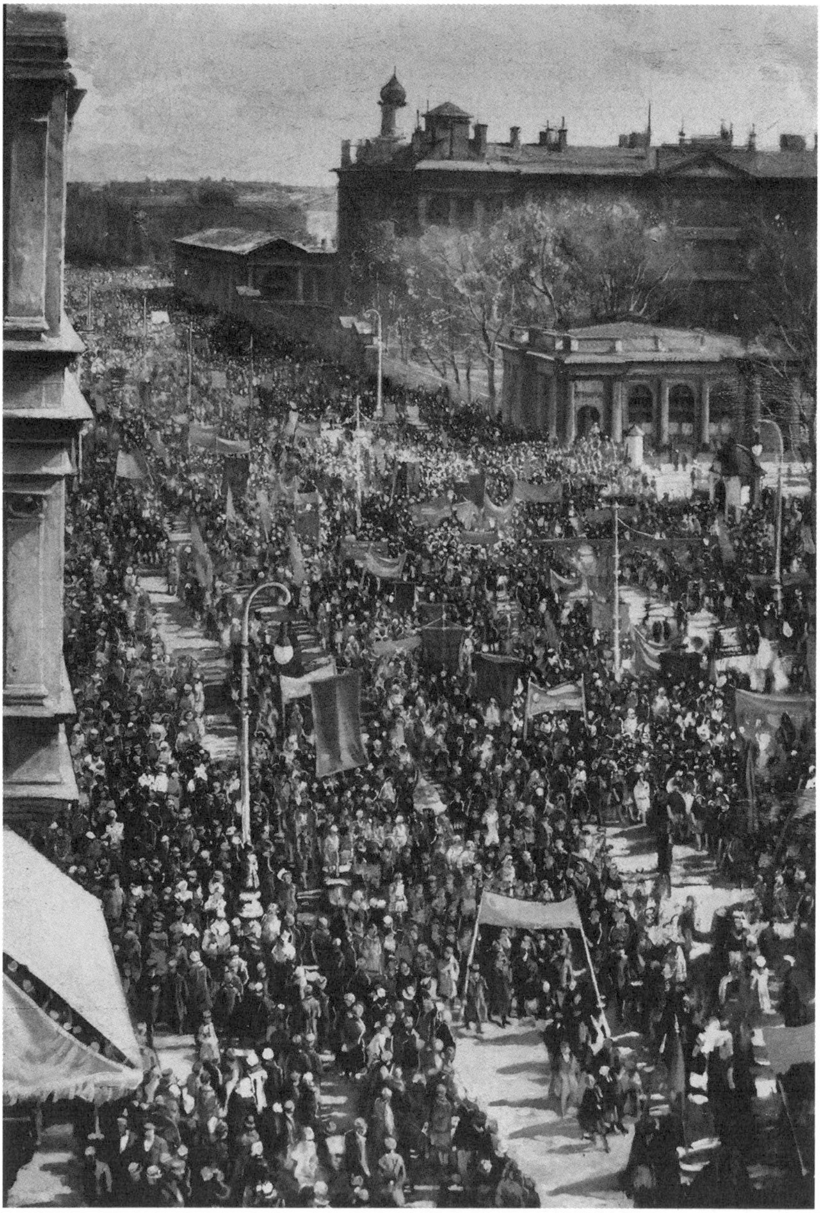

Figure 9.1 Isaak Brodsky, *Demonstration on 25th October Prospect*, 1934. Tretyakov Gallery, Moscow.

(*lozungi*), an agitprop technique that was widely used in urban official Soviet culture, but which Monastyrski has also compared to billboards.[19] During *Lozung*, the group suspended a red banner, not unlike the ones used in official demonstrations, between two trees on a hill above snow-covered ground.

As Monastyrski described the action:

> A piece of red cloth (1 x 10m) was hung between two treetops on a hill. The inscription in white stenciled letters said: "I DO NOT COMPLAIN ABOUT ANYTHING AND I ALMOST LIKE IT HERE, ALTHOUGH I HAVE NEVER BEEN HERE BEFORE AND KNOW NOTHING ABOUT THIS PLACE."[20]

Sabine Hänsgen has remarked that Collective Actions' transfer of slogans—which in the group's work function as demonstration fields within their specific natural contexts—from an urban context to the countryside, either in open fields or in clearings in a forest, represents one of the group's earliest means for reflecting on the perception of ideologically charged signs by changing their context: "The transition from the urban space into the rural landscape is connected to a process of semiotic reduction."[21]

The existing photographs of the suspended banner in this action are all taken from a distance, so that the writing on it is barely visible. And indeed, the slogan on the banner is unlike any used in official demonstrations. It would be highly unusual for a banner used in an official mass demonstration to make a direct reference to one single bearer ("I almost like it here"), and the presence of the unidentified first-person speaker provides for a certain ambivalence in our assessment of the situation. The banner's suspension between two trees in a forest further complicates the situation: who is speaking from or through this demonstration? The banner's odd positioning and its suspension between trees seem designed to press observers to concentrate less on its content than on their own experience of the

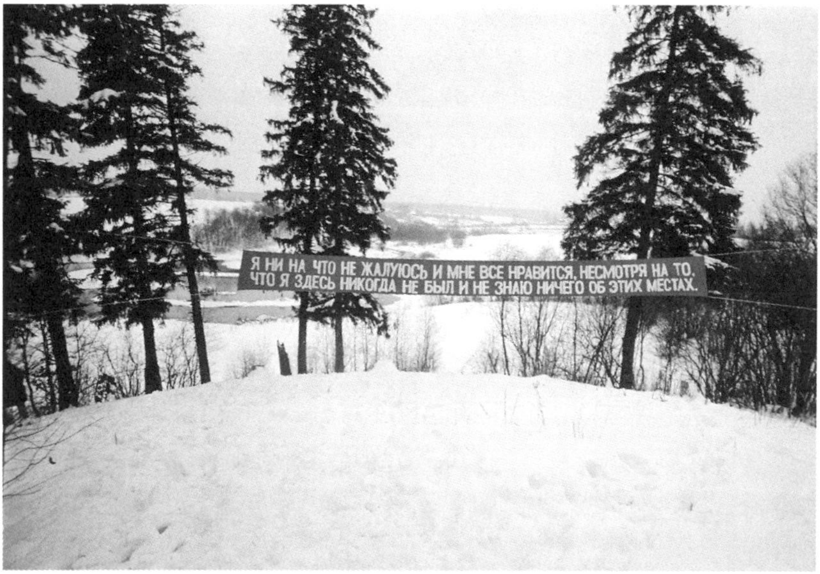

Figure 9.2 Collective Actions, *Lozung*, 1977. Image courtesy of Collective Actions.

demonstration and on the latter's medium.[22] As Octavian Esanu has noted, citing Kabakov, by the 1970s, many of the ideologemes that dominated life in the Soviet Union during previous decades had become mere decorations or free-floating "texts," which freed them for appropriation by artists who, like Kabakov, were interested in the different ways such texts constituted an (alternative) reality.[23]

It's not without interest, perhaps, that the German word *Losung*, which was adopted into Russian to refer to what in English is called a "slogan," can also refer to the password needed to enter a closed (and often secret) space. Indeed, it's as if the *Lozung* installed in the forest by the members of Collective Actions promised access to an alternative cognitive zone in which politics appears suspended without at the same time being fully eclipsed.

TAKING DEMONSTRATION BACK TO THE STREETS: EXTRA-GOVERNMENTAL CONTROL COMMISSION, RADEK COMMUNITY

During the post-perestroika decade, after the breakup of the Soviet Union in 1991, the streets of Moscow and, to a lesser degree, Saint Petersburg once again became the stage for sometimes unruly demonstrations and protests by interest groups ranging from students to disgruntled miners, thus returning political life to Russia. As Zinaida Starodubtseva has observed, during that time, public urban space was "desacralized," by which she means that it lost its status as a space exclusively reserved for officially sanctioned rituals.[24]

Unofficial artists also left the sanctuary of their apartments where they had been gathering, holding exhibitions, and organizing discussions, and began to stage demonstrations and other forms of public intervention in the streets of Moscow, a fact that appeared to mark the end of antipolitics. When in 1991 the group E.T.I. together with other volunteers spelled out the word *khui* (Russian for "cock," "dick") with their bodies near the Lenin Mausoleum on Red Square, they cleverly played on this shift: the scandal here is not only the word itself—ubiquitous in Russian slang, but also used freely by Moscow conceptualists, including Kabakov, in their work—and the action's proximity to the center of power, the Kremlin, but also the fact that the performers are present with their own bodies, turning the event from an abstract provocation into a demonstration whose stage is the body itself.[25]

The scandal of E.T.I.'s action, I argue, was not only its obscene referent and the way it violated a recent law against manifestations of obscenity in public, but also the fact that the artists took the act of pointing from the privacy of the studio back to the street. Demonstrations such as E.T.I.'s became the starting point for a series of artist demonstrations on the streets and public squares of Moscow and Saint Petersburg throughout the 1990s, marking a return to Gnezdo's earlier experimental efforts to take to the streets, and an implicit (or perhaps explicit) critique of Moscow conceptualism and its antipolitical postures.[26]

While there was an unmistakably political character to demonstrations such as E.T.I.'s or Aleksandr Brener's protest against the war in Chechnya, in 1991 on Red Square, wearing his underwear and boxing gloves ("Yeltsin, you coward, come outside!"), at the same time Brener and his fellow Moscow actionists clearly took note of the role played by the media in their increasing notoriety. Indeed, Igor Chubarov among others accused them of explicitly deploying their antagonistic strategies in a bid to increase their symbolic capital on the art market.[27] This also marks the difference between the actionists and, say, Gnezdo's 1978 *Art to the Masses*, which was staged at a time when Russian artists did not have to position themselves on a globalized art market, and when public demonstrations by artists still functioned as instances of more or less absolute transgression.

The artists associated with 1990s Moscow actionism (including, apart from Brener, Oleg Kulik, and Anatoly Osmolovsky,[28] who was behind E.T.I. and other radical initiatives at the time) used loosely scripted public performances to address the confluence of art and politics, and how their combination might bring about a kind of Rancièrian "redistribution of the sensible."[29] According to Gesine Drews-Sylla, the actionists hedged against

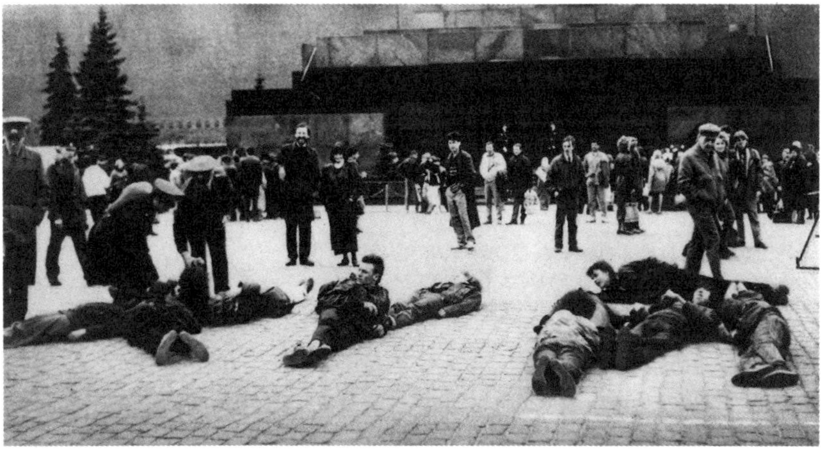

Figure 9.3 E.T.I., *Khooy (Хуй)*, 1991. Image courtesy of Anatoly Osmolovsky.

their own political ineffectuality by not giving up on their actions' status as art: "the protagonists of the radical art scene saw political protest as one of art's most important functions. However, from the beginning, they set up their own belief in the possibility of exerting real influence as merely utopian, so that we can sense in their often-radical political experiments an awareness that they operate within the closed realm of art."[30] As Matthias Meindl has pointed out, perhaps the chief concern for Brener and Kulik in the 1990s was not protest per se but the constant performative redefinition of its objects and goals.[31] In their often spectacular, sometimes violent demonstrations—barking at bystanders, squealing like a pig—Brener and Kulik again and again performed their own defense against what they perceived as a threatening social and political environment, brushing aside passersby, art institutions, the West, and even intelligible language as such. I have elsewhere described this strategy as a form of defensive abjection in Julia Kristeva's understanding of the term, whereby the Moscow actionists produce a form of "protest without object" whose ultimate target is language, understood as an instrumental system of referential signifiers; and of politics as the radical, even violent rejection of such enforced referentiality.[32]

In 1999, Extra-Governmental Control Commission (Vnepravitel'stvennaia komissiia), an association of artists, political activists, and intellectuals, was formed in the run-up to that year's elections for the Russian Chamber of Deputies (the Duma). The group started a campaign entitled *Against All Parties* (*Protiv vsekh partii*) that focused on an appeal to the Moscow electorate to "vote against all parties," a strategy Russian electoral law allowed at that time, and on the radical critique of liberal democracy more generally. Ten days before the elections, Osmolovsky and Oleg Kireev, who were among the main protagonists behind the campaign, unfolded a large red banner with the slogan "AGAINST EVERYONE" across the Lenin Mausoleum on Red Square, before being arrested by the police minutes later.[33]

Osmolovsky and Kireev had already worked with the name Extra-Governmental Control Commission a year before, when they staged a public demonstration on May 23, 1998, marking the thirtieth anniversary of the student protests of May 1968 in Paris. For that event, 250 artists, Russian and foreign art students, critics, and radical activists—including Avdey Ter-Oganyan, Osmolovsky, Dmitry Pimenov, Kireev, and Kirill Preobrazhensky—gathered on Gertsen and Nikitskaya streets in central Moscow, close to the Kremlin walls, for an action titled *Barricade* (*Barrikada*) made up of empty cardboard boxes, temporarily blocking traffic.[34] Attracting considerable media attention, the demonstrators raised banners that cited slogans similar or identical to the ones used in Paris in 1968 (some in French), including "Vous m'emmerdez" (You bother me), "Il est interdit d'interdire" (It is prohibited to prohibit), and "Soyez réalistes, demandez l'impossible" (Be realistic, ask for what is impossible). A black banner with the words "No money—no need for it" was draped over the boxes from which the barricade was constructed. Crucially, *Barrikada* not only made reference to May 1968 through slogans, but it also included art, as "large-format copies of works by modernist artists, such as Pablo Picasso, and original works by artists Avdei Ter-Oganyan, Dmitry Vrubel and Konstantin Zvezdochetov were positioned in front of the barricade."[35] The demonstrators' political agenda was broadly quotational and generally utopian ("no money—no need for it"). Their demands, again citing the student demonstrations of May 1968, asked, among other things, for free drugs for all participants, a monthly income for everyone, and the right to travel worldwide without visas.

In the way it bases its existence on the 1968 student *manifestations* rather than advancing an agenda of its own—or rather, by using 1968 as its agenda—*Barricade* functions as something akin to a carnivalistic "demonstration's demonstration." To be sure, it was not uncommon for street demonstrations to quote historical predecessors: think of the 1967 Shanghai commune, or the 1971 student strike in Paris, both of which made

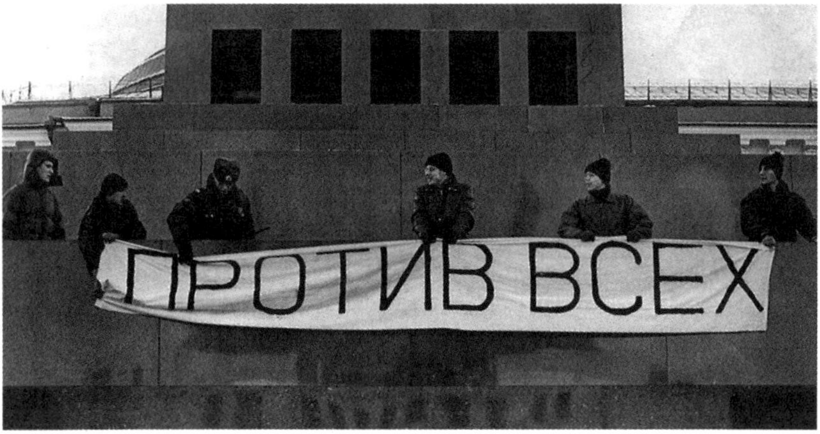

Figure 9.4 Extra-Governmental Control Commission, *Against Everyone* (*Против всех*), 1999. Image courtesy of Anatoly Osmolovsky.

reference to the Paris Commune of 1871. Yet such self-reflective citations do beg the question, already asked by scholars such as Chubarov and Meindl, whether a genuinely new politics can be founded on the citation of historical precedents, beyond merely rehearsing the impasse that was becoming increasingly obvious in Russia in the late 1990s—namely, that it was difficult or impossible to enter the neoliberal world order in a way that did not replicate that order. After three hours, Osmolovsky and the other demonstrators took down their barricade and started moving toward the Kremlin, confidently shouting a victory slogan before most of their inner circle, including Osmolovsky himself, were briefly detained by police and taken to different parts of the city.[36]

Osmolovsky had earlier provocatively marshaled demonstration as a means to challenge the antipolitical positions of Soviet-era unofficial art in a 1994 action in Amsterdam entitled *Exchange* (part II). As part of this action, Osmolovsky had constructed a series of houselike exhibition pavilions draped with a banner distinctly reminiscent of Collective Actions' *Lozung*. The banner read, in Dutch: "To see means to submit. Look into the bright light, you will go blind and attain freedom."[37] Once inside the pavilion, the visitor was confronted by a blinding light from a projector that momentarily made it impossible to see anything. Only after recovering from this shock were visitors able to see the pavilion's interior. The similarity between Osmolovsky's banner and the banner used by Collective Actions for *Lozung* is far from coincidental. As Osmolovsky has written, claiming in effect that his demonstration abandons the antipolitical strategies of Monastyrski's group: "You can partially see in this project [*Exchange*] a reference to the performance *Lozung* by Collective Actions. However, if *Lozung* was set up in a forest where no one saw it, in this case, the impact was the direct opposite: every visitor after reading the text went blind and 'attained freedom.'"[38] Apart from emphasizing the comparatively greater visibility of his demonstration, Osmolovsky's tongue-in-cheek comment seems designed to drive home the fact that *Exchange*—the word a key term in neoliberal economics, which was dominating Russia

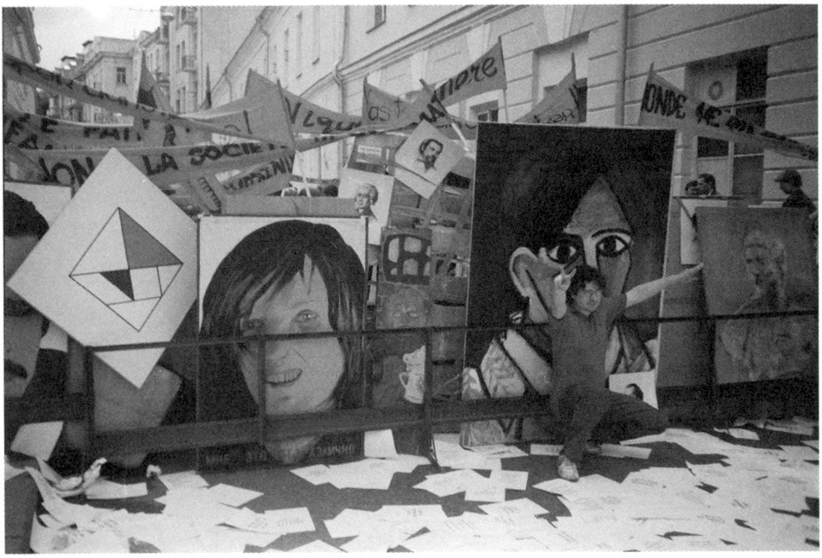

Figure 9.5 Extra-Governmental Control Commission, *Barricade* (*Баррикада*), 1998. Image courtesy of Anatoly Osmolovsky.

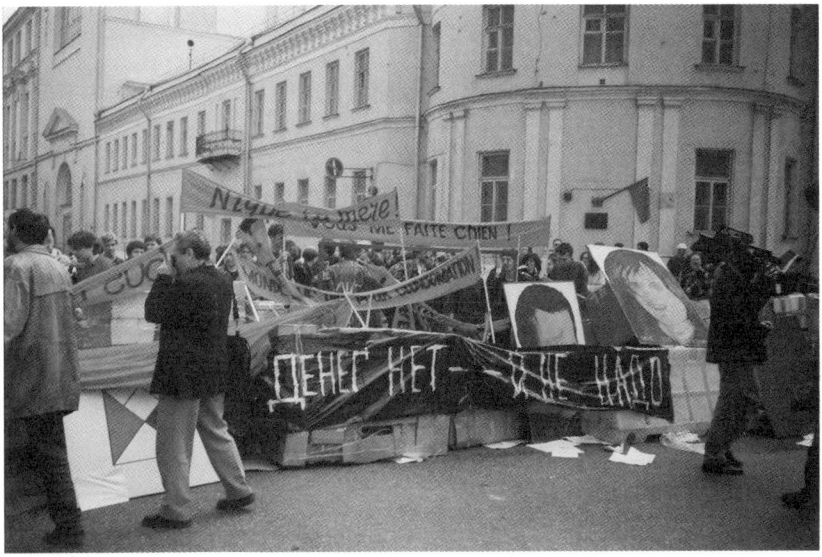

Figure 9.6 Extra-Governmental Control Commission, *Barricade* (*Баррикада*), 1998. Image courtesy of Anatoly Osmolovsky.

at the time—does not in fact present a viable alternative to the antipolitics of the Soviet era. While the post-Soviet period promises "freedom," that freedom is attained at a high price: Osmolovsky's visitor has to submit to a blinding sudden shock not unlike the economic shock therapy Russia and the countries of Eastern Europe underwent after 1989. Once "freedom" has been attained in this way, the visitor realizes that it is precisely blindness that now equals freedom. To put it differently, there is no viable exit from the totalizing space of the neoliberal world into which Russia has now been subsumed—although, crucially, we might say that the use of demonstration to enlighten the public to this fact, even where it cannot replace politics, marks a step forward.[39]

In 2000, the group Radek Community, again in central Moscow, performed a street action under the title *Demonstration* (*Demonstratsija*) that combined the continued critique of liberalism with renewed references to 1968. The action involved a few of the group's members who gathered at a busy street junction in Moscow, where the pedestrian red light showed for an especially long time. When the traffic light finally switched to green and the crowd began to cross the street, the artists placed themselves at its head and raised placards with anarchist or absurdist slogans ("Another World Is Possible"). In this way—in classic 1968 *Spaziergangsdemo* style—they were able to create the impression that many more people were taking part in their demonstration than was actually the case.[40]

Radek Community originated in Ter-Oganyan's esoteric "School for Contemporary Art," a didactic experiment that had led, in 1998, to the artist's notorious chopping up of prints of Russian Orthodox icons as a pedagogical exercise for "young atheists." With its 2000 *Demonstration*, the group wanted to highlight the fact that, in the mass media age, the public street no longer functions as a forum for the dissemination and discussion of revolutionary discourse.[41] The departure point for Radek Community's demonstration may have been Jean Baudrillard's realization that 1968 was made possible precisely by the understanding of the public street as a dynamic medium for immediate communication in multiple, hybrid

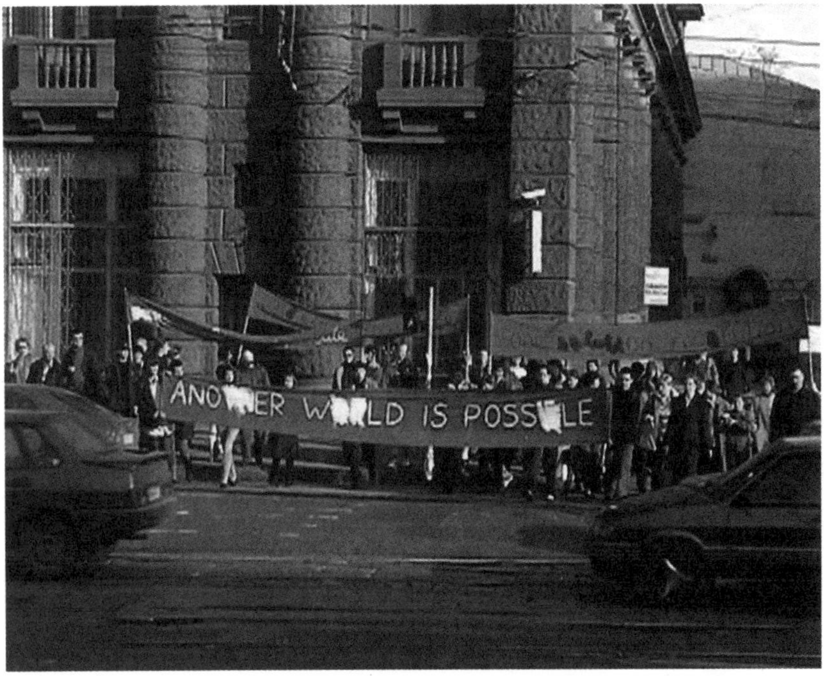

Figure 9.7 Radek Community, *Demonstration* (*Демонстрация*), 2000. Image courtesy of Petr Bystrov.

formats and without enforced consensus—as opposed to the homogenizing, formalized spectacle of communication established by the mass media. As Baudrillard wrote in the late 1970s,

> the real revolutionary media during May [1968] were the walls and their speech, the silk-screen posters and the hand-painted notices, the street where speech began and was exchanged—everything that was an immediate inscription, given and returned, spoken and answered, mobile in the same space and time, reciprocal and antagonistic. The street is, in this sense, the alternative and subversive form of the mass media, since it isn't, like the latter, an objectified support for answerless messages, a transmission system at a distance. It is the frayed space of the symbolic exchange of speech—ephemeral, mortal: a speech that is not reflected on the Platonic screen of the media. Institutionalized by reproduction, reduced to a spectacle, this speech is expiring.[42]

The street as "subversive mass media" that Baudrillard addresses involved a variety of social groups that included artists, students, and workers. Radek Community's *Demonstration*, conceived almost thirty years after Baudrillard wrote his analysis, starts with the realization that the communicative landscape that had enabled the 1968 student demonstrations was rapidly shifting; in Russia, the street had reverted, after the optimism of the perestroika years, to being a space of conformity and instrumentalized communication.

As members of Radek Community have written, their interest in 1968 was coupled from the beginning with a sense that the search for a new aesthetic language outside of neoliberalism—a language that might be able to reestablish or revive the communication channels that enabled 1968—had an uncertain outcome at best:

> We were fascinated by the aesthetics of 1968: posters, slogans, bombs, and terrorists. However, at the same time, we understood that we needed other technologies to affect the outer world, some other way of communicating. This is why we stand on a pedestrian crossing and wait for the traffic light to turn green. People keep coming and coming, finally forming a huge crowd. Each of them is going somewhere or another. Everyone is minding their own business; nothing connects any one with all the others, excepting the desire to cross the street. When the light finally turns green, we cross with all the others. And then, we raise red flags and banners above our heads. This is our "Demonstration." It is defined by our disappointment with and our hope for the prospects of finding a new language.[43]

Radek Community's demonstration is open to two mutually incompatible interpretations: on the one hand, by mingling with the crowd, the artists radically break down the boundary separating them from their audience, thus essentially making everyone a demonstrator in a way reminiscent of Debord's Situationist International. On the other hand, depending on which direction the banners are held, one half of their audience has their backs turned to the banners, which achieves the opposite effect. What this suggests is that the street, rather than being a forum for antagonistic, and hence genuinely political, communication (as in Baudrillard's reading of the 1968 demonstrations), is now a space where individuals mechanically follow programmed trajectories (red/green) or, on the contrary, a space where the SI's tactics, including the refashioning of the passive consumer into an active participant, is still an open, if uncertain, possibility.[44] Here again we can see that in post-Soviet Russian art, demonstration takes on the function of an experimental technique designed to test the possibilities for refashioning art's antipolitical orientation.

REANIMATING THE DIALECTIC: CHTO DELAT'S DEMONSTRATION POLITICS

If Moscow actionism of the 1990s with its conscious recourse to 1968 was a reflection on the perestroika years and the way they set Russia on a messy course of neoliberal economic policies, the artist group Chto delat, founded in 2003 in Saint Petersburg as a working group of artists, critics, philosophers, and writers, refuses to accept that Communism as a historical possibility failed together with the Soviet system.[45] Indeed, one of the group's core concerns, if not their main concern—at least before Russia's brutal invasion of Ukraine in February 2022—has been to work through what it calls the "lesson of *Perestroika*," setting out from the assumption that Communism, rather than being a closed chapter in the world's history, retains social and political potential, and that didactic activism, including art-as-demonstration, can lead to real change.[46]

One of Chto delat's recurring themes is therefore the need to "relearn Communism." If, for some, perestroika put the Soviet Union inexorably on a path toward Western liberal democracy and neoliberal economics, for others—the members of Chto delat included—the period, which came to a halt with the failed antigovernment coup of 1991, additionally represented a unique if unredeemed chance to revisit and relearn the history of the Soviet experiment in order to salvage from it what could be useful for a better future. In Chto delat's analysis, this opportunity—to revert to Soviet history and to treat it as an incentive for self-education, rather than as a closed historical chapter that needs to be forgotten—was squandered as oligarchs and former KGB operatives such as Vladimir Putin seized control: "In fact, for us, the event of *perestroika* gave us our first revolutionary chance in the fight for the oppressed (Soviet) past, and not for a comfortable bourgeois future. This past was foolishly squandered. It was obliterated by a party-state that proved capable of poisoning everything around it even as it lay dying, rising from the ashes under the control of former KGB officers, party apparatchiks, and young sycophants from the Komsomol, who all quickly found a common language with the capitalists of the world."[47] Against the actions of those who "squandered" Soviet history *and* the fake idealism of the liberal democrats, which also became the target of Moscow actionists such as Anatoly Osmolovsky, Chto delat assert perestroika's qualities as an event in Badiou's sense of that term. From the group's perspective, such an intervention—aimed at demonstrating the continued relevance of the Soviet experiment despite, or rather because of, the fact that in the political reality of the 1990s it seemed to have lost all relevance—is precisely what their activity aimed to achieve. For the group, what is important is less the radical leap into the future as a result of changes to representation—including its abolition—than interventions, including demonstrations and agitations, that may help recover the evental potential within existing reality itself. As Jacques Rancière puts it in one of the Chto delat newspapers, "art is about creating a space for unexpected capacities."[48]

"Relearning Communism" counts as such a capacity. The group's ideas about learning are poignantly Leninist ("the state of a creative lack of knowledge is the point of departure for action; it needs to be founded upon a clear historical analysis of the moment and the experience of emancipatory projects in the past")[49] and grounded in (self-)education, understood as the capacity to ask questions:

> We still do not know how to take action, nor do we know what our actions could bring. This is why we begin by asking questions. The situation of questioning is comparable to the consciousness of a child who has no ready answers. But unlike a child . . . we are forced to think the non-existent. This is precisely where we see the unbelievably provocative force of the Lenin quote: "Study, study, and study again to learn Communism in reality." We need to learn how to learn Communism, to learn something for which there are no ready recipes. Genuine education always sets itself the goal of learning the non-existent.[50]

Demonstrations have been a crucial element of the group's ambition to "learn how to learn Communism." Consider the project *Angry Sandwich People, or In Praise of Dialectics* (2006), which has participants—in the style of Buren's *Sandwich People* from 1968—walk around in Saint Petersburg's Stachek Square with signs containing words taken from Brecht's poem "In Praise of Dialectics" (1934):

Today, injustice goes with a certain stride,
The oppressors move in for ten thousand years.
Force sounds certain: it will stay the way it is.
No voice resounds except the voice of the rulers

And on the markets, exploitation says it out loud:
I am only just beginning.

But of the oppressed, many now say:
What we want will never happen

Whoever is still alive must never say "never"!
Certainty is never certain.
It will not stay the way it is.

When the rulers have already spoken
Then the ruled will start to speak.
Who dares say "never"?

Who's to blame if oppression remains? We are.
Who can break its thrall? We can.

Whoever has been beaten down must rise to his feet!
Whoever is lost must fight back!
Whoever has recognized his condition—how can anyone stop him?

Because the vanquished of today will be tomorrow's victors
And never will become: already today![51]

Chto delat's demonstration in a public square shows Brecht's poem as an open event rather than as a closed text: the questions and propositions cited on the placards that "sandwich" the participants directly address bystanders in the public square, as well as other members of the group. Chto delat understand dialectics, as did Brecht, as the unceasing necessity for things to change all the time ("Whoever is still alive must never say 'never'! / Certainty is never certain. / It will not stay the way it is"). In fact, the group draws a perestroika-inspired inference from Brecht's insight by literally "rebuilding" (*perestroit'*) Brecht's poem as part of their street action, so that a text like Brecht's cannot be considered as a closed form but rather is seen as an ongoing process, meaning that under its factual surface it holds possibilities for different historical directions.

With their address to bystanders on the square, Chto delat perform a double interpellation. If on the one hand they show the way in which subjecthood is conditional on ideology—the "sandwich people" look at first blush as if they were part of an advertising campaign—on the other hand, the process by which ideology creates a subject position—as a preexisting structure—may, by the same token, become the basis for resistance and struggle against oppression. This is an important distinction for the group, who do not believe in the possibility of a leap into an ideology-free world without careful organization and (self-)education.[52]

From the examples of didactic ostension in early Soviet art and culture to Gnezdo's early efforts to establish dialogue with an (elusive) public, to the more mediated demonstrational practice of Ilya Kabakov and Collective Actions' experiments in the peripheral "demonstration field," this chapter has sought to outline the contours of antipolitical art in the Soviet Union before pivoting to the post-Soviet era. In the 1990s especially, the Moscow actionists marshaled demonstration in a vain effort to ward off

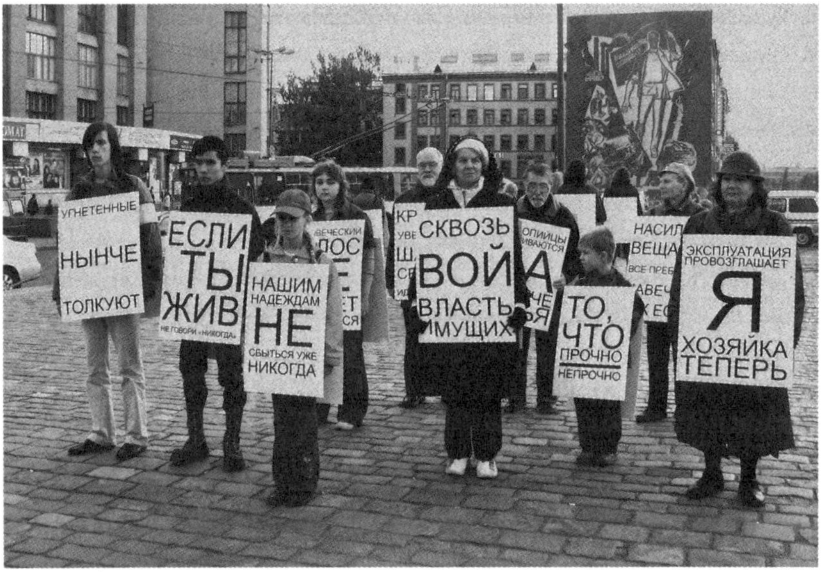

Figure 9.8 Chto delat, *Angry Sandwich People, or In Praise of Dialectics*, 2006. Image courtesy of Dimitry Vilensky.

neoliberalism and representational democracy, with the faint hope that some aspects of the revolutionary commons established in May 1968 might be salvaged. That hope appears amplified in Chto delat's use of demonstration to point to the "evental" structure of Communism as they revisit the perestroika years. As we now know, not only were these hopes optimistic even at the time, but they may have also prevented us from recognizing with the necessary sobriety what was going to come.

10

POSTSCRIPT: THE MIGRANT'S HANDS: BETWEEN DEMONSTRATION AND ARCHIVE IN SYLVAIN GEORGE'S *QU'ILS REPOSENT EN RÉVOLTE (DES FIGURES DE GUERRE)*

In this concluding postscript, I want to return to the problem of migrants and refugees raised in connection with Mladen Miljanović's *Didactic Wall*. I'd like to mobilize a distinction designed to help me grapple with two aspects of art-as-demonstration that have variously surfaced in the preceding chapters, referring to them as "demonstration" and "archive." In this distinction, the term archive names the perspective of narrative, by which I mean the subordination of facts to an overarching horizon of institutionalized meaning governed by the logic of cause and effect. By contrast, demonstration is associated with a different point of view, that of a present explained not with reference to institutional power and sovereignty but to acts of (self-)display and control over one's visibility.

I explain the antinomy between archive and demonstration on the example of Sylvain George's documentary film *Qu'ils reposent en révolte (Des figures de guerre)* (*May They Rest in Revolt [War Figures]*), which the director originally conceived as one part of a trilogy devoted to migration under the conditions of global neoliberalism, with the subsequent parts to be filmed in Greece and in the Spanish North African exclave of Ceuta and Melilla.[1] *Qu'ils reposent en révolte* was shot between 2006 and 2009 in and around the French port city of Calais, where undocumented migrants from different parts of the Global South but also from France itself have gathered since the 1990s to try to cross the English Channel by stowing away on trucks that would enter the ferries headed for the United Kingdom.[2]

With his documentary, George is committed to answering the question, in Debarati Sanyal's words, of "how . . . cultural forms such as cinema or photography frame the figure of the refugee and provide a symbolic platform for those denied the right to appearance and movement."[3] *Qu'ils reposent en révolte* couches its answer to these questions—and by extension its critique of contemporary French and European migration politics—in an experimental cinematic language that not only deploys the means and techniques of documentary film, but also includes a rich panoply of allusions to filmmakers who were members of the historical avant-garde, such as Sergei Eisenstein and Dziga Vertov, suggesting a perspective that merges aesthetics and politics at all levels of the film, with demonstration among one of its chief devices.

In a series of sequences separated from each other, *Qu'ils reposent en révolte* depicts the everyday activities of refugees in and around the so-called Calais jungle, including their efforts to evade the police, but also laughter, conversations, meals eaten together, and brief interactions with the filmmaker himself as the migrants speak, in English, into the camera. The film's second part depicts the buildup to a morning police raid on the Calais jungle in September 2009. Here, the presence of cameras, journalists, and hence the problem of documentation and documentary film comes to the fore in a more direct way than in the previous scenes, with camera and other recording equipment becoming part of the film.

Qu'ils reposent en révolte is not a conventional documentary in that it does not include a voiceover that explains and comments on the images shown. Instead, throughout the film, we hear a variety of voices in different languages, often untranslated, and we see images of objects or nature that appear curiously disconnected from the kind of summary history we expect documentaries to provide. Loosely edited and shot alternately with a conventional camera and a mobile phone, and full of cinematic effects such as close-ups, jump cuts, and fade-outs, the film ties the production of knowledge about the migrants and the space they inhabit to a perspective that often has us, the viewers, directly immersed in the migrants' lives as we follow their movements across this space. At other times, the documentary adopts a different perspective: we confront groups of police as they observe the migrants from afar or through binoculars, or try to control them by patrolling the jungle's perimeter or chasing them down the lanes of a park, as at the beginning of the film. This perspective is that of the authorities and the politicians who create policy and security narratives.

It is these two distinct perspectives developed in the film that I want to analyze with recourse to the opposition between archive and demonstration mentioned above, calling the immersive close-up associated with the migrants "demonstration," while referring to the surveillance view from the distance (for example by the police) as "archive." Archive here names the perspective of narrative, evidence, documentation, identification, and so on, all of which George's documentary associates with the police. Archives prove ownership, control identities, and cement claims to power, authority, and historical destiny, and they do so by tying assertions of ownership, home, and belonging to the past, to tradition, and ultimately to history.

While the records stored in the archive are functional and exert their claims whether or not they are being shown, the other perspective (demonstration) requires the presence of an individual who shows and points. In the register of demonstration, it is the act of showing itself, and the agency of the person behind that act, that matters; and it is to this act, and to this showing, that *Qu'ils reposent en révolte* devotes itself wherever it documents the migrants' attempts to become visible by *pointing to themselves* in a variety of ways.

The distinction between archive and demonstration bears a certain affinity to the difference between archive and repertoire established by the US performance scholar Diana Taylor. For Taylor, the difference between archive and repertoire is that while the archive safeguards and preserves the claims and titles of the powerful, the repertoire embodies these claims through performance and in-situ demonstration. As Taylor writes, "if performance did not transmit knowledge, only the powerful could claim social memory and identity."[4] The same can surely be argued for the migrants' canny deployment of demonstration in *Qu'ils reposent en révolte*.

Indeed, both archive and demonstration are on ample display in *Qu'ils reposent en révolte*. As far as archive goes, the European security regime demands from migrants that they be identifiable, that they register, and more generally that they be subject to classification. As we shall see, in this register, the efforts by the French police to control the migrants, check their papers, and so on, are always designed to enforce this archival logic. The material extension of this archive is the prohibitionary signage that dots the landscape around the jungle, from traffic signs to signs that prohibit entry, assigning the migrants a place by shutting them out on the basis of laws designed to protect the interest of the state and of private property.

This archive of rules and its signs differs dramatically from demonstration, which is by its very nature more than an interpellation to (not) do something, as it requires active participation. Demonstrations play a crucial role in *Qu'ils reposent en révolte*, especially during the raid on the jungle and after the French police clear the area, accompanied by activist French citizens who protest the actions of politicians and the police. The protesters shout their demands and hold large banners with their demands written on them, including the removal of the French interior minister and the cessation of flights to take migrants back to their home countries.

The migrants themselves also join in these demonstrations, holding up banners that plead for their right to a home and to be treated with respect. However, while the banners of the European protesters use only French and English, and generally appeal to broader concerns to do with human rights and French politics, the migrants' banners are not only multilingual (French, English, Arabic), they also self-reflexively mention the migrants' own presence in the jungle, which they refer to as their "home," a formulation that defies the authorities' view that the migrants are (unwelcome) visitors. In this way, the demonstration establishes a new, previously invisible perspective on the events around the jungle: that of the migrants themselves and their right to become visible.

During the demonstrations against the police's razing of the jungle with bulldozers and the threats of deportation of underage migrants to eastern France, the European press films the events, interviewing demonstrators as well as local and national politicians, and deploys reporters to pass commentary. And while the cameras' visible presence here hints at the presence of the movie camera in Vertov's 1929 *Man with a Movie Camera*, it's clear that for George, the emancipatory thrust associated with the camera's presence in Vertov's film can no longer be taken for granted. Instead, the cameras that take pictures of the anti-police protests in Calais and Lille feed a news cycle that helps perpetuate the migrants' invisibility as subjects in their own right.

After the bulldozers have cleared the jungle, we witness a particularly striking instance of demonstration by the migrants: not, this time, a political demonstration, but one that involves migrants combing the open field on which they previously sheltered, using their fingers to point to individual items they recognize as having once belonged to them, before their makeshift tents were destroyed. Picking up these items, they name them for each other ("these are my pants, this is my shirt"), carefully matching the name with the identified object.

The material objects scattered around the field and demonstrated by the migrants testify to their shared experience and in this way remain insulated from the abstract master narratives offered by the politicians, especially their constant references to a "humanitarian crisis." In this sense, these objects perform a function close to Walter Benjamin's view that what we contemplate as history needs to pay attention to the material surface structure of its constituent parts rather than to any larger ideological whole, of which these elements may form a part. Benjamin's use of the concept of contemplation in the preface to his book *The Origin of German Tragic Drama*

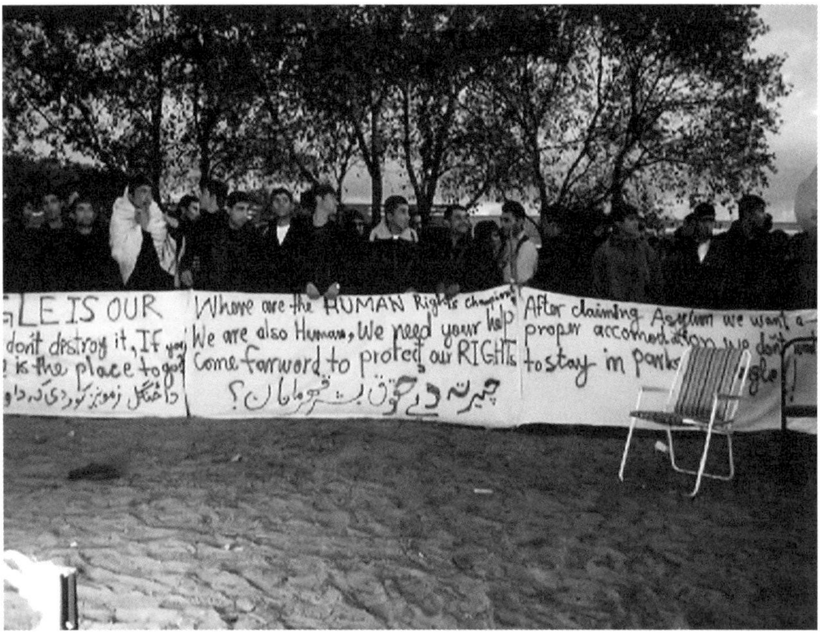

Figure 10.1 Sylvain George, *Qu'ils reposent en révolte (Des figures de guerre)*, 2010. Video still. © Sylvain George.

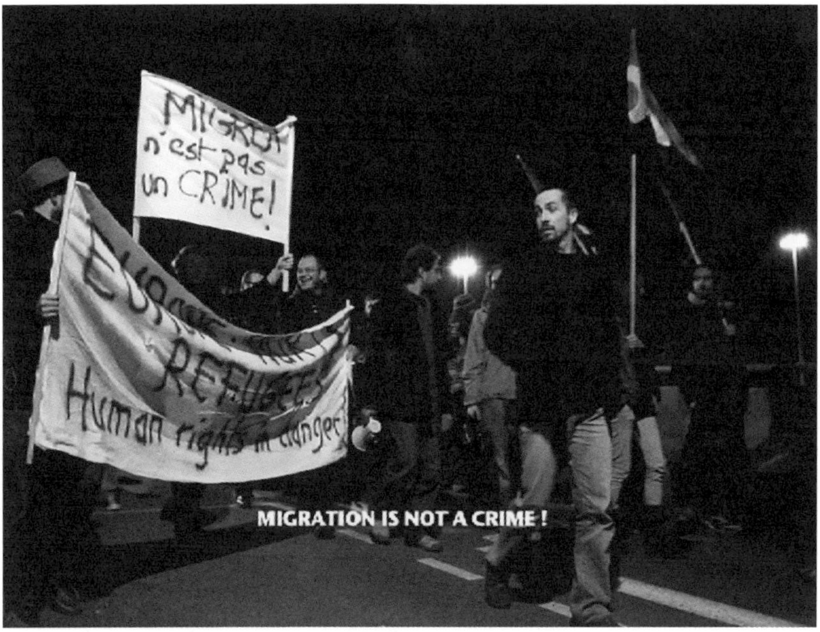

Figure 10.2 Sylvain George, *Qu'ils reposent en révolte (Des figures de guerre)*, 2010. Video still. © Sylvain George.

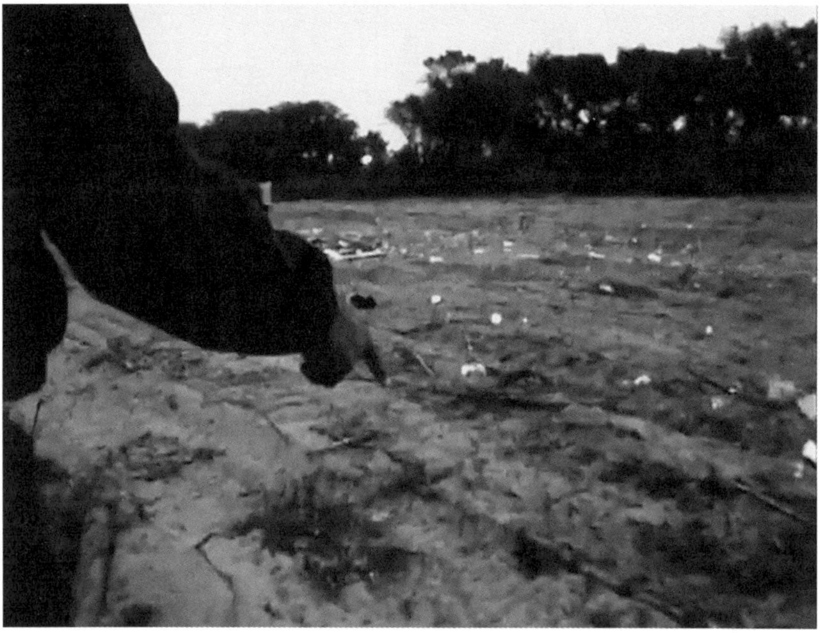

Figure 10.3 Sylvain George, *Qu'ils reposent en révolte (Des figures de guerre)*, 2010. Video still. © Sylvain George.

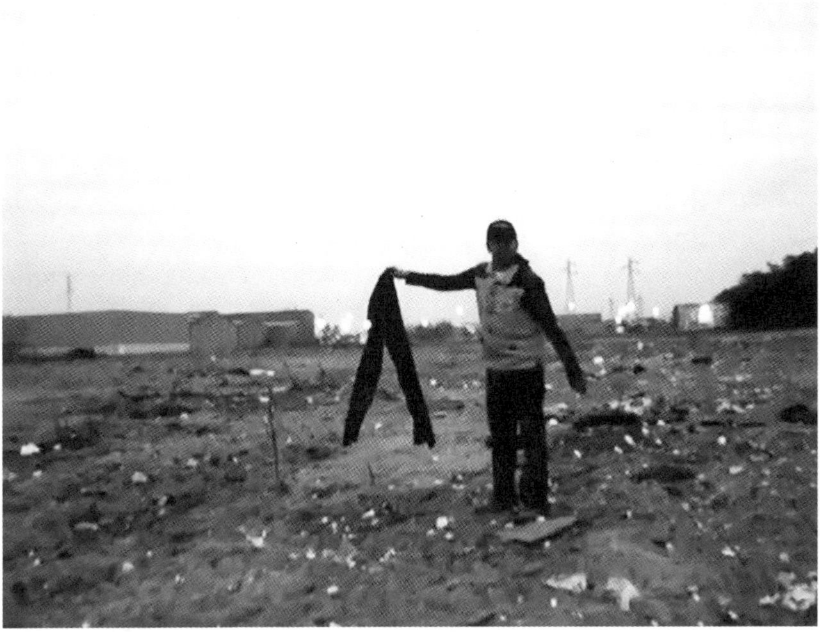

Figure 10.4 Sylvain George, *Qu'ils reposent en révolte (Des figures de guerre)*, 2010. Video still. © Sylvain George.

(1928), on which George wrote his master's thesis,[5] has little in common with the classic understanding of this term. For Benjamin, contemplation does not grasp an (art) object in its totality—in its truth—but instead serves to recognize that such truth is unfit for being grasped as a totality, as "the object of cognition does not coincide with truth. Cognition can become an object of inquiry, but not truth. Cognition is directed at the particular, but not immediately at the latter's unity [*Einheit*]."[6]

Qu'ils reposent en révolte invites contemplation in the sense invoked by Benjamin: its goal is not the the establishment of an archive, of ownership rights, or of an inventory of evidence, but—as with the two refugees in the field—the demonstration of presence ("We are here") by collecting, and pointing to, its material fragments. A similar understanding of demonstration is evident in other instances where the camera zooms in on individual material objects in the Calais environment. As Sanyal comments, "the camera weaves multiple elements of Calais's border scape into an ever-shifting tapestry in which living organisms, atmospheric phenomena, the elements, and inanimate things are in constant, nonhierarchical interaction (as in the echoes between whispering foliage and a refugee's song). In this ecology, no body or thing is out of place."[7] As instances of demonstration (rather than archive), these shots do not contribute to any overarching narrative, but they do allow us to make connections and establish parallels on a level far removed from the politicians' speeches and their abstract policy goals. In the process, these shots create a tangible role for documentary as a medium for protest and demonstration that exceeds the logic of representation.

The "archive," in George's film, enacts a machinery of classification based on protocols of identification to which the migrants react. In one scene we see a migrant from the chest down, holding a razor in one hand with which he peels the top layer off the skin of his fingers on the other hand. Shortly after, in a follow-up scene, we see a metal screw being turned around in a fire that is subsequently used by migrants huddled around the fire to scorch their fingertips. The goal in both cases is to prevent the police from assigning them an identity so they can be processed and possibly returned to their country of origin.[8] The identification of migrants is one of the key elements in European immigration policy and is used to process their deportation order. Migrants who lack identification—and thus are unable to show who they are—cannot be deported, either because it is unclear to what country they should be taken or because neither their countries of origin nor other countries in the Schengen area would accept them. By peeling off the skin from their fingertips, the refugees erase the possibility that they can be identified and hence deported. Soon another man in the group remarks: "If I could cut off this hand, I would do it," a phrase that takes us directly to the history of slavery. As is by now well known, in Belgian Congo and elsewhere in colonized Africa, the practice of severing the hands of insubordinate slaves was one of the most gruesome legacies of European colonial rule. One of the effects of this horrifying mutilation was the inability of the slave to point to herself, to demonstrate their body as a crucial way to identify themselves. In the colonial regime, the slave's identity was at the disposal of the colonizer: while the slave could be pointed to, they could no longer use their fingers to point to themselves. Seen in this light, the refugee's remark, "If I could cut off this hand, I would do it," serves as a reminder that "humanitarian" immigration practices—relying as they do on archival procedures of classification and categorization—have a dark underside: they literally repress the "freedom to demonstrate"—to become visible—and in ways much more far-reaching than this common phrase suggests. As another migrant says, "They are making us slaves, slaves of their own country."

An argument can be made that by mutilating their fingertips in order to escape forced identification, the migrants in George's documentary successfully adopt for themselves the brutal techniques of suppression once wielded by the colonizers, now to their advantage.[9] Yet while this scene may show that the migrants are not fully without agency—a fact the film

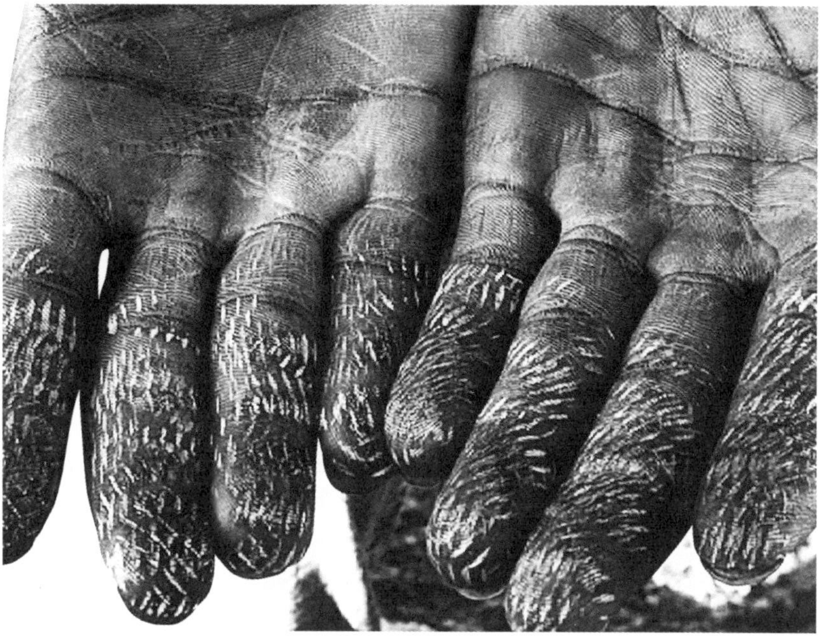

Figure 10.5 Sylvain George, *Qu'ils reposent en révolte (Des figures de guerre)*, 2010. Video still. © Sylvain George.

emphasizes throughout—what is more important may be the fact that *Qu'ils reposent en révolte* points to a common logic between colonial rule and humanitarian immigration policies: both deprive their subjects of the possibility of showing themselves, being visible, demonstrating that they exist.[10] And it is here, perhaps, that George's documentary can find its mission, by giving some degree of validation to the refugees' effort to point to themselves, in the present, through demonstration.

ACKNOWLEDGMENTS

Over the years this book has been in the making, many friends and colleagues have offered advice and conversation, generously sharing their time and expertise. At the MIT Press, I want to thank Victoria Hindley for the lively interest she has taken in my project from the beginning. Paula Woolley and Matthew Abbate edited the manuscript with care and precision. I thank the three anonymous peer reviewers for many invaluable suggestions and corrections. The book could not have been completed without Russell E. Coon, whose affection and support have sustained me over so many years. Keywan Tafteh has kept my spirits up and provided an artist's perspective. My students in several seminars at the University of California, Santa Barbara, and audience members in numerous lectures and talks have helped me connect my own ideas with the ideas of others. As always, my friends and coeditors at *ARTMargins* have provided encouragement and inspiration. For all manner of support, I also want to thank Ivana Bago, Jennifer Bajorek, Karen Benezra, David Crowley, Goran Djordjević, Maja Fowkes, Sabine Hänsgen, Angela Harutyunyan, Tom Holert, Emilia and the late Ilya Kabakov, Klara Kemp-Welch, Milan Knížák, Clemens Krümmel, Zsuzsa László, Matthias Meindl, Eckard Michels, Pavlína Morganová, Magdalena Moskalewicz, Dorotea Fotivec Očić, Michal Štochl, and Clemens von Wedemeyer.

NOTES

1 INTRODUCTION: ART-AS-DEMONSTRATION IN THE 1960S AND BEYOND

1. Bazon Brock, "Der Kopfstand—ein Markenzeichen?," in *Bazon Brock, Ästhetik als Vermittlung. Arbeitsbiographie eines Generalisten*, ed. Karla Fohrbeck (Cologne: DuMont, 1977), 764; translation mine.

2. With Reiko Tomii, I prefer the term "expanded 1960s" to the more customary "long 1960s" to suggest that the decade's expansion" is not limited to chronology. See Reiko Tomii, *Radicalism in the Wilderness: International Contemporaneity and 1960s Art in Japan* (Cambridge, MA: MIT Press, 2018), 27. In his study *Logics of a Failed Revolt* (1995), Peter Starr identifies as "1968" the period between the year 1965 (birth of *tiers-mondisme*, publication of Althusser's *For Marx*, etc.) and 1977, when a long process of disillusionment with the ideas of Marxism-Leninism that had begun with Khrushchev's secret speech in 1956 and the invasion of Hungary during that year appeared to come to a preliminary close. Peter Starr, *Logics of a Failed Revolt* (Stanford, CA: Stanford University Press, 1995), 4. See also James Meyer, *The Art of Return: The Sixties and Contemporary Culture* (Chicago: University of Chicago Press, 2019), esp. 36–38.

3. Fohrbeck, *Bazon Brock, Ästhetik als Vermittlung*, 381.

4. Andrew Stefan Weiner offers the following useful definition: "I will define an aesthetico-political activity whether an Action, a Happening, a Demonstration . . . as one that occurs at the intersection of aesthetics and politics, or in fact reconfigures our notion of these categories such that the very designations 'aesthetic' or 'political' enter into question." Andrew Stefan Weiner, "Times of the Event: On the Aesthetico-Political in West Germany and Austria circa 1968" (PhD diss., University of California, Berkeley, 2011), 13–14.

5. At the contemporary end, I'm thinking of the so-called educational turn of the early 2000s that was replete with projects and initiatives that opposed the neoliberal colonization and monetization of knowledge and education by engaging in grassroots projects, workshops, and the development of alternative pedagogies. However, it often lacked a historical perspective. See Irit Rogoff, "Turning," *e-flux journal* 0 (November 2008), https://www.e-flux.com/journal/00/68470/turning/; Paul O'Neill and Mick Wilson, eds., *Curating and the Educational Turn* (London: Open Editions/de Appel, 2010).

6. The English word is borrowed from Latin *dēmonstrātiō*, "action of pointing out, description, explanation," from late Latin, "deduction, proof." Meanwhile, the Latin verb *dēmonstrāre* means "to indicate, describe, show."

7. David A. Katz, "The Art of Effective Demonstrations" (2005), accessed October 3, 2021, https://www.ualberta.ca/centre-for-teaching-and-learning/media-library/catalysts/design-multidomain-demonstrations/effective-demonstrations.pdf.

8. Marshall Sahlins, "The Teach-ins: Anti-war Protest in the Old Stoned Age," *Anthropology Today* 1 (2009): 3, https://rai.onlinelibrary.wiley.com/doi/epdf/10.1111/j.1467-8322.2009.00639.x

9. Fredric Jameson, "Periodizing the 60s," *Social Text* 9–10 (1984): 192; emphasis mine.

10. See Meyer, *The Art of Return*, 19.

11. See Bogdan Suchodolski, *Einführung in die marxistische Erziehungstheorie* (Cologne: Pahl-Rugenstein, 1972), 99.

12. See Wolf Vostell, *Happening & Leben*, ed. Otto F. Walter (Neuwied/Berlin: Luchterhand, 1970), 99–100.

13. See Claire Bishop, "The New Masters of Liberal Artists: Artists Rewrite the Rules of Pedagogy," *Modern Painters* (September 2007): 87–89.

14. The only evidence we have of the readymade's physical existence is the 1920 painting by Duchamp's sister Suzanne.

15. Jacques Lacan, *Autres écrits* (Paris: Seuil, 2001), 408; emphasis mine. See also Roland Barthes, *Leçon/Lektion. Französisch und Deutsch. Antrittsvorlesung im Collège de France. Gehalten am 7. Januar 1977* (Frankfurt am Main: Suhrkamp, 1980), 30; Alain Badiou, *Le séminaire. Lacan. L'anti-philosophie 3. 1994–1995* (Paris: Fayard, 2013).

16. For a detailed discussion of this last demonstration, see Weiner, "Times of the Event," 48–57.

17. Heiner Stachelhaus, "Eine Demonstration (1964)," cited from *Kunst in Deutschland 1898–1973*, exh. cat. (Städtische Galerie am Lenbachhaus München, February 6–March 17, 1974), n.p.; translation and emphasis mine.

18. Howard Singerman, *Art Subjects: Making Artists in the American University* (Berkeley: University of California Press, 1999), 155–174.

19. See Peter Weibel, "Wolf Vostell und das Theater des Publikums," *Maske und Kothurn. Internationale Beiträge zur Theater-, Film- und Medienwissenschaft* 1–2 (2013): 11. Weibel's optimism finds its complementary counterpart in filmmaker Alexander Kluge's finding that in postwar Germany all learning processes have a "deadly ending," because the people live in a society where their "collective life programs disintegrate faster than they can produce new programs for living." Alexander Kluge, preface to Kluge, *Lernprozesse mit tödlichem Ausgang* (Frankfurt am Main: Suhrkamp, 1973), n.p.; translation mine.

20. Cited from Singerman, *Art Subjects*, 158.

21. Singerman, *Art Subjects*, 158. The original quotations are from Allan Kaprow, "Should the Artist Become a Man of the World?," *Art News* 63, no. 6 (1964): 34–59. The article is an attack on the Abstract Expressionists and argues for the professionalization of the artist. See also Helen A. Molesworth et al., eds., *Work Ethic* (University Park: Pennsylvania State Press, 2003); Philip Ursprung, *Kaprow, Smithson and the Limits to Art* (Berkeley: University of California Press, 2013); Julia Bryan-Wilson, *Art Workers: Radical Practice in the Vietnam War Era* (Berkeley: University of California Press, 2011).

22. Lucy R. Lippard, *Six Years: The Dematerialization of the Art Object from 1966 to 1972* (Berkeley: University of California Press, 1973), xvi.

23. Oskar Negt and Alexander Kluge, *Öffentlichkeit und Erfahrung. Zur Organisationsanalyse von bürgerlicher und proletarischer Öffentlichkeit* (Frankfurt am Main: Suhrkamp, 1972), 236.

24. Negt and Kluge, *Öffentlichkeit und Erfahrung*, 73; translation mine.

25. Antonio Gramsci, "Socialism and Culture," in *The Antonio Gramsci Reader*, ed. David Forgacs (New York: New York University Press, 2000), 57–58.

26. In his article on "Repressive Tolerance" (1965), Marcuse famously argued that in the capitalist Western democracies, the system promising such conditions is set up to make their operation impossible. See Herbert Marcuse, "Repressive Tolerance," in *The Essential Marcuse*, ed. Andrew Feenberg and William Leiss (Boston: Beacon Press, 2007), 32–59.

27. Rudi Dutschke, "Die geschichtlichen Bedingungen für den internationalen Emanzipationskampf," in *Rebellion der Studenten oder Die neue Opposition*, ed. Uwe Bergmann, Rudi Dutschke, et al. (Reinbek: Rowohlt, 1968), 76–77.

28. Dutschke even included a "reading list" for the 1968 student protesters in Dutschke, "Die geschichtlichen Bedingungen," 92. It should be noted that the belief in demonstrations as (auto-)didactic was not shared by everyone. In *Steal This Book* (1971), Abbie Hoffman, a proponent of theatrical elements in street demonstrations, argues against the view that such demonstrations should be educational: "Those who say a demonstration should

be concerned with education rather than theater don't understand either and will never organize a successful demonstration." Abbie Hoffman, *Steal This Book* (New York: Pirate Editions / Grove Press, 1971), n.p.

29. See also John Roberts, response to the Roundtable "What Is Radical?," *ARTMargins* 10, no. 3 (2021): 75–78. As Roberts argues, "The transformation of the demonstration may redefine what we want from manifestations of public resistance, but it settles nothing for art and politics as such."

30. Robert Stockhammer, *1967. Pop, Grammatologie und Politik* (Munich: Fink, 2017), 49–50. In 1977, Bazon Brock seemed to be responding to this call when he staged a public action entitled *Show Your Dearest Possessions!* (*Zeig Dein liebstes Gut!*), during which the artist appealed to Berliners to "finally also demonstrate demonstration itself" ("das Demonstrieren zu demonstrieren"). Cited in Peter Weibel, ed., *Beuys Brock Vostell. Aktion Demonstration Partizipation 1949–1983* (Ostfildern: Hatje Cantz, 2016), 363; translation mine.

31. See Kata Krasznahorkai, "Color-Blind and Color-Coded Racism: Angela Davis, the New Left in Hungary, and 'Acting Images,'" *ARTMargins Online*, February 2021, https://artmargins.com/color-blind-and-color-coded-racism-angela-davis-the-new-left-in-hungary-and-acting-images/.

32. See Oldrich Tuma, "Czechoslovakia," in *Dissent and Opposition in Communist Eastern Europe: Origins of Civil Society and Democratic Transition*, ed. Detlef Pollack and Jan Wielgohs (Burlington, VT: Ashgate, 2004), 34.

33. Jacek Kuroń and Karol Modzelewski, "Open Letter to the Party," in *Soviet Communism and the Socialist Vision*, ed. Julius Jacobson (New York: New Politics Books, 1972), 273.

34. Tomáš Štrauss, *Tri otázniky. Od päťdesiatych k osemdesiatym rokom* [Three question marks: From the 1950s to the 1980s] (Bratislava: H&H), 10, quoted from Andrea Bátorová, "Ostkunst, a Different yet Similar Art: Some Notes on the Complexity of Tomáš Štrauss's Thought," *ARTMargins Online*, May 2021, https://artmargins.com/ostkunst-a-different-yet-similar-art-some-notes-on-the-complexity-of-tomas-strausss-thought/.

35. See Marla Zubel, "Remembering the Global '60s: A View from Eastern Europe," *Cultural Critique* 103 (Spring 2019): 36. See also Gerd Koenen, *Das rote Jahrzehnt. Unsere kleine deutsche Kulturrevolution 1967–1977* (Frankfurt am Main: Fischer, 2002), 216–217; Adam Czirak, "Einleitung," in *Aktionskunst jenseits des Eisernen Vorhangs. Künstlerische Kritik in Zeiten politischer Repression*, ed. Adam Czirak (Bielefeld: transcript, 2019), 8–9.

36. Luiza Nader, "Transgressing the Imagination: The Zalesie Ball in 1968," in Claire Bishop and Marta Dziewańska, *1968–1989: Political Upheaval and Artistic Change* (Warsaw: Museum of Modern Art, 2009), 94–95. On the 1960s in Poland more generally, see Małgorzata Fidelis, *Imagining the World from Behind of the Iron Curtain: Youth and the Global Sixties in Poland* (Oxford: Oxford University Press, 2022).

37. See Boris Kanzleiter and Krunoslav Stojaković, *"1968" in Jugoslawien: Studentenproteste und kulturelle Avantgarde zwischen 1960 und 1975. Gespräche und Dokumente* (Bonn: J. H. W. Dietz, 2008).

38. The events that unfolded in 1968 in Poland, Yugoslavia, and Czechoslovakia were well known among student activists in Berlin and Paris. After the Soviet-led invasion of Prague, various West German student groups organized teach-ins and demonstrations in solidarity with the demonstrators. However, the Western students' parochial perspective on Eastern Europe—despite occasional personal visits and contacts—meant that the nuances of the situation were often lost on them. This was especially true of the Polish government's anti-Semitic campaign which, as Gerd Koenen has noted, was thoroughly misjudged by West German activists because they felt that anti-Semitism was "a German privilege." See Koenen, *Das rote Jahrzehnt*, 216–217. Koenen also mentions the blasé attitudes of Western participants at the 1968 seminar jointly held by the Slovak Communist Student Association and student representatives from the University of Tübingen in West Germany (218). See also Czirak, "Einleitung," 8–9.

39. See Annette Gilbert, "Von Witz und Schönheit der Schriftstellerei. Zu den Typewritings von Ruth Wolf-Rehfeldt," in *Ruth Wolf-Rehfeldt. 2021 Gerhard Altenbourg Preis*, exh. cat. (Lindenau-Museum Altenburg, 2021), 26.

40. For a chronicle of the events surrounding the sculpture's destruction, see Edit Sasvári, "'Long Live the Protest-Sign Forest!' Documents for the Protest-Sign Forest," accessed August 21, 2020, http://www.vividradicalmemory.org/htm/workshop/bud_essays/sasvari.pdf.

41. See Klara Kemp-Welch, *Antipolitics in Central European Art: Reticence as Dissidence under Post-Totalitarian Rule 1956–1989* (London: Tauris, 2014). Kemp-Welch does not regard "antipolitics" as synonymous with "nonpolitical" (5).

42. Luc Boltanski and Ève Chiapello, *The New Spirit of Capitalism* (London: Verso, 1999), 467.

43. Beuys is one of the most often cited examples of an instructionally oriented approach to art during the 1960s. However, to the extent that he remained associated with an ultimately romantic understanding of creativity as a genuine form of politics, and with the idea of the artist as an auratic figure of authority, he also stands at some degree of distance from the examples of art-as-demonstration art I discuss in the following chapters.

44. This is not to say, of course, that radical artistic gestures in the West were not also easily appropriated by "the system," or consumed as art rather than as an incentive for revolution. As Daniel Buren wrote in 1968 in a piece entitled "Is Teaching Art Necessary?": "Under these conditions, art in the factory will have as a positive result improvement of the working environment, no more, no less. Pushed to extremes, this will create

esthetic quarrels where otherwise the urge to revolution might have been born." Cited in Lippard, *Six Years*, 52.

45. See Noemi Smolik, "1968 in Prag—die andere Protestbewegung oder wer hört wem zu," in *Flashes of the Future. Die Kunst der 68er oder Die Macht der Ohnmächtigen*, ed. Andreas Beitin and Eckhart J. Gillen, exh. cat. (Ludwig Forum für Internationale Kunst Aachen, 2018), 460–465.

46. Smolik, "1968 in Prag," 460.

47. Andrea Bátorová, *Aktionskunst in der Slowakei. Aktionen von Alex Mlynárčik* (Berlin: Lit Verlag, 2009), 187.

48. See Wolfgang Klafki, *Studien zur Bildungstheorie und Didaktik* (Weinheim: Beltz, 1974), 72.

49. Alex Preminger, ed., *Encyclopedia of Poetry and Poetics* (Princeton, NJ: Princeton University Press, 1974), 190.

50. Preminger, *Encyclopedia*, 190.

51. Norbert Kössinger and Claudia Wittig, *Prodesse et Delectare: Case Studies on Didactic Literature in the European Middle Ages* (Berlin: De Gruyter, 2019).

52. See especially Leo Steinberg, *The Sexuality of Christ in Renaissance Art and in Modern Oblivion* (London: Faber, 1984). Steinberg's findings were controversial; see Charles Hope, "*Ostentatio Genitalium*," *London Review of Books* 6, no. 21 (1984), accessed July 6, 2022, https://www.lrb.co.uk/the-paper/v06/n21/charles-hope/ostentatio-genitalium.

53. Edgar Allan Poe, "The Poetic Principle," in Poe, *Selected Prose and Poetry* (New York: Holt, Rinehart and Winston, 1965), 416–417.

54. Luis Chamnitzer, *Conceptualism in Latin American Art* (Austin: University of Texas Press, 2007), 34.

55. Barbara Rose, "The Value of Didactic Art," *Artforum* (April 1967), 33–36.

56. Rose, "The Value of Didactic Art," 32.

57. As the negation of the art object and art's autonomy more generally, or as a critique of art's commercialism, didactic art remains largely "negative"; this, for Rose, is "its least interesting aspect." By contrast, "positive" didactic art, for Rose, is represented especially in film—she singles out Warhol's *Chelsea Girls*—but also in happenings and other time-based art forms that take their material from reality without at the same time aspiring to be either "art" (through editing or by otherwise creating an aesthetic form) or unedited "life."

58. Rose, "The Value of Didactic Art," 33.

59. Jack Burnham, "Systems Esthetics," *Artforum* 7 (1968). Subsequent citations are from this issue. The essay was later reprinted in Jack Burnham, *Dissolve into Comprehension:*

Writings and Interviews, 1964–2004 (Cambridge, MA: MIT Press, 2015), 115–125. On Burnham's article, see Caroline A. Jones, "Jack Burnham's 'Systems Esthetics,'" *Artforum* 9 (2012), accessed September 25, 2021, https://www.artforum.com/print/201207/caroline-a-jones-on-jack-burnham-s-systems-esthetics-32014; and Luke Skrebowski, "All Systems Go: Recovering Jack Burnham's System Aesthetics," *Grey Room* 30 (Winter 2008), 54-83.

60. Burnham, "Systems Esthetics," 31.

61. Burnham, "Systems Esthetics," 31.

62. In 1966 Lawrence Alloway coined the term "systemic painting" for his survey of "cool abstraction" at the Guggenheim Museum.

63. Marx developed the term *Entfremdung* in his early *Economic-Philosophical Manuscripts*, which were published for the first time in 1932.

64. As Luke Skrebowski writes, Haacke himself notes that it was Burnham who introduced him to systems aesthetics. Skrebowski, "All Systems Go," 60.

65. Skrebowski, "All Systems Go," 55.

66. Burnham, "Systems Esthetics," 35.

67. On more recent art historical takes on the contested divide, in Haacke's work, between early technophilia and the later "political" works, see Skrebowski, "All Systems Go," 59–60.

68. Burnham, "Systems Esthetics," 35. In this context, Burnham finds that that the Soviet productivists were crushed by teleology, as they were unable to resist Stalinist industrialization: "As a group dedicated to historical materialism and the scientific ethos, most of its members were quickly subsumed by the technological needs of Soviet Russia. . . . While the Productivist program might have had some basis as a utilitarian esthetic, it was crushed amid the Stalinist anti-intellectualism that followed it" (35).

69. See also Matthew Rampley, "Systems Aesthetics: Burnham and Others," *Vector* b, no. 12 (January 2005), accessed February 13, 2023, http://virose.pt/vector/b_12/rampley.html.

70. See for example Judith Rodenbeck, "Between the Personal and the Political: On Marianne Wex's *Let's Take Back Our Space*," *ARTMargins* (2022) 11 (12), 50–80.

71. Ivana Bago, email to author, September 29, 2022. In another work, *New Zagreb (People Behind Windows)*, 1979/2006), Iveković hand-colored a black-and-white newspaper photograph of Tito's motorcade to indicate how many people were not following the order to block their windows.

72. Iveković comments on her work in this way: "The action begins when I walk out onto the balcony and sit on a chair, I sip whiskey, read a book, and make gestures as if I perform

masturbation. After a period of time, the policeman rings my doorbell and orders that the 'persons and objects are to be removed from the balcony.'" Quoted from Ruth Noack, *Sanja Iveković: Triangle* (London: Afterall, 2013), 83.

73. On the tension between chance, diagrams, and geometry in Dada, see David Joselit, "Dada's Diagrams," in *The Dada Seminars*, ed. Leah Dickerman with Matthew S. Witkovsky (Washington, DC: National Gallery of Art, 2005), 221–239.

74. A Marxist sociologist and scholar, Tom Bottomore became known, in the early 1960s, as an editor and translator of Karl Marx's long-unknown early manuscripts of 1844, while in his book *Elites and Society* (1964) he examines theories of elitism in light of Marxist and other approaches, weighing in against the rejection of the Marxist notion of "a ruling class." The subject of Bottomore's book had a certain relevance in the former Yugoslavia, where the desire to return to the early ideals of the Yugoslav model of Socialism coupled with a vigorous critique of the country's political elite had been at the very heart of the 1968 student protests.

75. As the artist writes, "due to the construction of the balcony, only the person on the roof can actually see me and follow the action. My assumption is that this person has binoculars and a walkie-talkie apparatus." Cited in Noack, *Sanja Iveković: Triangle*, 83.

76. Brian Rotman, *Mathematics as Sign: Writing, Imagining, Counting* (Stanford, CA: Stanford University Press, 2000), 57.

77. Joselit, "Dada's Diagrams," 237.

78. See also Sven Spieker and Tom Holert, "Introduction: The Heresy of Didactic Art," *ARTMargins* 11 (2022), 3-9.

79. See Oliver Sukrow, "'Designing Freedom'—der Computer zwischen 'Freiheitsmaschine' und 'Kontrollaparat' im globalen Kontext der 68er," in Beitin and Gillen, *Flashes of the Future*, 414. See also Fred Turner, *From Counterculture to Cyberculture: Stewart Brand, the Whole Earth Network, and the Rise of Digital Utopianism* (Chicago: University of Chicago Press, 2006); Dieder Diederichsen and Anselm Franke, eds., *The Whole Earth. Kalifornien und das Verschwinden des Aussen* (Berlin: Sternberg, 2013).

2 OSTENTATIOUS NEUTRALITY (BERNAR VENET, DANIEL BUREN, ADRIAN PIPER)

1. John Willett, ed., *Brecht on Theatre: The Development of an Aesthetic* (New York: Hill and Wang, 1966), 75.

2. Willett, *Brecht on Theatre*, 76.

3. Willett, *Brecht on Theatre*, 72–73.

4. Fredric Jameson, *Brecht and Method* (London: Verso, 1998), 91.

5. In his *Letters on the Aesthetic Education of Man* (1794), Friedrich Schiller had linked what he called the "pedagogical and political artist's" agency to an ability to mediate between the opposed realms of beauty (art) and necessity (nature). See Friedrich Schiller, "Über die ästhetische Erziehung des Menschen in einer Reihe von Briefen," in Friedrich Schiller, *Werke*, vol. 4 (Frankfurt am Main: Suhrkamp, 1966), 262.

6. Walter Benjamin, "The Author as Producer," in Benjamin, *Selected Writings*, vol. 2, part 2, *1931–1934* (Cambridge, MA: Belknap Press of Harvard University Press, 2005), 777.

7. Benjamin, "The Author as Producer," 775.

8. Thierry de Duve, "'Tas de charbon' et 'Tubes': Les accusés de réception de Bernar Venet," in Bernar Venet, *Rétrospective, 2019–1959*, Musée d'Art Contemporain de Lyon (Paris: Éditions Dilecta, 2019), 338; translation mine.

9. "Entretien Bernar Venet / Hans Ulrich Obrist," in Venet, *Rétrospective, 2019–1959*, 150; translation mine.

10. "Interview entre Catherine Millet et Bernar Venet," in *Quatre/cztery*, exh. cat. (Galeria Foksal, 1974), 5.

11. "Entretien Bernar Venet / Hans Ulrich Obrist," 152; translation mine. On Venet's art practice of the 1960s and its connection with the university, see Howard Singerman, *Art Subjects: Making Artists in the American University* (Berkeley: University of California Press, 1999), 167–171.

12. Barbara Rose, "The Paradox of Coherence," in *Bernar Venet: The Paradox of Coherence*, exh. cat. (IVAM Centre Julio Gonzalez, 2010), 147.

13. At the same time, as Rose remarks, Venet took to heart Duchamp's admonition to begin the creation of art from mathematics and physics. See Rose, "The Paradox of Coherence," 145. See also Donald H. Karshan, *The Five Years of Bernar Venet: A Catalogue Raisonné* (New York: New York Cultural Center in Association with Farleigh Dickinson University, 1971), 7.

14. Such differentiation between (scientific) knowledge on the one hand and art on the other—disrupting their alliance in classical aesthetics—is a staple of avant-garde art.

15. Mersch argues that the natural sciences continue even now to idealize the relationship between truth and beauty (the "beauty of an argument" determines how convincing it is). See Dieter Mersch, *Epistemologien des Ästhetischen* (Zurich: Diaphanes, 2015), 76. See also George David Birkhoff, "A Mathematical Approach to Aesthetics," *Scientia* (1931). Conversely, the ideal truth content of a work of art could be measured, as Schiller argued in his *Letters on the Aesthetic Education of Man* (1794), through its aesthetic qualities.

16. See Hans-Christian von Herrmann, "Metatechnik," in *Ästhetik als Programm. Max Bense/Daten und Streuungen*, ed. Barbara Büscher, Hans-Christian von Herrmann, and Christoph Hoffmann (Berlin: Kaleidoskopien, 2004), 45. See also Max Bense, "Kybernetik oder die Metatechnik einer Maschine," in Büscher, von Herrmann, and Hoffmann, *Ästhetik als Programm*, 50–61; Max Bense, *Aesthetica (II). Aesthetische Information* (Baden-Baden: Agis, 1956).

17. "Interview entre Catherine Millet et Bernar Venet," 19.

18. In Eastern Europe, the ruling Communist parties—heir to the same type of technocratic modernity that governed on the other side of the Wall—likewise routinely stressed the central importance of the highly skilled expert.

19. Alain Badiou, *L'hypothèse communiste* (Paris: Éditions Lignes, 2009), 63.

20. This is what Benjamin argues for in "The Author as Producer" when he demands that the writer take up photography because "only by transcending the specialization in the process of intellectual production—a specialization that, in the bourgeois view, constitutes its order—can one make this production politically useful." Benjamin, "The Author as Producer," 775.

21. John Roberts, "Art after Deskilling," *Historical Materialism* 18 (2010): 83. See also Dave Beech, "Weberian Lessons: Art, Pedagogy and Managerialism," in *Curating and the Educational Turn*, ed. Paul O'Neill and Mick Wilson (London: Open Editions/de Appel, 2010), 56–57.

22. Joseph Beuys and Heinrich Böll, "Manifesto on the Foundation of a 'Free International School for Creativity and Interdisciplinary Research,'" in *Joseph Beuys in America. Energy Plan for the Western Man. Writings by and Interviews with the Artist*, ed. Carin Kuoni (New York: Basic Books, 1993), 149–150.

23. Boris Arvatov, *Art and Production* (London: Pluto, 2017).

24. Rose, "The Paradox of Coherence," 148.

25. See Jacques Bertin, *Semiology of Graphics: Diagrams, Networks, Maps* (Redlands, CA: Esri Press, 2010).

26. Bernar Venet, *Art: A Matter of Context. Writings, 1975–2003* (Lenox, MA: Hard Press Editions, 2004), 21. Venet used the term "monosemy" in writing for the first time in 1971, but claims to have read Bertin's book in the late 1960s.

27. "The univocity, the monosemic nature of these signs has no reality except on the level of their use as symbols. My works are not monosemic in and of themselves, but they employ monosemic signs. It is at this level that they are different from what we are familiar with in art." Venet, *Art: A Matter of Context*, 41.

28. Venet's conviction here is a compelling illustration of the position held by Immanuel Kant with regard to mathematical diagrams. In remarks devoted to geometry in his *Critique of Pure Reason* (1781/87), Kant contests the view, widespread in his time, that in mathematics, diagrams are poor, if not misleading, visualizations of concepts with which these visualizations have no essential connection whatsoever. By contrast, for the philosopher, the schematic presentation (*Anschauung*) of a geometric problem by means of a diagram was much more than a visualization; it *was* that problem and as such, exemplified its cognitive structure. See Birgit Schneider and Christoph Ernst, eds., *Diagrammatik-Reader. Grundlegende Texte aus Theorie und Geschichte* (Berlin: De Gruyter Akademie Forschung, 2016), 21–22.

29. Lucy Lippard and John Chandler, "The Dematerialization of Art," in Lippard, *Changimg: Essays in Art Criticism* (New York: Dutton, 1971), 255–276.

30. Diagrams are conventionally understood as a type of schematic drawing (often for purposes of teaching) that shows the structure, appearance, or working of something, often as a step toward a larger piece of work or research. See Susanne Leeb, ed., *Materialität der Diagramme: Kunst und Theorie* (Berlin: b-books, 2012).

31. Venet, *Art: A Matter of Context*, 26. Venet's position at the time also owed a debt to Ad Reinhardt's conception, spelled out most succinctly in his 1953 "Twelve Rules for a New Academy," of an art unencumbered by anything outside of itself. See Ad Reinhardt, excerpts from "Twelve Rules for a New Academy" (1953), *ArtNews* 56, no. 3 (May 1957): 37–38, 56; reprinted in Barbara Rose, ed., *Art-as-Art: The Selected Writings of Ad Reinhardt* (New York: Viking, 1975), 203–207.

32. See Liz Kotz, *Words to Be Looked At: Language in 1960s Art* (Cambridge, MA: MIT Press, 2007), 135–174.

33. Venet, *Art: A Matter of Context*, 95.

34. On the concept of the "educational image" (*Erziehungsbild*), see Tom Holert and Marion von Osten, eds., *Das Erziehungsbild. Zur visuellen Kultur des Pädagogischen* (Vienna: Akademie der Künste, 2010). Thierry de Duve makes a related point when he argues that Venet was not able to predict the reactions of the spectator and that "it was an error to confuse the semiotic and the aesthetic." De Duve, "'Tas de charbon' et 'Tubes,'" 340; translation mine.

35. Otto Neurath, "Pictorial Statistics Following the Vienna Method," trans. Sven Spieker, *ARTMargins* 1 (2017): 117–118.

36. Not coincidentally, in his 1967 essay "The Death of the Author," Roland Barthes had explicitly linked his argument for the disappearance of the author as an authoritative instance regarding his or her text's inherent meaning to the rise of information-as-literature

and semiology. Roland Barthes, "The Death of the Author," in Barthes, *Image. Music. Text* (London: Fontana, 1977), 142–148.

37. Lucy R. Lippard, *Six Years: The Dematerialization of the Art Object from 1966 to 1972* (Berkeley: University of California Press, 1973), 23.

38. This was important to Venet, who was eager to displace the innovative thrust of his works from form and expression to content. His idea was that if the scientific information was outdated after a certain period of time, it needed to be replaced, dealing another blow to the integrity of the artwork as object.

39. In 1969, Venet began his *Wall Street* series, presenting diagrams from a series of articles the economist Gem Margello published in the magazine *Newsweek* throughout 1969. Venet produced as many panels as Margello published articles in that year. "Interview entre Catherine Millet et Bernar Venet," 10.

40. "Interview entre Catherine Millet et Bernar Venet," 13.

41. "Interview entre Catherine Millet et Bernar Venet," 13.

42. "Interview entre Catherine Millet et Bernar Venet," 11.

43. "Interview entre Catherine Millet et Bernar Venet," 11.

44. Jack Burnham, *The Structure of Art* (New York: George Braziller, 1971), 152.

45. Venet's approach corresponds with the heightened interest during the mid- to late 1960s in efforts to describe the nature of epistemological ("paradigm") shifts in scientific thought, from Thomas Kuhn's *Structure of Scientific Revolutions* (1962) to Diana Crane's *Invisible Colleges* (1972).

46. Guy Debord and Gil J. Wolman, "A User's Guide to Détournement," *Les Lèvres Nues* 8 (May 1956), accessed November 8, 2021, http://www.bopsecrets.org/SI/detourn.htm.

47. Thomas Levin has discussed the importance of discussion and the didactic in Debord's films. See Thomas Levin, "Dismantling the Spectacle: The Cinema of Guy Debord," in *Guy Debord and the Situationist International: Texts and Documents*, ed. Tom McDonough (Cambridge, MA: MIT Press, 2002), 321–453. See especially 330, 370, 372, 365, 426, 428.

48. Theodor W. Adorno, *Minima Moralia* (Frankfurt am Main: Suhrkamp, 1979), 85; translation mine.

49. For Venet's views on Buren's work at the time, see Bernar Venet, "A Summary of Responses to Basic Questions, 1975," in Venet, *Art: A Matter of Context*, 46.

50. See Lippard, *Six Years*, 45. These activities were preceded by the famous demonstrations (*manifestations*) by Buren and his friends Olivier Mosset, Michel Parmentier, and Niele Toroni at the 18th Salon de la Jeune Peinture in January 1967. See Benjamin Buchloh,

"The Group That Was (Not) One: Daniel Buren and BMPT," *Artforum International* 46, no. 9 (May 2008), accessed January 1, 2022, https://www.artforum.com/print/200805/the-group-that-was-not-one-daniel-buren-and-bmpt-19959.

51. See the summary of these arguments in Sami Siegelbaum, "The Riddle of May '68: Collectivity and Protest in the Salon de la Jeune Peinture," *Oxford Art Journal* 35, no. 1 (2012), esp. 64.

52. Siegelbaum, "The Riddle of May '68," 65.

53. Siegelbaum, "The Riddle of May '68," 65.

54. The action's documentation consists of a ring binder with forty-four hand-annotated pages torn from Piper's paperback copy of the *Critique*, together with fourteen photographic self-portraits. On Piper's performance, see Sven Spieker, "Akusmatische Reduktion und Akusmatizität in der Kunst der 1960er Jahre (Robert Morris, Bernar Venet, Adrian Piper)," in *Akusmatik als Labor: Kultur, Kunst, Medien*, ed. Sven Spieker and Mario Asef (Würzburg: Königshauses & Neumann, 2023), 83–97.

55. Adrian Piper, "Food for the Spirit," in Adrian Piper, *Out of Order, Out of Sight*, vol. 1: *Selected Writings in Meta-Art, 1968–1992* (Cambridge, MA: MIT Press, 1996), 55.

56. Elizabeth Kaufmann, "Adrian Piper and Immanuel Kant: Toward a Synthesis of Art and Philosophy" (MFA thesis, University of Cincinnati, 2009), 30. Robert Storr underlines the point about Piper's didactic engagement when he writes that "Piper's education prompted her to become an educator. Among the many roles she has played in her professional life . . . all relate to this primary vocation. It was the least common of choices for artists. If they taught at all, most of them did so to sustain an aesthetic endeavor that eschewed didacticism of any kind. Contrary to that norm, and to its historical art for art's sake justification, Piper has mounted a spirited and articulate defense of the didactic mode. In essence she has revived the classical ideal, that, as well as please, art should, without qualm or dissemblance, instruct." Robert Storr, foreword to Piper, *Out of Order, Out of Sight*, vol. 2: *Selected Writings in Art Criticism, 1967–1992* (Cambridge, MA: MIT Press, 1996), xi. Piper's best-known instructional work is the collaborative performance *Funk Lessons* (1984/84). On Piper's didacticism, see also Grant H. Kester, *Conversation Pieces: Community and Communication in Modern Art* (Berkeley: University of California Press, 2004), 79–81.

57. Adrian Piper, "Talking to Myself: The Ongoing Autobiography of an Art Object," in Piper, *Out of Order, Out of Sight*, 1:30. See also Jörg Heiser, "Adventures in Reasonland," in *Adrian Piper: A Reader*, ed. Cornelia H. Butler and David Platzker (New York: Museum of Modern Art, 2018), 27–28.

58. See also Heiser, "Adventures in Reasonland," 25.

59. "Je stärker die Sinne bei eben demselben Grade des auf sie geschehenen Einflusses sich affiziert fühlen, desto weniger lehren sie. Umgekehrt: wenn sie viel lehren sollen, müssen

sie mäßig affizieren." Immanuel Kant, "Anthropologie in pragmatischer Hinsicht," §19, in Immanuel Kant, *Werkausgabe*, vol. 12: *Schriften zur Anthropologie, Geschichtsphilosophie, Politik und Pädagogik 2* (Frankfurt am Main: Suhrkamp, 1977), 452; translation mine, with emphasis added.

60. Sense (*Sinn*) "is the ability of contemplation in the presence of the object." The outer sense, according to Kant, is the one whereby the human body is affected by corporeal things; the inner sense, by contrast, is the one where it is affected by the soul (*Gemüt*). Kant, "Anthropologie in pragmatischer Hinsicht," §13, 445.

61. Piper, "Food for the Spirit," 55.

62. Piper, "Food for the Spirit," 55. See also Kaja Silverman, *The Female Authorial Voice in the Acoustic Mirror in Psychoanalysis and Cinema* (Bloomington: Indiana University Press, 1988), 187–234.

63. Piper, "Food for the Spirit," 55.

64. Piper, "Food for the Spirit," 55.

65. Martin Heidegger, "Was heißt Lesen?," in *Gesamtausgabe*, section 1, *Veröffentlichte Schriften 1910–1976*, vol. 13: *Aus der Erfahrung des Denkens* (Frankfurt am Main: Vittorio Klostermann, 2002), 111. The connection between *lesen* (reading) and *Sammeln* (collecting) is grounded in the etymological link between *lesen* and the Greek verb *legein* (to collect, gather). There are still some German compound nouns that preserve the etymology of lesen as "gathering," such as *Auslese* (vintage collection) or *Weinlese* (grape harvest). One other such (now obsolete) term, *Blütenlese* (in Greek, *anthología*), signifies a collection of meaningful utterances by historical personalities.

66. Adrian Piper, "Food for the Spirit," 55.

67. Hans-Georg Gadamer, *Truth and Method*, trans. Joel Weinsheimer and Donald G. Marshall (London: Continuum, 1989), 153.

68. One of the pioneering texts of this kind of criticism was David Bleich's *Readings and Feelings: An Introduction to Subjective Criticism* (1975). In 1967, the critic Stanley Fish published *Surprised by Sin*, which focused on the reader's experience of Milton's *Paradise Lost*. See Stanley Fish, *Surprised by Sin: The Reader in Paradise Lost* (1967; repr., Cambridge, MA: Harvard University Press, 1998).

3 BURLESQUE LECTURE DEMONSTRATION (ROBERT MORRIS, WALTER BENJAMIN)

1. See also Sven Spieker, "Unoriginal Pedagogies: 'Didactic' Art as Edification (Robert Morris, Walter Benjamin, Ilya Kabakov)," in *Ethos und Pathos. Mediale Wirkungsästhetik im*

20. Jahrhundert in Ost und West, ed. R. Nicolosi and T. Zimmermann (Munich: Böhlau), 413–423.

2. The neo-avant-gardist, student-run Galerie Aachen existed from 1965 to 1967. Its co-director was Valdis Abolins, the organizer of the festival at Technische Hochschule Aachen in July 1964. Among the many artist demonstrations organized by Abolins at the gallery were the protests staged by Jörg Immendorff and his LIDL Academy. See Renate Puvogel, "Wollt Ihr das totale Leben? 'Fluxus und Agit-Pop der 60er Jahre in Aachen.' Neuer Aachener Kunstverein, 14.1.–19.2.1995," *Kunstforum* 130 (1995), accessed July 14, 2022, https://www.kunstforum.de/artikel/wollt-ihr-das-totale-leben/.

3. See the archive collection of Galerie Aachen at Cologne University, December 1965 to 1967, accessed January 1, 2022, https://zadik.uni-koeln.de/homepage/bestand_personen.aspx?person=450&b_id=291.

4. Jacques Lacan, "My Teaching, Its Nature and Its Ends," in Lacan, *My Teaching* (London: Verso, 2008), 59–60.

5. Jacques Lacan, "So, You Will Have Heard Lacan," in Lacan, *My Teaching*, 94-95.

6. Lacan, "My Teaching, Its Nature and Its Ends," 60.

7. Jacques Lacan, "The Place, Origin and End of My Teaching," in Lacan, *My Teaching*, 26.

8. Sibylle Peters, "Von der Kunst des Demonstrierens. Zur Figuration von Evidenz in der Performance des Vortrags," in *"Intellektuelle Anschauung." Figurationen von Evidenz zwischen Kunst und Wissen*, ed. Sibylle Peters and Martin Jörg Schäfer (Bielefeld: transcript 2006), 201–222, https://doi.org/10.25969/mediarep/2398.

9. Friedrich Daniel Ernst Schleiermacher, "Occasional Thoughts about Universities in the German Sense: With a Supplement about a University Soon to Be Founded," in *Gründungstexte. Festgabe zum 200-jährigen Jubiläum der Humboldt-Universität zu Berlin, hg. v. Präsidenten der Humboldt-Universität zu Berlin* (2010), 161, accessed December 30, 2021, https://edoc.hu-berlin.de/handle/18452/5304.

10. The philosopher G. W. F. Hegel's lectures at the university of Berlin, which were often barely intelligible to his listeners, can serve as a good example of such proceedings.

11. The piece's title, *21.3*, was allegedly the number of an art history course Morris had taught at Hunter College, New York, during the early 1960s. See Gordon Hall, "Read Me That Part Again, Where I Disinherit Everybody," accessed December 13, 2021, http://gordonhall.net/files/read_me_that_part_a-gain_where_I_disin-herit_everybody_gordon_hall.pdf.

12. Rosalind Krauss, "The Mind/Body Problem: Robert Morris in Series," in *Robert Morris*, ed. Julia Bryan-Wilson (Cambridge, MA: MIT Press, 2013), 76. Maurice Berger has called *21.3* a "travesty." Maurice Berger, "The Politics of Experience: Robert Morris,

Minimalism, and the 1960s" (PhD diss., Graduate Center, City University of New York, 1988), 46, https://academicworks.cuny.edu/cgi/viewcontent.cgi?article=2660&context=gc_etds.

13. Erwin Panofsky, *Meaning in the Visual Arts* (New York City: Doubleday Anchor, 1955), 26.

14. Panofsky, *Meaning in the Visual Arts*, 23.

15. Panofsky, *Meaning in the Visual Arts*, 23.

16. Morris had meticulously noted the lecturer's movements in the script for his performance.

17. The title of Morris's piece is reminiscent of Cage's *4′33″*.

18. John Cage, "Lecture on Nothing," in Cage, *Silence: Lectures and Writings by John Cage* (Middletown, CT: Wesleyan University Press, 2011), 109.

19. Branden W. Joseph, "Robert Morris and John Cage: Reconstructing a Dialogue," in Bryan-Wilson, *Robert Morris*, 140–141. See also John Cage, *Work List Edition Peters* (New York: Edition Peters, 1962), 41.

20. Simon Aeberhard, "Writing the Ephemeral: John Cage's Lecture on Nothing as a Landmark in Media History," *Journal of Sonic Studies* 13 (2017), accessed September 23, 2018, https://www.researchcatalogue.net/view/323127/323128#323260.

21. Anael Lejeune, "21.3 (1964) de Robert Morris: L'iconologie et la forme au travail," in *Les conférences d'artistes: Entre fiction théorique et geste artistique* (Rennes: Presses Universitaires de Rennes, 2015), accessed January 17, 2022, https://dial.uclouvain.be/pr/boreal/object/boreal:135916. After Morris met his future wife, the choreographer Simone Forti, he developed doubts about his calling as an abstract painter. With her encouragement, he began to participate in the dance collective taught by Anna Halprin in San Francisco. See Carrie Lambert, "Moving Still: Mediating Yvonne Rainer's 'Trio A,'" *October* 89 (1999): 87–112; and Virginia Spivey, "Sites of Subjectivity: Robert Morris, Minimalism, and Dance," *Dance Research Journal* 35, no. 2 / 36, no. 1 (2003–2004): 113–130.

22. See Joseph, "Robert Morris and John Cage," 142.

23. John Cage, "In this Day . . .", in Cage, *Silence*, 94.

24. See Joseph, "Robert Morris and John Cage," 140–141.

25. See Lambert, "Moving Still," and Spivey, "Sites of Subjectivity."

26. Robert Morris, "Notes on Dance," *Tulane Drama Review* 10, no. 2 (1965): 179–186; emphasis mine.

27. Annette Michelson, "Yvonne Rainer, Part One: The Dancer and the Dance," *Artforum* 1 (1974): 59.

28. Jacques Derrida, *L'Université sans condition* (Paris: Galilée, 2001), 35; translation mine. Derrida's essay was originally delivered as a Presidential Lecture at Stanford University in 1998. This version can be found in *Jacques Derrida and the Humanities: A Critical Reader*, ed. Tom Cohen (Cambridge: Cambridge University Press, 2001), 24–57.

29. Derrida, *L'Université sans condition*, 36; translation mine.

30. The earliest reference to lecturing as (art) performance arguably occurred in 1917 when Katherine Dreier, the cofounder of the Society of Independent Artists and its head of public education, supported Marcel Duchamp and his friend Walter Arensberg in their efforts to organize a public lecture on "The Independent Artists in France and America" by the rebellious poet and boxer Arthur Cravan, author of the short-lived magazine *Maintenant* (1912–1914). After Cravan finally arrived, dead drunk, went on stage and, instead of delivering a lecture, began hurling insults at the audience and took off his clothes, Duchamp reportedly commented: "What a wonderful lecture." See Larry Whitham, *Picasso and the Chess Player: Pablo Picasso, Marcel Duchamp, and the Battle for the Soul of Modern Art* (Hanover, NH: University Press of New England, 2013), 125.

31. Tristan Tzara, "Lecture on Dada," in *The Dada Painters and Poets: An Anthology*, ed. Robert Motherwell (Cambridge, MA: Harvard University Press, 1981), 247.

32. Tzara, "Lecture on Dada," 247.

33. The following year (1987), a film was made of Benjamin's performance of the lecture at Belgrade University, this time in English. On Walter Benjamin and his activities as a performer, see Inke Arns, "Tripping into Art (Hi)Stories: Genealogy and/as Fiction. On the Exhibition 'What Is Modern Art?' (Group Show)," in *What Is Modern Art? (Group Show)*, exh. cat. (Künstlerhaus Bethanien Berlin, September 29–October 29, 2006), 7–8. While Benjamin's first lecture in Ljubljana was titled "Mondrian '63–'96" and was organized by the Marxist Center and ŠKUC Gallery, the second lecture, delivered in English, was recorded and later broadcast on Belgrade's public television program *TV Galerija*, with the title *Mondrian Lecture*. For the text of the lecture, see Walter Benjamin, "Mondrian '63–'96," in Benjamin, *Recent Writings* (Los Angeles: New Documents, 2013), 21–26.

34. Walter Benjamin, "The Work of Art in the Age of Its Technical Reproduciblity," in Benjamin, *The Work of Art in the Age of Its Technical Reproduciblity and Other Writings on Media*, ed. Michael W. Jennings et al. (Cambridge, MA: Harvard University Press, 2008), 19.

35. Benjamin, "The Work of Art," 21.

36. Benjamin, "Mondrian '63–'96," 23.

37. Benjamin, "Mondrian '63–'96," 24.

38. In his book *Philosophy and the Mirror of Nature*, Rorty distinguished between "edifying" and "systematic" philosophy, the latter involving reformulations of known truths or facts rather than truth's new foundation. While systematic philosophy seeks to find a new

way in which to ground an absolute truth, edifying philosophy searches for deviating or otherwise "abnormal" ways of speaking. In doing so, edifying philosophy, according to Rorty, does not question the need to search for, or teach, facts; it is more than anything interested in different ways of speaking about them, suggesting that any truth procedure is only one specific example of what may be a broad spectrum of possible narratives about what is or may be true. See Richard Rorty, *Philosophy and the Mirror of Nature* (Princeton, NJ: Princeton University Press, 1979).

39. Jacques Derrida, *Positions* (Chicago: University of Chicago Press, 1981), 43.

40. See Bojana Videkanić, *Nonaligned Modernism: Socialist Postcolonial Aesthetics in Yugoslavia, 1945–1985* (Montreal: McGill/Queens University Press, 2020).

41. A related and controversial argument is made by Boris Groys in his book *The Total Art of Stalinism: Avant-Garde, Aesthetic Dictatorship, and Beyond* (Princeton, NJ: Princeton University Press, 1992), where he argues that Stalinist culture takes up the goals and ambitions of the Soviet avant-garde.

4 FILM AS OPERATION (HARUN FAROCKI, PAWEŁ KWIEK)

1. See also Tom Holert, "Tabular Images: About *The Division of All Days* (1970) and *Something Self Explanatory (15 x)* (1971)," in *Harun Farocki: Against What? Against Whom?*, ed. Antje Ehmann and Kodwo Eshun, exh. cat., Raven Row (London: Koenig Books, 2009), 75–92. Farocki's didactics has become the subject of systematic study, for example at the 2020 workshop "'Wie man sieht': Zur Didaktik von Harun Farocki" at Siegen University in Germany, organized by Phillipp Goll and Anne Margarete Röhl.

2. In 1968, the German Film and Television Academy (dffb), where Farocki studied, was temporarily renamed "Dziga Vertov Academy."

3. Harun Farocki, "Die Votze ist kein Radio," in Farocki, *Schriften*, vol. 3: *Meine Nächte mit den Linken. Texte 1964–1975*, ed. Volker Pantenburg (Berlin and Cologne: Harun Farocki Institut/n.b.k and Verlag der Buchhandlung Walther König, 2018), 56; translations from Farocki are mine unless otherwise noted.

4. Farocki, "Die Votze ist kein Radio," 59–60.

5. Harun Farocki, "Staubsauger oder Maschinenpistolen. Ein Wanderkino für Technologien," in Farocki, *Schriften*, vol. 3, 59–60.

6. Harun Farocki, *Nicht löschbares Feuer, Harun Farocki Filme 1967–2005*, 5 DVDs (Absolut Medien, 2011).

7. In May 1967, a month after 125,000 people demonstrated against the Vietnam War in New York City, an antiwar arson attack was leveled against the department store

L'Innovation in Brussels, killing 322 people. The West Berlin-based Kommune 1 collective issued four flyers in which their authors expressed sorrow for the victims' families but also gratification about the empathy for Vietnam that the attack had elicited: "A burning department store with burning people for the first time in a European metropolis gave us that crackling Vietnam-like feeling of being there, of also being aflame that so far we are missing in Berlin." The authors of the flyers were indicted but eventually cleared of all charges. See Ulrich Enzensberger, *Die Jahre der Kommune I* (Munich: Goldmann, 2006), 135–145, my translation.

8. See Guntram Vogt, "Studenten- und Debütfilme im Umkreis der 68er Frühe Filme an der DFFB," *AugenBlick. Marburger Hefte zur Medienwissenschaft*, no. 42: *40 Jahre Erinnerung an 68—Tyrannei der Jahreszahl?* (2008): 43–65, https://doi.org/10.25969/mediarep/2066.

9. A crucial reference point for Farocki and his fellow dffb students during that time were the so-called Ciné tracts produced in 1968 by Jean-Luc Godard, Jackie Raynal, Alain Resnais, Philippe Garrel, Gérard Fromanger, and others. I thank Tom Holert for this important reference.

10. The arrows modify and direct our perception and rationalize the flow of information in an effort to expand the viewer's media competence. See Harun Farocki Institut, "November 2017: *Anleitung, Polizisten den Helm abzureissen*," accessed February 23, 2023, https://www.harun-farocki-institut.org/de/2017/11/30/november-2017-anleitung-polizisten-den-helm-abzureissen/.

11. Vladimir Ilich Lenin, *What Is to Be Done? Burning Questions of Our Movement*, Marxists Internet Archive, accessed January 11, 2022, https://www.marxists.org/archive/lenin/works/1901/witbd/iii.htm; emphasis mine.

12. Lenin, *What Is to Be Done?*; emphasis mine. The distinction between agitation and propaganda goes back to Georgii Plekhanov, the founder of the Russian Social-Democratic movement. According to him, while the propagandist demonstrates ideas to a number of people, the agitator focuses on a few ideas that they bring before a larger number of people.

13. Walter Benjamin, "The Author as Producer," in Benjamin, *Selected Writings*, vol. 2, part 2, *1931–1934* (Cambridge, MA: Belknap Press of Harvard University Press, 2005), 771.

14. Farocki, "Staubsauger oder Maschinenpistolen," 59–60. Farocki was using an Ampex film recorder at the time, see footnote 1 on p. 59.

15. Klafki's article "Zur bildungstheoretischen Bedeutung der modernen Didaktik" (On the importance of modern didacticism for the theory of education) appeared in 1959; Wagenschein's book *Verstehen lehren. Genetisch—Sokratisch—Exemplarisch* (Teaching how to understand: genetically—socratically—and by example) was published in 1968.

16. Harun Farocki, "Die Agitation verwissenschaftlichen," in Farocki, *Schriften*, vol. 3, 63.

17. "Leftist agitation cannot adopt the methods of didacticism, it has to transform them." Farocki, "Die Agitation verwissenschaftlichen," 72; translation mine.

18. Farocki, "Die Agitation verwissenschaftlichen," 72. For Walter Benjamin, the "operating writer" (*der operierende Schrifsteller*) is an example of how progressive politics and technical innovation depend on each other. Benjamin, "The Author as Producer," 770.

19. On Farocki's later development of the "operational image" and its links to his early film theory, see Volker Pantenburg, "Working Images: Harun Farocki and the Operational Image," in *Image Operations: Visual Media and Political Conflict*, ed. Jens Eder and Charlotte Klonk (Manchester, UK: Manchester University Press, 2016), 49–62.

20. Rudi Dutschke, "Die geschichtlichen Bedingungen für den internationalen Emanzipationskampf," in *Rebellion der Studenten oder Die neue Opposition*, ed. Uwe Bergmann, Rudi Dutschke et al. (Reinbek: Rowohlt, 1968), 86–87.

21. The killing inspired Joseph Beuys to found the Deutsche Studentenpartei (German Student Party) in 1967: "Beuys saw this party as a pedagogical party [*Erziehungspartei*] focused on the free academy, 'the education of human beings, by means of art, to be independent and autonomous,' and the expansion of political consciousness." Peter Weibel, ed., *Beuys Brock Vostell. Aktion Demonstration Partizipation 1949–1983* (Ostfildern: Hatje Cantz, 2016), 220; translation mine.

22. Both carry paper bags over their heads that have the royal couple's stylized faces printed on them. Ulrich Enzensberger reports that student protesters produced these bags, which had small openings for the eyes, from supermarket shopping bags on the eve of the shah's visit, and that these bags helped them protect their identities from German press photographers and from the agents of the Iranian secret police (Savvak). See Enzensberger, *Die Jahre der Kommune I*, 147.

23. Bahman Nirumand, *Persien. Modell eines Entwicklungslandes, oder die Diktatur der freien Welt* (Frankfurt am Main: Rowohlt, 1967). Nirumand's book, the first of its kind and written in German, tells the story of the exploitation of Iranian oil by outside powers including Britain and the United States. In June 1967, Nirumand gave a speech about the shah's visit at West Berlin's Free University before several thousand students.

24. Rudi Dutschke, "Vom Antisemitismus zum Antikommunismus" in Bergmann, Dutschke et al., *Rebellion der Studenten*, 79–80; Enzensberger, *Die Jahre der Kommune I*, 145, 147.

25. Cited from "The Words of the Chairman," accessed May 26, 2023, https://www.harunfarocki.de/films/1960s/1967/the-words-of-the-chairman.html.

26. Cited from "The Words of the Chairman."

27. Meins's militant three-minute instructional film shows a woman's hands adding an explosive liquid to a wine bottle and stuffing the bottle's opening with a rag that is then put on fire. The film ends, tellingly, with an image of the Berlin headquarters of Germany's most notorious right-wing publisher, Springer Verlag. The public destruction of Springer newspapers was a prominent form of protest in Germany in the late 1960s. For a critique that argues that student protesters in West Germany in 1968 confused symbolic actions with reality, see Jürgen Habermas, *Protestbewegung und Hochschulreform* (Frankfurt am Main: Suhrkamp, 1969). Habermas critiques this confusion as a *Scheinrevolution* (would-be revolution) (197–198).

28. Napalm, a jelly-like substance made of gasoline that was extremely flammable and sticky, had been used in World War II. By the late 1960s, when the US government handed all of its production over to a small chemicals company based in Michigan, Dow Chemical, its production using gasoline, benzene, and polystyrene was greatly simplified. See "Napalm and the Dow Chemical Company," article related to *Two Days in October*, on *The American Experience*, PBS, aired October 17, 2005, accessed August 15, 2022, https://www.pbs.org/wgbh/americanexperience/features/two-days-in-october-dow-chemical-and-use-napalm/.

29. Farocki, *Nicht löschbares Feuer.*

30. Farocki, *Nicht löschbares Feuer*; translation mine.

31. I thank David Crowley for pointing me to the relevance of Kwiek's work for my argument.

32. Farocki, "Die Agitation verwissenschaftlichen," 72.

33. Łukasz Ronduda, "SocArt, or the Attempt at Revitalising Avant-Garde Strategies in the [sic!] Polish Art of the 1970s," in Łukasz Ronduda and Florian Zeyfang, *1, 2, 3 . . . Avant-Gardes: Film/Art between Experiment and Archive* (Berlin: Sternberg Press, 2007), 51. See also Łukasz Ronduda, *Polish Art of the '70s* (Jelenia Góra: Polski Western/Ujazdowski Castle Centre for Contemporary Art, Warsaw, 2009), 232–236.

34. More specifically, the TV program was devoted to the Workshop of Film Form, an interdisciplinary group of students and graduates at the Leon Schiller National Higher School of Film, Television, and Theater in Łódź (with Paweł Kwiek among them). The group had formed in 1970 and subjected the school's didactic principles and curriculum to a fundamental critique. As Ronduda has written, the group operated at the intersection of film and the visual arts, effectively creating its own educational research program: Łukasz Ronduda, "The Workshop of the Film Form. Film Realizations from the Years 1970–1977," Monoskop, last modified October 21, 2022, https://monoskop.org/Workshop_of_Film_Form. See also http://www.exchange-gallery.pl/english/wff.html, especially for the workshop's roots in the 1960s Toruń-based art group Zero-61. Ronduda relates this

performance and other video projects of the time to Kwiek's interest in cybernetics. See Ronduda, *Polish Art of the '70s*, 286.

35. Paweł Kwiek, *Video C* (1975), Filmoteka Muzeum, Museum of Modern Art in Warsaw, accessed February 23, 2023, https://artmuseum.pl/en/filmoteka/praca/kwiek-pawel-video-c. Citation from Ronduda, *Polish Art of the '70s*, 287.

36. Citation from Ronduda, *Polish Art of the '70s*, 287.

37. Kwiek's creation of model situations like the one in *Video A* can be related to Debord's ideas concerning the creation of situations. Not coincidentally, Debord considered (documentary) film ideally suited for the education of the new Situationist generation: "Since the systematic construction of situations will give rise to previously unknown sentiments, film will find its greatest educational role in the dissemination of these new passions." Guy Debord, "Report on the Construction of Situations," in *Situationist International Anthology*, ed. Ken Knabb (Berkeley, CA: Bureau of Public Secrets, 2006), 40. Indeed, Debord's view of film—as strictly antirepresentational and demonstrative—is close in many ways to Kwiek's structural approach to the medium, and the latter's ambition to use his model to "observe what is over the horizon of everyday life" is as close to what the Situationists had in mind as it could be. See Debord, "Report on the Construction of Situations," 41. On Situationism in Poland, see Krzysztof Hoffmann, "Niech żyje sytuacjonizm (w literaturze polskiej)," *Czas Kultury* 2 (2018): 64–73.

5 TAKING IT TO THE STREET: EASTERN EUROPEAN ART DEMONSTRATIONS (MILAN KNÍŽÁK, JIŘÍ KOVANDA, ENDRE TÓT, MLADEN MILJANOVIĆ, CIPRIAN HOMORODEAN)

1. Cited from Eckhart J. Gillen, "Performative Aufklärung falschen Bewusstseins. Happening, Performance und Action-Teaching bei Beuys-Vostell-Brock 1960–1970," in *Flashes of the Future. Die Kunst der 68er oder Die Macht der Ohnmächtigen*, ed. Andreas Beitin and Eckhart J. Gillen, exh. cat. (Ludwig Forum für Internationale Kunst Aachen, 2018), 169.

2. Gillen, "Performative Aufklärung falschen Bewusstseins," 169.

3. Václav Havel, "An Anatomy of Reticence," in Havel, *Living in Truth: Twenty-Two Essays Published on the Occasion of the Award of the Erasmus Prize to Václav Havel* (London: Faber and Faber, 1987), 166–167. Klara Kemp-Welch adds that "artists in late socialist Eastern Europe might well also have yawned when they heard the word 'politics.'" Klara Kemp-Welch, *Antipolitics in Central European Art: Reticence as Dissidence under Post-Totalitarian Rule 1956–1989* (London: Tauris, 2014), 8.

4. Knížák became director of Fluxus East in 1965. He is known for organizing and performing the first happenings and Fluxus concerts in Czechoslovakia. In the late 1960s he visited the United States, but returned home disappointed.

5. Pavlína Morganová, *Czech Action Art: Happenings, Actions, Events, Land Art, Body Art, and Performance Art Behind the Iron Curtain* (Prague: Karolinum Press, 2014), 50.

6. The manifesto, originally published in the journal Tvár in 1965, was published in English. Cited in Pavlína Morganová, "Czech Action Art in the 1960s Press," in *Akce, Slovo, Pohyb, Prostor. Experimenty v umění šedesátých let*, ed. Vit Havránek (Prague: Galerie hlavního města Prahy, 1999). Aktual's goal was social enlightenment, and the group also created music, self-publishing (samizdat), mail art, and other activities, without always framing them as art.

7. Milan Knížák, "Aktual Art—An Aktual Walk around Nový Svět / Demonstration for All the Senses," in Pavlína Morganová, *A Walk through Prague: Actions, Performances, Happenings, 1949–1989* (Prague: Academy of Fine Arts, 2017), 32–33.

8. Milan Knížák, "Demonstration for One," in Morganová, *Czech Action Art*, 56–57. Morganová illuminates the affinities (and differences) of the artist's actions with Western-style happenings. With regard to *Demonstration for One*, she points out that "the costume for this action was not merely uniquely eccentric; in this period Knížak designed clothing that was both strangely provocative and a new fashion" (57).

9. Theodor W. Adorno, *Minima Moralia* (Frankfurt am Main: Suhrkamp, 1979), 89.

10. Milan Knížák, "Why Indeed. Lecture as Demonstration" (1964/65), unpublished manuscript.

11. Alain Badiou, *Being and Event* (London: Bloomsbury, 2007), 203. An "event," in Badiou's sense, "ruptures the appearance of normality . . . opening a space to rethink reality from the standpoint of its real basis in inconsistent multiplicity." Quoted in Andy McLaverty-Robinson, "An A to Z Theory: Alain Badiou: The Event," *Ceasefire*, December 15, 2014, https://ceasefiremagazine.co.uk/alain-badiou-event/.

12. Milan Knížák, "Why Indeed. Lecture as Demonstration," unpubl. ms.

13. "Szombathy, Bálint: Lenin in Budapest" (1972/2010), Ludwig Museum, Budapest, accessed January 10, 2022, https://www.ludwigmuseum.hu/en/work/lenin-budapest.

14. Overidentification is a form of subversive affirmation, whereby a position is expressed not negatively—in open opposition to what is being negated—but, on the contrary, by identifying with what one criticizes. See, most recently, Sylvia Sasse, *Subversive Affirmation. Denkt Kunst* (Berlin: Diaphanes, 2022).

15. Cited in Miško Šuvaković, "Szombathy Art," accessed April 19, 2023, http://www.acax.eu/muveszek/szombathy_balint.580.html?downloadType580=doc&download

File580=932. In a related project equally focused on recontextualization and entitled *Bauhaus* (1972), Szombathy placed a white cardboard with the name "Bauhaus" in various places around his own home, contrasting the disorder of a private abode with the legacy of a modernist institution known for its rationality and deliberateness.

16. "Alas, they control only an empty form that each addressee will fill with the meanings provided by his own cultural models. The strategic solution is summed up in the sentence 'We must occupy the chair of the Minister of Information' or even 'We must occupy the chair of the publisher of *The New York Times*.'" Umberto Eco, "Towards a Semiological Guerrilla Warfare," in Eco, *Travels in Hyperreality* (San Diego: Harcourt Brace Jovanovich, 1986), 142.

17. Eco, "Towards a Semiological Guerrilla Warfare," 142.

18. See Cécile Whiting, "Andy Warhol, the Public Star and the Private Self," *Oxford Art Journal* 2 (1987): 58–75.

19. *Europa* is also the name of one of the first Polish avant-garde silent films (dir. by Stefan and Franciszka Themerson), also named after Stern's poem.

20. I thank Wojciech Krukowski (Akademia ruchu's founder) and Krzysztof Żwirblis, a group member, for generously answering my questions about this action.

21. Kathrin Fahlenbrach, "Protestinszenierungen. Die Studentenbewegung im Spannungsfeld von Kultur-Revolution und Medien-Evolution," in *1968. Handbuch zur Kultur- und Mediengeschichte der Studentenbewegung*, ed. Martin Klimke and Joachim Scharloth (Stuttgart: Metzler, 2007), 13.

22. Mia Lee, "Umherschweifen und Spektakel: Die situationistische Tradition," in Klimke and Scharloth, *1968. Handbuch*, 101.

23. Lee, "Umherschweifen und Spektakel," 101. See also Uwe Bergmann, "Die Einleitung des Konflikts auf die Stadt," in *Rebellion der Studenten oder Die neue Opposition*, ed. Uwe Bergmann, Rudi Dutschke, et al. (Reinbek: Rowohlt, 1968), 25; Fahlenbrach, "Protestinszenierungen," 14.

24. See Kata Krasznahorkai and Sylvia Sasse, eds., *Artists and Agents: Performance Art and the Secret Services* (Leipzig: Spector Books, 2019).

25. Kata Krasznahorkai, "Black or White? Angela Davis, Bobby Seale und Black Power in den Akten der Staatssicherheit in den 1970er Jahren," in *Aktionskunst jenseits des Eisernen Vorhangs. Künstlerische Kritik in Zeiten politischer Repression*, ed. Adam Czirak (Bielefeld: transcript, 2019), 171.

26. Krasznahorkai, "Black or White?," 177, 179. See also Martin Klimke, *The Other Alliance: Student Protest in West Germany and the United States in the Global Sixties* (Princeton, NJ: Princeton Univesity Press, 2011).

27. On this action, see also Kemp-Welch, *Antipolitics in Central European Art*, 127.

28. It's unclear whether the police came and arrested the artist, as is often claimed, or he simply walked away.

29. For an extensive discussion of TOK, with particular emphasis on the group's environmental concerns, see Maja Fowkes, *The Green Bloc: Neo-avant-garde Art and Ecology under Socialism* (Budapest: Central European University Press, 2016), 127–149.

30. Fowkes, *The Green Bloc*, 118–119. Fowkes argues that the display of the abstract signs by TOK is not affirmative, serving instead to illustrate the group's view of "neo-figuration as an appropriate art style for public display" (143).

31. Tót began his career in the early 1960s as one of the more talented practitioners of Informel painting in Hungary, before abandoning the practice in the early 1970s.

32. To say that one is "glad that I can read Lenin" was provocative in both Eastern Europe and the West, but for different reasons.

33. See Klara Kemp-Welch, "Affirmation and Irony in Endre Tót's Joy Works of the '70s," in *Art History and Criticism 3, Art and Politics: Case-Studies from Eastern Europe*, ed. Liniara Dovydaityte (Kaunas, Lithuania: Vytautas Magnus University, 2007), 136–144.

34. Slavoj Žižek, *Tarrying with the Negative: Kant, Hegel, and the Critique of Ideology* (Durham: Duke University Press, 1993), 200.

35. The differences between Eastern and Western Europe were, of course, anything but categorical. For instance, Kemp-Welch cites Slovak critic Tomáš Štrauss's remark that even though demonstrations in West Germany were technically free, spontaneous demonstrations such as Tót's were as illegal in West Germany as they were in Eastern Europe. Kemp-Welch, *Antipolitics in Central European Art*, 183–184.

36. Irfan Hošić, *The Didactic Wall / Didaktički zid* (Bihać: Gradska galerija, 2019), 15.

37. Quoted in Sven Spieker, "One on One: The *Didactic Wall* (2019) by Mladen Miljanović," *ARTMargins Online*, July 1, 2020, https://artmargins.com/one-on-one-series-mladen-miljanovic-the-didactic-wall-2019/.

38. Sándor Gardó and Reiner Martin, "The Impact of the Global Economic and Financial Crisis on Central, Eastern and South-Eastern Europe: A Stock-Taking Exercise," European Central Bank/Eurosystem, Occasional Paper Series, no. 114, June 2014, https://www.ecb.europa.eu/pub/pdf/scpops/ecbocp114.pdf.

39. Homorodean's project belongs to a specific form of didactic artwork that is based on the idea of the manual. For a more recent example, see, for example, Bill Posters, *The Street Art Manual* (London: Lawrence King Publishing, 2019). Unlike Homorodean, Posters encourages not stealing but the insertion of artworks where they do not belong (hacking the city).

40. Ciprian Homorodean, *Survival Strategies: Take the Book, Take the Money, Run* (Paris: La Bibliothèque Fantastique, 2010), n.p., accessed September 2, 2021, http://www.ciprianhomorodean.eu/take-the-book-take-the-money-run/.

41. Homorodean, *Survival Strategies.*

42. Homorodean, *Survival Strategies.*

43. Homorodean, *Survival Strategies.*

44. Abbie Hoffman, *Steal This Book* (New York: Pirate Editions / Grove Press, 1971), n.p.

45. Hoffman, *Steal This Book.*

46. The term "New Communalists" was coined by Fred Turner. The citation is from Fred Turner, *From Counterculture to Cyberculture: Stewart Brand, the Whole Earth Network, and the Rise of Digital Utopianism* (Chicago: University of Chicago Press, 2006), 5.

47. Hoffman, *Steal This Book*, n.p.

48. Homorodean, *Survival Strategies.*

49. Homorodean, *Survival Strategies.*

6 LEARNING FROM THE SITUATION (ULRIKE MEINHOF, CLEMENS VON WEDEMEYER)

1. Wolfgang Klafki, *Studien zur Bildungstheorie und Didaktik* (1963; repr., Weinheim: Beltz, 1974), 75–76. See also Christoph Luth, "On Wilhelm von Humboldt's Theory of Bildung Dedicated to Wolfgang Klafki for His 70th Birthday," *Journal of Curriculum Studies* 30, no. 1 (1998): 43–60.

2. See Eva Borst, *Theorie der Bildung. Eine Einführung* (Baltmannsweiler: Schneider Verlag Hohengehren, 2011), 65.

3. Klafki, *Studien zur Bildungstheorie*, 56–57.

4. Walter Benjamin, "The Author as Producer," in Benjamin, *Selected Writings*, vol. 2, part 2, *1931–1934* (Cambridge, MA: Belknap Press of Harvard University Press, 2005).

5. Klafki, *Studien zur Bildungstheorie*, 94; translations from Klafki are mine unless otherwise noted.

6. Klafki, *Studien zur Bildungstheorie*, 55–56. In his theory, Klafki distinguishes between "material" and "formal" aspects of *Bildung*, associating the latter with the creation of subjective competences, and the former with normative knowledge.

7. Theodor W. Adorno, "Theorie der Halbbildung," in Adorno, *Gesammelte Schriften*, vol. 8: *Soziologische Schriften 1* (Frankfurt am Main: Suhrkamp, 1972), 93–121. As Douglas

Yacek has argued, Adorno's concept of *Bildung* is located between, on the one hand, the ideal of freedom and self-perfection as understood by Wilhelm von Humboldt and, on the other, the need to assimilate to the demands of society. See Douglas Yacek, "Dialectics of Education: Adorno on the Possibility of *Bildung* in Consumer Society," *Philosophy of Education* (2016): 204–213, https://educationjournal.web.illinois.edu/archive/index.php/pes/article/view/5262.pdf. On Adorno's concept of *Halbbildung*, see Borst, *Theorie der Bildung*, 124–136.

8. By contrast, Adorno's interlocutors point to the urbanizing or acculturating potential of the medium. See Theodor W. Adorno, *Erziehung zur Mündigkeit. Vorträge und Gespräche mit Hellmut Becker 1959–1969* (Frankfurt am Main: Suhrkamp, 1971), 50–69.

9. Hans-Georg Gadamer, *Truth and Method*, trans. Joel Weinsheimer and Donald G. Marshall (London: Continuum, 1989), 153. In German, visual art is sometimes referred to as *bildende Kunst*, implying a double reference to the verb *bilden*, meaning "to form" and "to educate."

10. Friedrich Nietzsche, "Schopenhauer als Erzieher," in Nietzsche, *Sämtliche Werke. Kritische Studienausgabe in 15 Bänden*, vol. 1 (Frankfurt am Main: Fischer, 1999), 341.

11. Theodore Roszak, *The Making of a Counter Culture: Reflections on the Technocratic Society and Its Youthful Opposition* (1969; repr., Berkeley: University of California Press, 1995), 1–41.

12. As Harun Farocki observes, "Mao actually provides a much easier access to a position of untroubled knowledge than classical Marxism. Marx warns with every word: 'Don't dare to engage with this issue before you have studied the entire intellectual history.'" Kaja Silverman and Harun Farocki, *Speaking about Godard* (New York: New York University Press, 1998), 121–122.

13. Herbert Marcuse, "Repressive Tolerance," in *The Essential Marcuse*, ed. Andrew Feenberg and William Leiss (Boston: Beacon Press, 2007), 48.

14. Jürgen Habermas, "Student Protest in the Federal Republic of Germany," in Habermas, *Toward a Rational Society: Student Protest, Science, and Politics* (Boston: Beacon Press, 1970), 30.

15. Reform schools such as the one featured in Meinhof's film were subjected to harsh critique during the late 1960s and '70s. Katharina Rutschky in 1977 coined the phrase "black pedagogy" (*schwarze Pädagogik*) to denounce the dehumanizing tendencies of a pedagogical tradition obsessed with progress and rationality, while publications such as the left-wing West German intellectual periodical *Kursbuch* issued broadly based denunciations of the Western school system and the educational theories that undergirded it. See *Schwarze Pädagogik: Quellen zur Naturgeschichte der bürgerlichen Erziehung*, ed. Katharina Rutschky (Berlin: Ullstein, 1977).

16. The subtitle *Fürsorge—Sorge für wen?* translates literally as "Foster care—for whom does it care?" See Jutta Ditfurth, *Ulrike Meinhof. Die Biografie* (Berlin: Ullstein, 2007), 103–104.

17. In 1979, a theater play based on Meinhof's film opened in the West German city of Bochum. The film itself was not shown on German regional public television channels until 1994. In 2008, a TV documentary about reform care in Germany during the 1960s was produced, called *In the Claws of the Fürsorge: The Fate of Children in Reform Schools during the 1960s.*

18. Already in 1967, Baader and Ensslin had carried out an attack against a prominent church in West Berlin, but this had remained largely symbolic.

19. Cited from Alois Prinz, *Lieber wütend als traurig. Die Lebensgeschichte der Ulrike Meinhof* (Frankfurt am Main: Suhrkamp, 2005), 165.

20. See Stefan Aust, *Der Baader Meinhof Komplex* (Munich: Goldmann, 2008), 121–186; more specifically on the film *Bambule*, see 100–108.

21. The history of the RAF became the subject of a sprawling (and controversial) exhibition at Berlin's Kunstwerke Gallery in 2005.

22. See "Conversation between Clemens von Wedemeyer and Eberhard Itzenplitz," unpubl. ms. (2011), para. 4. As Itzenplitz explains in his conversation with von Wedemeyer, the printed version of the *Bambule* script has a complex history and its details are not faithful either to Meinhof's text or even to the film. Zoltán Kékesi sees the completed film as a complete distortion of Meinhof's original intentions: "The original script and the notes and deletions of the director show clearly that the television film omitted the allusions that referred to the broader social context of the riot and to the political objectives of 1968. It also omitted the ironic reference to police authority (represented in the script at one point as a marionette). In this sense it can be stated that the television film was part of the state apparatus that maintained the symbolic order." Zoltán Kékesi, *Agents of Liberation: Holocaust Memory in Contemporary Art and Film Documentary* (Budapest: Central European University Press, 2015), 195. Meinhof's script, with many (unmarked) deletions and alterations by Itzenplitz and Dieter Waldmann, was published by Wagenbach Verlag in 1974; see "Conversation between Clemens von Wedemeyer and Eberhard Itzenplitz," para. 4. I disucss von Wedemeyer's film installation *Rushes*, which is based in part on Meinhof's film, in the second part of this chapter.

23. See Ditfurth, *Ulrike Meinhof*, on the real-life model of Frau Lack and her unconventional (and controversial) education methods at Eichenhof, which made her unpopular with her superiors (236).

24. See Gerd Koenen, *Das rote Jahrzehnt. Unsere kleine deutsche Kulturrevolution 1967–1977* (Frankfurt am Main: Fischer, 2006), 235.

25. Eichenhof was not the only institution of its kind. Another was Breitenau near the city of Kassel where Ulrike Meinhof also did research, although she was likely not aware that there had been a concentration camp there, since the local population withheld that information from everyone (I thank Clemens von Wedemeyer for this information). The Eichenhof juvenile reform institution was finally closed in the early 1970s, in response to increased public awareness of the awful conditions inside it.

26. See Norbert Frei, *Adenauer's Germany and the Nazi Past: The Politics of Amnesty and Integration* (New York: Columbia University Press, 2002).

27. Theodor W. Adorno, "Education after Auschwitz," *Philosophy of Education* 25, no. 2 (2019), https://pdfs.semanticscholar.org/66fe/aed4d856efdef4249a23d79c45e74ed61348.pdf?_ga=2.67537623.796808335.1627029566-1378727157.1627029566.

28. Adorno, "Education after Auschwitz."

29. Ditfurth, *Ulrike Meinhof*, 237; translation mine.

30. Adorno, "Education after Auschwitz." Adorno first used this phrase in his book *Dissonanzen. Musik in der verwalteten Welt* (Göttingen: Vandenhoeck & Ruprecht, 1956). It was repeated in the title of a radio broadcast of a discussion between Adorno, Horkheimer, and the historian Eugen Kogon at Hessischer Rundfunk (Hesse Broadcasting Station), on September 4, 1950: "Adorno / Horkheimer / Kogon: The Administered World, or The Crisis of the Individual," posted on YouTube by LK, March 8, 2019, accessed July 23, 2021, https://www.youtube.com/watch?v=89o2VYn7MJc.

31. Adorno, "Education after Auschwitz."

32. "Adorno / Horkheimer / Kogon: The Administered World, or The Crisis of the Individual."

33. Louis Althusser, "Ideology and Ideological State Apparatuses (Notes Towards an Investigation)," in *Lenin and Philosophy and Other Essays* (1968; repr., New York: Monthly Review Press, 2001), 105. Elsewhere in the same essay, Althusser defines false consciousness as a "'representation' of the imaginary relationship of individuals to their real conditions of existence" (109).

34. My reference to APO is no coincidence: when Irene boards a bus after her escape, the conductor mockingly addresses her as "APO."

35. In German, the word *Heim* literally means "home."

36. For the moment at least, Iv remains unimpressed. "Who has the night shift today?" she wants to know.

37. Bettina Röhl, "Bambule—No Good Act without a Good Motive?," in *Bambule: The Script / das Regiebuch*, ed. Clemens von Wedemeyer (Ostfildern: Hatje Cantz, 2012), 275. See also Prinz, *Lieber wütend als traurig*, 181.

38. Röhl, "Bambule," 285; translation mine.

39. Among these radio features was one also titled *Bambule*. Other titles included *Girls in Fürsorgeerziehung* for Hessischer Rundfunk, and *Bunker, Bunker* for Westdeutscher Rundfunk (WDR).

40. Ulrike Meinhof, "Vorbemerkungen," in Meinhof, *Die Würde des Menschen ist antastbar. Aufsätze und Polemiken* (Berlin: Wagenbach, 1981), 8. All translations from Meinhof's texts are mine.

41. Manfred Kappeler, "Einführung zum Fernsehspiel 'Bambule,'" accessed September 24, 2020, https://www.stiftungwaisenhaus.de/wp-content/uploads/pdf/gdkih/2017-12-05_Kappeler_Einführung_Bambule.pdf; translation mine. The cited passage comes from the radio feature *Guxhagen—Girls in Fürsorgeerziehung*, which aired on November 7 and November 10, 1969, on the radio station Hessischer Rundfunk.

42. Meinhof, "Vorbemerkungen," 8.

43. Meinhof, "Vorbemerkungen," 8.

44. Meinhof had taken a lively interest in pedagogy ever since her earliest days at the university where she studied, among others, Pestalozzi (about whom she wanted to write a dissertation) and Rousseau. See Prinz, *Lieber wütend als traurig*, 80.

45. "Conversation between Clemens von Wedemeyer and Eberhard Itzenplitz."

46. As it was, according to his own testimony, on the second day of filming, director Itzenplitz started the production when the girls had to go to class so that his crew's work would not be disrupted by large numbers of spectators. Still, there were always contacts between the crew and the reform school residents. See "Conversation between Clemens von Wedemeyer and Eberhard Itzenplitz," para. 21–23.

47. Ditfurth, *Ulrike Meinhof*, 237.

48. Cited from Aust, *Der Baader Meinhof Komplex*, 106.

49. Such an emphasis on the "aesthetics of production" was certainly not unusual for the 1960s and dovetails with multiple efforts to activate the reader/spectator.

50. Cited from Aust, *Der Baader Meinhof Komplex*, 104.

51. Prinz, *Lieber wütend als traurig*, 193, 195.

52. Röhl, "Bambule," 294.

53. Röhl is critical, if not of Meinhof's intentions, then certainly of their consequences: "On close inspection, it is apparent that Ensslin, Baader, and then Meinhof recruited their own terrorist disciples in the juvenile reform houses. . . . Removing young people from such places could be a good deed; to consign them to deprivation and neglect was not a

good deed; and the motive of recruiting comrades-in-arms hardly sheds a rosy light on the pre-RAF reform-home campaigns." Röhl, "Bambule," 306.

54. Ulrike Meinhof, "Falsches Bewusstsein," in Meinhof, *Die Würde des Menschen ist antastbar*, 117.

55. Karl Marx, "Thesen über Feuerbach," in Marx, *Frühe Schriften*, vol. 2 (Stuttgart: Cotta, 1971), 2; translation mine.

56. Meinhof, "Falsches Bewusstsein," 118.

57. Meinhof, "Falsches Bewusstsein," 118.

58. Meinhof, "Vorbemerkungen," 10.

59. Cited from Reinhard Mohr, "'Revolutionäres Gewäsch,'" *Der Spiegel* 33 (1996), 137.

60. Eberhard Itzenplitz, "Über die Filmarbeit mit Ulrike Meinhof" (1986), in Ulrike Marie Meinhof, *Bambule. Fürsorge—Sorge für wen?* (Berlin: Klaus Wagenbach, 2002), 126.

61. Itzenplitz, "Über die Filmarbeit mit Ulrike Meinhof," 117; translation mine.

62. "Conversation between Clemens von Wedemeyer and Eberhard Itzenplitz," para. 18; translation mine.

63. "Conversation between Clemens von Wedemeyer and Eberhard Itzenplitz," para. 18.

64. "Conversation between Clemens von Wedemeyer and Eberhard Itzenplitz," para. 20.

65. "Conversation between Clemens von Wedemeyer and Eberhard Itzenplitz," para. 4.

66. Itzenplitz, "Über die Filmarbeit mit Ulrike Meinhof," 125; translation mine.

67. Itzenplitz, "Über die Filmarbeit mit Ulrike Meinhof," 133.

68. Itzenplitz, "Über die Filmarbeit mit Ulrike Meinhof," 127.

69. Itzenplitz, "Über die Filmarbeit mit Ulrike Meinhof," 124.

70. Itzenplitz, "Über die Filmarbeit mit Ulrike Meinhof," 127.

71. Situationism reached the APO not least through Dieter Kunzelmann, one of the cofounders of Kommune 1 in West Berlin. See Aribert Reimann, *Dieter Kunzelmann. Avantgardist, Protestler, Radikaler* (Göttingen: Vandenhoek & Ruprect, 2009), 49–64.

72. Klaus Wagenbach, "Nachwort," in Meinhof, *Bambule. Fürsorge—Sorge für wen?*, 125.

73. Cited from Aust, *Der Baader Meinhof Komplex*. On the film *Bambule*, see 102.

74. Cited from Mohr, "'Revolutionäres Gewäsch,'" 136–137.

75. "Breitenau Concentration Camp," Wikipedia, accessed March 6, 2023, https://en.wikipedia.org/wiki/Breitenau_concentration_camp.

76. See the official website of the Breitenau memorial site, accessed July 27, 2021, https://guxhagen.de/tourismus-kultur/kultur/gedenkstaette-breitenau-und-kloster-breitenau/.

77. See Kékesi, *Agents of Liberation*, 190–194. The inclusion of Breitenau in Documenta 13 was part of curator Carolyn Christov-Bakargiev's plan to include the city of Kassel and its history in the show. In preparation, many participating artists visited Breitenau, and several of them developed projects in connection with it, von Wedemeyer among them. As part of Documenta 13, Christov-Bakargiev showed an audio-slide show about Breitenau's Nazi past, which had originally been created by Gunnar Richter for Documenta 7 in 1982. See Gunnar Richter, "Die Geschichte Breitenaus und die Gedenkstätte als besonderer Bezugspunkt der documenta (13)," accessed July 27, 2021, https://www.gedenkstaetten forum.de/uploads/media/GedRund172_16-28.pdf.

78. A film version based on the three segments was made for the German TV station 3sat.

79. Alain Badiou, *Saint Paul: The Foundation of Universalism* (1997; repr., Stanford, CA: Stanford University Press, 2003), 50.

80. "I consider dangerous the illusion that it is not just *particular* traditions which must repeatedly be shattered, but the continuity of history as such—that it is not just epochal relations of subjects to the symbolic systems of their world- and self-interpretation which must *repeatedly* be abandoned, but symbolic mediation as such." Habermas, "The Movement in Germany: A Critical Analysis.," Habermas, *Toward a Rational Society*, 39.

7 INSTRUCTIONS FOR SEEING (BAZON BROCK, WŁODZIMIERZ BOROWSKI)

1. Brock's action teachings included *A-Men, B-Men* (1966) and *The Artist's New Clothes* (1967).

2. See Andrew Stefan Weiner, "Times of the Event: On the Aesthetico-Political in West Germany and Austria circa 1968" (PhD diss., University of California, Berkeley, 2011), 3. Wolf Vostell defined his happenings as a way to teach his audience "LIFE." Cited in Peter Weibel, ed., *Beuys Brock Vostell. Aktion Demonstration Partizipation 1949–1983* (Ostfildern: Hatje Cantz, 2016), 104; translation mine.

3. The Documenta 5 catalogue would criticize this approach as "phenomenological."

4. Documenta 5 is generally hailed as the achievement of Harald Szeemann alone. Especially Brock rebelled against this view, positioning his *Besucherschule* as a central element of the exhibition. As he noted in 2001, "Szeemann may have been chief curator, but the critics owe the concept and the desired effect of documenta 5 to other minds, including my own." Cited in Heike Radek et al., "Podiumsdiskussion der Zeitzeugen. Harald Szeemann, Bazon Brock, Klaus Staeck, Georg Jappe," in *Wiedervorlage documenta 5* (Hofgeismar: Evangelische Akademie, 2002), 72.

5. Cited in Weibel, *Beuys Brock Vostell*, 243; translation mine.

6. See Marina Biryukova, "Bazon Brock's Visitors' School on Documenta in Kassel: Training for Reception of Contemporary Art," *JADE* 38, no. 1 (2019): 211.

7. At the show's press conference, a group of artists that included Brock emptied a bag full of pennies on the table in front of the documenta's organizers, and then proceeded to pour a jar of honey over the coins.

8. Bazon Brock, "Vom Action-teaching zur Rezeptionsästhetik—Hinweise zu einer Arbeitsbiographie," in *Bazon Brock, Ästhetik als Vermittlung. Arbeitsbiographie eines Generalisten*, ed. Karla Fohrbeck (Cologne: DuMont, 1977), 564; translation mine.

9. See Julia Friedrich, "Picasso, Shared and Divided," in *Picasso Shared and Divided: The Artist and His Image in East and West Germany*, exh. cat. (Cologne: Museum Ludwig, 2021), 44.

10. The *Didactic Exhibition* was recreated in 2016 by Jasna Jakšić at the Museum of Contemporary Art Vojvodina in cooperation with the Museum of Contemporary Art, Zagreb.

11. Jasna Jakšić, "Art on Tour: The Invention of an Audience," in Fokus Grupa, *Didaktička izložba. Didactic Exhibition*, exh. cat. (Rijeka/Zagreb: Muzej suvremene umjetnosti, 2016), 8. Jakšić's article, on which my summary is based, provides an excellent introduction to this crucial exhibition in the history of Eastern European curatorship.

12. Jakšić, "Art on Tour," 8. As Jakšić points out, Barr's show *Cubism and Abstract Art* (1936) began with a reproduction of Picasso's *Les Demoiselles d'Avignon*, a work included on the exhibition's checklist as "not exhibited" (10).

13. See also Bazon Brock, "Aus der Bürgerschule," in Fohrbeck, *Bazon Brock, Ästhetik als Vermittlung*," 681.

14. When the curtain went up after the end of the lecture, viewers became aware that the people on the stage were connected to each other by threads and were reading aloud passages from a text about torture, prisons, and resistance practices. Weibel, *Beuys Brock Vostell*, 241. See also Brock, "Aus der Bürgerschule," 681–684.

15. The work cited most often in this context is Umberto Eco's *The Open Work* (1962; Cambridge, MA: Harvard University Press, 1989).

16. See Celeste Resh, "Experimenting with Response to Literature," *Language Arts Journal of Michigan* 3, no. 1, article 3 (1987), https://doi.org/10.9707/2168149X.1727.

17. Brock, "Aus der Bürgerschule," 681; translation mine.

18. Bernd Blaschke, "Wahrnehmung oder Kommunikation. Schwierigkeiten einer Ästhetisierung der Vermittlung," *Paragrana* 2 (2006): 255.

19. See Karl Löwith, "Vermittlung und Unmittelbarkeit bei Hegel, Marx und Engels," *Revue Internationale de Philosophie* 101, no. 3 (1972): 323.

20. Brian O'Connor, "Adorno's Reconception of the Dialectic," in *A Companion to Hegel*, ed. Stephen Houlgate and Michael Baur (Oxford: Wiley-Blackwell, 2011), https://philarchive.org/archive/OCOARO-4. See also Theodor W. Adorno, "Subject and Object," trans. Andrew Arato and Eike Gebhardt, in *The Adorno Reader*, ed. Brian O'Connor (Oxford: Blackwell, 2000), 142.

21. Raoul Vaneigem, *The Revolution of Everyday Life* (Oakland, CA: PM Press, 2012), 85. On Vaneigem's conception of the everyday, see also John Roberts, *Philosophizing the Everyday* (London: Pluto, 2006), 81–86.

22. Vaneigem, *The Revolution of Everyday Life*, 80.

23. Vaneigem, *The Revolution of Everyday Life*, 81.

24. Vaneigem, *The Revolution of Everyday Life*, 76. And while this doesn't exclude knowledge, Vaneigem suggests all information be "converted into poetry" (85).

25. The title is often wrongly translated as "pictorial worlds," which misses the cumulative, rather than representational, thrust of the phrase.

26. The 1972 documenta was the first without the so-called "documenta council," and the *Realisatoren* acted as co-curators with Szeemann. The second concept for the show was developed by Brock. See Harald Szeemann, "Einführung," in Radek et al., "Podiumsdiskussion der Zeitzeugen," 20.

27. Harald Szeemann, (no title), in *documenta 5. Befragung der Realität*, 10–11; translation mine.

28. Bazon Brock, "Ein neuer Bilderkrieg—Wirklichkeitsanspruch in Bildwelten heute" in *documenta 5. Befragung der Realität*, 2: 2.1-2.19. See also Hans-Heinz Holz, "Kritische Theorie des ästhetischen Zeichens," in *documenta 5. Befragung der Realität*, 1: 1.2-1.3.

29. Only the "Audio-Visual Documentation" remained, a series of videos with interviews with artists, critics, and visitors. See Radek et al., "Podiumsdiskussion der Zeitzeugen," 21. Also Roland Nachtigäller et al., eds., *Wiedervorlage d5. Eine Befragung des Archivs zur documenta 1972* (Ostfildern: Hatje Cantz, 2001), 76–81.

30. The discussion was informed by cybernetics and behaviorism (B. F. Skinner), and by the possibility of developing machines for learning that would assume the role of a teacher and even have the capacity of adapting themselves to the specific pace of the student. The first such machine was developed by Sidney L. Pressey in 1926, and was based on a feedback mechanism that rewarded the students' ability to fill in the gaps in sentences where certain highly predictable pieces of information had been deliberately left out. Harun Farocki criticized the exploitative undercurrents of Pressey's machine and of behaviorist

learning models more generally from a Marxist perspective, arguing that they instrumentalize the student for a didactic system whose sole product is alienation, and whose "content" is glaringly subordinate to its mechanical process, much as industrial capitalism rewarded workers for the permanent reproduction of existing norms. See Harun Farocki, "Die Agitation verwissenschaftlichen und die Wissenschaft politisieren," in Farocki, *Schriften*, vol. 3: *Meine Nächte mit den Linken. Texte 1964–1975*, ed. Volker Pantenburg (Berlin: n.b.k, 2018), 68–72.

31. *documenta 5. Befragung der Realität. Bildwelten heute*, exh. cat. (Kassel, June 30–October 8, 1972), 2: 2.1; translation mine.

32. See "Robert Fleck: Atelierseminar with Bazon Brock," video, Bazon Brock website, accessed March 1, 2021, https://bazonbrock.de/mediathek/?id=8227&type=video&rubrik=94.

33. Weibel, *Beuys Brock Vostell*, 243; translation mine.

34. Dan Karlholm, "Developing the Picture: Wölfflin's Performance Art," *Photography and Culture* 3, no. 2 (2010): 207–215, 10.2752/175145110X12700318320512.

35. Zeynep Çelik Alexander, "Baroque Out of Focus: The Question of Mediation in Wölfflin," *New German Critique* 1 (2018): 80.

36. See "Robert Fleck: Atelierseminar with Bazon Brock."

37. Hans-Heinz Holz, "Kritische Theorie des ästhetischen Zeichens," in *documenta 5. Befragung der Realität*, 1: 1.2; translation mine.

38. Holz, "Kritische Theorie des ästhetischen Zeichens," 1: 1.2; translation mine.

39. Bazon Brock, "Kunst nach der documenta 5" (1973), in Fohrbeck, *Bazon Brock, Ästhetik als Vermittlung*, 316; translation mine.

40. Holz, "Kritische Theorie des ästhetischen Zeichens," 1: 1.3; translation mine.

41. Daniel Buren called Documenta 5 a "very didactic" show. See Daniel Buren, "Teaching without Teaching," in *Curating and the Educational Turn*, ed. Paul O'Neill and Mick Wilson (London: Open Editions/de Appel, 2010), 221.

42. Szeemann, (no title), in *documenta 5. Befragung der Realität*, 10; translation mine. The "Ereignisdocumenta"—a "100-day" event full of performances and actions—had dominated the first concept for the show, but was soon discarded as impractical.

43. Radek et al., "Podiumsdiskussion der Zeitzeugen," 66.

44. Cited in Caroline A. Jones, *The Global Work of Art: World's Fairs, Biennials, and the Aesthetics of Experience* (Chicago: University of Chicago Press, 2016), 187.

45. Beuys's bureau had existed since 1971; it involved the artist talking to the public for the duration of Documenta 5. The bureau's political platform found expression in the

slogan "Democracy from below," a phrase Beuys tirelessly explained and expounded (*vermitteln*), causing considerable consternation. See Weibel, *Beuys Brock Vostell*, 325.

46. As Brock argued, "In my mind museums can only continue to exist as schools." Bazon Brock, "Weshalb der Laienstandpunkt im Bereich der ästhetischen Praxis immer mehr abgebaut wird," in Fohrbeck, *Bazon Brock, Ästhetik als Vermittlung*, 249; translation mine.

47. Friedrich, "Picasso, Shared and Divided," 41.

48. Quote from an exhibition panel shown in Friedrich, "Picasso, Shared and Divided," 40; translation mine.

49. Werner Schmalenbach, cited in Friedrich, "Picasso, Shared and Divided," 41. As Julia Friedrich writes: "The subject of this didactic exercise is something that no longer directly bewilders, attracts or repels, and has thus lost its power." Friedrich, "Picasso, Shared and Divided," 42.

50. Hans Heinz Holz, "Critical Theory of Aesthetic Signs," in *documenta 5. Befragung der Realität*, 1: 1.64; translation mine.

51. The absence of the Socialist Realist works was made palpable by fact that the section in the catalogue that had been reserved for them remained empty.

52. Bazon Brock, "Ein neuer Bilderkrieg. Programmtext des audiovisuellen Vorworts der d5 synchron zu 2000 Dias der AV-Präsentation,"in *documenta 5. Befragung der Realität*, 2: 2.3; translation mine.

53. Brock, "Ein neuer Bilderkrieg. Programmtext," 2: 2.3; translation mine.

54. Bazon Brock, "Ein neuer Bilderkrieg—Wirklichkeitsanspruch in Bildwelten heute," in Fohrbeck, *Bazon Brock, Ästhetik als Vermittlung*, 268-269; translation mine. This text is a modified version of the program text for the documenta 5 *Audio-Visual Preface*. See note 28.

55. The early *Artons* (from 1958) lit up, while the later ones made from plastic did not. See Magdalena Moskalewicz, "Plastikowe *Artony* Włodzimierza Borowskiego" [Włodzimierz Borowski's Plastic *Artons*], *Artium Quaestiones* 19 (2008): 183–212.

56. In this sense, the customary translation of *pokaz* as "demonstration" is plausible, while *wsytawa* is the exact equivalent of the German *Ausstellung* and the English *exhibition*.

57. Włodzimierz Borowski, "Mirror Manifesto" (1966), in *Art Always Has Its Consequences: Artists' Texts from Croatia, Hungary, Poland, Serbia, 1947–2009*, ed. Dóra Hegyi, Zsuzsa László, Emese Süvecz, and Ágnes Szanyi (Berlin: Sternberg Press, 2011), 33; see also Włodzimierz Borowski Archive, Museum of Modern Art Warsaw, accessed July 24, 2022, https://artmuseum.pl/en/archiwum/archiwum-wlodzimierza-borowskiego/1167.

58. For an excellent discussion of this demonstration, see Luiza Nader, *Konceptualizm w PRL* (Warsaw: Fundacja Galerii Foksal, 2009), 124–127.

59. Włodzimierz Borowski, "IV Syncretic Showing," cited from Nader, *Konceptualizm w PRL*, 124–125. A partial translation can be found at Włodzimierz Borowski Archive, Museum of Modern Art Warsaw, accessed July 24, 2022, https://artmuseum.pl/en/archiwum/archiwum-wlodzimierza-borowskiego/1219.

60. Borowski, "IV Syncretic Showing," 124–125.

61. Borowski's dilemma is the dilemma of many artists in Eastern European countries who gave up painting during the 1960s, yet who were at the same time reluctant to abandon the idea of artistic autonomy: how to extend art practice beyond painting without compromising that autonomy?

62. Lisa Le Feuvre, ed., *Failure* (London: Whitechapel, 2010), 194.

63. Włodzimierz Borowski, "Fubki tarb," *Odra* 6 (1969). A translation entitled "Pubes of Taint" can be found at Włodzimierz Borowski Archive, Museum of Modern Art Warsaw, accessed November 15, 2022, https://artmuseum.pl/en/archiwum/archiwum-wlodzimierza-borowskiego/1187.

64. Think of Manzoni's 1960–1961 series of happenings entitled *Living Sculptures* during which the Italian artist designated a number of women as "art" by signing different parts of their bodies.

65. Borowski, "Fubki tarb."

66. Borowski, "Fubki tarb."

8 TEACHING WHAT DOES NOT EXIST (GNEZDO, ILYA KABAKOV)

1. The group's members, apart from Mikhail Roshal, were Viktor Skersis and Gennady Donskoy. Dmitry Ulyánov Street was named after the brother of Vladimir Lenin.

2. G. Donskoy, M. Roshal, and V. Skersis, *Gnezdo* (Moscow: n.p., 2008), 82.

3. On the Bulldozer Show, see Viktor Agamov-Tupitsyn, *Bul'dozernaia vystavka / The Bulldozer Exhibition* (Moscow: Ad Marginem, 2014).

4. This is the argument made about the group by Mary Nichols in a recent article. Nichols writes, "unlike many of their colleagues, the Nest shun command performances about dialogue for the possibility of engaging in actual conversation." Mary A. Nichols, "Reassessing Moscow Conceptualism: The View from the Nest," *ARTMargins* 11, nos. 1-2 (2022): 188.

5. The same impulse was behind the painted "masterwork" that Kabakov doggedly pursued around the same time, in 1957, as if to graduate himself into art history. See Il'ya Kabakov, "60-e–70-e . . . Zapiski o neofitsial'noj zhizni v Moskve," *Wiener Slawistischer Almanach* 47 (1999): 13.

6. Quoted in Matthew Jesse Jackson, *The Experimental Group: Ilya Kabakov, Moscow Conceptualism, Soviet Avant-Gardes* (Chicago: University of Chicago Press, 2010), 18.

7. Kabakov, "60-e–70-e," 47.

8. This view of things was from the 1980s, when Kabakov wrote the remark cited above, and when Moscow conceptualism as a communal pedagogical project was already taking shape, complete with the mystification of the artist as someone who, as a result of his isolation, is compelled but also empowered to lay the foundations for his own development as an artist, including self-education in subjects or movements—Dadaism, surrealism, cubism, etc.—not commonly taught at the Soviet art academy.

9. See Viktor Voronkov and Jan Wielgohs, "Soviet Russia," in *Dissent and Opposition in Communist Eastern Europe: Origins of Civil Society and Democratic Transition*, ed. Detlef Pollack and Jan Wielgohs (Burlington, VT: Ashgate, 2004), 111–113.

10. The Soviet educational system relied on canonical knowledge that had its (suppressed) counterpart in books and ideas that were banned from Soviet schools. Boris Groys has argued that nonofficial Soviet art and Moscow conceptualism picked up and reused this knowledge. Boris Groys and Anton Vidokle, "Art beyond the Art Market," in *East Art Map*, ed. IRWIN (London: Afterall, 2006), 402. See also Nichols, "Reassessing Moscow Conceptualism."

11. Jackson, *The Experimental Group*, 178.

12. Jackson, *The Experimental Group*, 178. Jackson attributes to Kabakov a "misdirected inspiration and pedagogical zeal" that "[radiates] from nearly every object and text" (178). He further notes that "the sociability of the Conceptual circle straddled the laboratory and the classroom. In Rubinstein's *Program of Works*, Collective Actions' *Trips Out of Town*, and Kabakov's *On Gray and White Paper*, a concern for the evidentiary and didactic predominates" (182; see also note 64).

13. In the late 1960s and the 1970s, cybernetic terminology became fashionable among members of the *nomenklatura* and in the official press. As a result, the Soviet mass media were saturated with the vocabulary of scientifically managed efficiency and transparency. As Slava Gerovitch has written: "Cybernetics became part of the dominant discourse that early cyberneticians despised, and they no longer wanted to call themselves cyberneticians." Slava Gerovitch, *From Newspeak to Cyberspeak: A History of Soviet Cybernetics* (Cambridge, MA: MIT Press, 2002), 289.

14. http://shvartsman-heritage.org/1-ENG%20-Biography.pdf

15. Mikhail Bakhtin, "Discourse in the Novel," in Bakhtin, *The Dialogic Imagination: Four Essays*, ed. Michael Holquist (Austin: University of Texas Press, 1981), 276. For a discussion of this passage in relation to other unofficial "truth seekers," notably Ernst Neizvestny and Vladimir Yankilevsky, see Jackson, *The Experimental Group*, 101–102.

16. See Kabakov, "60-e–70-e," 21.

17. Kabakov, "60-e–70-e," 22.

18. Roland Barthes, "The Reality Effect," in Barthes, *The Rustle of Language* (New York: Hill and Wang, 1986), 141–148.

19. Barthes, "The Reality Effect," 141–148.

20. Jackson, *The Experimental Group*, 83.

21. See Kabakov, "60-e–70-e," 24.

22. Kabakov, "60-e–70-e," 22.

23. Kabakov, "60-e–70-e," 23. See also Jackson, *The Experimental Group*, 74–75. For an expanded discussion of shimmering in Kabakov, see Daniil Leiderman, "The Strategy of Shimmering in Moscow Conceptualism," *Russian Literature* (February–May 2018): 51–76.

24. On Vasiliev's explorations of space, see Molly Brunson, "A Light on the Road: Oleg Vassiliev and Painterly Space," in *Space and Light: Oleg Vassiliev*, exh. cat. (New Brunswick, NJ: Zimmerli Museum, Rutgers University, 2014–2015).

25. Famous examples from the history of art include Arcimboldo's heads made of fruits and vegetables. The *Vexierbild* is related to anamorphosis, which is one of its subcategories.

26. Franz Kafka, *Kritische Ausgabe, Tagebücher* (Frankfurt am Main: Fischer, 1990), 47; translation mine.

27. Jackson, *The Experimental Group*, 62.

28. Kazimir Malevich, *The Non-Objective World* (Berlin, 1927).

29. Christina Lodder, "Man, Space, and the Zero of Form," in *Meanings of Abstract Art: Between Nature and Theory*, ed. Paul Crowther and Isabel Wünsche (New York: Routledge, 2012), 57–58.

30. Jackson, *The Experimental Group*, 62.

31. See Sabine Sanio, *1968 und die Avantgarde. Politisch-ästhetische Wechselwirkungen in der westlichen Welt* (Sinzig: Studio Verlag, 2008), 50–55.

32. Jackson, *The Experimental Group*, 64.

33. Jackson, *The Experimental Group*, 64.

34. Cited in Jackson, *The Experimental Group*, 97.

35. Jackson, *The Experimental Group*, 97.

9 DEMONSTRATION IN SOVIET AND POST-SOVIET SPACE (EXTRA-GOVERNMENTAL CONTROL COMMISSION, RADEK COMMUNITY, CHTO DELAT)

1. Devin Fore, "Demonstrate!," in *Revoliutsiia! Demonstratsiia!*, ed. Matthew S. Witkovsky and Devin Fore (New Haven: Yale University Press, 2017), 291.

2. Fore, "Demonstrate!," 291.

3. Fore, "Demonstrate!," 291.

4. Pamela Kachurin, *Making Modernism Soviet: The Russian Avant-Garde in the Early Soviet Era, 1918–1928* (Evanston: Northwestern University Press, 2013), esp. 3–36.

5. Kachurin, *Making Modernism Soviet*, 55. On these debates, see Maria Gough, *The Artist as Producer: Russian Constructivism in Revolution* (Berkeley: University of California Press, 2005), 21–59.

6. Yuri Tsivian, "Dziga Vertov and His Time," in *Lines of Resistance: Dziga Vertov and the Twenties*, ed. Yuri Tsivian (Gemona: Le Giornate del Cinema Muto, 2004), 9; emphasis mine.

7. As the art historian Kristin Romberg has pointed out, Gan's schooling in Marxist political and economic theory—resulting, among other things, in his manual entitled *Constructivism* (1922)—was itself based on didactic manuals such as Proletkult founder Alexander Bogdanov's *The Science of Social Consciousness: A Short Course on an Ideological Science in Questions and Answers* (1914). Kristin Romberg, *Gan's Constructivism: Aesthetic Theory for an Embedded Modernism* (Berkeley: University of California Press, 2018), 66.

8. See Gough, *The Artist as Producer*; Sven Spieker, *The Big Archive: Art from Bureaucracy* (Cambridge, MA: MIT Press, 2008), 105–129.

9. Leon Trotsky, "Proletarian Culture and Proletarian Art," in Trotsky, *Literature and Revolution* (Chicago: Haymarket Books, 2005), 161.

10. Through this process, the proletariat's class character would be dissolved: "Before the proletariat will have passed out of the stage of cultural apprenticeship, it will have ceased to be a proletariat." Trotsky, "Proletarian Culture," 161. Trotsky was wary of the idea of proletarian art that was being promoted by Bogdanov's Proletkult, even as he acknowledged Proletkult's effort to raise the working class's education level.

11. Boris Arvatov, *Art and Production* (London: Pluto, 2017), 85.

12. As Maria Zalambani points out, unlike Soviet constructivism, productivism was primarily a theory of social art production that advocated the merging of art with industrial production, and of the artist with the engineer: "We can assume then that the term constructivism refers to an art movement, while productivism constitutes a theoretical current that elaborates a social (rather than aesthetic) theory of art production." Maria Zalambani, *L'arte nella produzione. Avanguardia e rivoluzione nella Russia sovietica degli anni '20*

(Ravenna: Longo Editore, 1998), 117; translation mine. As an example of a productivist demonstration inserted into real-life practice, Zalambani cites Anton Lavinsky's project for a constructivist city (114).

13. Arvatov, *Art and Production*, 87.

14. Already in Maksim Gorky's novel *Mother* (first published in Russian in 1907), which is often referred to as the prototype of Socialist Realist representation, the novel's Socialist hero, Pavel, insists he will carry his banner in a demonstration against the authorities even if he risks being thrown in jail: "'Are you going to carry the banner?' the girl asked quietly. 'I am . . . It's my right.' 'Prison again?!' Pavel was silent." Maksim Gorky, *Mother*, trans. Hugh Aplin (London: Alma Classics, 2015), 121.

15. In Socialist Realist painting, Stalin is often shown as the master of multiple means and media of communication, thus refuting the separation of media technologies that characterized the historical avant-garde. See Sven Spieker, "Stalin as Medium: On the Sublimation and Desublimation of Media Technologies in Stalinist Culture," in *Sovetskaja vlast' i media*, ed. Hans Günther and Sabine Hänsgen (Saint Petersburg: Akademicheskij proiekt, 2006), 51–58.

16. Andrei Monastyrski, preface to *Trips Out of Town*, vol. 1, Moscow Conceptualism: Russian Conceptual Art website, accessed October 15, 2021, http://conceptualism.letov.ru/monastyrski-preface-to-1-volume.htm. As Octavian Esanu notes, in later years, a third factographic layer was added to the demonstration field in the group's self-theorization. See Octavian Esanu, *Transition in Post-Soviet Art: The Collective Actions Group Before and After 1989* (Budapest: Central European University Press, 2013), 112.

17. Andrei Monastyrski, preface to *Trips Out of Town*.

18. Participants included A. Monastyrski, V. Miturich-Khlebnikova, N. Alexeev, G. Kizevalter, N. Panitkov, A. Abramov, among others.

19. Sabine Hänsgen and Andrey Monastyrski, "A Dialogue on the Slogans of Collective Actions," Moscow Conceptualism: Russian Conceptual Art, accessed August 3, 2022, https://conceptualism.letov.ru/MONASTYRSKI-Haensgen-DIALOGUE.htm.

20. "Kollektivnye Deystviya (Collective Actions), The Descriptions of All the Actions, Photo and Video," Moscow Conceptualism: Russian Conceptual Art, accessed March 14, 2023, https://conceptualism.letov.ru/KD-ACTIONS-4.htm. The slogan on the banner was taken from Monastyrski's book *Nothing Happens*.

21. Sabine Hänsgen and Andrey Monastyrski, "A Dialogue on the Slogans of Collective Actions."

22. See also George Kieselwalter's account of a later incarnation of this action (1980): "Kieselwalter's Story: For G. Kieselwalter. George Kieselwalter, April 3, 1980," in

Collective Actions: Audience Recollections from the First Five Years, 1976–1981, ed. Yelena Kalinsky (Chicago: Soberscove Press, 2012), 59–62.

23. Esanu, "Transition in Post-Soviet Art," 139. Esanu quotes Kabakov: "'The posters, stands, slogans, banners, indications, time-tables and schedules do not correspond to anything in reality. These are clean, self-referential objects that contain utterances which do not refer to any known thing. These are TEXTS in the full sense of this word.'"

24. Zinaida Starodubtseva, "Performances in Moskau: von der Recherche bis zur Intervention," *Kunstforum* 223 (2013): 208, accessed July 29, 2022, https://www.kunstforum.de/artikel/performances-in-moskau-von-der-recherche-bis-zur-intervention/.

25. The acronym E.T.I. stands for the Russian equivalent of "Expropriation of Art's Territory." "'Э.Т.И.' Movement 1990–1992," accessed July 29, 2022, http://osmopolis.com/osmolovskiy_1989-1992.

26. "The transformation of public space after Perestroika went hand in hand with the 'desacralization' of official Soviet space." Starodubtseva, "Performances in Moskau," 208; translation mine.

27. See Matthias Meindl, *Reiner Aktivismus? Politisierung von Literatur und Kunst im postsowjetischen Rußland* (Cologne: Böhlau, 2018), 125–126.

28. Osmolovsky was also the editor of the journal *RADEK*, which appeared three times between 1993 and 1999. The name refers to Karl Radek, a Trotskyite member of the central committee of the CPSU until 1924.

29. Jacques Rancière, *The Distribution of the Sensible* (New York: Continuum, 2004).

30. Gesine Drews-Sylla, *Moskauer Aktionismus. Provokation der Transformationsgesellschaft* (Munich: Fink, 2011), 11.

31. Meindl, *Reiner Aktivismus?*, 59.

32. Sven Spieker, "Ekstasen der Kritik ohne Objekt: Zur verworfenen Moskauer Aktionskunst," in "Kultur—Sprache—Ökonomie," ed. Wolfgang Weitlaner, *Wiener Slawistischer Almanach* 54 (2001): 289–310.

33. See Meindl, *Reiner Aktivismus?*, 120–127, for an extended critique of this demonstration.

34. Oleg Kireev, "Russische Flash Mobs," *Transversal*, October 2004, accessed July 22, 2022, https://transversal.at/transversal/1202/kireev/de. For an analysis of *Barricade*, see also Meindl, *Reiner Aktivismus?*, 100–106. The "lightweight" nature of the barricade highlights the fact that, as Karl Marx already noted, barricades not only separate people but also bring the people on either side of them into contact with each other. As Anthony Vidler has written with reference to the Paris Commune, "face to face in the narrow street, divided only by a temporary wall of debris, the men and women of the revolt and the

troops of authority were for a brief instant forced to recognize each other, even to speak and argue, before consciously firing." In Anthony Vidler, "The Scenes of the Street," in Vidler, *The Scenes of the Street and Other Essays* (New York: Monacelli Press, 2011), 90.

35. "Anatoly Osmolovsky, The Extra-Governmental Control Group, The Barricade, 1998," Tate, accessed July 27, 2022, https://www.tate.org.uk/art/artworks/osmolovsky-extra-governmental-control-group-the-barricade-p82580.

36. For a detailed description, see "Action—Happening Barricade on Bolshaya Nikitskaya Street," accessed July 29, 2022, http://osmopolis.com/page128/pages/id_25.

37. According to Osmolovsky, the line is a quotation from a then-unpublished novel by the theorist and artist Dmitry Pimenov; see "Vtoraia chast' proekta 'Exchange,'" accessed July 31, 2022, http://osmopolis.com/videt_znachit_podchinyatsya. Pimenov has been critical of neoliberalism and its representatives in Russia since the early 1990s. See also Boryana Rossa, "The Last Sincere Artist in Russia," accessed July 31, 2022, https://boryana-rossa.livejournal.com/17089.html.

38. "Vtoraia chast' proekta 'Exchange,'" http://osmopolis.com/videt_znachit_podchinyatsya, accessed July 31, 2011; translation mine.

39. We can also see in this strategy the final rejection of the paradoxical metaphysical optics of Kazimir Malevich's *Black Square* (1913–1914) with its assumption, also common to Russian icons, that blindness is a form of seeing.

40. The action was repeated several times and filmed by artist Dmitry Gutov.

41. See *Performans v Rossii: 1910–1920. Kartografiia istorii*, exh. cat. (Moscow: Garazh, 2014), 164.

42. Jean Baudrillard, *Critique of the Political Economy of the Sign* (St. Louis, MO: Telos Press, 1978), 176–177.

43. "Radek Community /// In Search of Our Dream (Not Finished Yet)," *Chto delat Newspaper 9: What Do We Have in Common?*, accessed July 28, 2022, https://chtodelat.org/b8-newspapers/12-66/in-search-of-our-dream-not-finished-yet/.

44. On the relevance of the SI for Moscow actionism, see Meindl, *Reiner Aktivismus?*, 106–119.

45. The group's goal is to "merge political theory, art, and activism." See Chto delat, https://chtodelat.org. Apart from the production of a newspaper, Chto delat's educational activities have included workshops, street actions and performances, a blog, and the organization of a school.

46. At the same time, the group denounces the way in which the politicization of art has helped depoliticize society. As David Riff has remarked, "society is outsourcing its politics to art, and that has become extremely profitable." See David Riff and Dmitry Vilensky,

"From Communism to Commons?," Chto delat, accessed March 27, 2021, https://chtodelat.org/b9-texts-2/riff/from-communism-to-commons-david-riff-and-dmitry-vilensky/.

47. Dimitry Vilensky, "Introduction to 'Victory Over the Coup,'" *Chto delat Newspaper 14: Self-Education*, https://chtodelat.org/b8-newspapers/12-60/rancieres-lessons/, accessed March 27, 2021. https://chtodelat.org/b8-newspapers/12-51/introduction-to-qvictory-over-the-coupq/.

48. "Jacques Rancière – Chto delat: You Can't Anticipate Explosions," Chto delat, accessed January 10, 2022, https://chtodelat.org/b8-newspapers/12-57/you-cant-anticipate-explosions/.

49. Dmitry Vilensky, "Theses on Self-Education," Chto delat, accessed March 27, 2021, https://chtodelat.org/b8-newspapers/12-60/theses-on-self-education/.

50. Vilensky, "Theses on Self-Education."

51. Translation by Chto delat member David Riff. See "In Praise of Dialectics," Chto delat, accessed March 27, 2021, https://chtodelat.org/b8-newspapers/12-63/in-praise-of-dialectics/.

52. See "Erroristas Internationale (& Etcetera) /// Notes on De-Education and Errorism," *Chto delat Newspaper 14: Self-Education*, accessed March 27, 2021, https://chtodelat.org/b8-newspapers/12-60/theses-on-self-education/.

10 POSTSCRIPT: THE MIGRANT'S HANDS: BETWEEN DEMONSTRATION AND ARCHIVE IN SYLVAIN GEORGE'S *QU'ILS REPOSENT EN RÉVOLTE (DES FIGURES DE GUERRE)*

1. Debarati Sanyal, "Calais's 'Jungle': Refugees, Biopolitics, and the Arts of Resistance," in *Refugee Routes: Telling, Looking, Protesting, Redressing*, ed. Vanessa Agnew, Kader Konuk, and Jane O. Newman (Berlin: transcript, 2020), 165, https://openresearchlibrary.org/viewer/f5d7da19-c466-4be4-91f3-c07137334e85/5.

2. The production of George's film predates the height of the so-called European migrant crisis of around 2014–2015, but the landscape inhabited by the different groups of characters in his film was already referred to as "the jungle," a designation that gained universal notoriety a few years later.

3. Sanyal, "Calais's 'Jungle,'" 165.

4. Diana Taylor, *The Archive and the Repertoire: Performing Cultural Memory in the Americas* (Durham: Duke University Press, 2003), xvii.

5. Sanyal, "Calais's 'Jungle,'" 165.

6. Walter Benjamin, "Ursprung des deutschen Trauerspiels," in *Gesammelte Werke* (Frankfurt am Main: Suhrkamp), vol. I.1 (1), 209; translation mine.

7. Sanyal, "Calais's 'Jungle,'" 165.

8. In the history of Western film, the mutilation of one's fingertips to avoid identification is a well-known trick often used by criminals to avoid persecution by the police.

9. Sanyal speaks of a "subversive mimicry of state violence." Sanyal, "Calais's 'Jungle,'" 176.

10. As Jennifer Bajorek has written, "the refugee's body is, once again, subject to paradoxical regimes of visibility and invisibility, and even withdrawn from the sphere of representation." Jennifer Bajorek, "This Past Must Address Its Future: Uses of African Non-Contemporaneity in Contemporary Art from the French Borderscape," *ARTMargins* 12, no. 2 (2023): 69–80.

INDEX